The Face of Nature

The Face of Nature

WIT, NARRATIVE, AND
COSMIC ORIGINS IN OVID'S
METAMORPHOSES

Garth Tissol

PRINCETON UNIVERSITY PRESS
PRINCETON, NEW JERSEY

Copyright © 1997 by Princeton University Press
Published by Princeton University Press, 41 William Street,
Princeton, New Jersey 08540
In the United Kingdom: Princeton University Press, Chichester,
West Sussex

All Rights Reserved

Library of Congress Cataloging-in-Publication Data

Tissol, Garth, 1953–
  The face of nature : wit, narrative, and cosmic origins in Ovid's Metamorphoses / Garth Tissol.
    p. cm.
  Includes bibliographical references (p.) and index.
  ISBN 0-691-01102-8 (cloth : alk. paper)
  1. Ovid, 43 B.C.–17 or 18 A.D. Metamorphoses.   2. Latin wit and humor—History and criticism.   3. Epic poetry, Latin—History and criticism.   4. Mythology, Classical, in literature.   5. Cosmology, Ancient, in literature.   6. Ovid, 43 B.C–17 or 18 A.D.—Style.   7. Metamorphosis in literature.   8. Latin language—Style.   9. Narration (Rhetoric).   10. Rome—In literature.   11. Rhetoric, Ancient.   I. Title.
PA6519.M9T57 1997 883'.01—dc20   96-26943 CIP

ISBN 0-691-01102-8

This book has been composed in Galliard

Princeton University Press books are printed on acid-free paper
and meet the guidelines for permanence and durability of the
Committee on Production Guidelines for Book Longevity of
the Council on Library Resources

Printed in the United States of America by Princeton Academic Press

1 3 5 7 9 10 8 6 4 2

W. S. A.

donato iam rude

CONTENTS

Acknowledgments ix

Abbreviations xi

Introduction 3

CHAPTER 1
Glittering Trifles: Verbal Wit and Physical Transformation 11

Transgressive Language: Narcissus and Althea 11
Indecorous and Transformative Puns 22
Misunderstanding aura: *Cephalus, Procris, and the Pun* 26
Divinatory Wordplay: The Pun Overheard 30
Vox non intellecta: *Irony and Metamorphic Wordplay (Myrrha)* 36
Littera scripta manet—*Or Does It? (Byblis)* 42
Self-Cancelling and Self-Objectifying Witticisms 52
Wordplay, Personification, and Phantasia 61
True Imitation: Ceyx, Alcyone, and Morpheus 72
The House of Reception 85

CHAPTER 2
The Ass's Shadow: Narrative Disruption and Its Consequences 89

Some Exemplary Interruptions 89
Daedalus and Perdix 97
Cyclopean Violence and Narrative Disruption 105
Some Scandalous Passages 124

CHAPTER 3
Disruptive Traditions 131

Indecorous Possibilities: Callimachus's Hymn to Artemis and Ovidian Style 131
Elegiac Contributions: Propertius's Tarpeia and Ovid's Scylla 143
Epic Distortions: The Hecale *in the* Metamorphoses 153

CHAPTER 4
Deeper Causes: Aetiology and Style 167

Aetiological Wordplay 167
Ovid's Little Aeneid 177
Aetiology and the Nature of Flux 191

Conclusion 215

APPENDIX A
G. J. Vossius on *Syllepsis oratoria* 217

APPENDIX B
Syllepsis and Zeugma 219

APPENDIX C
Further Examples of Syllepsis in Ovid 221

References 223

Index locorum 231

Index 235

ACKNOWLEDGMENTS

I AM GRATEFUL to many who have assisted me at various stages in this project. When it was inchoate as a dissertation, William S. Anderson, A. W. Bulloch, and Peter Dale Scott offered many suggestions for improvement. The work is dedicated to Professor Anderson on the occasion of his retirement. I also owe much to Leonard Barkan, Peter Bing, Ann Cumming, Charles P. Reichmann, Florence Verducci, Stephen M. Wheeler, and two anonymous readers for Princeton University Press. For the opportunity to make further improvements and to add much I am indebted to two institutions: Emory University provided a grant from the University Research Committee; and the National Endowment for the Humanities provided a Fellowship for College Teachers and Independent Scholars. The editors of *Helios* and *Syllecta Classica* kindly allowed republication of two sections that originally appeared in those journals: "Polyphemus and His Audiences: Narrative and Power in Ovid's *Metamorphoses*," *Syllecta Classica* 2 (1990): 45–58; and "Ovid's Little *Aeneid* and the Thematic Integrity of the *Metamorphoses*," *Helios* 20 (1993): 69–79. Finally, I have received most welcome assistance and support from the staff of Princeton University Press.

ABBREVIATIONS

Abbreviated names of ancient authors and works follow the *Oxford Classical Dictionary*, except where expanded for clarity. I quote W. S. Anderson's text of Ovid's *Metamorphoses* (Leipzig, 1977), noting any divergences. Except where noted, all translations are my own. The following abbreviations for secondary sources appear in notes and references.

AAWW	*Anzeiger der Österreichischen Akademie der Wissenschaften in Wien, Phil.-Hist. Klasse*
AJPh	*American Journal of Philology*
ANRW	*Aufstieg und Niedergang der römischen Welt*
ASD	Desiderius Erasmus, *Opera omnia* (Amsterdam, 1969–)
AU	*Der altsprachliche Unterricht*
Bömer	F. Bömer, ed., *P. Ovidius Naso: Metamorphosen*, 6 vols. (Heidelberg, 1969–1986)
CJ	*Classical Journal*
CP	*Classical Philology*
CQ	*Classical Quarterly*
CR	*Classical Review*
CronErc	*Cronache Ercolanesi*
CWE	*Collected Works of Erasmus* (Toronto, 1969–)
GB	*Grazer Beiträge*
G & R	*Greece and Rome*
GRBS	*Greek, Roman, and Byzantine Studies*
H.	Callimachus, *Hymns*
H-E	M. Haupt, O. Korn, H. J. Müller, and R. Ehwald, eds., *P. Ovidius Naso, Metamorphosen*, vol. 1 (Books 1–7), vol. 2 (Books 8–15), rev. M. von Albrecht (Dublin and Zurich, 1966)
HSCP	*Harvard Studies in Classical Philology*
ICS	*Illinois Classical Studies*
JHS	*Journal of Hellenic Studies*
Keil	H. Keil, *Grammatici Latini*, 8 vols. (Leipzig, 1857)
MD	*Materiali e discussioni per l'analisi dei testi classici*
OLD	P.G.W. Glare, ed., *Oxford Latin Dictionary* (Oxford, 1968–1982)
PCPhS	*Proceedings of the Cambridge Philological Society*

Pf., Pfeiffer	R. Pfeiffer, *Callimachus*, 2 vols. (Cambridge, 1949, 1953)
RE	A. Pauly, G. Wissowa, et al., *Real-Encyclopädie der classischen Altertumswissenschaft* (Stuttgart, 1893–1978)
RhM	*Rheinisches Museum*
Roscher	W. H. Roscher, *Ausführliches Lexikon der griechischen und römischen Mythologie*, 7 vols. (Leipzig, 1884–1937)
SH	H. Lloyd-Jones and P. Parsons, *Supplementum Hellenisticum*, Texte und Kommentare 11 (Berlin and New York, 1983)
TAPhA	*Transactions of the American Philological Society*
Walde-Hofmann	A. Walde and J. B. Hofmann, *Lateinisches Etymologisches Wörterbuch*, 3 vols. (Heidelberg, 1938–1956)
WdF 92	M. von Albrecht and E. Zinn, eds., *Ovid*, Wege der Forschung 92, 2d ed. (Darmstadt, 1982)
ZPE	*Zeitschrift für Papyrologie und Epigraphik*

The Face of Nature

INTRODUCTION

WHILE WITTICISMS and jokes—especially indecorous ones, which call notions of appropriateness to mind, only to trounce them—rightly have a place in critical description of Ovid's *Metamorphoses* because of the enjoyment that readers take in them, my impulse to write the following pages arose from a conviction that they also have much to contribute to our understanding of the work. All elements of the narrative surface have more interpretive importance than they are commonly acknowledged to have. The same can be said for the texture of Ovid's text—the abruptly shifting character of his narrative, its variation in tone and the intrusion of incongruous elements into it, its deliberate arousal of expectations in the reader, which are then thwarted. Style shapes the reader's understanding of the work and embodies its meanings in the reader's experience.

The purpose of these pages is not to attempt a comprehensive view of Ovidian style, still less to produce an anatomy of it along the lines of Frécaut (1972) on wit and humor.[1] Its purpose is to encourage readers to consider the narrative surface and texture of the *Metamorphoses* as worthy of thought rather than dismissal. I develop discussion of stylistic features out of critical readings of tales and passages, and for the most part do not accumulate them in lists, both because context is everything in the discussion of style, and because in the *Metamorphoses* all elements of style and subject are ultimately inseparable. Such lists as I do include are necessarily incomplete. To my examples of the trope syllepsis, for instance, in Chapter 1, many more could be added; for syllepsis is a habit of Ovid's imagination, pervasive in the *Metamorphoses* and his other works, not a discrete phenomenon that rewards study in isolation from its innumerable contexts. The presence of an example in a list is only an interpretive suggestion that one might think about that example in a certain way as one reads and reflects upon it as part of the *Metamorphoses*.

One traditional and typical approach to Ovidian wit may be illustrated by a quotation, chosen almost at random, from Otis on King Midas. After witnessing a musical contest between Pan and Apollo, Midas declares the judgment in Apollo's favor to be unjust, and receives from the god ass's ears as a punishment (*Met.* 11.85–179): "But there is one feature of the Midas episode that lifts it above the level of mere wit or humour. It is the story not just of folly but of aesthetic insensitivity; its metamorphosis is thus the exact reverse of that in the corresponding *Pyg-*

---

[1] On the style of the *Metamorphoses* in general, see Kenney 1973.

malion. Pygmalion is the artist rewarded; Midas is the philistine punished or stigmatized."[2] What is most striking about this aesthetic allegory (which is of a very common type) is how much it excludes from significance. One could point to its denial of naked power-relationships behind the judgment in favor of Apollo; for the treatment Midas receives clearly shows why the judges do not allow their aesthetic sensitivity to stray from prudent courses. Otis's aesthetic preoccupation covers over Apollo's exercise of arbitrary power, along with any interpretive significance it might have for our reading of Ovid. For my purposes here, the terms applied to Ovidian wit are especially revealing. Aesthetic allegory "lifts" the story "above the level of mere wit or humour." From their position below higher considerations, wit and humor contribute nothing to interpretation; they are no longer in view. Many writers before and after Otis have pursued aesthetic considerations of this sort, from Fränkel (1945) to Solodow (1988). I ask my readers to descend and peer downward at the lowest and most indecorous features of Ovidian wit. In fact, I invite them to sink to the very depths, and contemplate the pun.

There is much of value in Otis, and more recent critics offer some laudable conclusions about style and the mercurial qualities of narrative texture, suggesting interpretive significance there that points the way to further reflection. Because I find myself so often dissatisfied with the practice of these critics, I cite at the outset summary conclusions that I can recommend with enthusiasm:

> Connected with this constant transmutation of tone and style is another basic, and obvious, characteristic of the Ovidian narrative, the rapidly moving succession of motifs and episodes. Ovid always surprises the reader ... by introducing unexpected developments. (Galinsky 1975, 12)

> The poem regularly invites us to look for patterns of order but then frustrates our search. (Solodow 1988, 2)

> One of its central concerns is to demonstrate the inadequacy of schemes and structures for making sense of the world. (Solodow 1988, 5)

> Narrative discontinuity parallels the ever-shifting nature of the physical world. As bodies are undergoing change, so does the narrative structure. (Segal 1985, 59)

> There is no rigid formal scheme in the *Metamorphoses*. Everything is in flux, and the ever-changing structure of the poem, and of many individual stories, reflects metamorphosis and, metaphorically speaking, *is* metamorphosis. (Galinsky 1975, 62)

[2] Otis 1970, 192–193.

As evidence for the informing vision small phenomena can be as valuable as large. (Solodow 1988, 5)

My own views arose in part out of a double response to the conclusions of these and other critics. How could I agree with so many of their conclusions, especially those expressed in summary terms, and yet find others unsatisfying, especially those more closely associated with readings of specific passages? Though I have no quarrel with the conclusions listed, I find that they too rarely inform the critical practice of their authors. Elsewhere we find Galinsky, for example, concluding that "metamorphosis as an actual subject does not matter to Ovid," whereas Solodow, despite his promising association of "informing vision" with "small phenomena," declares Ovid's epigrammatic *sententiae* "essentially ornamental" and his narrative transitions "decorative."[3]

Among these writers, the narrative surface, and stylistic considerations in general, are too readily separated from anything of serious interpretive interest. By contrast, the work of Bernbeck (1967) has long pointed the way to a deeper appreciation of Ovidian style. In his attention to anomalous features of the narrative, such as deliberate inconsistency and "inappropriate presentation" of subject matter, not without "surprising rupture of mood," Bernbeck offers a model reading of the tale of Ino in Book 4.[4] His discussion, though well known, has not been as influential as it deserves to be. To be sure, many writers on Ovid respect the principle, familiar in new-critical practice, that form and content are inseparable in a successful imaginative work. Yet their terms of critical description often reflect a lingering suspicion that some stylistic features, especially comic and indecorous ones, were extrinsically added and are not integral to the work, as if they were detachable ornaments, or froth that must be cleared away if one is to arrive at something solid.

Closely connected to this attitude is the suspicion that Ovid does not quite control his creative efforts, but slips into self-indulgent exhibition of stylistic tricks. There are two famous remarks cited by our earliest critic of Ovid, his contemporary Seneca the Elder: *nescit quod bene cessit relinquere*, "He does not know when properly to leave off" (*Controv.* 9.5.17), attributed to Aemilius Scaurus; *non ignoravit sua vitia sed amavit* (*Controv.* 2.2.12), "He was not unaware of his faults, but loved them." Many have over the centuries developed such remarks into more detailed complaints about Ovid's excessive verbal artifice and wanton failure to

---

[3] Galinsky 1975, 55; Solodow 1988, 49 and 28: "The connections suggested between his stories are in the end decorative; the parallels, balances, and antitheses are rhetorical in the narrowest sense. They convey no conclusions, no morals, no illuminations." For "decorative" and "ornamental anthithesis," see ibid., 134–135.

[4] Bernbeck 1967, 14, 24.

accommodate language to subject matter.[5] It would be easy to identify faults in the perspective of Scaurus and Seneca: *bene* and *vitia* reflect unexamined assumptions about what would be proper and why Ovid's faults deserve that name; these critics suggest that the evaluative relevance of their standards of decorum is too obvious to need explanation and defense. The first remark, attributing ignorance to Ovid, implies that if only he had known when properly to leave off, he would have done so. The notion that Ovid's facility and his tendency toward stylistic improprieties result from a failing on his part ought to require some defense if we are to accept it, or so one might suppose. Seneca, however, judged rightly that these unexamined assumptions would be shared by others. In recent times, Galinsky approves *amavit sua vitia* as a causal explanation for stylistic excesses attributed to the story of Tereus.[6] The first remark finds a more subdued but wider echo in modern critics, many of whom remark that Ovid "cannot help" pursuing a witticism or other excessive feature of style, as if he did not know how to forestall it. So Galinsky on Echo and Narcissus: "Ovid cannot resist the temptation to make the most of Echo's disability." Wilkinson on Byblis: "Now Ovid is overcome by the opportunity for conceits inherent in the situation." Anderson on Alcmaeon: "Ovid could not restrain the temptation to produce this witty zeugma." Otis on Olenos, Lethaea, and an unnamed man transformed to stone: "Finally Orpheus' numbed sensibility after the tragedy is likened to the petrifaction of three persons whom Ovid cannot resist mentioning at this point." Because I will discuss Ovidian puns, a remark of Redfern's on puns and punsters in general may be added to this list: puns "are a latent resource of language, and certain temperaments simply will not resist trying to mine and exploit this rich ore, because (like Everest) it is there."[7]

No doubt writings do reflect the temperaments of their authors, but there is no reason to suppose that Ovid's do so more than those of others. Perhaps Vergil could not resist imparting to the *Aeneid* a certain sadness, and Sophocles could not resist treating Antigone in a largely serious fashion. For all we know, Ovid may have been among "certain temperaments" of the punning sort. But his works' variety of tone, including even sustained seriousness from time to time, suggests that style may reflect Ovid's rhetorical designs upon his readers more than his own

---

[5] An eloquent example is the quotation below from Dryden's Preface to the *Fables* (1700). S. Hinds (1988) defends Ovid's works against three depreciatory generalizations, "The Shallow and Over-explicit Poet," "The Excessively Literary Poet," and "The Passive Panegyrist." In each case, Hinds counters a reductive cliché by examining the richness of Ovid's allusive texture.

[6] Galinsky 1975, 131.

[7] Ibid., 54; Wilkinson 1955, 207; Anderson 1972, 446; Otis 1970, 185; Redfern 1984, 9.

temperament. More often than not, we readers cannot resist following where Ovid leads. The significant "temptations" of Ovidian style may not be those to which Ovid supposedly yields, but those that he sets in our path.

I locate more of interpretive significance in narrative structure and stylistic features than critics usually do. Whereas those quoted above make assumptions about the author and his temperament, I make claims about the audience, and these warrant some examination. My readers will recognize this work's audience-oriented critical affiliations, which one might classify as a joining of reader-response practice and eclectic formalism.[8] Though I undertake to describe experiences of reading Ovid's text and attribute these to Ovid's readers, I do not claim to offer a complete description of any reader's experience. Rather, I propose the reading as applicable to some common features of readers' experiences. Such descriptions are necessarily partial, indeed closely tailored to the interpretations I offer. I do not claim that all readers' experiences of Ovid's text are the same, or have been so over the centuries, nor that a single individual, for that matter, experiences the work in the same way when returning to it for successive readings.

If one judges from the interpretations that Ovid's readers over two millennia have found acceptable, their experiences have indeed greatly varied. This fact in no way compromises the validity or value of new interpretation, which Ovid's work demands as insistently as ever. In a well-known discussion, Stanley Fish argues that interpretations of a work gain acceptance because the values and assumptions that shape them are shared with a larger interpretive community.[9] No doubt Ovid's first readers, for example, experienced his work in ways unique to them, as did rhetoricians of late antiquity, medieval theologians, and present-day students. And within such groupings, each individual brings different habits of mind to the act of reading. We who read ancient writings should acknowledge, without reproach, that we bring preoccupations of our own times to the task. Without such preoccupations, we could not begin to think about the ways in which antiquity warrants our attention. Their unavoidable presence does not lead us to suspect that reading is a static mirroring of preestablished views; for interpretations are, and ought to be, always under revision, always changing, always subject to many influences. Interpretive communities do not operate within a closed system. However much readers' values and presuppositions may

---

[8] Any reader-oriented discussion of the *Metamorphoses* owes much to the example of Due (1974), who constructs the expectations of Ovid's reader on the basis of the earlier works, then describes this hypothetical reader's encounter with representative portions of the *Metamorphoses*.

[9] Fish 1980, especially 1–17, 338–371.

contribute to their understanding of a text, other interpretations as well are likely to clamor for a hearing. These other interpretations will maintain a persistent challenge, seeking to dislodge competitors or to co-opt and transform them by affecting the values and presuppositions upon which competitors depend.

To offer but two examples, acceptance of moralizing allegorical readings in the *Ovidius moralizatus* of Pierre Bersuire (d. 1362) was no doubt accommodated by allegorizing habits of mind of Ovid's fourteenth-century readers. Yet Bersuire's work also influenced those readers' experiences of Ovid, winning many over to its interpretive model: its popularity is clear from its abundant manuscripts and translations.[10] The development of printing in the fifteenth century allowed still wider dissemination of moral allegories; yet the same century produced Raffaele Regio's austerely nonallegorical commentary (1493), a classicizing work, rich in identification of rhetorical tropes, following interpretive principles familiar in Quintilian rather than those of medieval allegory. These two models of interpreting Ovid long flourished among readers whose assumptions, values, and habits of reading easily accommodated the acceptance of either one. Though some readers must have found one more convincing than the other, I suspect that many were content to bring both interpretive models to their reading of Ovid—and perhaps others as well. For readers of the *Metamorphoses* ought to recognize that, though on the one hand the work demands interpretation, on the other it is as inexhaustible as the *mundus*, the cosmos it represents as its subject. Like the *mundus*, it will ultimately exceed our views of it, always suggesting that greater depths, greater potential for understanding, lie beyond our provisional appreciations. The *Metamorphoses* always remains an open interpretive field. As for my own descriptions of the reader's experience, I hope that they will be found recognizable and convincing as part of my interpretive model, and that thereby the interpretations will be the clearer and more acceptable to my readers.

Recent work on Ovid suggests to me that my own views can be seen as an individual extension of views in which many share. Writers pursuing one productive vein of stylistic criticism show manifold and diverse

---

[10] On Bersuire, see Ghisalberti 1933. Many earlier works would have prepared readers for Bersuire, such as *Ovide moralisé* of the preceding century, a more extreme moral allegory; see Rudd 1988, 28–29. A. Moss (1982) offers a sympathetic discussion of the Ovidian moralists: see 23–27 on Bersuire, 31–36 on the more sophisticated allegorical reading of Petrus Lavinius, *Tropologicae enarrationes* (Lyon, 1510). Grafton (1991, 31) remarks that Moss "has shown how successive generations of Ovidian allegorists modernized their methods and their use of evidence without ever fully abandoning the assumption that Ovid must be reconciled with Christianity—and thus kept the *Metamorphoses* fresh and instructive for very different audiences."

connections between figurative language and metamorphosis. As Barkan writes, "Ovid frequently uses similes as protometamorphoses, rhetorically pointing out the direction in which an individual will literally travel when his transformation takes place." Rosati traces amatory metaphors in particular, describing how they become literalized and reified in the transformative contexts of the *Metamorphoses*.[11] Pianezzola, on "Ovidian metamorphosis as narrative metaphor," illustrates Ovid's exploitation of ambiguous metaphorical expressions; ambiguity grants them a wide semantic range, one that facilitates a shift from metaphorical to literal: "Ovid has therefore developed the initial metaphor in narrative and descriptive terms." Viewed from a slightly different angle, the semantic shift necessary in the appreciation of such expressions figures metamorphosis in the experience of Ovid's readers. Pianezzola takes a crucial further step in connecting literalization of metaphor to Ovid's aetiological themes: through transformation, "human existence . . . is tied by infinite threads to the rest of the world: to rocks, trees, land animals, birds, and fish. But his newness of vision is actually made possible by the metaphorical nature of Ovidian metamorphosis."[12] Ovid's development of so large-scale a vision out of metaphor can be traced to ancient views of metaphor as substitution: one of Quintilian's categories of metaphor, *pro rebus animalibus inanima*, "Inanimate things substituted for animate" (Quint. 8.6.10), could also serve to describe many Ovidian transformations.

Following several paths traced by these writers within the vast range of Ovid's figurative expression, I begin, in the first chapter of this work, with paradoxical witticism and wordplay. Quintilian provides, as an example of the type of metaphor just mentioned, a line from an old tragedy: *ferrone an fato moerus Argivom occidit?* "Was it by the sword or fate that the Argive wall fell?" (*Trag. inc.* 35 Ribbeck). Such simultaneous play on literal and figurative senses is an instance of syllepsis, a favorite trope of Ovid's, and one that I will explore; for the double meaning present in this trope illustrates a close connection between puns and metaphorical expressions.[13] In puns, in syllepsis, and in paradoxical witticism, we can observe large-scale thematic concerns manifested in especially revealing ways in the experience of the reader. They all aim to surprise: they suddenly make us aware of a word's extended and unexpected applications.

---

[11] Barkan 1986, 20–21; see also 23: "Often the business of metamorphosis, then, is to make flesh of metaphors." Rosati 1983, especially 166–170.

[12] Pianezzola 1979, 83, 90; see also Schmidt 1991, 56–69.

[13] As Barkan (1986, 21) remarks on the transformation of Lichas in *Met.* 9, "Once we are aware of the parallel between emotional state and shape, the terms of description take on the force of puns."

Surprise and abrupt alteration of perspective are also the focus of the second and third chapters, in which I examine Ovid's ever-shifting narrative structures as thematically significant: they embody change in the experience of reading. We experience reading as a transformative process not only in the characteristic indirection and unpredictability of Ovid's narrative, but also in our memory of his predecessors; for he exploits allusion to them as part of the process. In the fourth chapter I show how Ovid subsumes Vergil's *Aeneid* into the *Metamorphoses* in an especially rich allusive exploitation, one that contrasts Vergil's aetiological themes with those of his own work. Throughout this discussion, my focus is on stylistic manifestations of instability and change, through which effects of Ovidian style become thematic reflections on the nature of things.

Chapter 1

GLITTERING TRIFLES: VERBAL WIT AND PHYSICAL TRANSFORMATION

Transgressive Language: Narcissus and Althea

In the Preface to *Fables, Ancient and Modern* (1700), John Dryden offers a hostile yet perceptive criticism of Ovid. He sets up a comparison between Chaucer and Ovid, and when he comes to consider the subject of propriety in thought and language, Ovid must endure an attack:

> The Vulgar Judges, which are Nine Parts in Ten of all Nations, who call Conceits and Jingles Wit, who see *Ovid* full of them, and *Chaucer* altogether without them, will think me little less than mad, for preferring the *Englishman* to the *Roman*: Yet, with their leave, I must presume to say, that the Things they admire are only glittering Trifles, and so far from being Witty, that in a serious Poem they are nauseous, because they are unnatural. Wou'd any Man who is ready to die for Love, describe his Passion like *Narcissus*? Wou'd he think of *inopem me copia fecit*, and a Dozen more of such Expressions, pour'd on the Neck of one another, and signifying all the same Thing? If this were Wit, was this a Time to be witty, when the poor Wretch was in the Agony of Death? . . . On these Occasions the Poet shou'd endeavour to raise Pity: But instead of this, *Ovid* is tickling you to laugh. *Virgil* never made use of such Machines, when he was moving you to commiserate the Death of *Dido*: He would not destroy what he was building.[1]

It may seem that I am setting up an easily demolished straw man, beginning a discussion of Ovidian wit by quoting this famous attack on it. But though I mean to praise Ovid, I in fact find much to admire here. For the sense of outrage in Dryden's criticism betrays a deeper response to Ovid's wit than do the discussions of more approving recent critics, many of whom claim to *like* Ovidian wit. By contrast to Dryden, they provide safe and comfortable readings of Ovidian wit that make it seem pretty much like "comic relief," a pleasant and agreeable interruption of seriousness. On their view, wit promotes the "genial tone"[2] they attribute to the *Metamorphoses*. Assigned to such a function, wit loses its power—

---

[1] Dryden (1700), in Kinsley 1962, 527. For an illuminating discussion of Dryden and Ovid, with special attention to Dryden's translations, see Hopkins 1988.
[2] Galinsky 1975, 159.

power to provoke and vex a reader. Serving only as a critical anesthetic, it works to forestall readers' emotional and intellectual engagement with the text.[3]

The term "comic relief" is not used much anymore, perhaps because it is felt to be too naive, too reductive. Whatever the case, let us turn to the term actually used by Solodow in his recent general book on the *Metamorphoses*: "Humor is the universal solvent doing away with all pretension."[4] The context shows that "universal solvent" is to be taken as an equivalent for comic relief: humor prevents Ovid's mythological subject matter from becoming too somber. The metaphor itself apparently has little force for its author, and soon gives way to others: "The injection of humor inoculates mythology against excessive solemnity."[5] Some critical analogies are more useful than others; that of the "universal solvent" is suggestive, and seems to lead us to reflect on possibilities of meaning beyond its context. Let us follow up on the notion that wit dissolves things; perhaps we can take these terms a step further and describe wit as the "universal corrosive."

There is much to be learned from Solodow and from other recent discussions of Ovidian wit. Many readers, however, have been dissatisfied with F. Ahl's treatment of punning anagrams, many of which seem accidental and without interpretive significance.[6] Walter Redfern's *Puns* (1984) has given much more helpful impetus to reflection, opening up the subject of wordplay through a discussion of its function in a vast range of contexts. From *On Puns*, edited by Jonathan Culler (1988), which follows up some of Redfern's explorations, I take this remark: "Puns present the disquieting spectacle of a functioning of language where boundaries—between sounds, between sound and letter, between meanings—count for less than one might imagine and where supposedly discrete meanings threaten to sink into fluid subterranean signifieds too undefinable to call concepts."[7] In discussing Ovidian wit, I wish to attribute this transgressive quality of the pun to wordplay in general, to show that it is interpretively significant through its corrosion of semantic boundaries.

---

[3] See Chapter 2 for a discussion of the nature and extent of readers' potential engagement with Ovidian narrative.

[4] Solodow 1988, 101.

[5] Ibid., 108.

[6] Ahl's polemics against scholarly neglect of wordplay (1985, 18–19; and 1988, 18–26) are of value as a caution against critical prejudice. But his positive contribution, narrowly focused upon anagrams, often frustrates the reader; for he discusses punning anagrams in isolation from Ovidian style in general, and his examples seldom contribute to a plausible interpretation of their context.

[7] Culler 1988, 3.

Let us begin with the paradox that Dryden found so bad: *inopem me copia fecit*, "Abundance has made me resourceless" (*Met.* 3.466). Dryden's example is typical of paradoxical wit in the *Metamorphoses*, and is one of many paradoxes that Narcissus utters. *Copia* and *inopia* are, of course, opposites, and each is most perfectly defined in contrast to the other. As for *copia*, we could ordinarily assume that it would cause a person to become richer, or at least less poor, to improve his circumstances in some measure; in any case, the one thing it would not do is to make him purely *inops*. By making abundance the cause of resourcelessness in Narcissus, Ovid equates the two in this context, making them interchangeable. We are accustomed to think of these opposite terms as extremes on a spectrum, and we are likely to imagine a large middle ground between them. Ovid's witticism makes an assault on our semantic categories; not only does he remove the middle ground between *copia* and *inopia*, he also dissolves any boundary between them. He destabilizes both terms, causing them to melt before our astonished eyes. That is what makes paradox shocking or offensive or incongruously funny—potent in eliciting some response from us, whether expressed by laughter or a groan.[8]

Inopia . . . dicitur e contrario, ubi nulla est copia, as we are told by Cassiodorus.[9] "*Inopia* receives its name from its opposite: where there is no *copia*." Their definition as opposites links *copia* and *inopia* by preexisting ties, which make them available for paradoxical wordplay. But they are tied still more closely by etymology. Ovid's paradox calls attention to the fact that *inops* and *copia*, from *co-opia, are etymologically connected.[10] The etymological element of wordplay facilitates the collapse of opposed meanings by showing that little more than the negative *in-* separated these terms in the first place.

Dryden's objection to such witticisms is based on ideas of decorum: "In a serious Poem they are nauseous." And his example of a serious poem is, as in so many later disparaging treatments of Ovidian style, the *Aeneid*. Narcissus's death scene could have measured up to the appropriate standard, Dido's death scene, had not Ovid destroyed it by piling on the paradoxical witticisms. Such criticism ignores the actual appropriateness of paradox to the specific narrative situation, which has few resemblances to the Vergilian tragedy that Dryden would have preferred to

---

[8] What Redfern says of puns can be (here as often) extended to wordplay in general: "By common consent, puns make people groan, squirm, flinch, grimace, or wince, as we do of course when we witness a physical collision, a painful conjunction, taking place" (Redfern 1984, 30–31).

[9] Cassiodorus *Expositio in psalmum* 87, 10 (*Corpus Christianorum* 98, ed. M. Adriaen [Turnhout, 1958], 798). For further etymological connections with *inops* in Roman sources, see Maltby 1991, 305.

[10] See Walde-Hofmann 1:270.

find. Narcissus has just come to recognize that his beloved is in fact his own reflection. Unable to reach toward the object of his desires without destroying it (by disrupting the water's surface), or even to look away without losing the reflection (*Met.* 3.433), Narcissus quickly arrives at a state of paralyzed inaction, for which the self-obliterating terms of his speech provide fitting expression. And more specifically, witticism provides a correlative to the confusion of subject and object that defines Narcissus's case.

Throughout the *Metamorphoses*, paradox is the preferred form of expression for characters who are unable to act, and for Ovid in describing them. Most of the story of Althea in Book 8, for example, represents no kind of narrative action, but a state of moral paralysis. Althea, long unable to decide whether to avenge her brothers by causing the death of her own son, finally decides to do so. But after many waverings from one unacceptable course of action to the other, her resolve is rather like a toss of the coin: a resolve, but not a resolution of the dilemma. It finds its perfect expression in paradox:

> et consanguineas ut sanguine leniat umbras,
> inpietate pia est.[11]
> (*Met.* 8.476–477)

And in order to assuage her kindred shades with blood, she is dutiful in her violation of duty.

In causing *pietas* and *inpietas* to implode or collapse together into the same thing, this paradox resembles Narcissus's treatment of *copia* and *inopia*. But in Althea's case the terms are far more highly charged for Roman readers. For them, little can have seemed more important than the distinction between *pius* and *inpius*, along with the understanding of how these terms are to be applied to human conduct. Such understanding, of course, depends on the opposition of these terms and the recognition of boundaries that separate them and keep them at a safe distance from each other. These are the very boundaries that are obliterated in Althea's situation and its representation in paradoxical language. When the ethical case is at a complete impasse, it finds its appropriate correspondence in semantic impasse. By making Althea's conflict of choices irreconcilable, Ovid robs *pietas* of the freedom necessary for its existence. The case is well embodied in terms that cancel each other out—a seman-

---

[11] Hollis (1970) dismisses *consanguineas . . . sanguine* as "a forced and almost pointless wordplay." As often, Ovid deserves to be defended against his commentators, in this case by Kenney (1973, 151 n. 108). This example, which plays upon conceptual and physical meanings, is especially apt and relevant; see below, "Self-Cancelling and Self-Objectifying Witticisms."

tic short-circuit, one may call it. As in all Ovidian paradoxes, this one assaults the normally well-protected mental categories of the reader. But an assault in *these* terms is more serious, more shocking than most. I suspect that is why Ovid introduces so many similar examples into the *Metamorphoses*: *facto pius et sceleratus eodem*, an expression used twice in this form (3.5, 9.408), "Dutiful and criminal in the same deed"; *scelus est pietas in coniuge Tereo*, "Crime *is* duty when your husband is Tereus" (6.635); *ne sit scelerata, facit scelus*, "Lest she be criminal, she commits a crime" (7.340); and so on.

To re-emphasize a point made earlier, Ovid's paradoxical witticisms are appropriate to the narrative situations he chooses—decorous in their lack of decorum. Paradox-laden speeches are typically the expression of characters who are in some state of paralyzed inaction, such as Narcissus and Althea. Marsyas has recourse to witticism—*quid me mihi detrahis?*, "Why do you tear me from myself?" (6.385)—once he has been tied up, and his flaying has begun.[12] We can observe rich thematic consequences in paradoxical wit when we consider that Ovid often sets such narratives of paralysis in contrast to the heroic action that might have been the subject of his story. Althea's dilemma, for example, is the climax of the tale of the Calydonian boar. This is an epic subject rich in heroic possibilities, all of which are defeated by Ovid through the resources of burlesque.[13] But nothing more surely defeats the heroic potential of the story than the fact that its events serve largely as an introduction to Althea's hopeless choice. Leaving behind all opportunities to exploit the action-packed heroics of the hunt, Ovid puts the emphasis on an internal description of moral paralysis, embodying it in a narrative surface that coruscates with self-cancelling witticisms.

Paradox has a place in the larger field of significant wordplay, many of whose paths will be traced in later discussion. We have seen how paradoxical wit erodes semantic boundaries and disturbs semantic values. In doing so it represents an extreme example of Ovidian wit in general. For infinitely varied as it is, Ovidian wit usually exhibits one consistent feature: it wrenches the meanings of words, creating sudden and unexpected semantic slippage. To return to Narcissus, we may consider his famous conversation with Echo—or rather, his verbal confrontation with Echo—in which she is able only to repeat the last words he has spoken. Echo manages to express her own views—entirely contrary to Narcissus's—by repeating, and thereby appropriating, the very words Narcissus has just spoken. When, for example, he wishes to confront the unknown person who is repeating all his utterances, and says *huc co-*

---

[12] Play on pronouns, a favorite Ovidian witticism, will be discussed below.
[13] See Anderson 1972, on *Met.* 8.324. For Ovid's burlesque mode, see Chapter 3 below.

eamus, Echo is able to fill *coeamus* with her own passionate desire, transforming its sense entirely:

>   perstat et alternae deceptus imagine vocis
>   "huc coeamus!" ait, nullique libentius umquam
>   responsura sono "coeamus!" rettulit Echo
>   et verbis favet ipsa suis egressaque silva
>   ibat, ut iniceret sperato bracchia collo;
>   ille fugit fugiensque "manus conplexibus aufer!
>   ante" ait "emoriar, quam sit tibi copia nostri";
>   rettulit illa nihil nisi "sit tibi copia nostri!"
>   (*Met.* 3.385–392)

> He stopped, and, tricked by the reflection of the voice answering him, said, "Let us come together"; Echo, who would never answer another utterance more gladly, replied, "Let us come together!" Her own words found favor with Echo herself, and she emerged from the woods to throw her arms around the neck she hoped for. He fled, and as he did so, said, "Keep your hands off me! I'll die before I let you get possession of me." She repeated only, "Get possession of me!"

For all the verbal constraint under which Echo must operate, she succeeds at making wordplay into an aggressive act: she robs Narcissus's words of their meaning. There is a clear correspondence between the sexual aggression occurring here in the events of the plot and the semantic aggression in Echo's wordplay, which embodies those events on the narrative surface.

Since the words exploited by Echo suddenly acquire *her* meanings in addition to those already allotted them by Narcissus, they function much like puns. Echo's punlike wordplay expands each word's meaning far beyond the boundaries set for it by the original speaker. We recognize and appreciate these boundaries in our effort to understand Narcissus's meaning, an effort that requires our restricting the initial application of *coeamus*, for example, to what we deem appropriate to the context, to what we have induced about Narcissus's intentions in using the word. Then Echo's wordplay dissolves the restrictive limits in which we have necessarily participated. Puns have a detonating effect; we are astonished by them, as we recognize semantic spaces opened up, unforeseen distances revealed within a single word. In the case of *coeamus*, mischievous delight as well as astonishment is a likely response, for the lubricious sense assigned by Echo to the word offers special stimulus to take pleasure in the dissolution of Narcissus's meanings. Yet in merely trying to understand the pun we have already felt its seductive power, as it invites us to cross semantic limits and proceed into regions that are all the more enticing for being unknown. Transformed by wordplay, the word escapes its usual banality and becomes unfamiliar. So Redfern recognizes in this description of the pun: "Language itself experienced as foreign."[14] This description aptly fits the present case. We initially understand Narcissus's words as he intends them, then witness a defamiliarizing effect as Echo gets hold of them and twists them.[15]

In opening vistas within a word, punlike wordplay is the inverse of the paradoxical sort exemplified above with *impietate pia est*. There, two opposed terms collapsed in a nullifying verbal paroxysm, as Althea finds no way out of her ethical paralysis. Here, each single word expands outward into new semantic fields, freed to generate multiple meanings—and to grant Echo freedom from divine punishment. Juno had punished Echo by depriving her of original speech, so that "her own words," *sua verba* (*Met.* 3.378), must be merely what others have said, scarcely her own at all. "Ovid, however," as John Brenkman has shown, "averts all these dangers by producing a series of utterances and echoes that opens Echo's speech to exactly the kind of reading that seemed threatened. The echoes are to be read as replies made by one character to another."[16] Wordplay makes communication possible for Echo, as she exploits the semantic extensions discoverable in Narcissus's words. In the process, "Juno's punishment is effaced"; Echo regains her character and identity. "We can say that the story of Echo emerges within the larger narrative as the drama of the self's identity and integrity restored. What could have been the mere play of significations left unattached to a speaker, a character, a consciousness, becomes the other side of an actual dialogue between autonomous speakers, between two equally realized characters."[17]

"When no known language is available to you, you must determine *to steal a language*"—so writes Roland Barthes. "All those—legion—who are outside power are obliged to steal language."[18] This remark may well apply to Echo, but those inside power are equally capable of committing such a theft. Another case like Echo's, in which we witness a word's unexpected potential for double meaning, occurs in the story of Aglauros in Book 2. Overcome by jealousy of her sister Herse, Aglauros sits in the doorway of the house to prevent Mercury's access to Herse, declaring that she will not move from the spot unless she repels him: *hinc ego me non sum nisi te motura repulso*, "I will not leave this place until you have been driven away" (2.817). "Let us agree upon these terms!" replies Mer-

---

[14] Redfern 1984, 1, quoting Sartre.

[15] For another stylistic context in which the "defamiliarization" of the Russian formalists is relevant, see Pianezzola 1979, 91.

[16] Brenkman 1976, 300. Though Brenkman does not discuss wordplay, his treatment is highly relevant here.

[17] Ibid., 300, 301.

[18] Barthes 1977b, 167.

cury, and he turns her to stone. He has deliberately misinterpreted her, seizing Aglauros's word *motura* and aggressively applying it in a different sense from that intended by her. The play on words is another theft of someone else's meaning, as in Echo's case, but here it functions as the casual expression of divine power. Mercury's play on *motura* initiates metamorphosis: he first transforms Aglauros's word, and then her body.

I wish to emphasize the link between metamorphosis and wordplay, especially the punning sort exemplified here. Critics usually treat events of plot, such as metamorphosis and divine mistreatment of human beings, as if they were entirely separate from Ovidian style—which is typically discussed in a separate chapter by itself. To separate wit from anything else that may be going on in the *Metamorphoses* is to trivialize it: it usually becomes mere "comic relief." Mercury's wordplay, by contrast, is both funny and chilling, for it represents both a typical joke and a typically brutal intervention of divine power. And in its larger thematic significance, it embodies, on the level of the narrative surface, the fluidity of form that is the work's principal subject.

To illustrate further the close connection between metamorphosis and wordplay, let us consider the trope referred to by modern convention as syllepsis, a favorite in Ovid's panoply of "verbal wit," whereby the figurative and literal significances of a word are both employed simultaneously. The trope is often called "zeugma." Ancient grammarians define neither syllepsis nor zeugma in terms that correspond to the most conspicuous feature of Ovid's usage, the joining of literal and figurative senses. The modern use of syllepsis to describe such a joining owes its currency to the influential eighteenth-century treatise of Dumarsais, *Des tropes, ou des différents sens* (1730). In the previous century, G. J. Vossius had defined *syllepsis oratoria* as a kind of wordplay: *cum vox anceps usurpatur communiter; sive, cum verbo ambiguo res unâ plures significantur*, "When a word of various meanings is used without discriminating between them, or, when several things are signified at the same time by an ambiguous word."[19] Vossius illustrates in his examples the simultaneous use of literal and figurative senses. Dumarsais, while drawing much from Vossius, including his examples, adapts the trope by setting it explicitly in the class of metaphor: "La *syllepse* (σύλληψις, comprehensio, complexio, συλλαμβάνω, comprehendo) oratoire est une espèce de métaphore ou de comparaison, par laquelle un même mot est pris en deux sens dans la même phrase, l'un au propre, l'autre au figuré" ("Rhetorical syllepsis is a kind of metaphor or comparison, by which the same word is taken in two senses in the same phrase, the proper sense and the figurative sense").[20] In Ovid's

---

[19] Vossius 1695–1701, 3:196. See Appendix A, "G. J. Vossius on *syllepsis oratoria*."
[20] Dumarsais [1730] 1988, 145. See Appendix B, "Syllepsis and Zeugma."

works this trope is widespread and noticeable; he first made it important, employing it with great originality for his specific thematic purposes.

In the *Metamorphoses*, as in other works of Ovid, we often observe syllepsis as a localized phenomenon involving only a few words: When Jupiter put a stop to Phaethon's ride, *animaque rotisque / expulit*, "He knocked him out of his wits and out of the chariot" (2.312–313). When Vulcan heard that his wife Venus was enjoying an adulterous affair with Mars, *et mens et quod opus fabrilis dextra tenebat / excidit*, "His spirits dropped, as did the work that the blacksmith's hand was holding" (4.175–176). *Actaque magni / Herculis inplerant terras odiumque novercae*, "The deeds of great Hercules filled the lands and fulfilled the animosity of his stepmother" (9.134–135). Alcmaeon, pursued by the Furies, is *exul mentisque domusque*, "An exile from his wits and home" (9.409). This list could go on and on.[21] The figure is not unknown in the *Aeneid*, and several Ovidian examples reflect Vergil's language at *Aen.* 5.508, *pariterque oculos telumque tetendit*, "At the same time he aimed his gaze and shaft." Vergil's only slightly metaphorical *oculos* gives the syllepsis a mild and unemphatic impact, whereas Ovid in parallel examples polarizes the conceptual and physical, so that their union produces a jolt (e.g., *Met.* 2.505–506: *pariterque ipsosque nefasque / sustulit*, "At the same time he removed the crime and its perpetrators"; 3.99–100: *pariter cum mente colorem / perdiderat*, "He had lost his color together with his courage").[22] In the case of syllepsis, as often, what is marginal and limited in Vergil has become central and widespread in Ovid. In its sheer pervasiveness, the figure takes on a larger impact than these few rather simple examples may suggest. So many words so frequently slide between their literal and metaphorical senses that the slippage becomes a conspicuous feature of the narrative surface. And it is a thematically suggestive feature. For once a word has suggested to us literal and metaphorical senses at the same time, it is but a small step to a similar linking of the physical and the conceptual. Ovid is certainly prepared to take that step, for it offers him a chance to blur the boundaries between words and ideas on the one hand, and things on the other. Thus syllepsis as a stylistic figure becomes directly connected with metamorphosis as a feature of plot; or, put another way, the easy shift in syllepsis from figurative to literal can be drawn upon to make an easy shift from the conceptual to the physical in metamorphosis. Ovid often plays on literal and figurative meanings in the description of metamorphosis, where there is often a connection between the character of the human being and the physical nature of that animal or plant into which he or she is transformed. We learn that Perdix, for

---

[21] See Appendix C, "Further Examples of Syllepsis in Ovid."
[22] See Anderson 1972, 23–24, and his index s.v. *pariter*.

example—changed from talented boy to swift bird—originally had a *velox ingenium*, and then had *veloces pedes* (8.254–255). To blur the boundaries between literal and figurative meanings is the perfect linguistic representation of metamorphosis.

This play on *velox* has perhaps taken us somewhat beyond syllepsis as it is usually defined and was illustrated in our original examples. But it is less useful to think of syllepsis (or of other types of Ovidian wit, for that matter) as separate categories, to be identified and classified, than to view them as habits of Ovid's imaginative expression. For his is what we could call a *sylleptic imagination*—one always ready to slip from the figurative to the literal, from the conceptual to the physical, and back, in creating a work on flux and the transformation of all forms and bodies. Puns often have a sylleptic quality. Redfern, quoting a writer on children's humor, remarks that "even simple puns tie a physical action or object to a mental concept or thought, such as the man taking a ruler to bed to see how long he slept."[23] That quintessentially simple fellow, Polyphemus in Book 13, offers a dazzling example of such a sylleptic pun, inspired to wit by his infatuation with the fair Galatea. When Telemus the prophet warns him that Ulysses will snatch away his single eye, the Cyclops replies with a laugh, *altera iam rapuit*, "Another has already snatched it" (13.775), drawing on the vocabulary of Roman erotic elegy, vocabulary familiar from Ovid's *Amores*—*nostros rapuisti nuper ocellos*, "You lately snatched my eyes" (*Am.* 2.19.19)[24]—and in a milder form from Propertius—*oculos cepisti*, "You captured my eyes" (3.10.15). Combining the figurative application of the elegiac *rapere oculos* with its physical application to Polyphemus, unrecognized by him, Ovid's ironic pun achieves a simultaneously grisly and hilarious effect:

> Telemus interea Siculam delatus ad Aetnen,
> Telemus Eurymides, quem nulla fefellerat ales,
> terribilem Polyphemon adit, "lumen" que, "quod unum
> fronte geris media, rapiet tibi" dixit "Ulixes."

---

[23] Redfern 1984, 149. A sylleptic pun is the first example of syllepsis addressed by Riffaterre (1980, 628–629), who comments on Mallarmé's use of *hymen* and a discussion of it by Derrida: "Our critic points out that the grammar prevents the reader from choosing between hymen as 'marriage,' a symbolic union or fusion, and as 'vaginal membrane,' the barrier to be broken through if desire is to reach what it desires." Riffaterre's aim is to extend the meaning of syllepsis to correspond to elaborate examples of intertextuality (see 637–638), but this discussion of *hymen*, a case of his "complementary" type of intertextuality, is most relevant to Ovidian syllepsis. Riffaterre notes that "it is rare . . . to find two normal, current meanings of the same word activated simultaneously" (629). In Ovid, examples are common, as if he sought them out, or discovered them everywhere.

[24] See also *Am.* 3.11.48. Schawaller (1987, 204–205) includes this play on *rapere* among her examples of "semantic wordplay." On the tone of this passage, see below, Chapter 2.

>   risit et "o vatum stolidissime, falleris" inquit,
> "altera iam rapuit."
> (*Met.* 13.770–775)

> Meanwhile, Telemus put in at Aetna—Telemus, whose notice no bird of prophecy escaped. He approached dreadful Polyphemus and said, "The single eye, which you have in the middle of your forehead, Ulysses will snatch away from you." Polyphemus laughed and said, "O most stupid of bards, you are wrong: another has already snatched it."

In its complexity of tone, this pun is far different from anything that could be reduced to "comic relief." Funny as it is, it has an intellectual seriousness and a relevance to its larger context that deserve to be recognized.[25] Some have said that Ovid was not really interested in metamorphosis at all;[26] tales such as this one are taken to support this claim, since hundreds of lines go by without the description of a single metamorphosis (only much later does the narrative sequence include Acis's transformation into a river of the same name). I maintain that, on the

---

[25] A work whose intellectual seriousness is less often doubted is *Paradise Lost*, in which Milton, no stranger to the *Metamorphoses*, avails himself of witticisms that much resemble Ovid's. Eve may be regarded as the first discoverer of syllectic wordplay; for she, upon seeing the forbidden tree, grants to "fruitless" an unaccustomed literal force: "Serpent, we might have spar'd our coming hither, / Fruitless to mee, though Fruit be here to excess" (*Paradise Lost* 9.647–648). Such puns then enter Adam's speech at his fall. After eating the fruit, he becomes witty, quickly adept at syllectic and etymological wordplay: "*Eve*, now I see thou are exact of taste, / And elegant, of Sapience no small part, / Since to each meaning savor we apply, / And Palate call judicious; I the praise / Yield thee, so well this day thou hast purvey'd" (*Paradise Lost* 9.1017–1021). Adam plays on the literal and figurative meanings of "taste" and calls attention to the etymological connection between "sapience" and "savor." Editors note an allusion to Cicero *De finibus* 2.8.24 (*nec enim sequitur ut cui cor sapiat ei non sapiat palatus*, "He whose mind is sapient will not necessarily lack a sapient palate [i.e., one able to taste]"). For more syllectic wit, see Adam's reproachful description of Eve: "All but a Rib / Crooked by nature, bent, as now appears, / More to the part sinister from me drawn" (*Paradise Lost* 10.884–886).

Milton's puns can have a transformative character, and seem especially Ovidian when linked to metamorphosis. As Satan enters paradise at *Paradise Lost* 5.181, he "at one slight bound high overleap'd all bound / Of Hill or highest Wall." Tillyard (1951, 71–75) associates the pun on "bound" with its stylistic context, emphasizing a tonal transformation from tragic to comic in the portrayal of Satan. Yet Milton's wordplay is also, like Ovid's, linked to metamorphosis as an event of plot: Satan has transformed himself into the shape of a "stripling Cherub" in true Ovidian fashion at *Paradise Lost* 3.634–644, and at his leap into Paradise shifts from cherubic to cormorant form. On Ovidian and Miltonic puns, see DuRocher 1985, 128, 135–136.

[26] "Metamorphosis as an actual subject does not matter to Ovid" (Galinsky 1975, 55). This is a theme of Galinsky's treatment; e.g., "A . . . most fundamental novelty of the *Metamorphoses*, compared to the earlier metamorphosis poems, is that they are *not* about metamorphosis" (Galinsky 1975, 3). For other such views and a useful corrective, see Solodow 1988, 14–15, 234 n. 13.

contrary, Ovid finds metamorphosis not only in events of plot but everywhere else as well. In fact, he is out to show that change is suffused throughout creation, and throughout every aspect of human experience. Fittingly, it is also embodied in the style of the *Metamorphoses*. Wit is constantly keeping matters in flux—paradox seeming to drain words of their semantic value, and wordplay seeming to superload them with extra. On the narrative surface, transformation is occurring as much in the tales of Althea and Polyphemus as in those that highlight, as a central event, the change of some human being into a tree or rock.[27]

Indecorous and Transformative Puns

In pursuing the dissolution of various kinds of boundary, it is only natural that Ovid would willfully violate stylistic decorums, including generic and tonal decorums; for such violation creates dissolution or breakdown in the elements of the reader's experience of the text, and one can view such disruptive events as part of the general pattern. Even in small-scale and localized disruptions, we are given a view of their larger relevance. According to Redfern, "The pun is obviously anti-decorum,"[28] and Ovid's puns certainly register a sense of violation and distress in some of his critics. The display of tears with which Ulysses begins his speech, as he begs the assembled Greeks for Achilles' arms, does not prevent him from making a pun that has proved unacceptable to some:

> quis magno melius succedit Achilli,
> quam per quem magnus Danais successit Achilles?
> (*Met.* 13.133–134)

> Who better succeeds great Achilles than he who succeeded at winning him over to the Greeks?

"Un jeu de mots intraduisible," says Lafaye, but not according to J. J. Hartman: *non lusus verborum . . . sed merae sunt ineptiae*, "Not a play on

---

[27] Paradox, wordplay, and syllepsis abound also in other works of Ovid's, some of which have little to do with the transformation of human beings into natural phenomena. Dissolution of semantic boundaries, however, is as much Ovid's concern in those works as in the *Metamorphoses*. To cite one paradoxical formulation in the *Ars Amatoria*: *saepe, quod incipiens fixerat esse, fuit*, "Often he was what at the start he had only pretended to be" (*Ars Am.* 1.616). One could argue that the context reveals an inward transformation, as the pretender to love (*simulator, Ars Am.* 1.615) actually begins to love; and that wit has a parallel function in both works. Yet this example has a deeper kinship with witticisms in the *Metamorphoses*: it likewise represents the collapse of opposed categories, here pretense and truth. D. F. Kennedy, who is not discussing paradox in particular, but the force of the passage as a whole, remarks, "At what point can 'feigned' love be said to have become 'real'? Such analyses tend to blur any distinction between 'real' and 'false.'" (Kennedy 1993, 67).

[28] Redfern 1984, 18.

words, but pure foolishness"; so he emends *successit* to *accessit*, eliminating the pun.[29] By setting *lusus verborum* and *merae ineptiae* in exclusive opposition, Hartman implies that the former could be safely accepted into the text, but not the latter; while Ovid may be permitted acceptable wordplay, *this* example is too much. Hartman resists our temptation to admit this case as wordplay, to fall for it, so to speak. But Ovid, I suspect, knew not only of the "hidden depths and traps" that characterize the pun,[30] but also of his readers' general willingness (though perhaps not everyone's) to fall into the pit opened by wordplay, even if it meant knocking against *merae ineptiae* at the bottom. Though the evaluative force of Hartman's term *ineptiae* should be rejected, the term is in a sense paradoxically appropriate: indecorous wit is not *aptus*, it does not fit, contrived as it is to stretch and burst its contextual limits. The result can be painful, for these limits often represent standards, like Dryden's criteria of a "serious Poem," which are well established in the reader's mind, and to which a sense of value has long been committed.

Though this may be Ulysses' most indecorous pun, it is not his only one:

> his umeris, his inquam umeris ego corpus Achillis
> et simul arma tuli; quae nunc quoque ferre laboro.
> (*Met.* 13.284–285)

On these shoulders, *these* shoulders, I tell you, I bore away Achilles' body together with his arms—which now also I am struggling to bear away/to win.

Here the pun has a sylleptic edge, for although *ferre* retains physical force—one "carries off" a prize—Ulysses' double use of the same verb in *tuli* and *ferre* points up the contrast between them, calling attention to the more metaphorical sense, "to win," in the latter.[31] Once the suggestive identification of conceptual and physical has been made, it spills over into the context. *Laboro* might have seemed a dull and ordinary metaphor for the rhetorical effort in which Ulysses is now engaged. But his emphatic reference to his shoulders' physical contribution to the earlier effort now enables him to play on the literal and the figurative in *laboro*, revivifying the metaphor by referring to its origin in physical labor.

---

[29] Lafaye 1928–1930, 3:59 n. 1. Hartman 1920, 433; the emendation was anticipated by Faber (see H. Magnus 1914, ad loc.). See Bömer 6:239.

[30] Redfern 1984, 6.

[31] Schawaller (1987, 201–202) discusses both examples as "semantic wordplay," with others from the *Metamorphoses* and *Heroides*. In semantic wordplay, as Schawaller characterizes it, Ovid uses a word twice in a single context, engaging in each case connotations widely separated on the semantic spectrum. This is a larger phenomenon than paronomasia and zeugma (i.e., syllepsis), from which she distinguishes it on formal grounds (211–213).

Then, later, *ferre* can reappear with a backward glance at its intensified double sense: *fortisque viri tulit arma disertus*, "The eloquent man carried off/won the brave man's arms" (*Met.* 13.383).

Let us consider the contribution of some other sylleptic puns to their contexts. We have already seen how Polyphemus, later in Book 13, can achieve this kind of wit in his riposte to Telemus. Polyphemus's ill-judged attempt to win Galatea's love through song, with its heap of epithets and ludicrous self-commendatory arguments, meets with total failure, as Galatea rejects him outright in favor of her Acis. Yet Polyphemus retains one rhetorical weapon in store. Before smashing Acis with a rock, he threatens Galatea with his intention to do so, and includes a transformative sylleptic pun:

> viscera viva traham divisaque membra per agros
> perque tuas spargam (sic se tibi misceat!) undas.
> (*Met.* 13.865–866)
>
> I shall tear apart his living guts and scatter his severed limbs across the fields
> and your own water—let him join with you that way!

In the expression *sic se tibi misceat*, Polyphemus plays on the "literal and transferred senses," as Kenney remarks, of *miscere*.[32] The metaphor of transference in figurative language is especially apt. It is sometimes said that in order to commit violence, one needs conceptually to objectify the victim, to move the victim, by any rhetorical means available, out of the human category. So here Polyphemus, abandoning his verbal appeal to Galatea and shifting to physical violence toward Acis, exploits the pun's semantic scope in an especially grisly fashion. The pun transfers Acis from his identity as Galatea's lover—denoted by the figurative sense of *miscere*—to his new identity as a dismembered, indeed partly liquefied, body, as denoted by the literal sense. Acis has been carried across a semantic gulf, and is then translated from the human to the natural realm.[33] When he turns into a stream, which is to be known thereafter by his name, metamorphosis completes the transformative process already initiated by Polyphemus's words, or rather re-enacts on the level of plot what the pun has already achieved.

A sylleptic instance of paronomasia, or punning repetition of a word, occurs as the shape-shifting deity Vertumnus is described taking on various disguises to gain access to Pomona. In a passage that seems deliber-

---

[32] Kenney 1986, 453.

[33] The same verb may be used of saints translated across a parallel gulf—but in another direction, so to speak—from earth to heaven: *fide Enoch translatus est ne videret mortem*, "By faith Enoch was translated, lest he see death" (*Ad Hebraeos* 11.5, translating μετετέθη). This verb also provides the metaphor of metaphor, μεταφορά, *translatio* (Quint. 8.6.4).

ately to blur disguise and self-transformation—both are specialties of Vertumnus—Ovid plays on physical and conceptual meanings of *putare*, "to prune" and "to think":

> falce data frondator erat vitisque putator;
> induerat scalas: lecturum poma putares.
> (*Met.* 14.649–650)

> Given a pruning-hook, he was a shearer and vine-pruner; when he had taken up a ladder, you would have thought him an apple-picker.

The semantic shift that we must make here offers a parallel on the stylistic surface to the fast-changing forms by which Vertumnus penetrates the defensive enclosure designed to protect Pomona. The context of this witticism is a literally transgressive act.

In a work where we are accustomed to understand *mutare* in the sense of physical change, Ovid takes his readers by surprise, slipping it in with a different sense, "to exchange," at the sacrifice of Iphigenia:

> victa dea est nubemque oculis obiecit et inter
> officium turbamque sacri vocesque precantum
> subposita fertur mutasse Mycenida cerva.
> (*Met.* 12.32–34)

> The goddess was won over. She set a cloud before their eyes and among the ceremonials and ado of the rite, and voices of praying participants, she is said to have brought in a deer and put it in Iphigenia's place.

Because Diana's substitution of a hind for Iphigenia is "itself a sort of metamophosis," as has been ingeniously pointed out,[34] Ovid's use of this verb calls attention to its double meaning. Once again, wordplay is linked to metamorphosis.

Ovid's retelling of Book 3 of the *Aeneid* offers him another opportunity for punning:[35]

> hunc Anius, quo rege homines, antistite Phoebus
> rite colebatur, temploque domoque recepit.
> (*Met.* 13.632–633)

> Anius, who protected his people as king and worshiped Phoebus as priest, received Anchises into his temple and home.

In this case, as in *mutasse*, Ovid introduces puns into allusive contexts, tragedy and the *Aeneid*, that are largely serious, yet are by no means

---

[34] Kenney 1986, 443.
[35] H-E, on *Met.* 13.632, notes this as an example of zeugma. For satirical elements in Ovid's Little *Aeneid*, see below, Chapter 3.

without puns of their own. Some readers will find Ovid's puns strikingly indecorous in view of the generic allusions of their contexts, others only mildly so. If readers do find their sense of propriety abused, Ovid will have gained a thematic point. Yet in any case, these puns superload the meaning of words, and thereby contribute to the thematic reference of Ovidian wordplay in general.[36]

Misunderstanding *Aura*: Cephalus, Procris, and the Pun

Whereas puns are examples of the semantic shifting that can occur as we readers apprehend and appreciate Ovid's text, there are also, as we have seen, many characters in the work who, as a parallel to our own experience, differently understand or misunderstand utterances. Echo willfully and deliberately changes the sense of Narcissus's words, and a similar change can result by accident, as in the tale of Cephalus and Procris. Procris mistakes her husband's innocent address to the breeze, *aura veni*, "Breeze, come!" (*Met.* 7.837), as an adulterous invitation to a mistress. Here the lack of any fixed distinction between words and names has fatal results for Procris.

As Cephalus tells the story, some rash informer (*temerarius index*, *Met.* 7.824) hears Cephalus extravagantly singing to the breeze on his solitary hunts, and reports his suspicions to Procris:

> vocibus ambiguis deceptam praebuit aurem
> nescio quis nomenque aurae tam saepe vocatum
> esse putat nymphae: nympham me credit amare.
> (*Met.* 7.821–823)

Someone listened and was deceived by the words of double meaning, supposed that the name *aura*, which I so often called out, was that of a nymph, and thought I loved a nymph.

In *vocibus ambiguis* Ovid explicitly calls attention to words that admit different interpretations from different parties, and he presents us with an expression, *nomen aurae*, that could mean either "the word breeze" or "the name Aura." The point is sometimes made that this long tale has

---

[36] Another instructive example of Ovidian punning occurs in Hercules' threat to Nessus at *Met.* 9.126: *vulnere, non pedibus te consequar*, "I will *attack* you with a wound, not *pursue* you with my feet" (hindered by the stream, Hercules shoots Nessus with an arrow). This is not a case of syllepsis, for both meanings of *consequar* are predominantly physical. But it is an impressive example of stretching a single word to embrace two very different simultaneous meanings. At *Met.* 10.557 (*pressitque et gramen et ipsum*, "Venus pressed both the grass and Adonis himself"), Ovid comically joins two different physical uses of *pressit* (Anderson [1972, 521–522] identifies this case as a zeugma).

very little metamorphosis in it.[37] But in fact, ambiguous language achieves the same result in the central narrative. Cephalus's misprision is a consequence of Procris's, and permits her to be killed as a game animal without actually becoming one. Misunderstanding *aura*, Procris enters the woods after Cephalus; when she hears her husband's passionate address to the breeze, she makes a rustling sound among the leaves where she is hiding, and Cephalus throws his unerring javelin. There is no need for physical transformation, for error has effectively made this change on the conceptual level. Because error can transform nothing into something, there is a special irony in Cephalus's remark about Procris's misunderstanding of *aura*: *quod nihil est metuit, metuit sine corpore nomen*, "She feared a mere nothing, she feared a word without a body" (*Met*. 7.830).[38]

Though Cephalus the narrator may have a less than adequate understanding of events, narrative gives him a second chance to gain interpretive control over them, and to instruct others, realizing his interpretation in their acceptance of it. I do not mean to be cynical about Cephalus's motives. One could easily regard him as unconsciously shaping his past to gratify present emotional longings. Memory can be as selective and self-serving as any operation of rhetorical skill. Perhaps, as Galinsky imagines, "for Cephalus, it is all heartfelt, personal experience."[39] In any case, it is the presence of an audience that enables Cephalus to recast his life as a satisfying tragic narrative. He has receptive listeners in the assembled Aeginetans, who are about to embark in support of Athens against

---

[37] What Otis would call a "true" metamorphosis is that of the hound and fox into stone (*Met*. 7.759–793), which in this tale seems almost like a digression. According to Otis (1970, 81), though Ovid "often introduced tales that were not true metamorphoses," such as that of Cephalus and Procris, "he usually followed them by, or incorporated in them, incidental metamorphoses of one sort or another." Anderson notes a structural function of the literal transformation of hound and fox in separating elements of the principal story: "Ovid breaks it carefully into two corresponding sections by inserting a slight metamorphosis at the center (759–93), which has little to do with the passionate love of Cephalus and his wife Procris" (Anderson 1972, 311).

[38] The pun on *aura* occurs within a larger context of *voces ambiguae*, "ambiguous terms" (*Met*. 7.821). The language within which Cephalus addresses the breeze is normally figurative and normally amatory, but he uses it with an uncommon literalness: *intresque sinus, gratissima, nostros, / utque facis, relevare velis, quibus urimur, aestus*, "Enter my breast, most pleasing delight, and, as you are doing, consent to relieve the heat with which I am burned" (*Met*. 7.814–815). Rosati's illuminating discussion emphasizes that the disjunction between amatory figurative sense and literal sense corresponds to the two different audiences: Procris, overhearing the words, and Cephalus, singing them to himself. "The Ovidian reader, in his competence, observes from above the tragedy of misunderstanding, which arises not only from a name, *aura*, but precisely from a special jargon, the lexicon of erotic eros: it recovers here, in the mouth of Cephalus, its primary and original sense, stripped of its accustomed metaphorical valences" (Rosati 1983, 100).

[39] Galinsky 1975, 151.

King Minos, but are now delayed. They have kindly intentions toward the elderly speaker and are entirely immobile, thanks to the contrary winds. And in Ovid's larger narrative scheme, the time is no less right: Cephalus can easily engage that other audience, ourselves, the readers, many of whom are always ready for a warm bath in tragic emotions—emotions that Ovid usually denies us.[40]

Indeed, the narrator himself gives the lead to the sentimental tragic interpretations of this story that some critics have chosen to make.[41] But such critics neglect the larger transformation that is taking place. As a narrator of his own story, Cephalus can cast a warm glow over it, leaving his audience as well as himself awash in tears: *flentibus haec lacrimans heros memorabat*, "In tears the hero recounted these events to his weeping listeners" (*Met.* 7.863).[42] Ovid's readers, if aware of other, more standard versions,[43] may suspect a revisionist selectivity in Cephalus's recollection of events. As if to clue us in to the workings of narrative, to let us watch a narrator transforming his material, while at the same time engaging us in it, Ovid has Cephalus leave in quite a few traces of the standard versions, enough to show how differently the story might have been told. "What Cephalus tells is not really the true or full story, but an edited version of it," Otis rightly remarks.[44] Cephalus's most glaring suppression is his silence about how he acquired the marvelous javelin: he had it in return for sexual favors, granted to a man who turned out to be his wife Procris in disguise:

> quae petit, ille refert et cetera: nota pudori,
> qua tulerit mercede, silet.
> (*Met.* 7.687–688)

Cephalus answered the request and told the rest of the story. But he kept quiet about a matter known to his sense of shame, the price he paid to get the javelin.

Procris's mistaken understanding of *aura* is another example. Though Cephalus may be innocent in his address to the breeze, Procris has good

---

[40] According to Galinsky, "Unmitigated tragedy comes to the fore" in Cephalus and Procris. But "Ovid narrates few genuinely tragic stories in the *Metamorphoses*" (Galinsky 1975, 67; see also 150–152).

[41] E.g., Pöschl 1959, and especially Segal 1978.

[42] Cephalus also began his narrative in tears: *lacrimis ita fatur obortis* (*Met.* 7.689).

[43] These versions, including Ovid's probable source, Nicander, are concisely discussed by Otis (1970, 410–413).

[44] Ibid., 179–180. In Otis's view, Cephalus offers "a version chastened and corrected by his respect for Procris's memory and by his continuing devotion" (180). I see it as corrected by guilt and a desire to control the past by narrative revision of it—impulses that coexist with his "grief for his lost wife," *tactusque dolore / coniugis amissae . . . ita fatur* (*Met.* 7.688–689). See also Mack 1988, 131–134.

reason to suspect his fidelity in view of his long-standing relationship with Aurora, conspicuous in the standard versions, which was mentioned long before (*Met.* 7.700–708, 721–722) and which now, at this point in the tale, is unlikely to hold the attention of listeners or readers.[45] There may, however, be an unconscious reminder of it for us, unnoted by Cephalus, in his conventional time-setting:

> postera depulerant Aurorae lumina noctem:
> egredior silvamque peto.
> (*Met.* 7.835–836)

Aurora's last lights had driven away the night: I set out and seek the woods.

Cephalus gains rhetorically by emphasizing the informer and omitting mention of other possible causes for Procris's suspicion; instead, we hear about how innocent he is, and how mistaken Procris was to suspect him. As he guides his audiences into the moving conclusion, his emotionally self-exculpatory goals in narrative are well served by the pleasure audiences take—ourselves as well as the listeners within the tale—in a well-elaborated but uncomplicated death scene, one from which all problematic elements have been cleared away. The emotional power of the scene receives a great boost from the clarity that Cephalus gives it. He resolves the *error nominis*, at last restricting *aura* to its proper meaning in context. Cephalus gains complete interpretive control over the situation, and is even permitted to instruct his wife in the correct understanding, in his view, of her own death:

> "ne thalamis Auram patiare innubere nostris!"
> dixit, et errorem tum denique nominis esse
> et sensi et docui.
> (*Met.* 7.856–858)

"Do not let Aura succeed me as your wife!" she said; and then at last I understood, and taught her about, her mistaken understanding of the word.

The clarity, comprehensibility, and decorum of this death scene require that *aura* no longer function as a pun. Cephalus has power over this story, and he makes it happen.

---

[45] Though I am skeptical of Ahl's pursuit of anagrams in this story (Ahl 1985, 204–208), I agree that "Cephalus' talk of Aura must remind his questioner of the narrator's earlier, admitted affair with Aurora" (207). But what reminds Procris of Aurora is principally the fact that the goddess, like the imagined Aura, was Cephalus's lover. In this case, the partial similarity of sound between the two names does have relevance to the context. The remarks of Davis (1983, 142–144) support a view that Cephalus's language in addressing Aura is transformative, for it shows a "zeal for personification" (143) in Cephalus that goes far toward making the breeze into a rival—just what Procris will understand it to be.

Divinatory Wordplay: The Pun Overheard

Many people who use puns in conversation intend them to wound the sensibilities of their listeners—so much, at least, we may infer of their intentions from their obvious delight at the groans and winces with which the listeners involuntarily express their pain. Procris's misunderstanding of *aura*, as we have seen, makes it a pun: a word becomes stretched to include an extra measure of meaning. Yet Cephalus, unlike the conscious punster, never intended a double meaning, nor did Procris understand *aura* in a double sense. Until recast by Cephalus in narrative form, *aura*'s double meaning escapes the awareness and control of both speaker and listener. *Aura* is an extreme example of the autonomy of language, of its potential to escape the bounds necessarily set for it by speakers, in their attempt to communicate or to express themselves, and by audiences, in their attempt to make sense of what they receive. Such uncontrolled wordplay works by overhearing, for *aura* would not be a pun at all if Procris did not overhear it by accident. Though she comes to the woods well prepared by her suspicions to interpret *aura* as she does, chance gives her suspicions a shape, facilitating her conclusion that *Aura* is her husband's mistress.

The fact that words can become puns by being accidentally overheard grants them a role in divination. For the gods can overhear a human utterance, if they choose, and give it new and unforeseen interpretations. Though the speakers are unaware of the divine interpretation granted their words, it is accessible to some human beings, of augural sensitivity, who may also hear them; they must be overheard twice. Divinatory wordplay, or kledonomancy, warrants illustration here, for it is an element both of the Romans' religious experience and of their understanding of how language functions. It is exemplified in several Ovidian transformations, and invites interpretation of double meaning in terms of its typical patterns of elucidation.

Livy concludes his fifth book with a classic case of a divinatory pun, or κληδών. The Romans, demoralized by the recent occupation of their city, are wondering whether to migrate to Veii. They hear a long, elaborate, and powerful speech by Camillus, who urges them to remain at Rome:

> movisse eos Camillus cum alia oratione tum ea quae ad religiones pertinebat maxime dicitur; sed rem dubiam decrevit vox opportune emissa, quod cum senatus post paulo de his rebus in curia Hostilia haberetur cohortesque ex praesidiis revertentes forte agmine forum transirent, centurio in comitio exclamavit: "signifer, statue signum; hic manebimus optime." qua voce audita et senatus accipere se omen ex curia egressus conclamavit et plebs circumfusa

adprobavit. antiquata deinde lege promisce urbs aedificari coepta. (Liv. 5.55.1–2)

Camillus is said to have moved them by this speech, especially where it treated religious matters. But what decided the doubtful issue was a saying, which slipped out at just the right moment. For when the Senate, a little afterward, was convened to discuss this matter in the Curia Hostilia, and the cohorts returning from sentry duty by chance were crossing the forum in a troop, and were now at the Comitium, their centurion called out, "Standard-bearer, fix your standard: here we will best remain." When they heard this saying, the Senate came out of the Senate house and shouted that they accepted the omen, and the people, surrounding them, voiced their approval. Then the proposed law was rejected, and the city began to be randomly rebuilt.

As Ogilvie notes on this passage, "It was a form of divination to pick up a chance word or remark and to accept it in a sense other than that intended by the speaker who casually uttered it."[46] Two elements are cru-

---

[46] Ogilvie 1970, 752. Kledonomancy has been usually discussed in Aeschylean tragedy, as by Peradotto (1969), Cameron (1970), and Zeitlin (1982), but is far more extensive. For the Romans, see Pease 1963 on Cicero *De divinatione* 1.103 (p. 286); McCartney 1919; and O'Hara 1996a. E. Riess (*RE* s.v. *omen* 373.67–378.27) lists many divinatory puns on both words and names. Impressive among the latter is the story of Regalianus (etymologically mispelled Regilianus in the *Historia Augusta*), who became emperor as a result of a pun on his name: *mirabile fortasse videatur, si, quae origo imperii eius fuerit, declaretur. capitali enim ioco regna promeruit. nam cum milites cum eo quidam cenarent, extitit vicarius tribuni qui diceret: "Regiliani nomen unde credimus dictum?" alius continuo: "credimus quod a regno." tum is qui aderat scolasticus, coepit quasi grammaticaliter declinare et dicere: "rex regis regi Regilianus." milites, ut est hominum genus pronum ad ea, quae cogitant: "ergo potest rex esse?" item alius: "ergo potest nos regere?" item alius: "deus tibi regis nomen inposuit." quid multa? his dictis cum alia die mane processisset, a principiis imperator est salutatus. ita quod aliis vel audacia vel iudicium, huic detulit iocularis astutia*, "It would perhaps seem a cause for wonder if I were to explain the origin of his reign; for he came to power through a capital joke. When some soldiers were dining with him, a vice-tribune got up to say, 'Where do we imagine Regilianus's name comes from?' Another said at once, 'From royal power, I imagine.' Then a schoolteacher who was present began, as it were, to give a grammatical declension and to say, '*Rex regis regi Regilianus.*' The soldiers—a type of people very quick to pursue what they have in mind—respond, 'Can he therefore be king?' Likewise another, "Can he therefore rule us?" and another, "The gods have set on you the name of king." What need for further explanation? When, after this discussion, he went forth the next day in the morning, he was greeted as emperor by the frontline troops. And so, what audacity or judgment granted others, he gained through jocular cleverness" (*S.H.A.* 24 [*Tyr. Trig.*], 10.3–7). Though no doubt unhistorical, this tale is valuable in its combination of comic absurdity with reflection on characteristic modes of thought about divine intentions. For the link between names and omens in Plautus, Seneca, and Petronius, see Petrone 1988. Henderson (1988, 127) explores the paradoxically auspicious and inauspicious name of Scaeva at Lucan 6.257: *Scaeva . . . felix hoc nomine famae*, "Scaeva, fortunate in this name of renown." One the one hand, "*Scaeva* always meant *infelix*"; on the other, the name is

cial to the operation of omens of this kind: the divine meaning must be beyond the intention and awareness of the human speaker, and its reception must be accidental. The absence of human intentionality gives scope to the divine; the gap between meanings as intended and as potentially understood allows a glimpse of divine intention to those able to perceive it. Effective as Camillus's speech is at moving his audience, the κληδών permits divine ratification of his argument, tipping the scales in its favor. Once the gods have so clearly shown their desire that the Romans stay, the matter is settled; and in a sense, Rome owes its continued existence to a pun. The semantic potential of *hic manebimus optime* allows the gods' intervention: they come between the limits of the words, revealing an extent of meaning greater than what any human listener could have suspected or foreseen. Within this expanded semantic space the gods stake out their area of interpretation.

Livy's summary description of this event highlights its paradoxical character: *rem dubiam decrevit vox opportune emissa*. An ambiguous case, offering a choice of alternatives, is decided by a *vox* that has multivalence, that offers a choice of meanings. Providential ambiguity, it appears, permits divine interpretation to present itself with such clarity. Like other puns, to be sure, κληδόνες can be misunderstood, as in the case of M. Crassus, who, hearing a street-seller hawking Caunian figs, *Cauneas*, failed to perceive the further meaning offered by this word, *cave ne eas*, "Beware of going" (Cic. *De divinatione* 2.84; Plin. *H.N.* 15.83); and so he proceeded to his disastrous expedition against the Parthians. Once, however, someone hits upon the understanding that the gods have of an omen, its meaning becomes ineluctably obvious. Plutarch, in his version of the κληδών just cited from Livy, emphasizes this heaven-sent clarity, representing the omen as not in need of any words to explain it. And in fact, an explanatory restatement might introduce new ambiguities and problematic complications. At the meeting of the Senate on the question of whether to migrate to Veii, Camillus calls upon L. Lucretius to give his opinion. Lucretius is about to speak when the omen occurs. The centurion's words are overheard at once by the speaker and the assembled listeners; and Lucretius simply "votes with" the gods: ἅμα δὲ τῷ καιρῷ καὶ τῇ περὶ τοῦ μέλλοντος ἐννοίᾳ καὶ ἀδηλότητι τῆς φωνῆς γενομένης, ὅτε Λουκρήτιος ἔφη προσκυνήσας τῷ θεῷ προστίθεσθαι

---

auspicious in recalling Mucius Scaevola, an exemplum of *virtus*. Among Lucan's etymological puns, an especially impressive example links *Caesar* and *caedere*: *tu, Caesar, in alto / caedis adhuc cumulo patriae per viscera vadis*, "You, Caesar, on a high heap of slaughter, still stride through the guts of your country" (Luc. 7.721–722); see Henderson 1988, 151.

An interesting parallel to the ambiguity of divinatory wordplay is the ambiguity in multiple aetiologies, which, according to Miller (1992, 24–28), allow the divinity concerned a choice between them, and are thereby similar to epithets in hymns.

τὴν ἑαυτοῦ γνώμην καὶ τῶν ἄλλων ἕκαστος ἐπηκολούθησε, "The saying happened just at the right moment, as they were pondering the future, in uncertainty about it; whereupon Lucretius, with a gesture of obedience, declared that he would add his vote to that of the gods; and each of the others followed his lead" (*Camillus* 32.2). There is no need for Lucretius to explain anything: once he calls attention to it, the divine interpretation instantly shifts from an opaque to an obvious one.

In another instance of divinatory wordplay, closer to Ovid's time, Octavian himself could identify and trace destiny's motions in the multivalence of names: *apud Actium descendenti in aciem asellus cum asinario occurrit: homini Eutychus, bestiae Nicon erat nomen; utriusque simulacrum aeneum victor posuit in templo, in quod castrorum suorum locum vertit*, "At Actium, as he went to enter the battle, a little donkey with its driver met him: the man's name was Eutychus, 'lucky,' the beast's Nicon, 'victorious'; the victorious Octavian set up a bronze statue of them both in the precinct into which he transformed the site of his camp" (Suet. *Aug.* 96.2).[47] While to irreverent readers Suetonius may appear less than respectful in translating Nicon by *victor*, thereby making perhaps too close a connection between the donkey and Octavian, it is primarily Octavian's own controlling vision that guides interpretation of this wordplay. Puns, though well suited to the debunking and anarchic verbal activity of those who aim to demolish constructions of a serious nature, are essentially indiscriminate, available to anyone who has the wit to take advantage of them. Contemporary readers of Ovid's indecorous wordplay were familiar with a broad range of verbal shape-shifting, including that promoted by Octavian for highly serious ends. No stranger to the power of language, Octavian opportunistically grasps the divinatory wordplay available in this chance encounter, latent in the names of man and donkey. His imaginative activity is of a traditional stamp and draws on cultural resources of linguistic play. Yet it *is* imaginative activity, and here at least, if seldom elsewhere, Octavian's thought runs in channels that Ovid was to explore. By setting up a statue of man and donkey to memorialize the omen,[48] Octavian even offers us later observers an Ovidian parallel to

---

[47] See also Plut. *Ant.* 65.3; Zonaras 10.30 (*Patrologia Graeca* 134.891 B–C). Suetonius includes this example in a long list of omens (*Aug.* 94–97).

[48] As the memorial of an omen, the shrine of Aius Locutius offers an instructive parallel. Located on the *Nova via* at the foot of the Palatine, it marks the spot where M. Caedicius heard "a voice in the silence of night, more distinct than a human voice, which bid him tell the magistrates that the Gauls were coming" (*vocem noctis silentio audisse clariorem humana, quae magistratibus dici iuberet Gallos adventare*: Livy 5.32.6). According to Livy, Camillus proposed monumentalizing the site soon after defeating the Gauls (Livy 5.50.5), thus establishing an early and permanent connection between word, site, and monument. See J. Aronen in Steinby 1993, 29.

reflect upon; for the landscape of the *Metamorphoses* is strewn with statues that serve as *monumenta* of transformative wordplay. We readers of Ovid may also contemplate the comic potential of this bronze ass-driver and donkey in a military monument that bristled with the rams of ships and other impressive spoils.[49]

Two incidents in the *Metamorphoses* can illustrate Ovid's adapation of traditional κληδόνες to his own transformative wordplay. We have already noted Mercury's encounter with Aglauros:

> cui blandimenta precesque
> verbaque iactanti mitissima "desine" dixit
> "hinc ego me non sum nisi te motura repulso."
> "stemus" ait "pacto" velox Cyllenius "isto."
> caelestique fores virga patefecit.
> (*Met.* 2.815–819)

> When he kept subjecting her to flattery, entreaties, and sweet-talk, she replied, "Stop! I will not leave this place until you are driven away." "Let us agree upon these terms!" said swift Mercury. With his heavenly staff he opened the door.

Aglauros fails to recognize the semantic vulnerability of *motura*, unaware that she is offering her word to a divinity, who can choose to interpret it as an omen and exploit its potential for double meaning. This κληδών resembles Livy's and other typical examples in most respects: to Aglauros, the divine interpretation is accidental, unforeseen and unintended by her; once made, it irrevocably defines her fate. This case differs in that there is no need for a human being to overhear and recognize divine participation in meaning. We readers perform the augural role: Ovid lets us directly see the operation of divine hermeneutics by Hermes himself. Ovid's representation of the gods as personal agents, so casually, it may seem, borrowed from the panoply of epic convention,[50] becomes frighteningly revealing when combined with the equally typical and familiar patterns of divination. Malice all too clearly gives rise to divine hermeneutics, as to most other form of divine behavior in the *Metamorphoses*.

---

[49] So Ovid, regarding the temple of Mars Ultor in the Forum Augustum, invites a comic and indecorous view of its cult images, the adulterous Mars and Venus, and of her husband Vulcan left outside the door: *stat Venus Ultori iuncta, vir ante fores*, "Venus stands joined to the Avenger; her husband stands outside the door" (*Tr.* 2.296; see Owen 1924, 174–176). The comic angle may have escaped Augustus. On the design of the Actian monument, see Murray and Petsas 1989; on Eutychus and Nicon, ibid., 93, 153.

[50] See Feeney 1991, 232–239, on Ovid's exploitation of the "divine realism" of traditional epic, "the epic norms of analogy and authenticating detail in representing the divine" (232).

It is especially appropriate that Ovid represents Mercury as the god of divinatory double meaning in this story, for Mercury's preeminently shifty character makes him the best-qualified divine punster. Socrates in the *Cratylus*, playing with etymological meanings in the name of his interlocutor, Hermogenes, remarks, ἀλλὰ μὴν τοῦτό γε ἔοικε περὶ λόγον τι εἶναι ὁ Ἑρμῆς, καὶ τὸ ἑρμηνέα εἶναι καὶ τὸ ἄγγελον καὶ τὸ κλοπικόν τε καὶ τὸ ἀπατηλὸν ἐν λόγοις καὶ τὸ ἀγοραστικόν, περὶ λόγου δύναμίν ἐστιν πᾶσα αὕτη ἡ πραγματεία, "Well then, this name Hermes seems to concern speech, as does the fact that he is an interpreter, a messenger, thievish and deceptive in discourse, a bargainer: all this activity concerns the power of speech" (Pl. *Cratylus* 407E–408A).[51] Not just any sort of speech, one might add. The occupations listed here for the god require the more audacious and risky uses of words—language at its most aggressive and transgressive. So the pun on Aglauros's word is especially suitable for Mercury. Known for unorthodox boundary-crossings, since he slipped through a keyhole at one day old,[52] he now physically opens the doors barred to him (*Met.* 2.819). At the same time, Ovid grants him a pun to achieve the same result on the stylistic surface.

A similar treatment of kledonomancy occurs a little earlier in Book 2. It is again Mercury who makes the omen work, and another human being is turned to stone. Battus is the only one to notice that Mercury has successfully rustled Apollo's cattle. Bribed to keep silence, he tells Mercury,

> "hospes,
> tutus eas! lapis iste prius tua furta loquetur,"
> et lapidem ostendit.
> (*Met.* 2.695–697)

> "You may go in safety, stranger; this stone will speak of your theft before I do." And he pointed out a stone.

When Battus does betray the theft to Mercury in disguise, his remark becomes an omen and, enforced by divine interpretation, defines his fate. Again, we readers are allowed to see how κληδόνες work from behind the scenes. Of course, Mercury grasps the intended meaning in Battus's ἀδύνατον, his supposedly shared assumption that for stones to speak would be an impossibility; but Mercury chooses to take a literal interpretation unforeseen by the speaker. He turns Battus physically into a stone. But this is not an ordinary dumb stone, as, one is to infer, stones are conceptually classified in Battus's remark; it is a metaphorically speaking stone, *qui nunc quoque dicitur index*, "which even now is called the

---
[51] See Redfern 1984, 36.
[52] *Hymn. Hom.* 4.145–147.

Informer" (*Met.* 2.706). Ovid contributes both the κληδών and the "appropriate" nature of Battus's punishment to the story he received from his sources, where it is only Battus's name, "the Talker," that points to his fate.[53] By augmenting its significant wordplay, Ovid brings the tale fully into the *Metamorphoses*, making it exemplify the work's characteristic stylistic flux. We observe once again the fluid interchange of literal and metaphorical, physical and conceptual.

Vox non intellecta: Irony and Metamorphic Wordplay (Myrrha)

The most rigidly defined categories are those whose boundaries everyone has a stake in maintaining. Among these are family relationships, hedged about by taboos against incest. Because Ovid elaborates several tales, notably those of Byblis and Myrrha, in which these taboos are violated, many have pondered the relevance of incest to a work on transformation, seeking connections between these tales and Ovid's larger concerns. Some see large-scale psychological preoccupations in Myrrha's *discordia mentis* (*Met.* 10.445);[54] for others, Ovid's interest in incest is ethical, as Orpheus, the narrator, finally tells a story that will fit his announced theme, forbidden desires deserving just punishment:[55]

> puerosque canamus
> dilectos superis inconcessisque puellas
> ignibus attonitas meruisse libidine poenam.
> (*Met.* 10.152–154)

> Let us sing that boys, loved by the gods, and girls, smitten by forbidden fires, deserved the penalty for their passion.

And for some, the theme of incest is purely functional, a variation of motifs found elsewhere in the work, granting it "unity and coherence" of a technical sort.[56] For my purposes, the relevance of incest lies in the terms used to justify and account for it, terms that not only further illus-

---

[53] See Forbes Irving 1990, 30.

[54] For Wilkinson, the soliloquies of Byblis and Myrrha illustrate "Ovid's interest in psychology" (Wilkinson 1955, 205).

[55] See Anderson 1972, 501; Solodow 1988, 39. According to Otis (1970, 229), Ovid reaches in the tale of Myrrha "the lowest point in his narrative of unnatural *libido* and perverted desire." Nagle, discussing Byblis and Myrrha, imagines different degrees of ethical revulsion balanced against different degrees of sympathy on the part of the two narrators, the epic narrative voice (identified as "Ovid") and Orpheus: "Ovid is consistently sympathetic toward Byblis, whereas Orpheus is ambivalent toward Myrrha, with his initial revulsion giving way to sympathy" (Nagle 1983, 301).

[56] See Galinsky 1975, 88–91.

trate the resources of wordplay that we have been considering, but also expand wordplay's reach beyond ordinary limits. Here Ovid incorporates irony among its resources, and establishes a still closer link between the dissolution of semantic boundaries and metamorphosis. Such a concern is in no way inconsistent with other emphases that readers have found in Myrrha's story, though I would call their attention to the inseparability of virtually any thematic concern from verbal wit. *Discordia mentis*, for example, is an expression that arises directly from the paradoxical joining of grief and joy in Myrrha's heart (*Met.* 10.443–445). No "depth" of psychological theme has an existence apart from the narrative "surface."

As Myrrha herself seems to recognize, it is possible to think of incest as existing only in the abstractions used to conceptualize it. Family relationships, after all, are inconceivable without the *nomina consanguinitatis* that define them. This fact becomes especially clear when Myrrha, feeling the power of taboos, draws back from her intention to justify incest with her father:

> et quot confundas et iura et nomina, sentis!
> tune eris et matris paelex et adultera patris?
> tune soror nati genetrixque vocabere fratris?
> (*Met.* 10.346–348)

You see how many ties and names you are confounding. Will you be your mother's rival and your father's mistress? Will you be called your son's sister and brother's mother?

By accusing herself of confounding ties and names, she insists upon recognition of the proper limits that they presumably must have, while her rhetorical questions represent the *nomina* as having self-evident claims. How could a *filia* allow herself to be *matris paelex*, *adultera patris*, and so on? Here Myrrha, at least for now, cannot imagine the absence of a firm link between *nomina* and the categories of relationship that they help to keep separated. For the moment, there appears to be a perfect match, and an obvious one, between the two. Yet their very representation as *nomina* allows the categories to be blurred.

Already in her first speech, Myrrha is struggling against the fixed terms of relationship between herself and her father, and gains some initial success through the resources of paradox: "Because he is already mine, he is not mine":

> ergo, si filia magni
> non essem Cinyrae, Cinyrae concumbere possem;
> nunc, quia iam meus est, non est meus, ipsaque damno
> est mihi proximitas: aliena potentior essem.
> (*Met.* 10.337–340)

> Therefore, if I were not the daughter of great Cinyras, I would be able to sleep with him; but as it is, because he is already mine, he is not mine. Our very closeness functions as my loss. I would have greater power if I were a stranger.

Although she protests that Cinyras is of course *not* hers, the paradoxical identification of *meus* and *non meus* also sets these terms semantically afloat, suggesting the possibility of a new configuration.[57] And in the event, her disguise and deception of Cinyras will reverse these terms, erasing the father-daughter relationship and setting Cinyras in the category of *non meus*, so that he can become *meus* in the relationship of lover. *Quia non meus est, nunc est meus*: this is the achievement of Myrrha's disguise, and of her verbal shape-shifting.

The opening of the tale is shot through with paradoxes, beginning with its first line, wherein we learn that Cinyras would have been thought happy if he had been childless:[58]

> qui si sine prole fuisset,
> inter felices Cinyras potuisset haberi.
> (*Met.* 10.298–299)

> Cinyras, who, if he had been without offspring, could have been considered among the fortunate.

Orpheus soon introduces paradoxical play on *scelus*: *hic amor est odio maius scelus*, "This love is a worse crime than hate" (*Met.* 10.315). And when Myrrha begins her long speech of alternate self-condemnation and self-justification (*Met.* 10.320–355), *scelus* is the term that she seizes upon; for in justifying incest, she has much to gain from its potential for semantic slippage:

> di, precor, et pietas sacrataque iura parentum,
> hoc prohibete nefas scelerique resistite nostro,
> si tamen hoc scelus est.
> (*Met.* 10.321–323)

---

[57] Schawaller (1987, 207–208) notes this among examples of "semantic wordplay."

[58] Herodotus provides the *locus classicus* for the common view that children constitute part of complete happiness. In Book 1, Solon's first example of happiness is Tellus of Athens: Τέλλῳ τοῦτο μὲν τῆς πόλιος εὖ ἡκούσης παῖδες ἦσαν καλοί τε κἀγαθοί, καί σφι εἶδε ἅπασι τέκνα ἐκγενόμενα καὶ πάντα παραμείναντα, κτλ, "While his city prospered, Tellus had fine children, and he saw children born to them all, all of whom survived" (Hdt. 1.30.4). Like Solon's audience, Croesus, Cinyras was proverbially wealthy and might therefore already have a claim to be *inter felices*: e.g., Κινύρου πλουσιώτερος, "Wealthier than Cinyras"; Κινύρου πλοῦτος, "The riches of Cinyras"; cf. Erasmus (1536) 3.1.75, *Cinyrae opes*, *ASD* 2:5.2075 (*CWE* 34:211). But in his case not even wealth *and* fatherhood could make him happy.

> I pray you, gods, duty, and sacred bonds of parents: prevent this wrong,
> oppose my crime—if indeed it is a crime.

Invocation of *pietas* puts Myrrha well on the path to that familiar Ovidian paradox, *scelus est pietas*, which we have seen employed by Procne (*Met.* 6.635). Arguing from the practice of incest among various animal species, Myrrha proceeds to its acceptance among human *gentes*:

> in quibus et nato genetrix et nata parenti
> iungitur, ut pietas geminato crescat amore.[59]
> (*Met.* 10.332–333)

> Among whom mother is joined to son and daughter to father, so that the
> sense of duty may increase with redoubled affection.

While *scelus* has now fully become *pietas*, the *amor* identified with *scelus* at 315 can now be included under the category of *pietas*: both *amor* and *pietas* have undergone transformation.

Myrrha's story, sometimes labeled a "tragedy,"[60] has much irony of a sort customarily associated with that genre. This, like all the tragic features of the story, is not simply a formal consequence of generic allusion, but is fully integrated into Ovid's stylistic spectrum. Irony offers multiple meanings in a single expression, and so can be readily subsumed into Ovidian wordplay.[61] When, for example, Cinyras asks Myrrha what sort of husband she wants,

> "similem tibi" dixit; at ille
> non intellectam vocem conlaudat et "esto
> tam pia semper" ait. pietatis nomine dicto
> demisit vultus sceleris sibi conscia virgo.
> (*Met.* 10.364–367)

> She said, "One just like you." But he, not understanding the statement,
> praised it, saying, "Be always so dutiful." When she heard the word for duty,
> the maiden cast down her eyes, aware of her guilt.

---

[59] The vulgate *ut . . . crescat* (read here instead of Anderson's *et . . . crescit*) identifies a beneficial result.

[60] So Anderson 1972, 476.

[61] So Barthes includes tragic irony in his discussion of amphibologies or "double words," words that invite reflection on double meanings instead of making clear that a choice among restricted meanings is desirable: "In the dossier of this double response: the *addâd*, those Arab words each of which has two absolutely contrary meanings; Greek tragedy, the space of a double understanding, in which 'the spectator always understands more than what each character utters on his own account or on that of his partners'" (Barthes 1977b, 73).

Both *similem tibi* and *pia* are differently understood by Cinyras and Myrrha. Unwittingly taken by Cinyras in senses that we, along with Myrrha, know to be limited, they may be compared with the conscious and aggressive misunderstandings practiced by Echo in her response to Narcissus, and by Mercury in response to Aglauros. Meanwhile, Myrrha's ironic understanding of *pia* reaffirms the tale's central paradox, the identification of *scelus* and *pietas*.

In the succeeding conversation between the Nurse and Myrrha, there are several cases where the single word *pater*, while referring to Cinyras in the minds of both speaker and listener, means something quite different to each. At 401, the Nurse, ignorant of Myrrha's problem, lists advantages that ought to comfort her, ending with what the Nurse supposes will be a consolatory climax: *vivit genetrixque paterque*, "Your mother and father are alive" (*Met.* 10.401). Hearing the word "father," Myrrha sighs deeply; the Nurse, figuring out that Myrrha is in love, yet only partly understands the situation, and intends as encouragement an offer of help that concludes, *nec sentiet umquam / hoc pater*, "Your father will never find out about this" (*Met.* 10.409–410).

These are rather standard ironies,[62] as is the Nurse's remark, when Cinyras asks how old is the maiden offered him, *"par" ait "est Myrrhae,"* "She is equal in age to Myrrha" (*Met.* 10.441). Yet these ironies are closely linked to wordplay in the superloading of meaning that they achieve. And specific to the stylistic character of the *Metamorphoses* is the ironic focus on *nomina*, those terms that define the very boundaries eroded by irony. When Cinyras receives Myrrha into his bed and offers some words of encouragement to her in her troubled state,

> forsitan aetatis quoque nomine "filia" dixit:
> dixit et illa "pater," sceleri ne nomina desint.
> (*Met.* 10.467–468)

Perhaps he even said "Daughter," using a name that fit her age; and she said "Father," that their crime might not lack names.

Filia and *pater* must have seemed unsatisfactory terms to both participants in this encounter, yet they feel the need to clothe their act in some sort of verbal dress. Here Ovid touches upon a great paradox implicit in language. People need it; they cannot do without it even when its limita-

---

[62] Lines 401–402, alluding, as editors note, to Phaedra's conversation with the Nurse in *Hippolytus* 309ff., readily exploit ironies already present in the tragedy. In the tale of Procne, Ovid introduces various forms of generic allusion to tragedy, among which is irony of this kind, e.g., *et luget non sic lugendae fata sororis*, "And she [Procne] grieves for the fate of her sister who deserved grief, though not for this reason" (*Met.* 6.570). Ovid here exploits a double application of *lugenda* (Procne thinks Philomela is dead).

tions are evident, casting about for the available resources it affords. But once uttered, or written for that matter,[63] language is open to potentialities of meaning well beyond what the speaker may have intended or even imagined.

Even more impressive than the ironies themselves is the semantically destabilizing effect that they have on their surroundings. *Virgo Cinyreia* (369) is a perfectly ordinary epic locution, or rather would be if it did not come in a context wherein single expressions, such as *similem tibi* and *pia*, occurring shortly before, have multiple senses. Normally the patronymic *Cinyreia* would only identify Cinyras as Myrrha's father, but here she is "Cinyras's maiden" in two senses, and *Cinyreia* now functions as a pun. In a tale where *meus* and *non meus* collapse together, the most banal and easily understood formulation can become strangely affected, denatured by its context.

From boundary dissolution on the stylistic level it is but a short step to physical metamorphosis. Cinyras, eager to recognize who his lover may be, brings in a light: *inlato lumine vidit / et scelus et natam*, "Bringing in a light, he saw both the crime and his daughter" (*Met.* 10.473–474). Syllepsis, blurring the distinction between conceptual and physical, fittingly introduces the section of the tale wherein Myrrha's transformation into the myrrh-tree will occur.[64] For her tears, those *expressions* of her extreme emotional state, literally squeezed out of a body by more than physical passions, become physicalized as drops of myrrh:

> quae quamquam amisit veteres cum corpore sensus,
> flet tamen, et tepidae manant ex arbore guttae.
> (*Met.* 10.499–500)

Although she lost her old emotions along with her body, yet she weeps, and warm drops flow from the tree.

At the moment of recognition, Cinyras draws his sword (475). But he does not use it, and, as often in the *Metamorphoses*, a climax of action promised by the narrative movement gives way instead to metamorphosis. Exceptional in this story, however, is the fact that Myrrha is permitted to define her transformation before it occurs. Praying to the divinities, she asks for transformation in paradoxical terms, terms that correspond to her ambiguous emotional state *inter mortisque metus et taedia vitae*, "Between fear of death and weariness of life" (*Met.* 10.482):

---

[63] The special problems of written communication will concern us in the story of Byblis, below.

[64] Sylleptic expressions already suffuse the earlier narrative, e.g., *curasque et corpora somnus / solverat* (*Met.* 10.368–369); *tremulasque manus annisque metuque* (*Met.* 10.414). Cf. also the pairing of *fidem* and *opem* at 395, a mild syllepsis.

> o siqua patetis
> numina confessis, merui nec triste recuso
> supplicium. sed ne violem vivosque superstes
> mortuaque extinctos, ambobus pellite regnis
> mutataeque mihi vitamque necemque negate.
> (*Met.* 10.483–487)

> Gods—if there are any accessible to my confession—I have deserved a grievous punishment, and do not refuse it. But lest I, surviving, violate the living, or, dying, violate the dead, drive me from both realms. Transform me, and deny me both life and death.

Formerly she desired to be both *filia* and *amans*; now she wants neither life nor death. Her goal is always to position herself between opposed categories. In the case of *filia* and *amans*, it was merely an attempt to reconcile the irreconcilable. But life and death are more extreme: unlike *filia* and *amans*, they are definitive opposites, and everyone is assumed to have one or the other. In their abstract character they necessarily exclude the middle ground that Myrrha demands. Yet the fact of her transformation suggests that she has attained this impossible middle ground, that metamorphosis somehow embodies verbal paradox. Ovid may have adapted from Nicander Myrrha's final line, *mutataeque mihi vitamque necemque negate* (*Met.* 10.487). A hexameter, possibly direct from Nicander's *Heteroeumena*, has slipped into the prose summary of Antoninus Liberalis: (ηὔξατο) μήτε παρὰ ζῶσι[ν] μήτ' ἐν νεκροῖς[ι] (or ἐν νεκύεσσι) φανῆναι, "[She prayed] that she appear neither among the living nor among the dead" (Ant. Lib. 34.4).[65] Close as Ovid's version is to this, he introduces a characteristic change, one precisely relevant to the thematic character of his version. For instead of rejecting inclusion in groups of people who can be characterized as "the living" and "the dead," Ovid's Myrrha rejects pure abstractions, "life" and "death." That way Ovid can offer the paradox in its most extreme form at this climactic moment. Paradox *is* the action of this story.

Littera scripta manet—Or Does It? (Byblis)

Myrrha's tale is in many ways a rewriting of Byblis's. They share an emphasis on paradox, and in fact some specific paradoxes employed by Byblis recur in the later story, differing only in their application to Byblis's special problem, her desire for her brother Caunus. She views her existing close relationship with him as paradoxically hindering the close rela-

---

[65] See H-E on *Met.* 10.487.

tionship she desires and, as Myrrha will do, imagines a case in which the real one does not exist:

> possim, si non sit frater, amare,
> et me dignus erat; verum nocet esse sororem.
> (*Met.* 9.477–478)

> I would be able to love him if he were not my brother, and he would be worthy of me; but the fact that I am his sister harms me.

> at mihi, quae male sum, quos tu, sortita parentes,
> nil nisi frater eris: quod obest, id habebimus unum.
> (*Met.* 9.493–494)

> But to me—unluckily allotted the same parents as you—you will be nothing but my brother. The one thing we will always have is what stands in our way.

Like Myrrha, Byblis has a long soliloquy, wavering between resolve and guilty self-reproach (*Met.* 9.474–516); she includes self-justificatory exempla of the gods' incestuous behavior (*Met.* 9.497–499, 555), just as Myrrha cites foreign peoples. And the two tales are linked by *discordia mentis*, an expression applied to both heroines (*Met.* 9.630, 10.445). But most relevant here is Byblis's focus on *nomina consanguinitatis*. As the lines just quoted show, the categories defined by *soror* and *frater* represent for Byblis obstacles to be overcome. There are two ways, however, in which Byblis's story is strikingly different from Myrrha's. First, Byblis is unsuccessful in her incestuous approach to Caunus; and second, she resorts to writing. Eventually, I aim to show that the two facts are related; for now, let us consider how, through her exploitation of the written word, we can gain a broader perspective on the thematic relevance of verbal wit. I have chosen to discuss Byblis after Myrrha, rather than in order of their appearance, because in Byblis's tale the advantages and dangers of writing are in the foreground. Through this emphasis Ovid here more specifically invites reflection on our present concern, the nature of language and its link to metamorphosis.

Byblis introduces the contrast between spoken and written communication at the climactic end of her first soliloquy, as she resolves to write Caunus a letter:

> poterisne loqui? poterisne fateri?
> coget amor: potero; vel, si pudor ora tenebit,
> littera celatos arcana fatebitur ignes.
> (*Met.* 9.514–516)

> Will you be able to speak? Will you be able to admit it? Love will force you:
> I will be able; or, if a sense of shame holds my tongue, a secret letter will
> confess my hidden fires.

The letter is an innovation of Ovid's, unknown in earlier versions of the tale, and draws on his past achievement in the *Heroides*.[66] Byblis's name lacks any association with writing in earlier versions, but Ovid makes of it an etymological pun, suggesting through his new emphasis a connection with βύβλος (or βίβλος), a written document.[67] If we compare this tale structurally to that of Myrrha, Byblis's difficulty in composing the letter corresponds to Myrrha's troubles in making herself understood to the nurse; and the letter's communicative task corresponds to that of the nurse. Whereas Myrrha's conversation gave ample scope to irony, Byblis's wax tablet is the perfect space for paradoxical and self-cancelling actions:

> dextra tenet ferrum; vacuam tenet altera ceram:
> incipit et dubitat; scribit damnatque tabellas;
> et notat et delet; mutat culpatque probatque.
> (*Met.* 9.522–524)

> Her right hand holds the stylus, her other holds the empty wax tablet. She
> begins and hesitates; she writes and curses the tablet; she inscribes words
> and erases them; makes changes, blames, approves.

The spoken word, once spoken, *volat irrevocabile*: it cannot be called back, as Horace says (*Ep.* 1.18.71); but the written word can always be *erased: scripta "soror" fuerat; visum est delere sororem*, "She had written 'sister'; she decided to erase 'sister'" (*Met.* 9.528), along with the relationship so denoted. Writing allows *soror* to be transformed from a conceptual abstraction to a physical object, which then can be obliterated. Byblis writes *amans* in its place, then perceives obstructive problems in that name as well, soon reaching the conclusion that to be without a name would be best. This, in fact, she defines as the goal of her desire, as if to equate namelessness with winning Caunus's love:

> quam nisi tu dederis, non est habitura salutem,
> hanc tibi mittit amans: pudet a! pudet edere nomen,
> et si, quid cupiam, quaeris, sine nomine vellem
> posset agi mea causa meo nec cognita Byblis
> ante forem, quam spes votorum certa fuisset.
> (*Met.* 9.530–534)

---

[66] See Otis 1970, 417.
[67] According to modern authorities, Byblis's name is of non-Greek origin (Bömer 4:412). On the pun, see Ahl 1985, 211.

> The greetings and good health, which, unless you give it, she will not have, your lover sends to you. She is ashamed, ah, ashamed to state her name. If you ask what I want, I would like to plead my case without my name, and not to be recognized as Byblis until my hopes are certain of their aim.

Earlier, Byblis had wished that she could be joined to Caunus *mutato nomine*, "with a changed name" (*Met.* 9.487). Now the wax tablet appears to offer a chance physically to erase all conceptual, but undeniably real, difficulties besetting her.

Right from the opening of the story, the capacity of names to fix one's identity and assign one irremediably to a category presents problems to Byblis, before she is even conscious of her incestuous desires. As she slides (*declinat*, 461) from the role of *soror*, she becomes uncomfortable with the name *soror*:

> iam dominum appellat, iam nomina sanguinis odit:
> Byblida iam mavult quam se vocet ille sororem.
> (*Met.* 9.466–467)

> Now she calls him "master," now hates the name of blood-relationship. She prefers that he call her Byblis rather than sister.

Her personal name, Byblis, allows semantic flexibility not accessible in *soror*. It could be a lover's address as well as a sister's; and so, in the letter she eventually writes, Byblis is the identification she chooses (533).

In *odit* we observe powerful resentment toward names that define relationships, resentment that seems to objectify, to realize names, making them well-defined targets to aim at, or at least forces against which one can struggle. Byblis *desires* semantic slippage. And similarly, in the erotic dream that follows (*Met.* 9.469–473), desire achieves its own realization, and does so in physical terms that mask the unreality of the situation: *saepe vidit, quod amat*, "Often she sees what she loves" (*Met.* 9.470). The language used to describe this self-deceptive process, wherein dreamy unrealities become more palpable to Byblis than her waking circumstances, emphasizes the physical and the sensuous. As with Narcissus, an *imago* nearly takes on a life of its own: *me miseram! tacitae quid vult sibi noctis imago?*, "Wretched me! What means this vision in the quiet night?" (*Met.* 9.474). This line alludes to Medea's exclamation at Apollonius Rhodius 3.636: δειλὴ ἐγών, οἷόν με βαρεῖς ἐφόβησαν ὄνειροι, "Wretched me, how much fear grievous dreams have caused me!" But Ovid's *imago*, replacing ὄνειροι, takes us beyond the dream to its reflective and imitative character, linking this context thematically to other deceptive *imagines* in the *Metamorphoses*.[68]

---

[68] Vergil gives Dido a closer imitation of Apollonius's words: *quae me suspensam insomnia terrent?* (*Aen.* 4.9). See Tränkle 1963, 463 and n. 4.

As Byblis finishes writing her letter, Ovid calls our attention more and more to the physical nature of written communication. Remarking that Byblis's letter-writing efforts are pointless, he passes immediately to her difficulty in getting it all on one tablet—she runs over into the margin—as if to suggest a link between vain purposes and a lack of writing space:

> talia nequiquam perarantem plena reliquit
> cera manum, summusque in margine versus adhaesit.
> (*Met.* 9.564–565)

> The tablet, now full, gave out as her hand pointlessly cut these words into the wax. The last line stuck in the margin.

Then a sylleptic expression further blends the conceptual and physical: *protinus inpressa signat sua crimina gemma*, "At once she sealed her own accusation, pressing it with a signet ring" (*Met.* 9.566). After Caunus receives and angrily spurns the letter, Byblis blames her ill-judged methods of approach in another long soliloquy, even finding fault at one point with the wax tablet itself: *fecit spes nostras cera caducas*, "The wax made my hopes fallible" (*Met.* 9.597). This is because, when she handed her letter to the messenger, it slipped from her hands (*Met.* 9.571–572), revealing—or in Byblis's view, causing—a bad omen. This is a hazard of written communication: once written down, words can be *dropped*. Because writing has taken Byblis's words into the physical sphere, her metaphorical *caducas* takes on a sylleptic edge. More than just fallible, her hopes actually fell.

Byblis's soliloquy continues to ring every change on the physicality of language. We already know how her words spilled over into the margin; now she complains of the tablet's physical limitations: *plura loqui poteram, quam quae cepere tabellae*, "There was more I could have said than what the tablet held" (*Met.* 9.604); so she should have addressed him in person. Amusing as some of Byblis's self-reproaches may be, they invite in us serious reflection on a long-standing debate about the merits of spoken and written communication. Manifold advantages and hazards of both modes of communication had been explored by writers at least from Plato's time; in this case Byblis, having failed with writing, expands upon the resources of speech:

> et tamen ipsa loqui nec me committere cerae
> debueram praesensque meos aperire furores!
> vidisset lacrimas, vultum vidisset amantis;
> plura loqui poteram, quam quae cepere tabellae.
> invito potui circumdare bracchia collo
> et, si reicerer, potui moritura videri
> amplectique pedes adfusaque poscere vitam.

> omnia fecissem, quorum si singula duram
> flectere non poterant, potuissent omnia, mentem.
> (*Met.* 9.601–609)

> Even so, I should have addressed him myself, not entrusted my case to the wax. I should have opened my passion to him in person. He would have seen my tears, he would have seen his lover's face. There was more I could have said than what the tablet held. I could have thrown my arms around his unwilling neck, and, if I were rejected, I could have seemed about to die: embracing his feet, prostrate, I could have begged for life. I would have done all these things, and if they individually were unable to bend his harsh mind, all together they would have been able to do so.

Speech require the speaker's presence, from which flow all the rhetorical advantages of gesture, of facial and bodily expression, and most importantly, of adjustment to the perceived response of the audience. None of this is possible with writing, which for Byblis offers only obstructions. Byblis originally saw her absence as an advantage in addressing Caunus. As the later proverb has it, *litterae non erubescunt*, "A letter does not blush":[69]

> si pudor ora tenebit,
> littera celatos arcana fatebitur ignes.
> (*Met.* 9.515–516)

> If a sense of shame holds my tongue, a secret letter will confess my hidden fires.

But now she perceives that the written word is vulnerable, helpless without its author to defend itself against an unwelcome reception.

In her reflections on the limitations and deficiencies of writing, Ovid's Byblis may remind some readers of Socrates in the *Phaedrus*. Of course, the two have different goals for writing. Socrates measures it against an ideal of communication between participants in a search for understanding, and finds that the words most likely to be "written" (γράφεται, Pl. *Phdr.* 276A) on a person's soul will have been heard in conversation, not read from a fixed text. For Byblis, the written word is purely functional, a manipulative tool contrived to win its reader over to a course of action that is admittedly shameful. But both Socrates and Byblis recognize the helpless vulnerability of the written word, once it is bereft of its author:

ὅταν δὲ ἅπαξ γραφῇ, κυλινδεῖται μὲν πανταχοῦ πᾶς λόγος ὁμοίως παρὰ τοῖς ἐπαΐουσιν, ὡς δ' αὕτως παρ' οἷς οὐδὲν προσήκει, καὶ οὐκ ἐπίσταται λέγειν οἷς δεῖ γε καὶ μή. πλημμελούμενος δὲ καὶ οὐκ ἐν δίκῃ λοιδορηθεὶς

---

[69] Walter 1963–1986, 2:2.13906b.

τοῦ πατρὸς ἀεὶ δεῖται βοηθοῦ. αὐτὸς γὰρ οὔτ' ἀμύνασθαι οὔτε βοηθῆσαι δυνατὸς αὑτῷ. (Pl. *Phdr.* 275 D–E)

> Every speech, when once it has been written down, knocks about everywhere, alike among those who give heed to it and those who take no concern in it at all; and it does not know whom to address and whom not to. When abused and unjustly reviled it always needs its parent's help; for on its own it can neither protect nor help itself.

Much has been made in recent years about the "death of the author," that is, the potential of writing to have an autonomous existence independent of its author.[70] But this hazard was well known to ancient writers and their audiences. Ovid goes beyond reflection on the dangers faced by written words when he explicitly represents the rejection of Byblis's letter by its intended audience. Caunus reads only *part* of the letter: *proicit acceptas lecta sibi parte tabellas*, "Receiving the tablet, he threw it down after reading only part of it" (*Met.* 9.575). Byblis's concern about the amount of discourse that she can write on one tablet turns out to be misplaced, for an audience's potential to neglect or misuse a written text can defeat any author's efforts, however long and well developed they may be. Had she, like Myrrha, enjoyed the services of a nurse, her outcome might have been different.

In this exploration of the rigidity of writing, and its vulnerability to its own audience, Ovid's tale of Byblis offers an ironic comment on well-known positive claims for writing: that it grants words permanence and allows them to transcend time and decay, thereby assuring the author, in a sense, of survival. Such claims for writing occur often enough in Ovid's work, but instead of considering them amid the complexities of various contexts there, let us think of them for now in the abstract, as neatly distilled in a later proverb, *littera scripta manet*, "The written letter remains." This proverb is sometimes expanded, in a pentameter version, to make the contrast with the spoken word explicit: *littera dicta perit, littera scripta manet*, "The spoken letter perishes, the written letter remains."[71] Such an expression clearly implies the superiority of the written word, even its primacy. To refer to the spoken word as the "spoken letter" seems to suggest that speech is but incomplete and unrealized writing. Another pentameter expansion makes an absolute dichotomy between *littera* and *verbum*: *littera scripta manet, verbum ut inane perit*, "The written letter remains, just as the empty word perishes."[72] Though this dichotomy may appear to suit a claim for the fixity of published writings,

---

[70] See R. Barthes, "The Death of the Author," in Barthes 1977a, 142–148.

[71] Walter 1963–1986, 2:8.919a3.

[72] Ibid., 2:2.13903. From such expressions it is but a short step to the legal maxim *littera scripta valet*, "The written word has force" as judicial evidence.

at least those which have the good fortune to remain extant, such a claim is largely illusory. A published text may enjoy physical survival, but cast adrift to be received by any audience, its meaning will be variously interpreted; and some audiences will reject it outright. Byblis's written but unpublished letter may seem well aimed to overcome this problem of audience: she directs her text to a single person, well known to her; but Caunus's refusal to read or heed it shows how a written text can perish as utterly as any speech.

These proverbs are postclassical, but the permanence of the written word and the author's consequent survival were commonplace notions by Ovid's time, and they also find expression throughout Ovid's oeuvre, as in the emphatic but conditional *vivam*, "I will live," at the end of the *Metamorphoses*. Modern critics, favoring themes of artistic permanence and transcendence, have greatly emphasized their presence in the *Metamorphoses*, and have simplified that presence, overlooking the more complex and problematic examinations of writing to be found there.[73] I do not mean to suggest that the perspective developed in Byblis's tale is any more Ovidian than its opposite. What is most Ovidian is the exploration of paradox, not the exposition of any single perspective.

Perhaps the greatest paradox in the status of the written word, as it is explored in this tale, is its combination of inflexible permanence and erasability; for Byblis, as we have seen, finds erasure, not permanence, one of the advantages of writing. Therefore it is appropriate that Byblis be transformed into a spring, for this natural feature handily embraces both permanence and fluidity, continuity and ceaseless movement. While the spring Byblis possesses a fixed place and an established name, its fluid nature requires that it remain unstable, literally in flux, its boundaries never quite the same, nor ever precisely to be determined. As in Myrrha's tale, metamorphosis begins on the stylistic level, initiated by a characteristic syllepsis: *patriam fugit ille nefasque*, "He [Caunus] fled both country and crime" (*Met.* 9.633), giving his name to a new city; immediately thereafter, Byblis dissolves into the spring that still bears her name:

> vertitur in fontem, qui nunc quoque vallibus illis
> nomen habet dominae nigraque sub ilice manat.
> (*Met.* 9.664–665)

> She turned into a spring, which even now in that valley holds the name of its mistress, and flows beneath a black ilex.

---

[73] Solodow takes the critical emphasis on artistic transcendence to extremes in his sixth chapter, "Art" (Solodow 1988, 203–231). See Chapter 3 of the present work for aetiological notions of permanence.

I am taking Byblis's transformation as an allegorical symbol, an embodiment of paradoxical flux in fixity. Myrrha's transformation may be seen the same way. She, as a myrrh-tree, is rooted in one spot, but she is also porous, exuding myrrh, and flowing with it: *flet tamen, et tepidae manant ex arbore guttae,* "Yet she weeps, and warm drops flow from the tree" (*Met.* 10.500). Fixed though she is, there is no precise and final boundary to her new form. In both Myrrha and Byblis, tears are the liminal fluid that links human bodies to the natural, extra-human realm. Myrrha's tears cross over to that realm as myrrh-drops, while Byblis is consumed by her own tears, *lacrimis consumpta suis* (*Met.* 9.663). Though it would be possible to regard a tree that exudes and a spring that flows as very different phenomena, Ovid wants us to associate them in our minds. A simile places both exudation and dissolution on a sort of liquid continuum:

> protinus, ut secto piceae de cortice guttae
> utve tenax gravida manat tellure bitumen,
> utque sub adventu spirantis lene favoni
> sole remollescit, quae frigore constitit unda,
> sic lacrimis consumpta suis Phoebeia Byblis
> vertitur in fontem.
> (*Met.* 9.659–664)

At once, just as drops of pitch flow from cut bark, or as sticky tar from the swollen ground, or as water, frozen solid with cold, melts in the sun at the coming of the softly blowing zephyr, so Byblis, Phoebus's descendant, consumed by her own tears, turned into a spring.

Pitch, flowing from a tree, is much like myrrh. Tar brings the comparison closer to Byblis's final state, as it seeps from the ground. Finally ice, dissolving, seems to flow directly from the figurative to the literal spheres, as simile gives way to narrative event. The simile makes clear how much the transformations of Byblis and Myrrha have in common. Furthermore, comparison of these two transformation scenes illustrates the easy interchange between Ovidian figurative language and "straight" narrative description. Myrrha's tears *become* natural exudations, physical expressions of her emotional state; Byblis's tears *are like* such exudations. In the *Metamorphoses*, what is figurative language in one story can become narrative event in another, and vice versa. That the shift occurs so easily and naturally shows how integrated our experience of the work can become to its imaginative world.

At the beginning of my discussion of Myrrha, I mentioned that ethical interpretations were among those favored by writers on both Myrrha and

Byblis. Some follow Orpheus *narrans* in condemning incest directly; others—perhaps recognizing that daughters and sisters have but little need of cautionary tales about incest, when fathers and brothers are in fact more likely culprits—shift the ethical emphasis to self-deception.[74] And indeed, both heroines, deploying so much rhetorical ingenuity against their hesitations, deceive themselves in supposing that their aims will meet with a worthwhile outcome. As an ethical theme, self-deception also has the advantage of linking these tales to others in the work where incest is not an issue, like that of Scylla in Book 8, who argues herself into a mistaken belief that Minos will love her if she betrays her city. Though I have set such concerns aside in my attention to the stylistic surface and my claim for Ovid's serious interest in the nature of language, I now turn briefly to self-deception. My intention is not to draw new ethical admonitions from Ovid, but to claim that style is inseparable from this concern, as from all others—and not only style, but verbal wit in particular. For wit, as we have seen, expands the already rich potential of language in general for semantic slippage. That Myrrha and Byblis should rid themselves of the *nomina consanguinitatis* by exploring the semantic extensions of words and names shows how closely verbal wit can be bound up with self-deceptive fantasy. As we witness Myrrha pushing the application of *pietas* until it will embrace incest, or Byblis erasing *soror* and *amans* in favor of her name because it will allow either *soror* or *amans* or both to be understood, we observe language stretched and exploited, made to promote the worse argument over the better. And we also observe how this deception can be made to occur. Semantic slippage allows desire to work its way into our conception of the realities that face us, preparing fertile ground for both the generation and the reception of specious arguments.

Many writers have observed the rhetorical character of these two tales, which indeed has been identified as the most notable thing about them.[75] Because an influential treatise places Plato and Ovid on opposite ends of a spectrum of attitudes toward rhetoric,[76] I wish to note that Plato, who attacks rhetoric because it makes falsehood more appealing than truth, has quite a lot in common with Ovid, who analyzes and exposes the power of rhetoric to replace obstructive realities by pleasing fantasy. The

---

[74] According to Nagle (1983, 307 n. 22), Byblis and Myrrha are "atypical" as case studies of incest. Self-deception is a major emphasis of Anderson's commentary; e.g., "Byblis now begins to describe her fancies in positive terms as she longs to live in her imitation world and ignore the everyday world. The next step, of course, is to reverse the two worlds, to intrude her dreams deliberately upon waking reality" (Anderson 1972, 452–453).

[75] See Wilkinson 1955, 226–228.

[76] See ch. 2 of Lanham 1976, "The Fundamental Strategies: Plato and Ovid," 36–64.

principal difference, perhaps, is that for Ovid, language is inherently and inescapably rhetorical. For even as his work invites our reflective scrutiny of his characters' words and behavior, the stylistic surface is always inviting us to follow the imaginative courses of those characters, wherever these might lead. Ovid does not appear to believe, like some moderns, that language creates reality, but rather that we cannot conceptualize anything without language. Consequently, we are always vulnerable to it. It is always there to prey upon our minds, making our understanding of the world dangerously unconnected to reality. Because of the inevitability of this process, and its general application beyond the subjects of these incest narratives, we need to look beyond the moral hazards of self-deception to something more fundamental, the link between language and desire.[77]

Self-Cancelling and Self-Objectifying Witticisms

The many and various examples of wordplay that we have been considering illustrate a heaping-up or multiplication of meaning. Yet there is also, as we saw earlier in the description of Althea, a reverse effect of paradoxical wit, the dissolution of meaning:

> et consanguineas ut sanguine leniat umbras
> inpietate pia est.
> (*Met.* 8.476–477)

> And in order to assuage her kindred shades with blood, she is dutiful in her violation of duty.

Semantic accumulation and dissolution can indeed be seen as two sides of the same coin, and both can occur in proximity to each other. *Pietas* and *inpietas* collapse together, as if cheated of their definitive opposition, in the context of a sylleptic pun on *consanguineas*, "related by blood," which is here juxtaposed with the more physical *sanguine*.[78] Ovid here combines the blurring of conceptual and physical with paradoxical self-cancelling expression, achieving thereby no mere flourish, but a profound correspondence between witticisms of the narrative surface and the larger pattern of figurative expression. For Althea's inner conflict appears just before as an image of distraction:[79]

---

[77] After all, the ostensibly moral purpose of both tales (Byblis's, too: *Met.* 9.454) includes disclaimers that are at least as likely as not to inflame the reader's salacious interest, like Chaucer's disingenuous "Turne over the leef, and chese another tale" (*Prol. of Miller's Tale*, 1.3177).

[78] *Sanguine* here suggests a literally bloody death; but it will turn out to be largely figurative, as Meleager dies of inward fire, *sine sanguine*, "without blood" (*Met.* 8.518).

[79] See Anderson 1972, 373 on *Met.* 8.464.

> pugnat materque sororque,
> et diversa trahunt unum duo nomina pectus.
> (*Met.* 8.463–464)

Mother and sister are at war, and two names tear apart one breast.

One could say that the meaning of this expression is some ethical or psychological proposition, which one may abstract from Ovid's figurative terms. Yet although they do invite us to draw conclusions beyond their figurative elements, these terms also enact semantic transformation along the same lines as the paradoxes that succeed them. "Two names tear apart one breast." That insubstantial names should be able to act violently upon a living being of material substance is not *just* a figure of speech, nor is such a figure necessarily subordinate to ethical and psychological allegories that readers may choose to pursue. For in itself it represents the free interchange of words, ideas, and physical phenomena that characterizes Ovidian transformation.

Names again have a physically damaging force at a climactic moment of Althea's last soliloquy, just before she abandons self-paralyzing argumentation and takes action:

> quid agam? modo vulnera fratrum
> ante oculos mihi sunt et tantae caedis imago,
> nunc animum pietas maternaque nomina frangunt.
> (*Met.* 8.506–508)

What am I to do? Now the wounds of my brothers are before my eyes, and the image of so great a slaughter; now duty and the name of mother break my resolve.

Here the transformative effect of figurative language can be observed in process: the physical wounds of her brothers present themselves as an imaginary mental image, yet are spoken of as before her eyes, as if perceptible to the senses, while the purely conceptual *pietas* and abstractly definitive "name of mother" break apart her soul, or her resolve, as if they were physical agents.

Meleager's death brings this process to an impressive climax. There has existed a talismanic connection between the fatal log and Meleager's life from his birth, when the Fates set it in the fire, and Althea rescued it:

> ille diu fuerat penetralibus abditus imis
> servatusque tuos, iuvenis, servaverat annos.
> (*Met.* 8.458–459)

It had long been hidden away in the deepest recesses of the house: preserved there, it had preserved the young man's years.

CHAPTER 1

Now that Althea has added the log to the fire, the absent Meleager dies as it is consumed. His story conventionally has a place on the list of those "only tangentially connected with a metamorphosis,"[80] in this case that of his sisters into guinea hens, *meleagrides* (*Met.* 8.526–546). But, to take a less literal-minded perspective, the close connection between a nonhuman, natural object, the log, with a human life serves the function of metamorphosis to conclude the tale. Ovid represents this connection, and makes it still more intimate, by willfully defeating his readers' efforts to discriminate literal from metaphorical, efforts that are ordinarily a necessary and expected part of the act of reading. First, the log resembles its human counterpart in groaning, or appearing to groan:

> aut dedit aut visus gemitus est ille dedisse
> stipes et invitis correptus ab ignibus arsit.
> (*Met.* 8.513–514)

> The log either gave a groan or seemed to do so, and seized by the unwilling flames, it burned.

Here the natural object participates, or seems to participate, in the human; at least we can be sure that the log is literally burning up. But next, in the language used to narrate Meleager's death, Ovid carries metaphor beyond its ordinary limits. Accustomed as we may be to take fire as a conventional, indeed banal, metaphor for pain, it is here not merely that:

> inscius atque absens flamma Meleagros ab illa
> uritur et caecis torreri viscera sentit
> ignibus ac magnos superat virtute dolores.
> (*Met.* 8.515–517)

> Absent and unaware, Meleager is burned by that flame; he feels his guts roasted by hidden fires, and valorously overcomes his great pain.

Meleager really is being burned up, as his body, though absent, physically participates in the consumption of the log. Literal and metaphorical become indistinguishable in the end:

> crescunt ignisque dolorque
> languescuntque iterum: simul est extinctus uterque,
> inque leves abiit paulatim spiritus auras
> paulatim cana prunam velante favilla.
> (*Met.* 8.522–525)

[80] Galinsky 1975, 4.

> The fire and pain increase, then die away again; they both were simultaneously extinguished. Little by little, his life withdrew into thin air, as likewise white ash covered the coals.

Having first lulled us readers with an impression of the familiar, Ovid disorients us, arresting our attention with an unexpected ambiguity in the reference of terms. We would normally take *extinctus est* literally of a fire, metaphorically of human pain; but here no such distinction holds. In the collapse of this distinction Ovid achieves virtual metamorphosis through the resources of style. Meleager need not be changed into a log in order to burn up, just as Procris did not have to become a game animal in order to die as one; so completely do conceptual notions and physical realities flow together at the conclusion of these tales.

Parallel to images of distraction in Althea's story, and its paradoxes, are other witticisms that appear to drain words of their meaning. A well-known example occurs after the fall of Icarus:

> at pater infelix, nec iam pater, "Icare" dixit,
> "Icare" dixit "ubi es?"
> (*Met.* 8.231–232)

> But the unhappy father—no longer a father—said, "Icarus, Icarus, where are you?"

Ovid's joke invites his readers to be more literal-minded than usual, as it suggests two different views of the acceptable semantic range of *pater*. One could normally call someone a father whether his children were alive or not; and no reader, while still at the threshold of the line, and contemplating *at pater*, is likely to find the word *pater* inapplicable to Daedalus. But when we get to *nec iam pater*, a comic insistence on precision asks us to consider that Daedalus, suddenly without children, cannot be a father.[81] The word *pater* suffers a sudden semantic loss to parallel the loss just suffered by Daedalus.

Daedalus, though not physically transformed, undergoes change in losing his son. We observe this change in process as we take the repeated *pater* in a double sense, a "divided sense" in Dumarsais's language of tropes, adapted in this case from Aristotle.[82] For among tropes, the "di-

---

[81] As Regio (1493, l.i.r) notes, *pater quia genuerat, non pater quia filius iam erat mortuus*, "A father because he had engendered a son, not a father because his son had now died." Galinsky notes that Ovidian humor often arises from the development of "'logical' incongruity" (Galinsky 1975, 179–184). On the disruption of tone in this passage, see below, Chapter 2.

[82] As Douay-Soublin remarks on Dumarsais ([1730] 1988, 296–297), the categories "combined sense" and "divided sense" belong to the *Sophistici Elenchi* of Aristotle. "Can a bad cobbler be good? No, in the combined sense, because he cannot be a good cobbler;

vided sense" is most suitable to change and transformation. Dumarsais first exemplifies it in the terms used to refer to biblical miracles:

> Quand l'Évangile dit, *les aveugles voient, les boiteux marchent* (Matthieu XI.5), ces termes, *les aveugles, les boiteux*, se prennent en cette occasion dans le sens divisé, c'est-à-dire, que ce mot *aveugles* se dit là de ceux que étaient aveugles, et qui ne le sont plus; ils sont divisés, pour ainsi dire, de leur aveuglement; car les aveugles, en tant qu'aveugles, ce qui serait le sens composé, ne voient pas.[83]

> When the Gospel says, *the blind see, the lame walk* (Matt. 11:5), these terms, *the blind, the lame*, are taken in this case in the divided sense; that is, the word *blind* is spoken there of those who were blind and are no longer so. They have been divided, so to speak, from their blindness; for the blind, while blind—this would be the combined sense—do not see.

In apprehending a word in a divided sense, we witness the presence of change: the divided sense stylistically represents the miraculous transformation from blindness to sight. Dumarsais takes a further example from the terms Ovid uses to account for Agamemnon's participation in the sacrifice of Iphigenia:

> postquam pietatem publica causa,
> rexque patrem vicit.
> (*Met.* 12.29–30)

> After the public cause had defeated familial obligation, and king had defeated father.

"Ces dernières paroles sont dans un sens divisé. Agamemnon, se regardant comme roi étouffe les sentiments qu'il ressent comme père" ("These last words are in a divided sense. Agamemnon, regarded as king, stifles the emotions which he feels as father").[84] When a father is to kill his own daughter, a cleavage of identity is grimly serviceable, facilitating the action. Faced with opposed claims of *publica causa* and *pietas*, Agamemnon becomes doubly objectified, separated into *rex* and *pater* to correspond with each claim, whereupon the first can stifle the second. He has been separated from his identity as father. His division is closely parallel to

---

yes, in the divided sense, because he can be a good man" (adapted from *Sophistici Elenchi* 177b20). Aristotle is discussing fallacious arguments based on the combination and division of words: ἂν γὰρ διαιρούμενος καὶ συντιθέμενος ὁ λόγος ἕτερον σημαίνῃ, συμπεραινομένου τοὐναντίον λεκτέον, "For if the expression signifies something different when divided and when combined, as the opponent draws a conclusion one must take the expression in a contrary sense" (*Sophistici Elenchi* 177a20).

[83] Dumarsais [1730] 1988, 203.
[84] Ibid., 204.

Althea's—*pugnat materque sororque*, "Mother and sister fight" (*Met.* 8.463)—except that both claims upon her fall within *pietas*.

In Ocyroe's prophecy we observe once again the integrity of absolute terms compromised. She describes her father as *nunc inmortalis*, "Immortal for the time being" (*Met.* 2.649). Chiron was born divine, but, tormented by the Hydra's poison after being accidentally shot by Hercules' arrow, he will be allowed to die by a special dispensation of the Fates (*Met.* 2.649–654). So he is only temporarily immortal. Nothing is left of *inmortalis* when it is limited—literally as well as grammatically—by *nunc*. But Ovid makes such impossibilities paradoxically possible, extending the domain of change into the definitively changeless.

D. Lateiner describes several types of "mimetic syntax" in the *Metamorphoses*: "More than other Latin poets, Ovid orders words in one or more verses to make them imitate an aspect of the event that they narrate. Protean syntax, modified to suit the situation, reinforces the protean theme of mutability."[85] Juxtaposition is among his types of syntactic expressiveness, for Ovid often represents semantic disintegration by physical juxtaposition of words that embody it: *heu quantum Niobe Niobe distabat ab illa*, "Alas, how greatly changed was Niobe from that former Niobe" (*Met.* 6.273). So he describes Niobe changed by the death of her sons—not yet physically, though these terms already presage her eventual transformation.[86] Here language almost becomes physical. The two Niobes are set side by side, the first in the nominative case, the second— her decline registered symbolically—sinking downward into the ablative.[87] Viewed on the page, the second Niobe does not visibly differ from the first, for in the transliterated Greek name they both appear the same; but it reflects *distabat* more subtly. The grammatical context requires us to

---

[85] Lateiner 1990, 204; see 214–215 for examples of juxtaposition; also Schawaller 1987, 208–209.

[86] This form of stylistic transformation is reinforced by the larger context of Niobe's tale, wherein metaphorical language of the emotions becomes physicalized in metamorphosis. "Metamorphosis," as Pianezzola (1979, 83) remarks, "has developed the initial metaphor in narrative and descriptive terms."

[87] Ancient grammarians called the nominative and vocative *casus recti*, the "straight" cases, as if they represented the word in its simple, unaltered state. On this view, the *casus obliqui*, the "oblique" cases, are formed by changing the nominative. By a standard etymology of *casus*, the oblique cases represent a "falling" away from the word's nominative form: Donatus (Keil 4:377): *casus sunt sex . . . ex his duo recti appellantur, nominativus et vocativus, reliqui obliqui*, "There are six cases. . . . Of these, two are called 'straight,' the nominative and vocative, the others 'oblique.'" Diomedes (Keil 1:301): *casus sunt gradus quidam declinationis, dicti quod per eos pleraque nomina a prima sui positione inflexa varientur et cadant. alii sic, casus sunt variatio conpositionis in declinatione nominis per inmutationem novissimae syllabae*, "The cases are steps in the declension, so called because through them most nouns, as they are inflected from their initial position, are altered and fall. Others say this: the cases are variation in the makeup of a noun in its declension, through alteration of the last syllable."

see the second Niobe as changed, just as, in the larger narrative, we readers observe her already undergoing an inward transformation—one that would be imperceptible to an imagined viewer—well before she is turned to stone. Thus the function of the repetition of her name parallels that of paronomasia, a pun on repeated terms. *Anadiplosis (conduplicatio)* applies generally to juxtaposed repetition of a word; Vergil, for example, employs the trope at *Aen.* 10.180–181: *sequitur pulcherrimus Astur / Astur equo fidens*, "There follows most handsome Astur, Astur trusting in his horse." Specifically Ovidian is the clash between opposed sense and juxtaposed terms; uniquely Ovidian is the symbolic function and thematic relevance of the trope.

In general, Ovid likes to represent separation by physical juxtaposition of words. Sometimes they are of contrasting meaning, as in *unum duo* in the image of Althea's distraction: *et diversa trahunt unum duo nomina pectus*, "And two names tear apart one breast" (*Met.* 8.464). Sometimes the same word appears in different cases, as in the river-god Achelous's account of erosion by flood: *a silvis silvas et ab arvis arva revulsi*, "I tore away woods from woods and fields from fields" (*Met.* 8.585). Combining physical closeness with semantic distance, word order itself becomes paradoxical.[88]

These cases of change embodied in the altered repetition of terms may remind us of the self-cancelling repetition of *pater*, noted above, in the story of Daedalus: *at pater infelix, nec iam pater* (*Met.* 8.231). Therefore, it is revealing to note that Dryden, for all his expressed disapproval of Ovidian wit, adapted the juxtaposed repetition of a word, so typical of Ovidian paradoxical expression, to his rendering of Ovid's words on Daedalus: "The wretched Father, Father now no more." Dryden did not translate the story of Daedalus for the *Fables*, but he read it, retaining this expression in his mind for the tale of Meleager later in Book 8. It applies to Oeneus after his son Meleager's death:

> The wretched Father, Father now no more,
> With Sorrow sunk, lies prostrate on the Floor,
> Deforms his hoary Locks with Dust obscene,
> And curses Age, and loaths a Life prolong'd with Pain.[89]
> (*Meleager and Atalanta* 369–372)

> pulvere canitiem genitor vultusque seniles
> foedat humi fusus spatiosumque increpat aevum.
> (*Met.* 8.529–530)

---

[88] Cf. *Met.* 12.621: *deque armis arma feruntur*, "Arms are taken over arms," i.e., those of Achilles. On repetition of words, juxtaposed or in close proximity, see Bömer 2:302–303 on *Met.* 5.300.

[89] Kinsley 1962, 620.

> With dust the father dirties his white hair and aged face; sprawled on the
> ground, he blames his long life.

Dryden makes Ovid's lines more Ovidian, for the original lacks both the semantically disintegrative witticism and the anadiplosis, the juxtaposed repetition of "father." If in theory Dryden's *Preface* remains the harshest condemnation of Ovidian wit, his practice restores the balance with its deepest appreciation.[90]

Ovid also achieves the embodiment of separation through repetition in another well-known type of witticism, the play on pronouns.[91] *Quid me mihi detrahis?* "Why do you tear me from myself?" asks Marsyas (*Met.* 6.385), when Apollo, having won his musical contest, proceeds to flay the loser. As Marsyas becomes physically divided from his skin, the narrative surface represents this division with comic and grisly accuracy, repeating the reflexive pronoun in different cases. Fränkel introduced the expression "cleavage of identity" for his interpretation of Ovid in terms of psychological allegory,[92] but the expression could also function, applied to Ovidian style, as a representation of physical change. For once the self is represented by a signifier, in this case a pronoun, there is nothing to prevent the signifier from appearing twice in the same clause, as if cleft. Play on pronouns is part of Ovid's general stylistic tendency in the *Metamorphoses* to physicalize and objectify words. Metamorphosed in this way, words can have violence done to them, as when Ajax, about to stab himself, first objectifies himself as a pronoun, and cuts that apart: *"hoc" ait "utendum est in me mihi,"* "Against myself I must make use of this sword" (*Met.* 13.388). Ajax then commits suicide in a context of self-cancelling expressions. He distances himself from himself by using the third person instead of the first: the subject (*Aiax*) performs the action on itself as object (*Aiacem*)—while also narrating the event:

> quique cruore
> saepe Phrygum maduit, domini nunc caede madebit,
> ne quisquam Aiacem possit superare nisi Aiax.
> (*Met.* 13.388–390)

> This sword, often drenched in Trojan blood, shall now be drenched by its
> master's slaughter, lest anyone except Ajax be able to conquer Ajax.

---

[90] Cf. Hopkins 1988, 170, on another context: "As so often, Dryden's stated critical position is in direct conflict with his poetic practice." Lee (1953, 42) well remarks that Dryden "can not only reproduce Ovidian epigram but can father epigrams of his own on Ovid, and no one who did not know the original could tell the difference."

[91] See Bömer 1:317–318, on *Met.* 2.303; Herter 1980, 205–206; Lateiner 1990, 215–216.

[92] Fränkel 1945, 81; cf. 79 on Io: "confused and divided identity." For critiques of Fränkel's psychological interpretations, see Herter 1980, 188ff.; Schmidt 1991, 48–55.

If suicide as an event in the plot offers a parallel to the play on pronouns, the most common such event is naturally metamorphosis. From Marsyas's expression it is but one step to *ille sibi ablatus fulvis amicitur ab alis*, "Removed from himself, he is clothed in tawny wings" (*Met.* 5.546). In this case of Ascalaphus, changed into a screech-owl, separation from one's identity *is* metamorphosis. The same is true of Atalanta in Book 10, in whose story most features of the narrative surface that we have been considering—paradox, syllepsis, pun, and play on pronouns—unite to reveal their intimate connection to metamorphosis. When she consults an oracle about her prospects for a husband, Atalanta's success as a competitive runner gives the oracle an opportunity for sylleptic wordplay and paradox:

> scitanti deus huic de coniuge "coniuge" dixit
> "nil opus est, Atalanta, tibi. fuge coniugis usum.
> nec tamen effugies teque ipsa viva carebis."
> (*Met.* 10.564–566)

> When she asked about a husband, the oracle said, "You do not need one, Atalanta: avoid having a husband. And yet you will not escape having one, and while living, you will lack yourself."

The oracle plays on the semantic range of *effugere*, "to escape" a husband by physically outrunning him, and "to avoid" a husband by not marrying him. The play on pronouns, *teque ipsa viva carebis*, describes a cleavage of identity that will be achieved when Atalanta and her husband Hippomenes are transformed into lions (*Met.* 10.698–704).

Characters in the *Metamorphoses* often experience metamorphosis as a separation from themselves. The play on pronouns is part of this larger pattern, which can take other forms as well. Closely related is the paradoxical identification of *suus* and *non suus*, "one's own" and "not one's own," referring to parts of a body in transformation. Here the very elements of one's proper self, one's definitive identity, become their opposite, paradoxically alien to oneself. As Actaeon turns into a stag, he finds himself unable to express his misery in speech, and can only groan:

> ingemuit: vox illa fuit, lacrimaeque per ora
> non sua fluxerunt; mens tantum pristina mansit.
> (*Met.* 3.202–203)

> He groaned: that was his voice, and tears flowed down a face that was not his own; only his mind remained unchanged.

In *non sua* Actaeon has undergone a complete estrangement from his own body. Scylla likewise loses familiarity with her body as it is transformed, and tries to flee, initially in disbelief, from the monstrous appendages that are now part of herself:

> ac primo credens non corporis illas
> esse sui partes refugitque abigitque timetque
> ora proterva canum, sed, quos fugit, attrahit una
> et corpus quaerens femorum crurumque pedumque
> Cerbereos rictus pro partibus invenit illis.
> (*Met.* 14.61–65)

And at first not believing that they were part of her own body, she fled from the dogs' clamorous mouths, and pushed them away in fear; but dragged along with her what she was fleeing. As she looked for her body, comprising thighs, legs, and feet, she found the jaws of Cerberuses in place of those parts.

Ovid also employs his disjunctive repetition of pronouns for shape-shifting divinities, divinities in disguise, and protean figures such as Erysichthon's daughter, *a se / se quaeri gaudens*, "Delighted to find herself questioned about her own whereabouts" (*Met.* 8.862–863). Mercury hears of his own thefts from Battus, and responds, *me mihi, perfide, prodis?* "Do you betray me, treacherous man, to myself?" (*Met.* 2.704). Vertumnus and Cipus are trying to deceive their audiences when they objectify themselves as pronouns, though with different aims in view. The god wants to seduce Pomona, as he gives a good recommendation to his own character, *neque enim sibi notior ille est, / quam mihi*, "For nobody knows Vertumnus better than I do" (*Met.* 14.679–680). The man wants to rescue his listeners, the Roman people, from the tyranny that will ensue if he is allowed to enter the city:

> sed nos obstitimus, quamvis coniunctior illo
> nemo mihi est.
> (*Met.* 15.599–600)

But I stood in his way, though no one is more closely related to him than I.[93]

Wordplay, Personification, and *Phantasia*

Still more revealing, in its transformative character, is Ovid's use of such play on pronouns in contexts of personification. When, after the conflagration caused by Phaethon's disastrous ride, Tellus appears in person,

---

[93] Cf. *Met.* 1.641: *seque exsternata refugit*, "Io fled in terror from herself," after seeing her bovine reflection in the river. At *Met.* 14.580, Ovid represents metamorphosis with a sylleptic pun on *deplangere*, "to beat the breast" and, less physically, "to mourn for," whereas *suus* extends to Ardea both before and after transformation: *ipsa suis deplangitur Ardea pennis*, "Ardea [the city] is lamented / Ardea [the heron] beats her breast with her own wings." Parallel expressions less directly connected to metamorphosis are *Met.* 4.461 (*voluitur Ixion et se sequiturque fugitque*, "Ixion, as he rolls, pursues and flees himself"); *Met.* 2.383 (*lucemque odit seque ipse diemque*, "The sun hates his light, hates his very self, hates the day"). Cf. Bernbeck 1967, 110; Herter 1980, 190.

Earth personified, to lodge a protest with Jupiter, Ovid characterizes her along lines reminiscent of that comically irate divinity, Juno. Endowed with the power of speech, indeed with rhetorical skill, Tellus also receives physical details appropriate to a matron of some dignity, such as a concern for her appearance: *tostos en adspice crines!*, "Look at my scorched hair!" (*Met.* 2.283). But she retains a "double aspect," in Bernbeck's expression, remaining earth as well as matron.[94] Her double identity is created by the play on reflexive terms, which permit her simultaneous representation more than once in the same clause. Earth sinks into the earth at the conclusion of her speech, *suumque / rettulit os in se*, "She buried her face in herself" (*Met.* 2.302–303). According to Bernbeck, "The paradox lies less in the thing than in the expression."[95] Such an attempt to privilege the "thing" as something autonomous, and potentially independent of "expression," is misleading; and Ovid's paradoxical expression suggests that we might imagine the thing as equally paradoxical. But Bernbeck's comment is acceptable in the sense that one need not speak of earth in this way. For a different work, a less ambitious author could adopt a deeply serious mimetic pose, tastefully avoiding such witticisms. Haupt describes this example as "tasteless" wordplay,[96] and one can readily imagine the sources of critical discontent with wit of this kind. Ovid is throwing away rhetorical opportunities that only high seriousness can offer, flouting the author's duty to accommodate language to agreed-upon decorums. Perhaps through tasteful language, scrupulously attentive to the readers' sense of decorum, one could convince readers that they are viewing unmediated realities directly, realities unclouded by any manifest disjunction between "expression" and "thing." But in the *Metamorphoses*, language does not possess such transparency, if such were possible. For that would require insistence on a firmer distinction between words and putative realities; and this is among the distinctions that Ovidian wit erodes. Words, abstractions, and things are always in a process of reshaping. Through personification they appear to shift categories entirely. In personification one can again see, in Rosati's expression, "the contradictory nature of the real," to which paradoxical language gives a conceptual shape.[97]

There are many such small-scale explorations of paradox in personification, all encouraging us to take simultaneously both a literal-minded and an allegorically interpretive view. These show a notable continuity between representations of divinity and those of personification. Ovid and

---

[94] On the "double aspect" of divinities, see Bernbeck 1967, 112–113.
[95] Ibid., 113.
[96] H-E on *Met.* 2.303.
[97] Rosati 1983, 155.

his audiences were long familiar with representation of divinities as either persons or natural phenomena; Ovid typically engages both modes at once, exploiting the incongruities, often comic, that result. The river-god Inachus, having lost his daughter Io, "adds to his waters by weeping," *fletibus auget aquas* (*Met.* 1.584). At Orpheus's death, "rivers are said to have swollen from their own tears," *lacrimis quoque flumina dicunt / increvisse suis* (*Met.* 11.47–48).[98] There is sometimes no clear means of distinguishing a divinity from a personification, as in the case of Mount Tmolus, who takes a seat "on his own mountain" to witness the musical contest of Midas and Apollo:

> monte suo senior iudex consedit et aures
> liberat arboribus; quercu coma caerula tantum
> cingitur, et pendent circum cava tempora glandes.
> (*Met.* 11.157–159)

> The aged judge took a seat on his own mountain and freed his ears of trees; his blue-green hair is only fringed with oak, and acorns hang about his temples.

Ovid here draws on Vergil's representation of Atlas (*Aen.* 4.246–251); and, as usual, critical response shows a greater appreciation of Vergil's effort than of Ovid's: "heavily indebted to Vergil's description of Atlas," but "playful and decorative where Vergil's is symbolic and functional."[99] In fact, Vergil's description is also playful, while Ovid's is also symbolic and functional. For in blurring the boundary between Tmolus as natural phenomenon and as divine being, Ovid's descriptive language keeps his readers' attention closely focused on his most important and pervasive themes.

Nowhere are these themes more relevant than in his elaborate personifications of Invidia (*Met.* 2.760–832), Fames (*Met.* 8.799–822), Somnus (*Met.* 11.592–649), and Fama (*Met.* 12.39–63). These are justly famous for their originality and later influence on allegorical description. D. C. Feeney has discussed their literary background and considered them in terms of epic preoccupations, especially poetic authority and the "authenticating detail" made available to Ovid by the epic tradition.[100] Too often, however, they are dismissed as "grotesque" fantasies only casually related to the larger narratives in which they occur, and even less

---

[98] Paradoxically, the river Achelous serves his guests wine undiluted with water: *in gemma posuere merum*, the serving-nymphs "served unmixed wine in goblets of precious stone" (*Met.* 8.573). (I owe this example to M. Musgrove.)

[99] Kenney 1986, 438.

[100] Feeney 1991, 242–249. For Invidia's connection to the theme of *indicium*, and a programmatic interpretation, see Keith 1992, 124–131.

64   CHAPTER 1

directly relevant to metamorphosis.[101] They are indeed fantasies, *phantasiae*, in an intellectually serious sense of that term. Ancient critics apply the term φαντασία, "manifestation," or "visualization," to the description of divinities in epic, when they appear actively participating among human characters. It is "a word used to describe the process by which the poet makes something 'appear before the eyes' of the audience, in vivid imaginative actualization."[102] Descriptions of *phantasia* depend on a metaphor of visual perception for an imaginative activity of the audience: *quas* φαντασίας *Graeci vocant, nos sane visiones appellemus, per quas imagines rerum absentium ita repraesentantur animo ut eas cernere oculis ac praesentes habere videamur*, "Let us use the term *visiones* for what the Greeks call *phantasiae*, through which images of absent things are represented to the mind in such a way that we seem to perceive them with our eyes and have them present before us" (Quint. 6.2.29). Ps.-Longinus represents the author as first having formed these visual images, ὅταν ἃ λέγεις ὑπ' ἐνθουσιασμοῦ καὶ πάθους βλέπειν δοκῇς καὶ ὑπ' ὄψιν τιθῇς τοῖς ἀκούουσιν, "Whenever from inspiration and emotion you appear to see what you are describing, and you set it in your hearers' sight" (Ps.-Longinus 15.1).[103] Regio, using the standard term *prosopopoeia* for personification as such, applies *phantasia* to Ovid's richly elaborate personifications.[104] They do develop out of the stylistic resources of epic. Yet Ovid, as we shall see, took this form of imaginative actualization far beyond its origins, making of it a thematic principle, an embodiment of transformation itself. His personifications digress from their contexts only to extend, develop, and concentrate thematic elements of those contexts. Personification embodies the transformative nature of Ovidian language in an especially extreme form, and nothing could be more closely bound up with Ovidian metamorphosis.

In the view of M. Quilligan, allegorical works, however diverse, share

---

[101] With the introduction of Fames, according to Galinsky (1975, 8), Ovid "transposes us into the world of the wondrous and fantastic. And he will continue in the same grotesque and fantastic vein without ever returning to the realities of the early part of the story." This account is highly exaggerated, for nothing in any narrative ought to be so simply characterized as "reality." But Galinsky's point is that earlier details in the story of Erysichthon may suggest to Ovid's Roman readers elements of their own religious experience, whereas the description of Fames has little or no relevance to experience. By contrast, Solodow (1988, 196–202) includes discussion of personification in his chapter entitled "Metamorphosis." He rightly emphasizes the evocative power of visual images in Ovid's descriptions, but I cannot agree that they are examples of a "general striving for clarity" opposed to "the uncertain flux of experience" (197).

[102] Feeney 1991, 51.

[103] See Russell 1964, 121.

[104] For *phantasia*, see Regio 1493, d.iii.r (on Invidia) and p.iii.r (on the House of Somnus), both quoted below; and *prosopopoeia* p.iii.v (on Somnus himself).

"the generation of narrative structure out of wordplay."[105] This description will well suit Ovidian personification, if understood as applying to Ovid's free extensions of his mercurial style, rather than, as in Quilligan, to the generic requirements of later formal allegory. In Quilligan's texts, especially *Piers Plowman* and *The Fairie Queene*, allegory's high-profile generic status grants wordplay and personification a privileged condition that they ordinarily lack: they are both normal and expected, for the author necessarily adopts them in deciding to write allegory. This unwonted normalcy conditions our responses in a thoroughgoing way. We always know that the other meanings promised in the very name of *allegoria* are to be expected at every turn. Ovid's personifications arise more directly out of the narrative surface, developed as immediate extensions of the wordplay that flourishes there. They turn up unexpectedly from time to time as one reads along, and are unannounced by any generic signals. Despite these differences, Quilligan's account of personification as a fundamental "linguistic disposition," upon which allegory is based, will serve for Ovid's mode of personification: "Relying upon the process of making inanimate nouns animate," personification "requires a curious treatment of language. The violation of grammatical categories necessary for personification emphasizes the very operation of language and, having become self-conscious about the grammar, it is only logical for poet (and reader) to become sensitive to other surface verbal structures."[106]

In the case of Invidia, Mercury's sylleptic pun on *non motura* brings the story to its climax, and, as we have seen, metamorphosis issues directly from wordplay in Aglauros's petrification. Personification makes a fitting preparation for this event, for in it the association of wordplay and narrative is already very close. In Invidia, Ovid generates a story out of an abstraction. While Invidia's function is to cause a specific individual, Aglauros, to become envious, she is herself a collection of the effects of envy as manifested in countless examples.[107] As Regio remarks, *Eleganti Phantasia Invidiae et corpus et figuram humanam et actiones attribuit. Ea vero omnia describit quae invidis inesse solent*, "With an elegant *phantasia* he attributes to Envy a body, and a human shape and actions. But in fact he is describing all those things that are within envious people."[108] Just as an envious person may be sleepless, or unsmiling except at another's grief, so is Envy. She embodies, in abstract form, all characteristics attributable to individual cases:

> risus abest, nisi quem visi movere dolores,
> nec fruitur somno vigilacibus excita curis,

---

[105] Quilligan 1979, 22. Cf. Feeney 1991, 243–247.
[106] Quilligan 1979, 42.
[107] See Dickie 1975.
[108] Regio 1493, d.iii.r, on *Met.* 2.770.

> sed videt ingratos intabescitque videndo
> successus hominum carpitque et carpitur una
> suppliciumque suum est.
> (*Met.* 2.778–782)

There is no smile, except when pain she observes produces one. Kept awake by vigilant anxiety, she enjoys no sleep. With displeasure she looks upon human success, the sight of which eats away at her. She slanders and is slandered in turn; she is her own punishment.

Personification differs, however, from abstraction in general, because through sensuous language it presents an imaginatively powerful image. Here Ovid represents an essentialized conception as a body, causing the purely conceptual to gain such an elaborate appeal to the senses that it appears transformed into a physical being. By a sort of reverse mimicry, Invidia is made to evoke, in concentrated form, the unspecified cases that supply her characteristics:

> pallor in ore sedet, macies in corpore toto,
> nusquam recta acies, livent rubigine dentes,
> pectora felle virent, lingua est suffusa veneno.[109]
> (*Met.* 2.775–777)

Her face is pale, her whole body shrunken, her gaze never direct; her teeth are discolored with scurf, her breast green with bile; her tongue drips poison.

Ovid's narrative of physical realization grants Invidia "vividness"; that is, it encourages us readers to imagine Invidia as perceptible to the senses, and thereby willingly to make an imaginative extension that clashes with our knowledge that she is "really" a conceptual abstraction. Personification shows Ovidian wit at its most audacious. On it Ovid lavishes all the resources of authenticating detail, as if to flaunt the fact that words need not imitate things, but can create them *ex nihilo* before the eyes of an approving audience.

Invidia, after infecting Aglauros, creates an insubstantial *imago* before her eyes:

> germanam ante oculos fortunatumque sororis
> coniugium pulchraque deum sub imagine ponit
> cunctaque magna facit; quibus inritata, dolore
> Cecropis occulto mordetur.
> (*Met.* 2.803–806)

---

[109] Solodow (1988, 202) well remarks on "the use of words which have both physical-real and abstract-figurative applications.... *Livent* means both 'be livid, discolored' and 'be envious.' *Virent* means both 'be green' and 'be blooming with, full of.' The language is perfectly apt for the portrait of an abstraction given physical reality."

Before Aglauros's eyes she set her sister, her sister's lucky marriage, and the
god himself in a lovely image; she made everything large. Cecrops's daughter is goaded by these sights, and a hidden pain gnaws at her.

It is this *imago* that induces Aglauros to take action in opposing Mercury's access to her sister Herse, just as the wounds of Althea's brothers, forming an image *ante oculos*, "Before her eyes" (*Met.* 8.507), bring her at last to act. With such expressions Ovid seems to introduce the language of criticism into his poetry, for he represents a process of visualization in his characters that recalls the critics' accounts of how readers experience a poet's visualizations. Ovid realizes a simultaneous double application of *phantasia*, one implicit in critical descriptions like Ps.-Longinus's ὑπ' ὄψιν τοῖς ἀκούουσιν, "In the hearers' sight" (Ps.-Longinus 15.1). In imagination, we hearers have a sense of sight to match that of the characters in the story. The term εἰδωλοποιΐα, "image-production," which Ps.-Longinus gives as a synonym, preferred by some, for φαντασία, can also have this double application. Just as the Homeric divinity and Ovidian personification send forth εἴδωλα, *imagines, umbrae*, to affect the visual perception of characters, so the author induces a parallel visualization in the audience. Our experience as readers mirrors that of Aglauros, in that we have, just before, witnessed the personification of Invidia as a richly detailed *imago* before our eyes, so to speak. Yet our awareness separates us from Aglauros, who is simply deceived. Ovid has more to achieve with us than Invidia with Aglauros—to engage us in the power of the narrative while also permitting us to witness its operation in process.

As with Invidia, the personification of Fames grows directly out of its stylistic context in the story of Erysichthon (*Met.* 8.738–778). Here Ovid is characteristically exploring the paradoxical nature of the real and the imaginary; and we can observe, with special clarity, the close connections between elaborated personification and the small-scale instances of wordplay that we have considered above. Personification is a large-scale expansion of the narrative surface to engulf, as it were, the surrounding context, or rather our perception of it: personification becomes the main event of Erysichthon's story. Though it develops out of the stylistic raw material of the context, personification also transforms our understanding of the surrounding narrative, showing all elements of the tale to be consubstantial with the witticisms of its narrative surface.

After Erysichthon impiously destroys Ceres' grove, the goddess wishes to punish him with a devouring hunger; but to cause hunger is the opposite of Ceres' definitive function. Ovid expands upon a paradox already familiar from Narcissus's self-description: *copia* causes *inopia*. In shaping the structure of the narrative, Ovid frames the personification of Fames with variations of this paradox. First, he explores it in a comic account of the logistical difficulties of divine punishment: the goddess cannot be polluted by personal contact with Hunger, and must send an oread instead to search her out, *neque enim Cereremque Famemque / fata coire sinunt*, "For the Fates do not allow Ceres and Hunger to come together" (*Met.* 8.785–786). Here the author not only asserts a power greater than the Fates' by allowing Ceres and Fames to come together, physically juxtaposed in the line, but also effects through word order a paradoxical contradiction of his own statement. Ceres and Fames meet at the very moment we are learning that they can never meet. Then, after the description of Fames, Ovid restates the paradox in terms of the antithetical function of Ceres and Fames:

> dicta Fames Cereris, quamvis contraria semper
> illius est operi.
> (*Met.* 8.814–815)

Hunger performed Ceres' commands, though always opposed to her function.

Enclosed within these passages is the personification of Fames. She is similar to Invidia in that she embodies the accumulated effects that hunger has on individual human beings, but she is a more extreme case. In personifying Fames, Ovid makes an absence into a body, a lack into a character—one vividly imaginable, like Invidia, in terms of sense impressions. Fames is paradoxical in uniting opposites—absence and presence, richness and deprivation:

> quaesitamque Famem lapidoso vidit in agro
> unguibus et raras vellentem dentibus herbas.
> hirtus erat crinis, cava lumina, pallor in ore
> labra incana situ, scabrae rubigine fauces,
> dura cutis, per quam spectari viscera possent;
> ossa sub incurvis exstabant arida lumbis,
> ventris erat pro ventre locus; pendere putares
> pectus et a spinae tantummodo crate teneri;
> auxerat articulos macies, genuumque tumebat
> orbis, et inmodico prodibant tubere tali.
> (*Met.* 8.799–808)

After a search, she found Hunger in a rocky field, plucking sparse plants with her nails and teeth. Her hair was shaggy, her eyes hollow, her face pale, her lips gray with mold, her throat rough with scurf, her skin hard, through which her innards could be seen; her bones stood out dry beneath her curved loins; instead of a stomach there was a place for a stomach; you would have thought her breast was hanging, just held by the basket of the rib-cage; shrunkenness had made her joints larger; her knees were swollen, and her ankles projected with excessive swelling.

For all its appeal to the reader's visual imagination, this passage simultaneously demands a more abstract engagement with its terms. *Ventris erat pro ventre locus* is not a description of the stomach but of its absence. It substitutes absence for a visually evocative image, for the context would cause us to expect one like that introduced by direct second-person appeal to the reader's conceptual imagination: *putares*, "You would have supposed."

Once Fames has infected Erysichthon, his unquenchable hunger takes narrative form as a torrent of paradoxical expressions: *adpositis queritur ieiunia mensis / inque epulis epulas quaerit*, "With tables set before him he complains of hunger, and among feasts he searches for feasts" (*Met.* 8.831–832). In the end, Erysichthon's hunger comes very close to a literal embodiment of Narcissus's self-cancelling expression, *inopem me copia fecit* (*Met.* 3.466):

> quo copia maior
> est data, plura petit turbaque voracior ipsa est,
> sic epulas omnes Erysichthonis ora profani
> accipiunt poscuntque simul: cibus omnis in illo
> causa cibi est semperque locus fit inanis edendo.
> (*Met.* 8.838–842)

The greater his abundance, the more he seeks, and he is greedier because of the ready supply; thus the mouth of impious Erysichthon receives and demands all feasts at the same time; in him all food is the cause of more food; a place always becomes empty through eating.

These paradoxes are the stylistic issue of the personified Fames; they seem at this point to overwhelm the narrative, just as Erysichthon's hunger threatens to engorge the whole world.[110]

As he transforms Invidia and Fames into physically realized beings, Ovid goes beyond their appearance to their effect on human beings, which is also physically represented: they function like poisons. Ceres had ordered that Fames "bury herself in the criminal heart of the impious man," *ea se in praecordia condat / sacrilegi scelerata* (*Met.* 8.791–792). She is carried on the wind (*Met.* 8.815), an airborne pestilence like Lucretius's *mortifer aestus*, "death-bearing surge" (Lucr. 6.1138), yet she

---

[110] So Barkan (1986, 92–93) selects this passage as "a precis of the poem's cosmos" to exemplify the symbolic links between metaphor and metamorphosis.

remains personified as well. She has arms to embrace him even as she breathes herself into the man:

> geminis amplectitur ulnis
> seque viro inspirat faucesque et pectus et ora
> adflat et in vacuis peragit ieiunia venis.
> (*Met.* 8.818–820)

> She embraces him with both arms and breathes herself into the man, blowing through his throat, breast, and mouth, and spreading hunger in his empty veins.

In this process there is nothing insubstantial in Fames.[111] Medical authorities believed that the arteries conducted air to all parts of the body; so here the deadly contagion spreads.[112] In Invidia as well, we find the verb *inspirare* and the only partly metaphorical idea of infection by poisonous air:

> inspiratque nocens virus piceumque per ossa
> dissipat et medio spargit pulmone venenum.
> (*Met.* 2.800–801)

> She breathes into her a noxious poison, spreads a pitchy poison through her bones and scatters it in the middle of her lungs.

In representing a powerful emotion as an infection, in gruesomely physical terms, Ovid is partly drawing on the epic tradition, especially the *Aeneid*. In similar language Allecto, *infecta venenis*, "infected with poisons" (*Aen.* 7.341), taking on a serpent's form, breathes a noxious influence into Amata, *vipeream inspirans animam*, "breathing a viperous breath into her" (*Aen.* 7.351). In her function as the specialized servant of a major divinity, summoned to infect a human being with destructive passion, Allecto is more recognizably the parent of Invidia and Fames than are Vergil's personifications, such as Atlas and Fama in the *Aeneid* (*Aen.* 4.173–188, 246–251). But Allecto is an intermediate figure between abstract emotion and its individual instantiation. Ovid's personifications are more extreme than Allecto, for traditional epic readily sup-

---

[111] The remark of Hollis (1970, 142) on *Met.* 8.815 is misleading: "Hunger is so insubstantial that she floats on the breeze." In fact, Fames, carried by the wind, is already being treated in physical terms, transformed into a deadly contagion. Just so Lucretius's plague of Athens arose in Egypt, then, "having traversed much air," *aera permensus multum* (Lucr. 6.1142), it settled on the people of Athens.

[112] *Vena* is a general term, including both blood-bearing veins and air-bearing arteries (cf. *OLD* s.v. *vena* 1). Cicero distinguishes the two: *sanguis per venas in omne corpus diffunditur et spiritus per arterias*, "Blood is conducted to the whole body through veins, and breath through arteries" (*De natura deorum* 2.138). On the ancient belief that air was conducted by the arteries, see Pease 1955–1956, 911.

plies hellish creatures, which the poet can summon from the infernal regions as needed. Ovid himself does much the same in Book 4 with Tisiphone, who plucks a pair of snakes from her head with which to infect Ino and Athamas with madness:

> at illi
> Inoosque sinus Athamanteosque pererrant
> inspirantque graves animas.
> (*Met.* 4.496–498)

> But the snakes, gliding through the breasts of Ino and Athamas, breathe into them grievous influences.

By contrast to Tisiphone, Ovid's personifications of Invidia and Fames, taking a single leap from abstract to physical, are far more audacious than convention would warrant for underworld figures of epic.

Farther removed than Allecto from Ovid's personifications are the divinities of the *Aeneid*, even though Ovid draws many details from their portrayal, and invites us to think of their function as parallel to that of his personifications. Venus in *Aeneid* 1, resolved to induce in Dido a passionate love for Aeneas, instructs Amor to deceive her by taking the form of Ascanius. Here we find the verb *inspirare*—Amor is to breathe contagion into Dido—along with poison and deception, all aimed, as in Ovid's Invidia, at ruinous emotional manipulation of a mortal. Venus's speech must have been an inspiration to Ovid, for it also offers him a model for the juxtaposed repetition of a word, *pueri puer* (*Aen.* 1.684), to represent Amor's transformation into a reduplicated Ascanius:

> falle dolo et notos pueri puer indue vultus,
> ut, cum te gremio accipiet laetissima Dido
> regales inter mensas laticemque Lyaeum,
> cum dabit amplexus atque oscula dulcia figet,
> occultum inspires ignem fallasque veneno.
> (*Aen.* 1.684–688)

> Deceive her by a trick: a boy yourself, put on the well-known face of the boy, so that, when delighted Dido takes you in her lap, among the royal tables and wine, when she gives you embraces and places sweet kisses on you, you may breathe a hidden fire into her and deceive her with poison.

There are other parallels to the juxtaposition of *pueri* and *puer* in the *Aeneid*, but these less resemble Ovid's examples, lacking the thematic relevance to transformation.[113] The crucial difference between this infection and those achieved by Invidia and Fames is that Amor is the divinity

---

[113] *Aen.* 3.329, 4.83, 5.569, 10.600.

himself, not an abstraction represented along the lines of divinity. Epic divinities already have bodies, and they have had them from the start. There is nothing incongruous in the fact that Athena in the *Iliad*, when stepping into a chariot, causes it to creak loudly (*Il.* 5.838–839). In such a case, Homeric scholars will inform us very seriously that Homeric conceptions of divinity embraced the attribution of physical weight.[114] Vergil adapts his divinities to Homeric traditions of representation, as does Ovid, though Ovid emphasizes and exploits comic incongruities of every kind, including those available in the bodily nature of traditional epic divinity.[115] But in personification, as opposed to divine representation, Ovid undertakes a more radical achievement, the transformation of what is definitively insubstantial into something with bodily presence.

True Imitation: Ceyx, Alcyone, and Morpheus

The cave of Sleep, along with its inhabitants, occupies our attention for many lines in the midst of the vast tale of Ceyx and Alcyone (*Met.* 11.592–649). These are perhaps the richest of Ovid's personifications. Here again, Ovid's critics tend to see the relation, if any, between this extended passage and its context as one of digressive irrelevance. Like comic relief as the presumed purpose of Ovidian wit, this complex of personifications, "full of Ovidian whimsy and ingenuity," according to Galinsky, supposedly "offsets the pathos of the conclusion of the episode." On this view, "whimsy and ingenuity" are not intellectually serious, nor do they promote emotional and imaginative engagement on the reader's part; on the contrary, they characterize Ovid's expansion of the traditional story "to alleviate the *gravitas* of its central, traditional facts, the death of Ceyx and the anguish of Alcyone."[116] Informing this view of personification is the assumption that the larger tale has little to

---

[114] Kirk 1990, 146: "The gods can be conceived as having many corporeal attributes." Aristarchus athetized these lines ὅτι οὐκ ἀναγκαῖοι καὶ γελοῖοι καί τι ἐναντίον ἔχοντες, "Because they are unnecessary, laughable, and illogical" (*Schol. Graec.* 2.111 Erbse). According to Kirk, "It was probably the theological implications of Athene's sheer weight that distressed him."

[115] Among the innumerable examples that could be cited is Diana in Book 3. That divine bodies are larger than those of their attendants makes Homer's description of Artemis, and Vergil's of Diana, more impressive and awesome: πασάων δ' ὑπὲρ ἥ γε κάρη ἔχει ἠδὲ μέτωπα, "She held her head and face above them all" (*Od.* 6.107); *gradiensque deas supereminet omnis,* "As she strode, she towered above all the divinities" (*Aen.* 1.501). Ovid adapts these expressions in making Diana's greater size a cause of comically awkward embarrassment; Actaeon sees her bathing because she stands so much taller than her attendants: *Met.* 3.181–182 (*altior illis / ipsa dea est colloque tenus supereminet omnes,* "The goddess herself stood taller, and projected above them all as far as her neck"). On physicalizing wit, see below, Chapter 2.

[116] Galinsky 1975, 146, 145. On "detachment," see Chapter 2.

do with metamorphosis. After all, in so long a story, the actual transformation of Ceyx and Alcyone into kingfishers (*Met.* 11.731–742) requires but a few lines near the end: *ambo / alite mutantur*, "Both are changed into birds" (*Met.* 11.742), we learn in summary fashion, as if from an epitome. Galinsky includes this story on a list meant to show that "the main subject of the poem, if one has to specify one, is love rather than metamorphosis," in this case "the altruistic and conjugal love of Ceyx and Alcyone."[117] Many readers have indeed found the story moving because of its treatment of conjugal love, which can offer an emotional bath of the familiar "tragic" sort, its appeal similar to that of the story of Cephalus and Procris but without the complications of deception, murder, and so on. Yet there is no need to narrow one's attention or engagement only to the emotional appeal of its subjects, as some have done.[118] Once a reader's interest has been limited in this way, the cave of Sleep will indeed seem uninteresting.

Our first engagement with the love of Ceyx and Alcyone is with a paradoxical reference to it, made by Alcyone at her first appearance. Ceyx is ready to join in attacking the monstrous wolf that is devastating the herds of his guest Peleus, when Alcyone suddenly rushes in to prevent him from endangering himself:

> colloque infusa mariti,
> mittat ut auxilium sine se, verbisque precatur
> et lacrimis, animasque duas ut servet in una.
> (*Met.* 11.386–388)

Throwing herself on her husband's neck, she entreats him with words and tears to send help without going himself, and so preserve two souls in one.

No harm is to come to Ceyx in this incident, but Alcyone's fear of separation and loss proves well founded in the sequel, for Ceyx goes off to consult the oracle at Clarus and is drowned on his sea journey. No less than her fear for his safety, her description of their love in paradoxical terms also proves prophetic: it turns out to be definitive for the whole tale of Ceyx and Alcyone. Two is actually one, and separation is actually nonseparation. These may seem rather ordinary and familiar paradoxes of amatory language;[119] but they have already become more than that in the

---

[117] Galinsky 1975, 97.

[118] According to Wilkinson (1955, 204–205), "The story of Ceÿx and Alcyone, one of the best in the *Metamorphoses*, is moving in the same way as that of Cephalus and Procris or Protesilaüs and Laodamia, because it deals with deep conjugal affection." For a judicious general account of this tale, see Fantham 1979.

[119] Cf. *Am.* 2.13.15–16: *in una parce duobus: / nam vitam dominae tu dabis, illa mihi*, "Spare two lives in one: for you will give life to my mistress, and she will give life to me"; *Met.* 2.609: *duo nunc moriemur in una*, "We two shall now perish in one." In *Her.* 18

Metamorphoses. Though the love of Narcissus for his reflection may appear superficially to have little in common with that of Alcyone for her husband, they share the same fundamentally paradoxical nature. Narcissus addresses his reflection in terms very similar to Alcyone's: *nunc duo concordes anima moriemur in una* (*Met.* 3.473). Earlier we examined other paradoxes in Narcissus's story as stylistic enactments of transformation. As explored and developed in the tale of Ceyx and Alcyone, Alcyone's paradoxical language also becomes transformative; it engages central themes of the *Metamorphoses* and joins the host of significant paradoxes that inhabit the work. In short, Ceyx and Alcyone are first defined as an inseparable unity. Next, they are physically separated. Then, for most of the story, they are reunited in various metaphorical, verbal, and conceptual ways. This process continues unabated at the death of Ceyx, in fact becoming more intense and imaginatively powerful thereafter, especially in the cave of Sleep and Alcyone's subsequent dream. Finally, in metamorphosis Ceyx and Alcyone become physically reunited; transformation re-enacts what language and thought have already realized.

At the height of the storm, paradox is the natural expression of Ceyx's thoughts about his wife:

> Alcyone Ceyca movet, Ceycis in ore
> nulla nisi Alcyone est et, cum desideret unam,
> gaudet abesse tamen.
> (*Met.* 11.544–546)

Alcyone moves Ceyx, and no one but Alcyone is in Ceyx's mouth, and though he longed for her alone, yet he rejoiced that she was absent.

Despite her literal absence, Alcyone is present to Ceyx in more than recollection and thought: their names join them. The fact that her name is literally present in Ceyx's mouth, *in ore*, seems to give Alcyone presence in a sense that passes beyond the strictly metaphorical. Ovid's form of expression further serves the process of nominal reunification by juxtaposing the two names in the line: *Alcyone Ceyca movet*. This, another verbal joining, is yet not purely verbal, for to the listener's ear, and reader's eye, these names are physically perceptible in juxtaposition. And they invite, through the spatial symbolism of word order, a conceptual joining in the mind of the audience. Already at this point in the story,

---

(19).149–150, the notion of two people rescued by a single act is expanded into sylleptic wordplay. *Pendet* serves two semantic functions in a single word, as Hero appeals to Neptune: *da veniam servaque duos! natat ille, sed isdem / corpus Leandri, spes mea pendet aquis*, "Favor him and preserve two people! He is doing the swimming, but in the same waters hang my hopes as well as Leander's body."

Ovid encourages the audience to ponder transformative themes: the conceptual and physical set adrift, a potential conflation of names and things.

While clinging to a fragment of his ship and about to drown, Ceyx continues to name Alcyone despite the physical difficulty, thus giving further emphasis to the identification of absence and nonabsence:

> dum natat, absentem, quotiens sinit hiscere fluctus,
> nominat Alcyonen ipsisque inmurmurat undis.
> (*Met.* 11.566–567)

While he swims, he names absent Alcyone whenever the floods let him open his mouth; and he murmurs Alcyone in the waves themselves.

A little earlier, Ceyx joins his memory of Alcyone, and his continued pronunciation of her name, to a wish that she later find and bury his body:

> plurima nantis in ore est
> Alcyone coniunx: illam meminitque refertque,
> illius ante oculos ut agant sua corpora fluctus,
> optat, et exanimis manibus tumuletur amicis.
> (*Met.* 11.562–565)

Most often in the swimmer's mouth is Alcyone his wife: her he remembers and recalls to mind; he wishes that the floods might bring his body before her eyes, and that when dead he might be buried by friendly hands.

The expression *ante oculos* here has a literal and physical reference, but as we saw with Invidia and Althea, it often refers to the hovering presence of an *imago* before someone's mind;[120] and so it will happen in this story. Alcyone actually will discover her husband's body on the shore, but only after he has first become fully realized as an *imago*, presenting itself to her mind's eye.

As if in a partial and compensatory response to Ceyx's wish, Juno initiates the process of making an *imago* of Ceyx to be sent to Alcyone in sleep. Of course, Juno really has her own interests in mind: Alcyone is polluting the goddess's altars by her unwitting entreaties for her dead and unburied husband, and a news-bearing *imago* will ensure that she stops doing so. Juno orders Iris to pay a visit to the court of Sleep:

---

[120] Ovid and his audiences were familiar with the expression *ante oculos* in Vergil's representations of dreams (*Aen.* 3.150) and visions (*Aen.* 2.270), notably, for the context of this tale, Aeneas's vision of his wife Creusa: *infelix simulacrum atque ipsius umbra Creusae / visa mihi ante oculos et nota maior imago*, "Her likeness, the shade of Creusa herself, appeared before my eyes, her image larger than I had known it" (*Aen.* 2.772–773).

> vise soporiferam Somni velociter aulam
> exstinctique iube Ceycis imagine mittat
> somnia ad Alcyonen veros narrantia casus.
> (*Met.* 11.586–588)

Quickly visit the slumber-bearing court of Sleep and bid him send, in the image of dead Ceyx, dreams to Alcyone that tell of true events.

Ovid introduces the personification of Somnus with a formal description of his cave. Much as with Invidia and Fames, an appeal to the reader's sensuous imagination first gains momentum in elaboration of the setting, and this momentum is then transferred to the abstract personification. The Cave of Sleep much exceeds the earlier settings in length and detail; more significantly, it receives a negative description. Ovid lavishes all the evocative powers of sensuous language to tell us what the cave lacks:

> quo numquam radiis oriens mediusve cadensve
> Phoebus adire potest; nebulae caligine mixtae
> exhalantur humo dubiaeque crepuscula lucis.
> (*Met.* 11.594–596)

Where never Phoebus rising, at midday, or setting can approach; fogs mixed with darkness are breathed from the ground, and a twilight of doubtful light.

Though sunlight never penetrates its gloom, he most fully evokes its soundlessness:

> non vigil ales ibi cristati cantibus oris
> evocat Auroram, nec voce silentia rumpunt
> sollicitive canes canibusve sagacior anser;
> non fera, non pecudes, non moti flamine rami
> humanaeve sonum reddunt convicia linguae:
> muta quies habitat.
> (*Met.* 11.597–602)

There the wakeful cock does not summon Aurora with a song from its crested head, nor do dogs, when disturbed, break the silence with their voices, nor does the goose, more keen than dogs; no wild beasts, no sheep, no branches moved by the breeze, no outcry of human tongue make a sound: dumb quiet dwells there.

The climactic absence is that of human voices, natural enough, perhaps, in a cave, but striking when the cave is presently reconceived as a house. There are no doors to creak on their hinges, and no doorkeeper to announce the visitor's name:

GLITTERING TRIFLES 77

> ianua nec verso stridorem cardine reddit:
> nulla domo tota est, custos in limine nullus.
> (*Met.* 11.608–609)

Nor does a door cause creaking as its hinge turns: there is no door in the whole house, and no doorkeeper at the threshold.

Indeed, a doorless threshold does not really function like a threshold at all, to mark off inside and outside with a definite boundary; instead, it contributes to the amorphous, inchoate character of this house. And we who have just witnessed Ceyx exerting so much vocal effort to name Alcyone in the midst of the storm may well be struck by the absence of voices here. Voices, if present, might with clamorous insistence give shape to the chaoslike formlessness of Somnus's domain.[121] Silence, along with the *dubiae crepuscula lucis* with which the description begins, makes the perfect setting for *phantasia*.[122] Who knows what one is hearing or seeing in such a place? The setting offers raw material, so to speak, for the creation of images.

Barely able to raise himself to recognize his visitor, Somnus at last appears, realized in comically literal detail, and forming a brief but perfectly realized personification. As Regio remarks, *eleganter gestus describit poeta eorum qui gravi somno praemuntur. est autem prosopopoeia. Rei enim corpore carenti corpus attribuit,* "The poet elegantly describes the bearing of those who are pressed by deep sleep. This is, moreover, a case of personification; for he attributes a body to a thing that lacks a body."[123] So also appear the attendant dreams, which Iris must clear away in order to approach Somnus (*Met.* 11.616–617). From such a context, wherein the insubstantial is becoming elaborately reified, naturally arises another self-objectifying play on pronouns:

> vix oculos tollens iterumque iterumque relabens
> summaque percutiens nutanti pectora mento
> excussit tandem sibi se.
> (*Met.* 11.619–621)

---

[121] It is the creative character of this description that makes it so evocative, both as an image of formlessness and as a fertile field for the creation of *phantasiae*. To imagine the house of Somnus, we must first presuppose a typical Roman house with all its customary attributes, then rid this conception of doors, sound, etc. As Culler (1981, 115) remarks, "In most cases the logical presuppositions of positive and negative propositions are the same, but rhetorically, pragmatically, literally, negations are far richer in presuppositions."

[122] See Regio 1493, p.iii.r, on *Met.* 11.594: *pulchra poetae phantasia*, "The poet's lovely *phantasia*."

[123] Ibid., p.iii.v, on *Met.* 11.619.

> Scarcely lifting his eyes, sliding back again and again, and striking his upper chest with his nodding chin, at last he shook himself out of himself.

With Somnus, word and thing are once again in flux. The personified dreams add a further element, transformative imitation. They lounge about the cave (or house), a notably physical presence there, until called upon to imitate some shape:

> hunc circa passim varias imitantia formas
> somnia vana iacent totidem, quot messis aristas,
> silva gerit frondes, eiectas litus harenas.
> (*Met.* 11.613–615)

> Around him lay scattered empty dreams, imitating different shapes—as many as the ears of grain borne by the harvest, leaves by the forest, grains of sand tossed on the shore.

Variety is one attribute of these shapes, but what Juno cares about is their truth: her emissary Iris calls them *somnia, quae veras aequant imitantia formas*, "Dreams that imitate and equal true shapes" (*Met.* 11. 626),[124] reflecting Juno's own description of them, *somnia . . . veros narrantia casus*, "Dreams that tell of true events" (*Met.* 11.588). Indeed, these dreams transform events into shapes. Ceyx's death, an event unknown to Alcyone, is soon to take shape as an *imago* of his body as he died, *exanimi similis*, "Like one dead" (*Met.* 11.654).

The truth of dreams is their verisimilitude, as becomes clear with Somnus's choice of Morpheus as the dream best qualified to take on the task of representing Ceyx. Morpheus's name defines his power to become the perfect appearance of shape, μορφή, in his case human shape; and Ovid's description seems to arise directly from etymology, a "true account" of Morpheus:

> non illo quisquam sollertius alter
> exprimit incessus vultumque sonumque loquendi;
> adicit et vestes et consuetissima cuique
> verba, sed hic solos homines imitatur; at alter
> fit fera, fit volucris, fit longo corpore serpens:
> hunc Icelon superi, mortale Phobetora vulgus
> nominat.
> (*Met.* 11.635–641)

Ovid represents his dreams as specialized stage-actors, as Dryden, though not Ovid's modern commentators, recognizes:

---

[124] Anderson reads *somnia, quae veras aequant imitamine formas*, "Dreams that through imitation equal true shapes."

> *Morpheus* of all his numerous Train express'd
> The Shape of Man, and imitated best;
> The Walk, the Words, the Gesture cou'd supply,
> The Habit mimick, and the Mien bely;
> Plays well, but all his Action is confin'd;
> Extending not beyond our human kind.
> Another Birds, and Beasts, and Dragons apes,
> And dreadful Images, and Monster shapes:
> This Demon, *Icelos*, in Heav'ns high Hall
> The Gods have nam'd; but Men *Phobetor* call.
> (*Ceyx and Alcyone* 327–336)

The other dreams are, like Morpheus, specialized, and hence passed over by Somnus as he casts his mini-drama. The specialist in animals has two names, which re-emphasize the associations of this context with dramatic imitation: Icelos, "similar," reflects verisimilitude, an aesthetic aspect of performance; Phobetor, "frightener," the evocation of fear in an audience, an affective consequence. Phantasos even brings to mind the critical vocabulary of commentaries, reminding us that the context is one to which the term *phantasia* is suitable:

> est etiam diversae tertius artis
> Phantasos: ille in humum saxumque undamque trabemque,
> quaeque vacant anima, fallaciter omnia transit;
> regibus hic ducibusque suos ostendere vultus
> nocte solet, populos alii plebemque pererrant.
> (*Met.* 11.641–645)

> A third is *Phantasus*, whose Actions roul
> On meaner Thoughts, and Things devoid of Soul;
> Earth, Fruits and Flow'rs, he represents in Dreams,
> And solid Rocks unmov'd, and running Streams:
> These three to Kings, and Chiefs their Scenes display,
> The rest to th' ignoble Commons play.[125]
> (*Ceyx and Alcyone* 337–342)

If there is truth in acting, it paradoxically lies in the ability to deceive. The important thing is to convince the audience of a truthful representation, both in the theater and in Somnus's stagecraft.

Because the purpose of Morpheus's acting, of his power of imitation, is to cause Alcyone to form a perfectly realized conception of Ceyx, it would be possible to see a parallel between Morpheus's imitation of forms and the powerfully suggestive *phantasia* of the author, addressed

---

[125] Kinsley 1962, 721.

to the imagination of his readers. In suggesting such a parallel I hasten to discount the modern association of Morpheus with sleep as such, often without reference to shape-creating dreams; this association no doubt results from a conflation of Somnus and Morpheus.[126] In Ovid their functions remain distinct. Morpheus does not put Alcyone to sleep, nor, to pursue the parallel, did Ovid's work ever induce sleep in a reader capable of intellectual and emotional engagement with his text. Somnus's importance to this parallel lies not in his specific function, but in the fact that he is a personification, a reification of language. In Morpheus's mimetic creation of shapes we can see an embodiment of *phantasia*, or more specifically εἰδωλοποιΐα, image production. Just as Morpheus serves Somnus, image production serves personification, helping to turn words into things. Thus it shares in the transformative themes of the whole work. The vocabulary of Morpheus's imitative transformation—*mutare, forma, corpus*—is that with which Ovid characterized his own work at its beginning. I suggest this parallel not as a full-blown allegory, in which we would miss much if we did not see Ovid in Morpheus; nor do I wish to join the search for "artist-figures" in the *Metamorphoses*. I do propose that both Ovid's artistic self-consciousness and the reader's thematic awareness are more fluid and more pervasive than they appear in attempts to single out characters and tales as allegories of Ovidian art—Pygmalion and his tale, for example.[127] In my view, the style and content of the

---

[126] See Kenney 1986, 442, on *Met.* 11.635. On the function and literary background of Morpheus, see Fantham 1979, 337–341.

[127] Since Fränkel (1945, 96) described Pygmalion's tale as "one of the finest apologues on the marvel of creative imagination," Pygmalion has been often praised as an artist-figure, and his tale as an allegory of artistic transformation. Rosati's discussion is unusually sensitive and restrained (Rosati 1983, 58–67); more typical is the celebratory mode of Solodow (1988, 215–219): "The greatest, or nearly the greatest, artist in the poem is Pygmalion" (215). Romantic notions of the artist as hero strongly influence such interpretations, but are seldom acknowledged by their promoters. An older and wiser view associates Pygmalion with themes of perverse passion, madness, and self-delusion. Montaigne, in the essay "On the Affection of Fathers for Their Children," discusses the Platonic notion of intellectual parenthood, usually something admirable; but Pygmalion provides him with an impressive counterexample to conclude the essay: "And as for those raging vicious passions which have sometimes inflamed fathers with love for their daughters, or mothers for their sons, similar ones can be found in this other kind of parenthood: witness the tale of Pygmalion who, having carved the statue of a uniquely beautiful woman, was so hopelessly ravished by an insane love for his own work that, for the sake of his frenzy, the gods had to bring her to life: *tentatum mollescit ebur, positoque rigore / subsedit digitis* [When touched, the ivory softens; laying aside its hardness, it yields to his fingers: *Met.* 10.283–284]" (Montaigne [1595] 1993, 451–452). Montaigne's summary characterizes Pygmalion's tale as a wish-fulfillment story, calling attention to the fact that transformation here results from divine intervention, not artistic genius. Only by special pleading can Pygmalion sustain his burden as archetypal artist: he is more like the lottery winner of modern times, who through pure accident receives a large reward for having made a poor investment.

Metamorphoses are the same, and every element of the work invites our minds to return to its fundamental themes. Physical transformation in the natural world, literary creation, and the histrionic imitation practiced by Morpheus are all capable of resembling each other in significant ways, of having, so to speak, the same shape.

Alcyone's dream, in which Morpheus appears to her in the role of Ceyx, brings the tale to its climax. It reunites the pair on the conceptual level, but this time more fully and intensely, for an elaborately realized *imago* now represents Ceyx to the dreamer's visual imagination. This *imago* is analogous to others we have considered; Invidia, like Somnus, is a personification that sends out an *imago* to do its work. But with Morpheus Ovid achieves something more, through specific attention to an imitative process and the reception of *imagines*. Thereby he can offer another view of metamorphosis—conceptual metamorphosis so closely resembling physical that it seems to defy such a distinction, challenging any effort to keep the distinction in focus. Ovid makes so much here of verisimilitude, and the consequent power of imitation to produce in the audience a conviction of truth, because therein lies imitation's transformative character. Morpheus can "truly" become Ceyx if he can be recognized by Alcyone. She is, after all, his wife, not just any audience but the perfect test-case for imitative shape-shifting. Hence Morpheus prepares his role by taking on every detail of Ceyx's physical appearance:

> positisque e corpore pennis
> in faciem Ceycis abit sumptaque figura
> luridus, exanimi similis, sine vestibus ullis
> coniugis ante torum miserae stetit; uda videtur
> barba viri madidisque gravis fluere unda capillis.
> (*Met.* 11.652–656)

> Removing the wings from his body, he assumes Ceyx's shape and takes on his appearance: pallid, like one dead, without any garments, he stood before the wretched wife's bed; his beard looked sodden, and water seemed to weigh down and drip from his wet hair.

Most human actors at least somewhat resemble themselves when in costume, but Morpheus can outdo any costume designer's resources: his shape-shifting abilities allow him to take realism far beyond the mimetic compromises that the stage requires. In the domain of the word, however, formal conventions rule both dreams and stages; the power of the word is so great that it must be kept at the cost of verisimilitude. Morpheus may be *exanimi similis*, "like one dead," but he finds it useful to retain the power of speech, so unrealistic in a corpse. A word is worth at least a thousand pictures. Like the playwright exploiting soliloquies and asides, Morpheus gains rhetorical advantages in addressing his audience directly. Thus he can offer Alcyone pre-formed interpretations of the visual impressions she is already receiving:

> agnoscis Ceyca, miserrima coniunx?
> an mea mutata est facies nece? respice: nosces
> inveniesque tuo pro coniuge coniugis umbram.
> (*Met.* 11.658–660)

> Do you recognize Ceyx, wretched wife? Or has death so greatly changed my appearance? Look again: you will recognize and find your husband's shade in place of your husband.

There is much irony in this emphasis on precision in labeling Alcyone's perception—not your husband, but his shade—since we know it to be really Morpheus acting the part. The irony soon becomes still greater when Morpheus insists on his own unproblematical authenticity as an informant. This would be, if possible, the most perfect rhetorical victory: to convince the audience that one's words are interpretively transparent, not requiring any interpretation at all:

> non haec tibi nuntiat auctor
> ambiguus, non ista vagis rumoribus audis:
> ipse ego fata tibi praesens mea naufragus edo.
> (*Met.* 11.666–668)

> No ambiguous authority makes these announcements to you, nor do you hear them from wandering rumors; I myself, in person, the shipwrecked man, tell you of my own fate.

Here this scene begins to verge on the broadly comic, a send-up of the very issues of credibility in representation that are at the heart of *phantasia*.

Morpheus adds the proper intonation and gesture to his performance, and it proves entirely successful (*Met.* 11.671–673). Alcyone moves her body to embrace the insubstantial *imago*. Her attempt to bridge the gap between *corpus* and *umbra* resembles and recalls many comparable embraces in epic, but it is here perfectly matched to the transformative themes of this context. Their presence is stylistically signaled by the double application of *movet*:

> ingemit Alcyone; lacrimas movet atque lacertos
> per somnum corpusque petens amplectitur auras
> exclamatque "mane! quo te rapis? ibimus una."
> (*Met.* 11.674–676)

Alcyone groaned. She set her tears and arms in motion; seeking his body in sleep, she embraced the air; she shouted, "Stay! Where are you hurrying? We will go together."

Alcyone's attempted embrace shows that a conceptual reunification has occurred at least in her mind, at least for the moment, as does her insistence that the two depart together. Once she awakens and recognizes that Ceyx is dead, one might expect her to regard her link to Ceyx as broken along with her illusion. But in fact *ibimus una* simply shifts valence, accommodated to new circumstances. Now Alcyone's voice must take over the task of giving expression to the tale's central paradoxes: presence in absence, nonseparation in separation. Because she and Ceyx are a unity, she reasons, she herself must no longer be alive:

> "nulla est Alcyone, nulla est" ait, "occidit una
> cum Ceyce suo."
> (*Met.* 11.684–685)

"There is no Alcyone, there is none," she said; "she died together with her Ceyx."

This paradox grows directly out of her experience of the dream, wherein *phantasia* granted authenticity to her impressions by fully matching the experience of the senses. Ceyx was a shade, but a "manifest" shade, one that could almost be grasped in one's hand:

> vidi agnovique manusque
> ad discedentem cupiens retinere tetendi.
> umbra fuit, sed et umbra tamen manifesta virique
> vera mei.
> (*Met.* 11.686–689)

I saw him, I recognized him; I stretched out my hand to him as he left, wanting to hold him back. He was a shade, but a manifest shade, the true shade of my husband.

Here again this tale may bring Narcissus to mind, for it was he of whom we read, *corpus putat esse quod umbra est*, "He supposes that to be a body which is in fact a shade" (*Met.* 3.417).[128]

All elements of the stylistic embodiment of paradox become concentrated when Alcyone pursues her description of Ceyx's death as her own:

> nunc absens perii, iactor quoque fluctibus absens
> et sine me me pontus habet.
> (*Met.* 11.700–701)

---

[128] Reading *umbra* for the *unda* of Anderson and others; see Magnus 1914, ad loc.

Dryden well represents in English Alcyone's simultaneous self-cancellation and reduplication:

> Now I die absent, in the vast profound;
> And Me without my Self the Seas have drown'd.[129]
> (*Ceyx and Alcyone* 423–424)

Not only does Alcyone perish *in absentia*, she also is permitted to narrate the event, perfectly representing it in the disjunctive repetition of pronouns. From here it is but one step to an impressive example of virtual metamorphosis. Claiming that she will be Ceyx's "companion" in death, she seems dissatisfied with the largely metaphorical sense in which the notion of companionship applies; and so she transfers their names into the physical sphere and joins them there in written form. Unlike Byblis, Alcyone requires fixity of the *littera scripta*, not wax but stone. The names Ceyx and Alcyone will be physically next to each other on an inscription she proposes to execute, while her present utterance also joins them, taking advantage of the symbolic resources of word order:

> et tibi nunc saltem veniam comes, inque sepulcro
> si non urna, tamen iunget nos littera, si non
> ossibus ossa meis, at nomen nomine tangam.
> (*Met.* 11.705–707)

> Now at least I will go as your companion; if the urn within the tomb shall not join us, yet the letters on it shall; if I shall not touch your bones with mine, yet I shall touch your name with mine.

We may now recall that the shifting relation of *nomen* to *corpus* was already taking thematic shape at the beginning of the story, where Alcyone, fearing for her husband's safety, pondered the function of cenotaphs physically to substitute an inscribed name for the body of the deceased: *et saepe in tumulis sine corpore nomina legi*, "And often on tombs I have read names without a body" (*Met.* 11.429).

There is but one shift remaining in the reunification of the pair. Voice made Alcyone present to Ceyx in the storm, and image brought Ceyx to Alcyone in dreaming; now that their joined names have linked them, the process is re-enacted by their bodies. Alcyone once again recognizes her husband, this time as his corpse is washed to shore. When she throws herself from the pier, she becomes a bird and is reunited with Ceyx as he also undergoes transformation; Alcyone's name remains, transferred to her form as kingfisher.

---

[129] Kinsley 1962, 723. See Hopkins 1988, 187; Hopkins's discussion of this tale (179–190) sensitively illustrates Dryden's adaptation of Ovidian style.

THE HOUSE OF RECEPTION

Somnus, unlike Invidia and Fames, receives less elaborate description than his setting; and Morpheus's far richer personification is likely to displace him in our attention. In Fama, Ovid further develops patterns established there. When, after the sacrifice of Iphigenia, Ovid tells us that rumors of the Greek expedition had reached Troy, he prefaces the Trojan war with an account of Fama and her house (*Met.* 12.39–63). Here again a description becomes so prominent that it casts a symbolic coloring over its larger context. It concentrates our attention on the war as a report, its character and identity dependent on the version that the poet chooses to create in collaboration with his readers' memory of other versions.[130] In contrast to his treatment of Somnus, Ovid here shifts the emphasis further from person to setting, passing still more briefly over the central figure. Fama herself is indeed personified, and inhabits her house in person: *famam autem incorpoream tanquam corpus habentem describit*, "Though she is incorporeal, he describes her as if she had a body."[131] Yet she receives no descriptive elaboration, nor do the other personifications who inhabit her house—*Credulitas, temerarius Error, vana Laetitia*, "Credulity, rash Error, empty Joy" (*Met.* 12.59–60)—and the rest live there as simple embodiments of their names, not unlike the personified attendants of Sol in Book 2, who cluster about his throne: *a dextra laevaque Dies et Mensis et Annus*, "On his right and left stood Day, Month, and Year" (*Met.* 2.25), along with generations, hours, and personified seasons (*Met.* 2.26–30). It is instead the house that Ovid represents to us in a rich *phantasia*, for in this case a complex of significances becomes realized not principally as a body but as a place.

In some ways the house of Fama forms an expansive variation on that of Somnus. This one is even more radically porous:

> innumerosque aditus ac mille foramina tectis
> addidit et nullis inclusit limina portis:
> nocte dieque patet; tota est ex aere sonanti,
> tota fremit vocesque refert iteratque, quod audit.
> nulla quies intus nullaque silentia parte.
> (*Met.* 12.44–48)

She added innumerable approaches to the building, and a thousand openings. With no doors did she shut its threshold: it lies open night and day.

---

[130] Feeney (1991) discusses the house of Fama in connection with his themes of poetic authority; Zumwalt (1977) ably describes how it introduces Ovid's retelling of Homeric subjects.

[131] Regio 1493, p.vi.r, on *Met.* 12.43.

> The whole house is of resounding brass, produces a roar, echoes and repeats what it hears. There is no quiet within, silence in no quarter.

Because its purpose is to admit and echo sound, its fabric is as open as possible, designed for free access and without any concern to separate inside from outside. The unbounded character of the house matches the semantic limitlessness of rumors themselves, which offer an extreme case of the capacity of language to undergo transformations of every kind:

> hi vacuas inplent sermonibus aures,
> hi narrata ferunt alio, mensuraque ficti
> crescit, et auditis aliquid novus adicit auctor.
> (*Met.* 12.56–58)

> Some fill empty ears with talk, others report to another what has been told them; the measure of the fiction grows; each new authority adds something to what he heard.

For all its descriptive elaboration, the house remains highly undefined. The description suggestively promotes attempts in the reader's mind to form a mental picture, while withholding the means to do so. This is in a sense *phantasia* functioning as anti-*phantasia*: Ovid brings home the meaning of the passage by defeating his readers' efforts—for which his own earlier personifications have trained them—to engage their visual imaginations in the vividness of descriptive detail. To succeed in doing so would be to give Fama's house an inappropriate sense of definition. Even its location, though precisely fixed, defeats understanding. Situated at the highly indeterminate boundaries of the *mundus*, it stands between the familiar categories of earth, sea, and sky, just beyond our capacity to grasp its place:

> orbe locus medio est inter terrasque fretumque
> caelestesque plagas, triplicis confinia mundi;
> unde, quod est usquam, quamvis regionibus absit,
> inspicitur, penetratque cavas vox omnis ad aures.
> (*Met.* 12.39–42)

> There is a place at the middle of the world, between land, sea, and the heavenly region, at the boundary of the threefold universe. From here one can see anything anywhere, however distant its place; and every voice comes to one's hollow ears.

More than its appearance, Ovid wants us to have a sense of the house's sound; but here also clarity and stability of perception are not the goal, but a fundamental indistinctness:

> nec tamen est clamor, sed parvae murmura vocis,
> qualia de pelagi, siquis procul audiat, undis
> esse solent, qualemve sonum, cum Iuppiter atras
> increpuit nubes, extrema tonitura reddunt.
> (*Met.* 12.49–52)

Yet there is not noise, but a murmuring of small sounds, such as the sea's waves make, if one hears it from a distance; the sort of sound the last thunder makes, when Jupiter has made the dark clouds rumble.

Out of these confused sounds arise the personified rumors, whose description immediately follows:

> atria turba tenet: veniunt, leve vulgus, euntque
> mixtaque cum veris passim commenta vagantur
> milia rumorum confusaque verba volutant.
> (*Met.* 12.53–55)

A throng occupies its halls; they come and go, a light crowd; lies mixed with truth wander here and there by the thousands; and the confused words of rumor roll about.

Though Ovid outdoes his own mode of personification in the house of Fama, passing beyond descriptive precision and vividness to evoke a willfully indefinite and confused impression, he presents these rumors in a fashion that is largely familiar. They resemble Somnus's dreams in their emphatic physicality, while their semantic identities grant them a place in the conceptual sphere. They are defined in terms of significance, "lies mixed with truth," at the very moment that personification is endowing them with an impression of physical shape. Consistent with Ovidian personification in general is the conflation of physical and conceptual in *leve vulgus*. Normally a banal figurative expression, "the fickle crowd," it here gains an unexpectedly literal sense, "the light crowd," in a sylleptic pun on *leve*. As they flit about the house, these rumors are no less light than fickle.

In obliterating boundaries between physical and conceptual, personification here as elsewhere reveals its connections to the witticisms and tropes with which we began. Yet there are further thematic and stylistic patterns of which the house of Fama presents a symbol. The expression "lies mixed with truth" to characterize the host of rumors makes a pointed interpretive comment on the epic tales whose retelling is already under way. It calls attention to the questionable nature of narrative authority, whether one may choose to question Ovid's, or that of his predecessors, or both. The description of the house as a receptive echo chamber is also suggestive. Both the production and the reception of narratives is potentially unstable, and the reader's judgment is consequently never at rest. Though the reader receives Ovid's version of a tale together with the echoes of other versions that it calls to life in the memory, at the same time Ovid's own version may cause the reader's judgment to undergo many revisions. Ovid perceived in narrative structure, no less than in wit, an opportunity to embody metamorphosis and flux in the experience of his readers. We now turn to this feature of his transformative style.

Chapter 2

THE ASS'S SHADOW: NARRATIVE DISRUPTION AND ITS CONSEQUENCES

Some Exemplary Interruptions

As we look beyond wordplay to larger-scale patterns of Ovid's narrative style, it will be worthwhile to consider that the aggressive power of wordplay—its power to disarm readers and forcibly seize their attention—potentially extends to any element of Ovid's style. Within that style, wordplay has a true home, as can best be seen if one views style rhetorically, with a view to the engagement and manipulation of audiences. Before proceeding with Ovid's narratives, let us consider a tale of an orator and jurymen, which can serve as an exemplum, defining through analogy one possible relation between poet and audience. It is an anecdote of Demosthenes, included by Zenobius in his collection of proverbs and reworked by Erasmus, whom I quote. It illustrates a proverb, "the ass's shadow," and thereby mirrors the link between small-scale stylistic features and the depth of narrative that can inform and illuminate them.

De asini umbra

Ὑπὲρ ὄνου σκιᾶς, id est, *Super asini umbra*, pro eo, quod est: de re nihili. . . . Proinde sunt qui credant hoc adagii primum ab autore Demosthene natum fuisse fabulam huiusmodi referentes: Cum aliquando Demosthenes quendam in causa capitali defenderet ac iudices haberet parum attentos, sed dicenti obstreperent, ille "Paulisper," inquit, "aures mihi praebete, siquidem rem narrabo novam ac lepidam atque auditu iucundam." Ad quae verba cum illi iam aures arrexissent, "Adulescens," inquit, "quispiam asinum conduxerat rerum quiddam Athenis Megaram deportaturus. Inter viam autem cum aestus meridianus ingravesceret nec inveniret quonam umbraculo solis ardorem defenderet, depositis clitellis sub asino sedens eius umbra semet obtegebat. Caeterum id agaso non sinebat hominem inde depellens clamansque asinum esse locatum, non asini umbram. Alter item ex adverso tendebat asseverans etiam umbram asini sibi conductam esse. Atque ita inter eos acerrima rixa in longum producta est, ita ut etiam ad manus venerint, hoc pertinaciter affirmante non conductam esse asini umbram, illo pari contentione respondente umbram etiam asini conductam esse. Demum in ius ambulant." Haec locutus Demosthenes, ubi sensisset iudices diligenter auscultantes, repente coepit a tribunalibus descendere. Porro revocatus a iudicibus rogatusque, ut reliquum fabulae pergeret enarrare, "De asini," inquit, "umbra libet audire, viri causam de vita periclitantis audire gravamini?"[1] (Erasmus *Adagia* 1.3.52, from Zenobius 6.28)

About an ass's shadow. That is, about a thing of no moment. . . . There are some who think that this adage was first derived from Demosthenes as its author, and they tell this story: Once when Demosthenes was defending someone on a capital charge, and he had judges who were inattentive but interrupted constantly, he said, "Lend me your ears for a little while, and I will tell something new and amusing, and merry to hear." At these words they pricked up their ears to listen to him. "A certain young man," he said, "had hired an ass to carry goods from Athens to Megara. On the way, as the midday sun grew stronger, and he could not find a tiny bit of shade to shelter him from the sun, he took off the pack-saddle and sat under the ass, protecting himself with its shade. However the owner would not allow this, and dragged the man out, shouting that he had rented the ass but not the ass's shadow. The other held the opposite view, and declared that he had paid for the ass's shadow too. The quarrel between them dragged on until they came to blows, the one stoutly asserting that the ass's shadow had not been paid for, the other declaring on the contrary that he had hired it as well. Finally they went to law." Having got thus far, when he knew the judges were listening carefully, Demosthenes suddenly began to leave the rostrum. The judges called him back and asked him to go on with the rest of the story. "Do you mean to say," he said, "that you will listen to something about an ass's shadow, but you can't bother to hear the cause of a man in peril of his life?"

With this tale in mind, let us consider the ways in which authors entrap their audiences. For our present purpose, the consideration of Ovidian narrative style, this anecdote is revealing not so much for what it tells us about authors' designs upon audiences—for Demosthenes and Ovid aim to elicit rather different responses—but for what it tells us about audiences themselves. Demosthenes' jurors and Ovid's readers have, I would claim, notable similarities.

With his concluding rhetorical question, Demosthenes aims to chasten his listeners and to concentrate their responsible attention on the serious case at hand—attention that he now controls, at least for the moment. Yet rhetorical questions may tempt unruly listeners to supply them with answers, in this case to defy the speaker by answering the question in the

---

[1] *ASD* 2:1.252; trans. M. M. Phillips, *CWE* 31:278–279. Erasmus adapts and translates the story from Zenobius 6.28, providing additional citations of the proverb; see also Tosi 1991, §488; for Zenobius's text, see Leutsch and Schneidewin 1839–1851, 1:169–170.

affirmative. One can easily imagine a case in which the jurors refused Demosthenes' appeal to duty and demanded stories, for events have already shown an anarchic power in narrative. The speaker himself invited them to release their attention from the case; he judged that they could become engrossed in a story, and succeeded at telling it with just that effect. The jurors' minds, now absent without leave, may or may not be called back to duty. Demosthenes expects his listeners to distinguish appropriate engagement (in a serious case) from inappropriate (in a trivial tale), but his demonstration shows that listeners become engrossed in the details of a well-told tale, regardless of the appropriateness of their doing so.

The jurors' engagement results from the immediate power of narrative to shape events, to render them pleasingly comprehensible through ordered structures. By leaving the rostrum, Demosthenes provokes his listeners and reveals their craving for the rest—for continued gratification along lines established by the narrative, and for the resolution and closure that it appears ultimately to promise them. Any storyteller knows that skillful exposition of a few details is enough to develop a craving in the listeners to hear the rest, and that listeners are normally ready and eager to occupy their attention in details of a story. As long as they can be kept in a state of unsatisfied anticipation and longing, pleasure will secure their engagement, whether the narrative structures are simple or elaborate, sustained or fast-changing, serious or comic.

As our consideration of wordplay suggested, an invitation to throw aside efforts at decorous placement of our attention is surely omnipresent in the *Metamorphoses*. Other features of Ovid's narrative style point to the same conclusion. Yet Ovid, unlike Demosthenes in the anecdote, does not mark off a sharp line of separation between the pleasurable frivolity of narrative and the serious concerns he has in mind, nor does he ask us to reject the former in favor of the latter. Instead, as is also exemplified in wordplay, he introduces frivolity directly into serious contexts, and makes the resulting violations of decorum meaningful. Disruption itself becomes thematic: from a mixed and indecorous style arises what is intellectually serious in the *Metamorphoses*, if not always serious in tone.

I propose, in the following pages, to describe the rhetorical structure of several typical narrative sections of the *Metamorphoses*, and to illustrate significant aspects of its stylistic and tonal character: its disruptiveness and unpredictability, its purposeful tendency first to develop expectations in the audience and then to thwart them, its deliberate aim to induce a loss of narrative bearings on the part of the audience; for Ovid's narrative persona often leaves the rostrum just as a tale is taking shape, leaving us at a loss, at least for a time, about its outcome. The impact of such a work upon its readers may well be different in nature from that of narratives more sustained in style—narratives that gratify the plot expectations they have encouraged and maintain the stylistic and tonal decorums they have first established. But careful examination of Ovidian narrative structures will illustrate their affective function to promote and encourage engagement no less intense and powerful, and no less contributive to the meaning of the work.[2]

If, as I suggest, Ovid's narrative structures embody his thematic preoccupations in the experience of his readers, I assume a higher degree of engagement, both emotional and intellectual, with Ovid's text than is often granted by his critics. In my discussion of paradoxical witticism, I took the reader's engagement largely for granted, for puns and related witticisms manifestly engage the attention; even torpid and inattentive audiences will be brought up short by a pun, which tends to provoke a response—laughter, groans, grimaces—that they experience almost as involuntary. A speaker must win over an audience to receive most kinds of discourse, but the pun gains instant access, whether delightful or painful, to the listener's mind. With a narrative one must seduce one's audience, winning over its willing participation. Ovid can accomplish this task in short order, and his audiences are as willing as Demosthenes' jurors to become engrossed in a tale; but many modern critics fail to recognize engagement so promptly achieved, imagining "distance" and "detachment" as the typical condition of the Ovidian reader. This was not always the case, and it will be worthwhile briefly to review some views on emotional engagement.

Our earliest writer on Ovid, Seneca the Elder, associates him with the schools of rhetoric in which he was trained, and thereby with the potentially useful, potentially dangerous power to persuade.[3] Among the moderns, Kenney is noteworthy in his emphasis on Ovid's power to move, asserting that "direct emotional appeal to the reader" is a quality "in which Ovid excels," and describing Ovid as "an emotional engineer."[4] By

---

[2] That the "affective function" of narrative structures has a place in critical discourse is the contribution of reader-response critics, of whom Iser (1978), Jauss (1982), and Fish (1980) may be singled out as notably influential. For Ovidian studies, especially valuable are Due 1974, and Verducci 1985, especially 22–32; also Konstan 1991.

[3] For a useful discussion of Seneca the Elder's references to Ovid, see Higham 1958, 32–48. Modern writers on Ovid and rhetoric who admire their author—such as Higham and Arnaldi (1958, 23–31)—tend to distance him from the supposed frigidity and irrelevance of the rhetorical schools. For the ancients, however, rhetoric meant not merely *inanes rhetorum ampullae*, "The empty perfume-flasks of the rhetoricians" (Verg. *Catal.* 5.1), but also the power to move the passions of one's hearers and to affect their actions: "The equation of language with power, characteristic of Greek thought at least from the time of Gorgias the rhetorician, explains the enormous energies devoted to the study of rhetoric in the ancient world" (Tompkins 1980, 203–204).

[4] Kenney 1964, 375, 374.

contrast, for Galinsky, "detachment" and "distance" define the characteristic relation of Ovid's reader to the text: the "intent" of Ovid's narrative is "to let the reader be a critical observer and not to let him be naively or romantically drawn into the fictitious story, because that would lessen the sophisticated, intellectual pleasure which Ovid wants us to derive from his mythological storytelling." Consistent with this perspective, the self-consciously fictitious nature of Ovid's mythological subjects provides "the objective basis for his detached attitude that he wants the reader to adopt also."[5]

Galinsky's distanced "intellectual pleasure" may perhaps be the experience of some readers. But it is highly unlikely that Ovid "intended" it as an ideal response to his work, and there is much to suggest that he wants us "drawn in," the sophisticated no less than the naive. I wish to reassert the older view of Ovid as a writer of rhetorical power, and also to go beyond this reassertion to a new understanding of thematic significance in the experience of reading Ovid. If our engagement in a stylistically disruptive text permits that text to have a powerful impact upon us, then Ovid's theme of flux—*omnia mutantur*, "Everything changes" (*Met.* 15.165)—becomes far more than a summary proposition, easily hypostatized and isolated from the work; it becomes a rich and vast range of experiences for Ovid's reader.

One assumption I wish to deny is that because Ovidian style is disruptive and ever-shifting, one cannot be engaged while reading it as one can be in reading works whose style is more sustained and tonally consistent.[6] In doing so, I wish to distinguish Galinsky's disengagement from the "aesthetic distance" posited by H. R. Jauss as a necessary feature of the aesthetic experience of any text. Jauss's description of aesthetic experience is indeed useful for the present purpose. He maintains that aesthetic experience comprises both "elementary pleasure," that is, "the direct sensuous surrender of self to object," and "an additional element" of contemplative "aesthetic distance." By this distance Jauss does not mean to suggest any sort of disinterested remoteness on the reader's part; on the contrary, he defines it as the imaginative participation of the audience—its constitutive contribution to the act of reading, which is so much the focus of Jauss's theory of reception: "The aesthetic attitude demands that the distanced object be not merely contemplated disinterestedly, the viewer should also participate in producing it as an imaginary object—

[5] Galinsky 1975, 35, 37; see also 159. Detachment is also assumed by Solodow to be the affective result of Ovidian style, but he gives it little emphasis: a "slackening of emotional intensity" is presumed to be the result of epigram; in Ovid's description of the flood in Book 1, "the wavering tone holds us at some distance" (Solodow 1988, 50, 119).

[6] Galinsky's discussions of detachment occur in contexts that treat "verbal conceits and bathos" and other forms of indecorous wit (see especially Galinsky 1975, 35 and 159).

like the world of play into which one enters as a fellow player. The distancing act in the aesthetic experience is at the same time a form-creating act of the imagining consciousness."[7] While Jauss's conceptions of pleasure and distance are intended to apply generally to literary works—those of Vergil and Sophocles, for example, as well as Ovid—they have a special appropriateness in Ovid's case. Through them one can understand how the reader's emotional and sensuous surrender, encouraged by Ovid's narrative, can coexist with such contemplative activities as recognizing allusions, pondering thematic conceptions, and in general reflecting upon one's experience of reading.

It is revealing to recall Dryden's Preface to the *Fables* in this context, for, in his hostile rejection of *inopem me copia fecit*, he links paradoxical witticism to tonal collapse and other disruptions of narrative on a larger scale: Ovid "destroys what he was building." Like many, Dryden wants a stable edifice and gets indecorous stylistic collapse instead; but unlike some, he is well aware of a reader's inclination to become engaged in Ovid's text, and his discussion is partly in terms of the effects that Ovidian wit has upon its audience. Not content to criticize Ovid's "Conceits and Jingles" for being "unnatural," Dryden also says that they are "nauseous" for that reason. His annoyance at the portrayal of Narcissus's death results from its tendency to produce a response of inappropriate laughter. Dryden suggests that in violating decorum, Ovid also violates the reader's sensibility: "Virgil never made use of such Machines" is a protest against a kind of manipulation of the reader's emotions. Vergil would not have sought to move the reader by means that Ovid regularly employs, and Dryden is disturbed as well as annoyed by this fact. Dryden enjoyed the *Metamorphoses*—so much so that when he set out to translate some of it, he was led on by sheer pleasure to translate much more than he had originally intended[8]—but he recognized that this most enjoyable poem is also disturbing and provoking. His perception that Ovid would—as Vergil would not—"destroy what he was building" is an accurate insight into Ovid's unsettling narrative technique. Ovid does often disrupt his own narrative with incongruous elements, and often sets up

---

[7] Jauss 1982, 30–31. Jauss's "Sketch of a Theory of Aesthetic Experience" (3–51) is especially valuable for its acknowledgment of both pleasure and reflection in the aesthetic experience: "This state of balance between pure sensuous pleasure and mere reflection has probably never been described as concisely as in a Goethe aphorism which also already anticipates the turning of the receptive into a productive act and thus comes closest to modern theories of art: 'There are three kinds of reader: one, which enjoys without judgment, a third, which judges without enjoyment, and the one in the middle which judges as it enjoys and enjoys as it judges. This latter kind really reproduces the work of art anew'" (36).

[8] Dryden explains near the beginning of the Preface how the "pleasing Task" of translating Ovid expanded as he proceeded (Dryden [1700], in Kinsley 1962, 520–521).

expectations in his readers' minds, then deliberately subverts them. We may, if we choose, join in Dryden's censure, or acknowledge that among the results of all those "glittering Trifles" are amusingly and cruelly accurate perspectives on the world, which we may yet find worth serious pondering.

Dryden, objecting that in "a serious Poem" intrusive wit is "unnatural," places himself in a critical tradition that goes back to antiquity and can be illustrated by Seneca the Younger's comments on the flood in Book 1 (*Met.* 1.272–347). Readers of Ovid's "lengthy and dignified description"[9] of the flood (*Met.* 1.272–292) cannot fail to be surprised when the tone of the narrative abruptly changes, and we find ourselves reading about the wolf swimming among the sheep and the water carrying along tawny lions (*Met.* 1.304). Seneca thinks this intrusion highly inappropriate. He first quotes an impressive line from earlier in the description: *sicut illud pro magnitudine dixit: "omnia pontus erat, deerant quoque litora ponto"* [*Met.* 1.292] *ni tantum impetum ingenii et materiae ad pueriles ineptias reduxisset: "nat lupus inter oves, fulvos vehit unda leones* [*Met.* 1.304],* "So also he said the following, appropriate to the greatness of his subject: 'All was sea, and the sea lacked shores'; except that he brought such force of talent and theme down to boyish foolishness: 'The wolf swims among the sheep, the waves carry tawny lions'" (*QNat.* 3.27.13). Seneca's annoyance results from the fact that the flood is to his mind a serious matter, and he neither expects nor wants humorous treatment: *non est res satis sobria lascivere devorato orbe terrarum,* "To play, while the whole world is being consumed, is an insufficiently serious undertaking" (*QNat.* 3.27.14). Though Seneca may polemically describe Ovid's startling violation of decorum as *pueriles ineptiae*, it cannot be seriously maintained that Ovid is not in control of his material, especially since he calls attention to principles of decorum by an irreverent allusion to Horace's *Ars poetica*. Horace gives an example of how a poet's grossly excessive variation of a single subject leads to unnatural description:

> qui variare cupit rem prodigialiter unam
> delphinum silvis appingit, fluctibus aprum.
> (*Ars P.* 29–30)

> He who wants to vary a single subject to monstrous lengths paints a dolphin among the woods, a boar among the waves.

---

[9] Galinsky 1975, 184; Galinsky rightly emphasizes that Ovid here establishes a serious tone only to introduce humor hereafter. The flood is commonly classed among Ovid's "sublime" descriptions, as by Zarnewski (1925, 6). M. von Albrecht (1963) notes the combination of sublimity and humor in this passage (*WdF* 92, 420–421).

Ovid audaciously identifies himself with Horace's negative example by including Horace's exemplary details in his own description: *silvasque tenent delphines*, "Dolphins occupy the woods" (*Met.* 1.302); *nec vires fulminis apro . . . prosunt*, "Nor does the boar's strength benefit him" (*Met.* 1.305–306). By this allusion Ovid flaunts the fact that his treatment is no longer *pro magnitudine rei*.[10] Since the disintegration of serious tone cannot be foreseen, Ovid has taken unexpected advantage of his readers, simultaneously amusing them and letting them know that they have been deceived. He has destroyed what he was building; he has also slyly victimized his audience.[11]

Abrupt change from epic seriousness to irreverent humor in the same passage is typical of the *Metamorphoses*. It is the only kind of narrative disruption that attracts the notice of Ovid's critics, who occasionally note it as if it were a phenomenon isolated from other aspects of the poem. But in fact it is part of a larger tendency that characterizes the whole work. Ovid disrupts virtually every element of the narrative: style, tone, plot structure, thematic development, characterization, and so on. Unpredictable change controls the progress of the narrative as one reads, just as it defines the subject matter of most tales. If meaning and significance may be claimed for a poem still sometimes dismissed as a frivolous entertainment,[12] it is to be found in experience of the ever-changing narrative surface.

In Ovid's description of the flood, violation of decorum reveals with special clarity the link between the larger narrative texture and witticism, a more localized disturbance. By first appealing to standards of decorum, then compromising them, Ovid re-enacts on a larger scale the disruptive impact of paradoxical witticisms and puns, which, as we have seen, first invite normal restriction of their terms' semantic range, then defeat such a process. Structural disruption of the continuity of the reader's experi-

---

[10] See Galinsky 1975, 81. Ovid may be thinking of the *Ars poetica* also at *Met.* 8.359, where *vulnificus sus*, "The wound-dealing swine," at the end of the hexameter recalls, by sound and rhythm, Horace's *parturiunt montes, nascetur ridiculus mus*, "The mountains are giving birth; a ridiculous mouse will be born" (*Ars P.* 139). Vergil could write *sub ilicibus sus*, "A swine beneath the holm-oaks" (*Aen.* 3.390 = 8.43), in imitation of Ennius's roughness (for more examples, see H-E on *Met.* 8.359). Ovid, in his burlesque-heroic hunt of the Calydonian boar, wants us to remember both the Ennian tradition of monosyllabic line-endings and Horace's ridicule of it.

[11] A. J. Boyle (1988, 1) offers a concise appreciation both of Ovidian indecorum and of its value as a stylistic resource for later writers: Ovid's "rejection of Augustan classicism (especially its concept of *decorum* or 'appropriateness'), cultivation of generic disorder and experimentation (witness, e.g., *Ars Amatoria* and *Metamorphoses*), love of paradox, absurdity, incongruity, hyperbole, wit, and focus on extreme emotional states, influenced everything that followed."

[12] An extreme example is the view of G. Williams (1978, 100) that Ovid chose mythological subject matter in the *Metamorphoses* as a means of "escape or retreat" from reality.

ence is parallel to the disruptive impact of witticism, and both embody themes of the work in the experience of reading. While wit enacts transformation, narrative disruption makes flux as much a feature of Ovidian style as of Ovidian perspectives on the nature of things.

Daedalus and Perdix

A story in many ways typical of Ovid's narrative style is that of Daedalus in Book 8, one of the best loved and most easily trivialized stories in the *Metamorphoses*. Critics conventionally consider this "an attractive story"[13] and praise it for its charm, preferring to ignore the fact that a shocking irruption of violence may complicate so pleasant an effect: Daedalus, at first touchingly portrayed as a dutiful father, ends his part in the poem as a child-murderer. Here, as usual, Ovid deliberately destroys the impressions that he has first painstakingly developed. After the metamorphosis of Scylla, Ovid turns to Minos and lightens the tone of the narration with characteristic Alexandrian humor derived from the introduction of concern for bourgeois respectability into traditional myth. Pasiphae's adultery and its result, the minotaur, have become an increasing embarrassment to Minos:

> creverat opprobrium generis, foedumque patebat
> matris adulterium monstri novitate biformis.
> (*Met.* 8.155–156)

The disgrace to his family had increased, and, thanks to the strangeness of the two-formed monster, its mother's foul adultery was becoming obvious.

Consequently, Minos has the labyrinth built to conceal the source of family shame. Daedalus enters the poem in this amusing context (*Met.* 8.159), and then becomes a figure of some fun in the description of the labyrinth, which he so expertly designs that it almost prevents its designer from reaching the threshold (*Met.* 8.166–168). When, after the comically foreshortened story of Ariadne,[14] the narrative focuses on Daedalus, a note of sadness enters, and in a few quick strokes he becomes a touching and sympathetic character:

> Daedalus interea Creten longumque perosus
> exilium tactusque loci natalis amore
> clausus erat pelago
> (*Met.* 8.183–185)

---

[13] Hollis 1970, 57.

[14] By Ovid's time, the story of Ariadne's abandonment had become excessively familiar in literature and art, and Ovid himself had exposed it to parodic treatment in *Her.* 10, "whose dominant mood is universal travesty" (Verducci 1985, 246).

> Meanwhile Daedalus, hating Crete and his long exile, and touched by love
> for his native place, had been barred from it by the sea.

In order to facilitate our sympathy for Daedalus, Ovid alters details of the traditional story. According to the usual account, Minos becomes angry with Daedalus (and in some versions imprisons Daedalus and Icarus in the labyrinth), either because Daedalus helped Theseus to escape from Crete (so Apollod. *Epit.* 1.12) or because he made the hollow wooden cow for Minos's wife Pasiphae, in which she could receive the embrace of her beloved bull (so Diod. Sic. 4.77.5; Hyginus 40).[15] Ovid makes no connection between Daedalus and the wooden cow, which is mentioned only once, some time before, in a speech of Scylla (*Met.* 8.131–133).[16] Clearly Ovid is passing over anything unpleasant or unflattering in the earlier career of Daedalus, just as, to cite a well-known example, he cleaned up the story of Cephalus and Procris in the previous book.[17] Most important is the fact that in the lines quoted above he omits the cause of Daedalus's exile: the development of a sympathetic portrayal will permit no mention here of Daedalus's brutal attempt to murder his own nephew. Only the *doctus lector* may feel some discomfort at what Ovid is serving up here as a characterization of Daedalus. In mention of the *longum exilium* there is scarcely a hint of the grim twist with which the story will conclude.

Further details sustain and develop the portrayal of Daedalus. In an impressively defiant speech, he declares that though Minos closes off land and sea, he will escape by air (*Met.* 8.185–187); these three lines replace a long speech of pleading to Minos in Ovid's earlier version of the story in the *Ars amatoria* (2.33–42), and a reflective speech that follows it (2.33–42). By contrast, Daedalus's construction of wings receives brief mention in the *Ars* (2.45–48), but here there is a careful and detailed description (*Met.* 8.189–195), which produces two distinct impressions. First, it emphasizes the skill of Daedalus, whose craftsmanship produces a *mirabile opus*, "marvelous work" (*Met.* 8.199–200). Second, it introduces a note of homely domesticity in a simile comparing the wings to a *rustica fistula*, "rustic pipe" (*Met.* 8.191–192). Ovid introduces the boy Icarus at just the right moment to increase the impression of "homely realism" so admired by some:[18]

---

[15] The first version is older; the latter is thought to go back to Euripides (*RE* s.v. Daidalos 4.2000–2001). See Bömer 4:58 on Ovid's divergences from "the classical versions."

[16] In a later tale, the wooden cow provides Iphis with an exemplum (*Met.* 9.739–740).

[17] See above, Chapter 1. For the view that Ovid's changes to the tradition are aimed at producing an uncompromised "tragic" impact, see Segal 1978, 175–205; Galinsky 1975, 150–152; other references in Segal 1978, 175 n. 1.

[18] Hollis 1970, 58.

> puer Icarus una
> stabat et ignarus, sua se tractare pericla,
> ore renidenti modo, quas vaga moverat aura,
> captabat plumas, flavam modo pollice ceram
> mollibat lusuque suo mirabile patris
> inpediebat opus.
> (*Met.* 8.195–200)

The boy Icarus stood with him, and, unaware that he was handling things dangerous to him, now tried to catch feathers—which the passing breeze had set in motion—in his shining mouth, now softened the yellow wax with his thumb, and in his play impeded his father's marvelous work.

With perfect control of tone Ovid combines pathetic foreshadowing with a gently amusing picture of the boy playing and getting in the way of his father's work. As has often been noted, ancient reliefs and vase paintings show Icarus as a young man;[19] by making him a child Ovid can contribute many details to the increase of pathos, greatly expanding what he had written in the *Ars* (2.49–50). What Anderson calls "the poignantly innocent behavior of young Icarus"[20] has its parallel in the pathetic solicitude of Daedalus. All details are contrived to build him up as a conscientious and dutiful father, as he carefully instructs his son not to fly too high or too low and to follow his lead closely (*Met.* 8.203–209). The following description, after Daedalus has fitted wings to Icarus's shoulders, is a masterpiece of concise characterization and skillfully sustained appeal to sympathy from the audience:

> inter opus monitusque genae maduere seniles,
> et patriae tremuere manus. dedit oscula nato
> non iterum repetenda suo pennisque levatus
> ante volat comitique timet, velut ales, ab alto
> quae teneram prolem produxit in aëra nido,
> hortaturque sequi damnosasque erudit artes
> et movet ipse suas et nati respicit alas.
> (*Met.* 8.210–216)

Amid the work and instruction, the old man's cheeks were moist, and the father's hands trembled. He gave kisses to his son that would never be repeated. Rising on his wings, he flew ahead, and feared for his companion, like a bird, who has led her tender offspring from the high nest into the air; he urges him to follow and teaches him fatal skills; he moves his wings and looks back at those of his son.

---

[19] See ibid., 59, on *Met.* 8.195–200.
[20] Anderson 1972, on *Met.* 8.195.

Daedalus's tears, the trembling of his hands, the kisses, the simile of the bird teaching its young to fly, and so on—everything reinforces the presentation of Daedalus, while strongly foreshadowing Icarus's fall. By such explicit irony as *oscula non iterum repetenda* and *damnosas artes*, Ovid intentionally invites us, it seems, to indulge in a complacently sentimental awareness of the truth of Daedalus's fears. Those who enjoyed weeping over Cephalus and Procris can, for the time being, relish the anticipation of another sustained tragedy. The tragic foreshadowing gains particular richness in *et patriae tremuere manus* (8.211), an allusion to Vergil's *bis patriae cecidere manus* (*Aen.* 6.33), said of Daedalus *after* the fall of Icarus. Escaping from Minos, Daedalus dedicates a temple to Apollo at Cumae and fashions on its doors the story of Minos, Pasiphae, the minotaur, the labyrinth, and Ariadne's escape, but cannot bring himself to depict the death of his son:

> tu quoque magnam
> partem opere in tanto, sineret dolor, Icare haberes:
> bis conatus erat casus effingere in auro,
> bis patriae cecidere manus.
> (*Aen.* 6.30–33)

You too, Icarus, would have a large part in so great a work, if grief allowed.
Twice he had tried to shape the fall in gold; twice the father's hands fell.

By alluding to this passage, Ovid appropriates its pathos through the reader's recollection.

The famous picture of the fisherman, shepherd, and plowman gazing in astonishment at Daedalus and Icarus aloft (*Met.* 8.217–220) sustains the homeliness of the tale and reinforces the impression of Daedalus's marvelous achievement. The subsequent description of Icarus's overeager flight is likewise consistent with what we heard earlier of his playful innocence:

> puer audaci coepit gaudere volatu
> deservitque ducem caelique cupidine tractus
> altius egit iter.
> (*Met.* 8.223–225)

The boy began to rejoice in his bold flight: he left his guide, and, drawn by a
desire for the sky, drove his journey higher.

By placing *audaci* next to *puer* Ovid makes the adjective pathetic: this is no act of culpable arrogance by a responsible person, but rather a child's play. Though the boldness is that of a little boy, Ovid's *audaci volatu* shows awareness of one traditional interpretation of Icarus's fall as exemplifying hubris punished.[21] So Horace (*C.* 1.3.34) makes Daedalus an example of *audax omnia perpeti gens humana*, "The human race, audacious enough to undertake anything" (*C.* 1.3.25–26). Ovid calls attention to this tradition only to reject it—or rather, replace it.

Up to this point Ovid has improved every opportunity to sustain consistent tone, characterization, and narrative development. Now, however, there are some unexpected twists. As Icarus's wings disintegrate we seem to be coming to the climax of the story, but "the actual fall," as Bömer writes, "is not mentioned."[22] Icarus's story is over very suddenly, before one is even aware:

> rapidi vicinia solis
> mollit odoratas, pennarum vincula, ceras.
> tabuerant cerae: nudos quatit ille lacertos
> remigioque carens non ullas percipit auras,
> oraque caerulea patrium clamantia nomen
> excipiuntur aqua, quae nomen traxit ab illo.
> (*Met.* 8.225–230)

Nearness to the swift sun softened the fragrant wax that bound his wings. The wax melted; he flapped his bare arms. Now oarless, he did not grasp any air, and his face, shouting his father's name, was received by the blue water, which drew its name from him.

The *aition* in line 230 is a flat and abrupt insertion; the next line is even more jarring: *at pater infelix, nec iam pater, "Icare" dixit* (*Met.* 8.231). The intrusive witticism on *pater* in the "divided sense" may remind one of other instances, such as in the flood discussed above, where Ovid shatters a well-developed serious tone; but especially disruptive is this macabre joke on Daedalus's fatherhood, the one element of the story from which Ovid has been deriving the most pathos. Earlier we considered the semantic division of *pater* and the thematic seriousness of verbal paradox. Ovid's manipulation of tone reinforces and enlarges the relevance of the witticism. As the change of tone corresponds to abrupt change in our perspective on Daedalus's identity, we discern change in the heart of things, and are made to feel it as well. Some readers may well wish that Ovid had omitted *nec iam pater* and allowed us to forget that universal flux prevails both in events of the poem and in our own experience of it. Ovid's narrative can produce a sudden nostalgia, sharply jolting the reader into longing for the sustained joys of an earlier passage.

Another surprise immediately follows, when Daedalus has finished

---

[21] *Cupido* in line 224 may strengthen an impression that Ovid alludes to the tale's potential for moralizing interpretation.

[22] Bömer 4:81, on *Met.* 8.229–230.

calling out to Icarus and has spied the wings in the water. At this point the prior development of the narrative would lead one to expect concentration of Daedalus's paternal grief in a long and moving speech or description, something that would sustain the tragic potential of the story and provide a gratifying climax to the emotional involvement that the story has encouraged in its readers. Instead, the barest summary disposes of Daedalus's reaction to the death of his son:

> pennas adspexit in undis
> devovitque suas artes corpusque sepulchro
> condidit, et tellus a nomine dicta sepulti.
> (*Met.* 8.233–235)

> He spied the wings among the waves, cursed his skills, and buried the body in a tomb. The land received its name from that of the one buried there.

A burial and an *aition* ought normally to offer a sense of closure, especially when familiar formulaic language reinforces their conclusive impact; but here the formulas are cut short, and the events flash by so quickly that any sense of conclusion is minimal: the reader's attention is projected forward, not invited to linger. That these lines are devoid of pathetic elaboration is surprising enough; a ruder shock follows, when it becomes clear that Ovid has mentioned the burial of Icarus in order to elaborate an expression of *joy* at his death:

> hunc miseri tumulo ponentem corpora nati
> garrula limoso prospexit ab elice perdix
> et plausit pennis testataque gaudia cantu est:
> unica tunc volucris nec visa prioribus annis
> factaque nuper avis, longum tibi, Daedale, crimen.
> (*Met.* 8.236–240)

> As he lay his wretched son's body in the burial mound, a chattering partridge caught sight of him from a muddy ditch; it clapped its wings and bore witness to its joy by singing. At that time it was the only such bird, unseen in earlier years, and but lately made a bird—a charge of long standing against you, Daedalus.

Charm, homeliness, pathos have abruptly vanished, replaced by a disquieting harshness. Ovid plays up the terms of the partridge's reaction to the death of *puer Icarus* to make this scene ugly and repulsive in contrast to what went before. Especially striking is the partridge's first introduction (237), where the meanness of the subject matter (jabbering partridge, muddy ditch) jars with the elegant Vergilian chiastic line used to express it.[23] As the tale proceeds, one disturbing element after another

---

[23] So Anderson 1972, on *Met.* 8.237.

enters it. Daedalus had tried to murder his own twelve-year-old nephew, envious of the boy's inventive talent. When Daedalus pushed him off the Athenian acropolis, Pallas changed him, as he fell, into a partridge. The words *longum tibi, Daedale, crimen* (240), placed at the end of their sentence and emphasized by the apostrophe, identify the bird as a continuing charge against Daedalus; it is an eternal reminder of the crime. This intrusion of violence shatters our conception of Daedalus, which in the preceding account Ovid had so carefully developed. It is the feature of Perdix's tale that most forcefully "makes us," as Mack observes, "completely reassess what we have just heard about Daedalus."[24] The *longum exilium*, initially presented as if a reason for sympathy for Daedalus, now turns out to have had good cause. Daedalus's skill, so impressive earlier, is outmatched by a child's, and becomes the cause not of marvelous achievement but of malicious envy.[25] No other source for the story of Perdix mentions his metamorphosis into a bird;[26] Ovid makes much of how the partridge's behavior permanently reflects the terrible experience of the boy:

> non tamen haec alte volucris sua corpora tollit
> nec facit in ramis altoque cacumine nidos;
> propter humum volitat ponitque in saepibus ova
> antiquique memor metuit sublimia casus.
> (*Met.* 8.256–259)

Yet this bird does not lift its body aloft. It does not make its nest in the branches and high treetops; it flies along the ground and sets its eggs in hedges, and mindful of its ancient fall, it fears the heights.

Line 257 produces a disconcerting echo of the simile describing Daedalus as he introduced Icarus to flight:

> velut ales, ab alto
> quae teneram prolem produxit in aëra nido.
> (*Met.* 8.213–214)

Like a bird, who has led her tender offspring from the high nest into the air.

There, *velut ales* showed Daedalus at his most solicitous and parental; here, a real bird corrects a false impression.

There is a grim revelation in the words *factaque nuper avis* (240): Daedalus was a child-murderer just a little before he played the touching role of dutiful father. Ovid's earlier withholding of this information is a

---

[24] Mack 1988, 110.

[25] The careful description of Perdix's inventions (*Met.* 8.244–249) balances that of Daedalus's earlier (*Met.* 8.189–195).

[26] Holland (1902, 22) suggests that Boios's *Ornithogonia* may have been Ovid's source for the metamorphosis. See also Hollis 1970, 63; Forbes Irving 1990, 256–257.

striking example of how he deliberately manipulates and deceives his audience by the power of narrative. Shortly before, he spared no trouble to induce sympathy for the father about to lose his son. Now it becomes clear that Daedalus (if not Icarus) deserved what happened. As Bömer remarks, "The death of Icarus, who likewise fell from the heights, was in relation to Daedalus an instrument of compensatory justice."[27]

The fates of Icarus and Perdix are parallel. Ovid intends them to be compared, and Daedalus's part in the fall of Perdix is meant to qualify and revise the audience's impression of his part in Icarus's story. That is why Ovid moved the tale of Perdix from its traditional place in the narrative *before* the fall of Icarus. In all other versions in which Icarus and Perdix (usually called Talos, sometimes Kalos) are both included, the narrative proceeds chronologically.[28] The sequence of events as they appear in these is no doubt what was familiar to Ovid. By at first omitting the story of Perdix, Ovid can develop his initially sympathetic Daedalus; by introducing it afterward, he makes it disruptive. This is how Ovid makes the story his own and makes it consistent with the whole texture of the *Metamorphoses*, a work throughout which abrupt and unexpected disruption is a most conspicuous element of narrative style.

One result of Ovid's treatment of Perdix is to destroy the sentimental indulgence in pathos that the earlier part of Daedalus's story had encouraged in its readers. Perhaps that is why most commentators on the story of Daedalus treat Perdix almost as if he did not exist in the poem at all,[29] thereby dismissing all of Ovid's major innovations in the story except for the pathetic characterization of Daedalus and Icarus.[30] By denying significance to the intrusive violence, critics make Ovid's work frivolous. They fail to see that he wants to complicate our experience, and they often

---

[27] Bömer 4:82 headnote. Haedicke (1969, 74) makes a similar point: "Fate requites like with like."

[28] The fullest accounts are Apollodorus 3.15.8; Diodorus Siculus 4.76–77; Hyginus 39–40.

[29] Otis (1970, 168) abstracts "Paternal Grief" from Daedalus and Icarus, and so labels the story on a chart; Perdix's name (without comment) appears only there. "Paternal Grief" is a misleading summary of the story's content, enabling Otis to make Daedalus balance Dryope ("Maternal Grief") in Book 9 (324–393). In his effort to perceive structural symmetry in the *Metamorphoses* by means of such tenuous parallels as Daedalus/Dryope, Otis neglects the obvious parallel between Icarus and Perdix in their relation to Daedalus. He discusses the story's content only in terms of a contrast between Daedalus and Nisus as fathers, and Scylla and Icarus as children (353). Other writers deny significance to the story of Perdix. Anderson 1972, 355: "Ovid now tacks onto the story of Daedalus' dramatic escape a minor story." Hollis 1970 36: "The episode is of little importance here, except to provide variety and to justify the presence of Daedalus and Icarus in a work devoted to transformations."

[30] Vergil's lines discussed above (*Aen.* 6.30–33) anticipate Ovid's characterization of Daedalus and Icarus, and may well have suggested to Ovid the potential of a developed scene between father and son.

assume instead that a warmly complacent sentimentality is all that Ovid at his best intends us to feel. In fact, Ovid does sometimes encourage facile responses, but only to wrench his readers out of their easy entertainment by some shock.

Cyclopean Violence and Narrative Disruption

Reading the story of Daedalus in this way, I represent it as a "deceptive paradigm,"[31] useful in understanding Ovidian narrative more generally. Elements of the tale's narrative style, its tone, its characterization, all make surprise thematic. The tale is paradigmatic not in the sense that Ovid patterns many tales in a closely similar fashion; rather, he tends to introduce disruption and surprise into any narrative, whatever qualities he has chosen to establish for it. The story of Polyphemus in Book 13 is an especially rich example of disruptive narrative structure, its affective consequences, and their thematic significance. In offering the following description, I maintain that even though this tale may be more elaborately developed than most, it is stylistically typical and representative. If one wonders how the disruption of narrative patterns could occur again and again in a long work without defeating all sense of expectation on the reader's part, it is, I aim to show, because of the nature of the engagement encouraged by Ovid's text. For the the most part Ovid does not direct our attention to large formal schemes, but engages us locally in the features of the story at hand. Plot, characterization, tone, and all other narrative features are quickly established in a story. When developed consistently they begin to give the story a certain character in our minds, and must produce an expectation that more of the same will follow—at least, they must do so for a reader who recognizes consistent patterns in the narrative and who has no knowledge or exact recollection of what will happen next; for the reader's incomplete awareness of the future makes disruption possible. Once it has occurred, and the reader is temporarily at a loss, Ovid is quick to supply new patterns of consistency, often along entirely different lines. These again shape our expectations in potentially misleading ways. Thus the *Metamorphoses* offers us an experience that is always reshaping itself, often abruptly and surprisingly. Our reflections about the nature of what we are experiencing are both demanded by the consistent patterns that Ovid establishes, and made questionable and provisional by his intentional breakdown and re-forming of those patterns.

Although surprise continues to be a feature of the narrative through-

---

[31] This term Anderson (1989) employs for the tale of Lycaon as a model of divine justice; I borrow it for narrative deception.

out the *Metamorphoses*, Ovid's readers will always learn from their experiences, and the nature of their engagement can be expected to evolve as they progress through the text. The reader will come to expect that expectations, though inevitable, are seldom a reliable guide. Narrative disruption will become familiar, though not necessarily less intensely felt. In fact, familiarity may give it greater impact, whether for the first-time reader, who simply does not know what lies ahead, or for the experienced, whose many readings of the work and long reflection upon it will ensure a more mature and deeper astonishment.

As readers experience narrative disruption, the text invites them to reflect upon it; for the *Metamorphoses* is not a series of shocks and jolts to a purely vulnerable reader, nor does the work invite us to suspend reflection and let its intensities inundate us, stimulating unmediated responses. Reading is an active and participatory process. A reader must take up a book and read it, must make an effort to concentrate, knowing that any instruction or pleasure depends on such an effort; and a reader's experience is richer to the extent that it is more engaged. This much may be said of any text, and Ovid's, like others texts, also rewards efforts to understand and interpret it with maturity and depth of appreciation. But it differs from most by allowing readers less ultimate mastery, less control; for such mastery and control would be self-defeating for Ovid. The process of reading the *Metamorphoses* will most fully gain a transformative nature, and thereby be most richly thematic, if the work can establish an intense reflective engagement on the part of its readers, while simultaneously eluding their grasp, remaining in motion, just out of intellectual reach. As Ovid's readers become canny and familiar with his disruptive style, and their experience of his narrative comes to embody the fluidity of his theme, they ought to arrive at larger and larger thematic views, recognizing, over the extent of fifteen books and so many individual tales, the all-embracing character of transformation.

If one's apprehension is always evolving as one proceeds, it will never be a repetitive experience. This is why multiple readings of the *Metamorphoses* never compromise its surprising and disruptive character: as readers become more and more familiar with the text, their minds are brought closer to it; their apprehension, altered and transformed, makes them responsive in new ways. An experienced and learned reader of the *Metamorphoses* can expect to remain disoriented by it, and the nature of this disorientation will shift over any one reading or multiple readings. The *Metamorphoses* is uniquely elusive, and the process of reading it uniquely changeable. Apuleius's *Metamorphoses* offers an instructive contrast in its spectacular and large-scale instance of narrative surprise, the narrator's conversion to the worship of Isis in Book 11, the final book. This event requires of readers an interpretive backward glance at all that has preceded. J. J. Winkler traces eccentricities and problematic features of the new "Isiac interpretation" of earlier events, which Mithras, priest of Isis, presents with all signs and trappings of authority.[32] Mithras's "privileged" re-reading of experiences already undergone by both narrator and reader of Books 1–10 causes a cataclysmic narrative shift: "The basic rules of meaning are changed near the end of the game."[33] However problematical this shift may be, it must affect any second reading of the work: only a first-time reader could be unaware of it and so vulnerable to being surprised by it.[34] Its presence makes any second reading of Books 1–10 fundamentally different from any first reading. Winkler, admitting that he is himself a second-time reader, must call upon "critical fiction" to reconstruct a hypothetical first reading and to restore the interpretively significant unawareness with which an ideal first reader progresses through the work.[35] Though to some extent my reading of Daedalus and Icarus also refashions a lack of awareness on the reader's part, Ovid's text requires far less reconstruction of this sort than does Apuleius's. The lostness of the reader, on which Ovidian narrative surprise depends, is a more pervasive condition and one that continually re-establishes itself. Those experienced with Ovid's work will still find themselves lost in it: their lostness will be that of more mature and cannier readers, but parallel to that of the less experienced. The understanding of Ovid's *Metamorphoses* and of Ovidian transformation is unlikely to be a single and unalterable event, a move from ignorance to knowledge, darkness to light, confusion to clarity. Instead, it will be an endless process, an uncompleted journey, as the apprehension of change reflects its nature.

Consequently, first-time readings and multiple readings of Ovid's work are likely to be parallel and not radically distinct. Even in encountering narrative disruption and surprise, experienced readers lack a privileged position and fundamental advantages over the first-time reader, who has already made a beginning in the unending process. The first-time reader of Book 15 will have experienced much along the way; such a reader will not be naively vulnerable to narrative surprise, but will be more appreciative of it than before; even more appreciative will be one who has often read the *Metamorphoses* before, and returns to it with renewed anticipation and wonder. As inexperienced readers progress from Book 1 to Book 15, they may feel themselves comprehending more and more while losing confidence in their efforts to grasp the whole. Correspondingly, only readers who have carefully read the *Metamorphoses* many times can

---

[32] Winkler 1985, 209–215.

[33] Ibid., 9.

[34] On "suspense and surprise" under conditions of such sharply distinct styles of reading, see ibid., 142–144.

[35] Ibid., 10.

approach the work with a full appreciation of their own lack of intellectual mastery in its presence, and the significance that this lack possesses.

In its allusive richness, the tale of Polyphemus is an especially clear example of how Ovid exploits his reader's memory of earlier versions as a part of the creative process, and how this exploitation of the reader's memory supports and sustains engagement in a radically unsustained narrative, one characterized by flux. Indeed, all features of narrative, including allusion, can be viewed as rhetorical, and hence can contribute to a thematically significant experience of the text. In this regard they function like the tropes and intrusive witticisms of the narrative surface, contributing to the sudden expansion of the reader's perspective on events. G. B. Conte, in an influential essay, claims allusion as a trope, closely analogous to metaphor in particular.[36] Metaphorical language produces its special meanings through its "twofold nature": it creates a tension or gap between literal and figurative senses. Just so, allusion generates meanings that result from its twofold reference, uniting two significant contexts in the reader's mind. "The reader's collaboration is indispensable to the poet if the active phase of allusion is to take effect."[37] From the perspective of affective stylistics, the allusive character of this tale offers particularly clear examples of authorial designs upon the reader, since Ovid here exploits his readers' memory of earlier treatments of Polyphemus in Theocritus 11, *Odyssey* 9, and Vergil's *Eclogues*—which are also available to us. For Ovid, allusive technique is a consistent part of his larger affective aims, since allusions, associating the present text with some other literary structure, contribute much to the setting-up of expectations. The works Ovid alludes to—far from being "models" that the author can substitute for original invention—function as a store of recollections laid up in the reader's mind, which the author can draw upon with an allusive passage or line. By significant allusion, Ovid brings the reader's memory to bear on the understanding of the text presently at hand, and enriches the experience of that text by exploiting the power of past experience. Thus allusions, never mere ornaments or mere opportunities for learned ostentation, constitute a significant part of the literary structure, one that both defines and intensifies the reader's engagement with the text by appeal to recollections beyond it.[38]

---

[36] Conte 1986, 38, 53.

[37] Ibid., 35.

[38] Visual narratives, demanding the active collaboration of the observer, create a parallel mode of engagement. E. W. Leach, in a perceptive discussion of narrative in Roman painting, show that the Polyphemus and Galatea landscape from the villa Boscotrecase involves the spectator "in the integration of incongruous scenes": "Its images juxtapose two events in the history of Polyphemus as literature has shaped it—one is his pastoral courtship of Galatea, the dramatic situation of Theocritus' eleventh *Idyll*, the other his vengeful stoning

Characteristic overall of Ovidian stylistic disruptiveness is this story's abruptly surprising conclusion: after much virtuoso exploitation of the Cyclops in love for his comic possibilities, Ovid suddenly introduces stark and gruesome violence at the end. Corresponding to the unexpected plot development is an equally abrupt shift in tone; both correspond to a shift in allusive reference from Theocritus to Homer. In beginning to trace Ovid's narrative continuum as it is experienced, with special attention to its allusive reference, we immediately encounter conspicuous contrasts between Ovid's version and our memory of Theocritus. Though much of Polyphemus's speech in Ovid (*Met.* 13.789–869) calls attention to itself as manifestly adapted from Theocritus 11.19–79, it is very noticeable that Ovid has removed Theocritus's frame for Polyphemus's speech (Theoc. 11.1–18, 80–81), and with it the application or moral that the speech is meant to illustrate, namely the power of the Muses to cure love's anguish. Theocritus begins with an address to his friend Nicias, who, since he is a doctor and is also preeminently loved by the Muses, should be well aware of this cure:

> οὐδὲν ποττὸν ἔρωτα πεφύκει φάρμακον ἄλλο,
> Νικία, οὔτ' ἔγχριστον, ἐμὶν δοκεῖ, οὔτ' ἐπίπαστον,
> ἢ ταὶ Πιερίδες· κοῦφον δέ τι τοῦτο καὶ ἁδύ
> γίνετ' ἐπ' ἀνθρώποις, εὑρεῖν δ' οὐ ῥᾴδιόν ἐστι.
> γινώσκειν δ' οἶμαί τυ καλῶς ἰατρὸν ἐόντα
> καὶ ταῖς ἐννέα δὴ πεφιλημένον ἔξοχα Μοίσαις.
> (Theoc. 11.1–6)

There is no other cure for love, Nicias, neither ointment, it seems to me, nor poultice, other than the Muses. This is a light cure and sweet for human beings, but not easy to find. I suppose that you know well of it, as a doctor, and as one highly loved by the nine Muses.

The tone of friendly intimacy in this opening address extends to the introduction of the Cyclops in the next lines, whom Theocritus calls "my fellow countryman" (ὁ παρ' ἁμῖν)[39] and whose experience he commends to the understanding and sympathy of Nicias, and by implication the reader. The picture of the youthful Polyphemus consoling himself by song could not be farther from the Homeric tradition of Cyclopean char-

---

of the departing ship of Odysseus, an incident drawn from an epic context. Because these two separate actions are linked neither closely in temporal succession nor consecutively in a pattern of cause and effect, the panel is not strictly a continuous narrative, yet it effectively invites the spectator's creation of a narrative by the very fact of its generic and mythic disparities" (Leach 1988, 339). Throughout her discussion, Leach emphasizes the observer's participation in shaping details of a visual image into narrative.

[39] See Gow 1952, on Theoc. 11.7.

acter: cruelty, destructiveness, and anthropophagy are gone. The only suggestion of violence in Theocritus 11 is the wound that Polyphemus himself has received from Aphrodite's shaft:[40]

> ἔχθιστον ἔχων ὑποκάρδιον ἕλκος,
> Κύπριδος ἐκ μεγάλας τό οἱ ἥπατι πᾶξε βέλεμνον.
> (Theoc. 11.15–16)
>
> Having a painful wound beneath his heart, which the shaft from great Cypris had pierced in his liver.

Theocritus's portrayal invites identification with Polyphemus, whose self-consolation provides an example to be imitated.[41] The very idea of Polyphemus as a worthy model would have struck many of Theocritus's readers as comic, accustomed as they were to Homer's portrayal of Polyphemus as the opposite of everything civilized.[42] Contemporary readers were indeed familiar with a comic tradition of Cyclopean representation beginning with Epicharmus's mythological burlesque *The Cyclops* in the early fifth century B.C., and continuing through Cratinus's comedy Ὀδυσσῆς, Euripides' satyr-play *The Cyclops*, and Philoxenus's dithyramb *Cyclops* or *Galatea*. The last of these influenced Theocritus the most, for Philoxenus represented the Cyclops in love, consoling himself "by means of the Muses."[43] But Philoxenus also includes the most violent incident of Homer's version, the blinding of Polyphemus, as does Euripides and, most likely, the others as well. It is a conspicuous innovation of Theocritus that he eliminates from his version all mention of Odysseus together with all traces of the violence of Homer's account. In using Theocritus 11, Ovid chose the one version from which Homeric violence was most notably absent.

From a perspective of critical hindsight, knowing that Acis's grisly death will conclude the story, we can already draw some conclusions about Ovid's aims in setting up his complex of allusions to Theocritus: he wants to heighten comedy and engage us in enjoyment of the ridiculous at this point in the story. His larger goal, in terms of the emotional manipulation of his audience, is to intensify the later intrusion of vio-

---

[40] Elsewhere Theocritus could mention τὸν κρατερὸν Πολύφαμον, ὃς ὤρεσι νᾶας ἔβαλλε, "Mighty Polyphemus, who pelted ships with mountains" (Theoc. 7.152), but in Poem 11 all details of Homeric violence are conspicuously absent.

[41] For a sensitive discussion of Polyphemus in Poem 11 as a positive exemplum of self-knowledge, see Holtsmark 1966.

[42] Mondi (1983, 25–28) elaborates the idea that the author of the *Odyssey* intended the Cyclopes to contrast with the ideally civilized Phaeacians.

[43] τὸν Κύκλωπα Μούσαις εὐφώνοις ἰᾶσθαί φησι τὸν ἔρωτα Φιλόξενος, "Philoxenus says that the Cyclops healed his love by means of the sweet-voiced Muses" (Plut. *Mor.* 622C). On the pre-Theocritean versions, see Holland 1884.

lence. And so he invites our recollection of Theocritus here, with two aims: first, to associate his own initial portrayal of Polyphemus with a Theocritean lack of violence; and second, to disassociate his version from Theocritus's positive themes, setting his readers interpretively adrift. Both results contribute to form a rhetorical set-up. In no way does our intellectual recognition of an allusion invite or necessitate the emotional disengagement of a Galinskian "critical observer." On the contrary, Ovid exploits his reader's memory to intensify emotional engagement with the text at hand.

Even Ovid's parodies of Theocritus and Vergil, though they may distance us from their ridiculed subtexts, do not invite disengagement from his own text: rather, they encourage a free-wheeling emotional abandon, a destructive delight that lures us into complicity with the seductively naughty authorial voice. It is not inappropriate that Ovid sets his adaptation of Theocritus 11 into his retelling of the *Aeneid* (*Met.* 13.623–14.608), since he performs a similar operation upon both originals, robbing them of their consolatory interpretations of human experience and making their subject matter ridiculous. With consummate skill, he grotesquely distorts his predecessors' works in order to bring them into line with the themes and narrative patterns of the *Metamorphoses*. When Aeneas's wanderings after the fall of Troy bring him to Scylla and Charybdis, Ovid employs the monster Scylla to confuse the narrative bearings, seeming to follow Vergil's account closely while in fact deflecting the narrative into unforeseen directions. In the introduction of Scylla, Ovid specifically alludes to a prophetic speech of Helenus in *Aeneid* 3, wherein Scylla appears among the dangers that Aeneas must face:[44]

> dextrum Scylla latus, laevum inplacata Charybdis
> obsidet.
> (*Aen.* 3.420–421)

The right side Scylla, the left implacable Charybdis occupies.

> Scylla latus dextrum, laevum inrequieta Charybdis
> infestat.
> (*Met.* 13.730–731)

The right side Scylla, the left unresting Charybdis infests.

Ovid reduces what follows in Vergil, first a description of Charybdis (*Aen.* 3.421–423), then one of Scylla (*Aen.* 3.426–427), to summary. When he comes to Vergil's account of Scylla's maidenly face and torso, *prima hominis facies et pulchro pectore virgo / pube tenus*, "In front her appearance is human, a virgin with fair breast as far as the waist" (*Aen.*

---

[44] Helenus and his prophecies are first mentioned a few lines earlier, at *Met.* 13.720–724.

3.426–427), he seizes upon *virgo* to interrupt the story for some characteristic debunking:

> virginis ora gerens et, si non omnia vates
> ficta reliquerunt, aliquo quoque tempore virgo.
> (*Met.* 13.733–734)

> She had the face of a virgin and—unless the bards have left us nothing but fictions—at one time she really was a virgin.

By Book 13 we have encountered many such narrative intrusions, which abruptly call into question the reliability of the story being told; but this one is especially disruptive, since it not only interrupts Ovid's narrative, but also introduces inappropriate wit into our memory of Vergil. It is comically disrespectful of Ovid to summon before his readers' minds the solemn and, in context, unimpeachably accurate prophecy of a Vergilian *vates*, only to interject a story, not mentioned by Vergil, in which the bards may have left nothing but falsehoods. Yet there is still more to the audacity of Ovid's two lines: as M. von Albrecht remarks, they are "a malicious travesty of *Aen.* 1.315,"[45] where Venus presents herself to her son Aeneas disguised as a huntress, *virginis os habitumque gerens*, "Having a maiden's face and dress."

With this interruption Ovid abandons Vergil's subject matter, not to return to Aeneas and his fleet for over 300 lines (at *Met.* 14.75). He now seems to be beginning an account of Scylla's earlier history, to show how "at one time she really was a virgin," and is now a monster:

> hanc multi petiere proci; quibus illa repulsis
> ad pelagi nymphas pelagi gratissima nymphis
> ibat et elusos iuvenum narrabat amores.
> quam, dum pectendos praebet Galatea capillos
> talibus adloquitur referens suspiria dictis.
> (*Met.* 13.735–739)

> Many suitors sought her; she rejected them and, as a favorite of the sea-nymphs, went to the sea-nymphs and recounted the loves she had escaped of young men. Galatea, when offering her hair to be combed, sighed deeply and addressed Scylla in the following words.

Hanc multi petiere proci (735) is almost formulaic, so often do similar expressions occur as Ovid sets up a tale of love or rape. Nine earlier tales in the *Metamorphoses* include such a statement near the beginning, which is soon followed by introduction of the one suitor who is most signifi-

---
[45] *WdF* 92, 435.

cant in each story;[46] therefore we have every reason to believe that this story will follow the same pattern. Instead, it is almost immediately interrupted by Galatea's story; into that story is set Polyphemus's long-winded song. Glaucus, in love with Scylla, does not appear for 170 lines (at *Met.* 13.906). This arrangement of tales like Chinese boxes is similar to but more elaborate than the narrative sequence in *Met.* 5.1–6.45, where stories involving Minerva provide the frame. Like all of Ovid's means of linking stories together, it shows masterly and ingenious control of material on the part of the author, while keeping the reader always at a loss about the direction of the narrative.

The first part of Galatea's story, which turns out to have replaced Theocritus's opening address to Nicias, develops from the situation as Theocritus portrays it, but Ovid now invites us to view it from a comically enlarged perspective. Galatea, of course, has nothing to say in Theocritus, whose entire focus is on Polyphemus, his character, problems, and solution. She does, of course, react to him by fleeing; but even that fact we must infer from his pleadings. Ovid has us look at the situation from Galatea's point of view: she narrates the whole story, including Polyphemus's song. What is the experience of a nymph who receives the unwelcome attentions of an amorous Cyclops? Such a question has no place in Theocritus 11, but Ovid introduces it at the beginning. The lines just quoted above establish the intimate scene of a women's toilette, where Scylla and Galatea can freely (and at length) discuss the injuries they have received from males. Galatea compares what she suffered from her own monstrous pursuer with the easily repelled importunity of Scylla's suitors:

> "te tamen, o virgo, genus haud inmite virorum
> expetit, utque facis, potes his inpune negare.
> at mihi, cui pater est Nereus, quam caerula Doris
> enixa est, quae sum turba quoque tuta sororum,
> non nisi per luctus licuit Cyclopis amorem
> effugere," et lacrimae vocem inpediere loquentis.
> (*Met.* 13.740–745)

---

[46] *Multi illam petiere* (*Met.* 1.478); *divitibus procis . . . petebar* (2.571); *multi illum iuvenes, multae cupiere puellae* (3.353); *multorumque fuit spes invidiosa procorum* (4.795 = 9.10); *undique lecti te cupiunt proceres* (10.315–316); *Chione, quae dotatissima forma mille procos habuit* (11.301–302); *multorum frustra votis optata procorum* (12.192); *multae illum petiere* (12.404). In other works of Ovid: *mea virginitas mille petita procis* (*Her.* 16.104); *nequiquam multis saepe petita procis* (*F.* 6.108). For an expansion of the formula, see also *Met.* 14.326–334; see *Met.* 10.568 for a related expression. On expressions of this type, see Tissol 1992.

"You, maiden, are sought by the mild host of men, and you can say no to them with impunity, as you are doing. But I—whose father is Nereus and whom green-blue Doris bore, and who was protected by a crowd of sisters—I could not escape the Cyclops's love without a struggle"; and tears impeded her voice as she spoke.

Scylla wants to hear the whole story (*Met.* 13.746–748), and Galatea begins, removing all explicit mention of violence from the beginning. Galatea's remark quoted above, *at mihi . . . / non nisi per luctus licuit Cyclopis amorem / effugere*, is too general to indicate more than that the story will end in grief; it, along with her tears, is only a hint of gruesome violence to come. When, at the start, Galatea introduces her beloved Acis, it is without any mention of his fate:

> Acis erat Fauno nymphaque Symaethide cretus
> magna quidem patrisque sui matrisque voluptas,
> nostra tamen maior; nam me sibi iunxerat uni.
> (*Met.* 13.750–752)

Acis was the son of Faunus and the nymph Symaethis, a great pleasure to both father and mother, but more to me; for he had joined me to himself alone.

Acis is unknown to us before this account, as he may have been to Ovid's audience.[47] In any case, it is certainly Ovid's innovation to bring into Acis's story a distinctly Theocritean Polyphemus. Galatea's description of the Cyclops in love (*Met.* 13.759–788) comically exaggerates details in Theocritus. One result of Polyphemus's distraction by love is that his sheep must wander back to the fold unattended:

> πολλάκι ταὶ ὄιες ποτὶ τωΰλιον αὐταὶ ἀπῆνθον
> χλωρᾶς ἐκ βοτάνας.
> (Theoc. 11.12–13)

Often his sheep returned to the fold by themselves from the green pasture.

Ovid adapts this detail twice: *uritur oblitus pecorum*, "He burns, forgetful of his sheep" (*Met.* 13.763), and somewhat later, *lanigerae pecudes nullo ducente secutae*, "His wool-bearing sheep returning without a leader" (*Met.* 13.781). He adds to the Cyclops's love-symptoms a ludicrous *cura placendi* (*Met.* 13.764). The Cyclops adapts tools of his rustic livelihood

---

[47] On suggested sources, see H-E's headnote on *Met.* 13.750–897; Bömer 6:410–411. Holland (1884, 272–276) argues that Callimachus's lost *Galatea* is the source for the story of Acis, but Pfeiffer on Callim. fr. 378 denies that anything about Callimachus's *Galatea* can be derived from Ovid's version. Mewalt (1946) suggests that Nicander's *Heteroiumena* is the source for Ovid's story of Acis and Galatea.

to a program of self-beautification, combing his hair with a rake, trimming his beard with a pruning-hook, and composing his face by looking Narcissus-like into a pool:[48]

> iam rigidos pectis rastris, Polypheme, capillos,
> iam libet hirsutam tibi falce recidere barbam
> et spectare feros in aqua et conponere vultus.
> (*Met.* 13.765–767)

> Now you comb your stiff hair with a rake, Polyphemus, now it is your pleasure to clip your shaggy beard with a pruning hook, to gaze at your wild expression in the water, and to compose it.

According to Haupt-Ehwald on this passage, "Manifest everywhere is Ovid's exaggerated rhetoric, which intensifies, expands, and transforms what he has received."[49] The result is a funnier and less touching Cyclops than Theocritus's, but at this point equally harmless. In fact, while Theocritus portrays a peaceful Cyclops in implicit contrast to the Homeric tradition, Ovid's Galatea makes this contrast more directly:

> caedis amor feritasque sitisque inmensa cruoris
> cessant, et tutae veniunt abeuntque carinae.
> (*Met.* 13.768–769)

> His love of slaughter, his savagery and huge thirst for blood cease; and ships come and go in safety.

Ovid emphasizes the Cyclops's harmlessness here in order to prepare a more shocking intrusion of violence later. Yet from the vantage of hindsight it is noteworthy that even here, Ovid has incorporated some Homeric details not present in Theocritus 11, such as Cyclopean inhospitality and contempt for the gods:

> οὐ γὰρ Κύκλωπες Διὸς αἰγιόχου ἀλέγουσιν.
> (*Od.* 9.275)

> For Cyclopes take no thought for aegis-bearing Zeus.

> visus ab hospite nullo
> inpune et magni cum dis contemptor Olympi.
> (*Met.* 13.760–761)

> No guest sees him with impunity; he holds great Olympus and the gods in scorn.

---

[48] See H-E, on *Met.* 13.765 and 767. They also note that Polyphemus is following the advice of *Ars amatoria* 1.518: *sit coma, sit scita barba resecta manu*, "Let your hair and beard be cut by a skilled hand."
[49] H-E, on *Met.* 13.765.

Any Homeric fierceness suggested by these allusions or by such adjectives as *inmitis* (*Met.* 13.759) and *terribilis* (*Met.* 13.772) is qualified by the prevailing comic treatment. Yet Ovid's free intertwining of Homeric and Theocritean elements may seem disconcerting at the same time it is amusing, since whereas Theocritus's portrayal is consistent and sustained, always keeping Homer's at a distance, Ovid's contaminated portrayal hints of violence just below the comic surface. As we have seen, even that most gruesome event in Homer's account, the blinding of Polyphemus, here gives occasion for a grotesque pun:

> Telemus interea Siculam delatus ad Aetnen,
> Telemus Eurymides, quem nulla fefellerat ales,
> terribilem Polyphemon adit "lumen," que "quod unum
> fronte geris media, rapiet tibi" dixit "Ulixes."
> risit et "o vatum stolidissime, falleris" inquit,
> "altera iam rapuit."
> (*Met.* 13.770–775)

> Meanwhile, Telemus put in at Aetna—Telemus, whose notice no bird of prophecy escaped. He approached dreadful Polyphemus and said, "The single eye, which you have in the middle of your forehead, Ulysses will snatch away from you." Polyphemus laughed and said, "O most stupid of bards, you are wrong: another has already snatched it."

In Homer, the Cyclops ruefully recalls Telemus's prophecy after the blinding (*Od.* 9.507–512). Ovid, though he follows Theocritus 6.23–24 in making Polyphemus earlier scorn the prophecy, makes it clear that Homer is his source for it, closely adapting one line:

> Τήλεμος Εὐρυμίδης, ὃς μαντοσύνῃ ἐκέκαστο
> (*Od.* 9.509)

> Telemus, son of Eurymus, who excelled at prophecy.

> Telemus Eurymides, quem nulla fefellerat ales.
> (*Met.* 13.771)

> Telemus, son of Eurymus, whose notice no bird of augury escaped.

The sylleptic pun, Ovid's own contribution, produces a tone unlike that of either predecessor. Such wit invites perhaps more laughter at the punning Cyclops than at the pun itself, which, as we saw earlier, engages the metaphorical language of elegiac love-poetry. Simultaneously, the literal meaning of the pun calls attention to grisly events to come for Polyphemus, well known from Homer's description (*Od.* 9.371–398). In the *Metamorphoses*, humor never cancels out gruesomeness, but rather the two become combined. Ovid often aims to elicit a laugh and a shudder at the same time, and through this mixed tone heightens the uncertainty and unpredictability of the narrative.

When Galatea describes Polyphemus climbing up and straddling a promontory to pipe and sing, the description again expands on Theocritus; yet to the comic Cyclopean excesses, such as a *fistula* of a hundred reeds instead of the usual seven (*Met.* 13.784), there are again added a few Homeric features. The adjective *ferus* intrudes upon a description otherwise closely adapted from Theocritus:

καθεζόμενος δ' ἐπὶ πέτρας
ὑψηλᾶς ἐς πόντον ὁρῶν ἄειδε τοιαῦτα
(Theoc. 11.17–18)

Sitting on a high rock, looking out over the sea, he sang as follows.

huc ferus adscendit Cyclops mediusque resedit.
(*Met.* 13.780)

The Cyclops climbed up there and sat in the middle.

The tree, which though big as a mast serves Polyphemus as a staff, comes from the *Odyssey* (*Met.* 13.782–783; cf. *Od.* 9.319–324), where it is mentioned because of its usefulness to Odysseus as a weapon for the blinding.

Despite these reminders of Homer, violence quickly fades from view in the next part of the story, the comically preposterous love-song of Polyphemus. This lengthy effusion falls into three parts (*Met.* 13.789–809, 810–839, 840–869). Ovid uses Homer only for a few details of Cyclopean pastoral life in the second part, where Polyphemus lists the many gifts he can offer Galatea. Of these, Homer provides the lambs and goats in separate folds (*Met.* 13.327–328; cf. *Od.* 9.219–220), as well as some cheese (*Met.* 13.829–830; cf. *Od.* 9.246–249), but no details of violence. Most of the song freely expands upon Theocritus 11, with many reminiscences of passages in the *Eclogues* where Vergil adapts material from Theocritus.[50]

---

[50] In the example just mentioned of the cheese, all three earlier writers—Theocritus and Vergil as well as Homer—have something to contribute to the composition of two lines: *lac mihi semper adest niveum: pars inde bibenda / servatur, partem liquefacta coagula durant*, "I always have snowy milk, part of it kept for drinking, and dissolved rennet curdles part of it" (*Met.* 13.829–830). Since Polyphemus's song, the general context of these lines, is adapted from Theocritus, Ovid's *lac mihi semper adest niveum* alludes principally to Theocritus 11.36–37: τυρὸς δ' οὐ λείπει μ' οὔτ' ἐν θέρει οὔτ' ἐν ὀπώρᾳ, / οὐ χειμῶνος ἄκρω, "Cheese does not fail me in summer or fall, nor in the depth of winter." Yet Ovid's expression clearly recalls Vergil's close adaptation of Theocritus's lines in *Ecl.* 2, where Corydon desperately boasts to the absent Alexis: *lac mihi non aestate novum, non frigore defit*, "Fresh milk does not fail me in summer or winter" (*Ecl.* 2.22). For the rest of *Met.* 13.829–830,

The first part of Polyphemus's song expands two lines of Theocritus (11.20–21) into twenty. As Theocritus's Polyphemus begins, he praises Galatea in four rustic comparisons:

> Ὦ λευκὰ Γαλάτεια, τί τὸν φιλέοντ' ἀποβάλλῃ
> λευκοτέρα πακτᾶς ποτιδεῖν, ἁπαλωτέρα ἀρνός,
> μόσχω γαυροτέρα, φιαρωτέρα ὄμφακος ὠμᾶς;
> (Theoc. 11.19–21)

> White Galatea, why do you reject your lover?—whiter than cheese to look upon, softer than a lamb, more nimble than a calf, shinier than an unripe grape.

Such praise, drawing its terms from Polyphemus's pastoral way of life, is both touchingly naive and comically so. As before, the humor is what Ovid develops and heightens; his Polyphemus pours forth a torrent of comparisons:

> candidior folio nivei, Galatea, ligustri,
> floridior pratis, longa procerior alno,
> splendidior vitro, tenero lascivior haedo,
> levior adsiduo detritis aequore conchis,
> solibus hibernis, aestiva gratior umbra.
> (*Met.* 13.789–793)

> Galatea, whiter than the leaf of the snowy privet, more flowery than fields, taller than a long alder, shinier than glass, more nimble than a tender goat, smoother than shells worn by the unceasing sea, more pleasing than sun in winter, shade in summer.

H. Dörrie discusses the sources of humor in this passage, noting that though the Cyclops is inept in the language of erotic symbolism, his comparisons themselves are only ridiculous in part, and become much more so from their grotesque accumulation.[51]

After this heap of miscellaneous epithets, Polyphemus proceeds to enumerate, at even greater length, the products of field and wood that he can offer Galatea (*Met.* 13.810–839). A few short passages in Theocritus 11 (36–37, 40–41, 45–48) give rise to this prodigious list, swollen with many additional examples. Some of these are adapted from Homer and

---

Ovid contrasts the following lines in Homer's account of Polyphemus, where ἥμισυ ... ἥμισυ corresponds to *pars* ... *partem*: αὐτίκα δ' ἥμισυ μὲν θρέψας λευκοῖο γάλακτος / πλεκτοῖς ἐν ταλάροισιν ἀμησάμενος κατέθηκεν, / ἥμισυ δ' αὖτ' ἔστησεν ἐν ἄγγεσιν, ὄφρα οἱ εἴη / πίνειν αἰνυμένῳ καί οἱ ποτιδόρπιον εἴη, "At once, curdling half of the white milk, he collected and stored it in woven baskets; half he set in pails, so he could take from it and drink, so it would be his supper" (*Od.* 9.246–249).

[51] Dörrie 1969, 87.

some from Vergil's *Eclogue* 2, in which the lament of Corydon, unable to win the affections of Alexis, includes a complex of allusive parallels to Theocritus's Polyphemus.[52] Now the Cyclops waxes rhetorical, unconcerned for the ludicrous disjunction between rustic subject matter and language suitable to the presentation of evidence in court:

> de laudibus harum [i.e., pecudum]
> nil mihi credideris: praesens potes ipsa videre.
> (*Met*. 13.824–825)

> There's no need for you to trust my praises of these sheep: you can see for yourself in person.

With this fine-spoken appeal to the principle of *res ipsa loquitur*,[53] Polyphemus, disclaiming the need for any encomium of such obvious excellence, invites Galatea to see for herself *ut vix circueant distentum cruribus uber*, "How his animals' legs can hardly surround their bulging udders" (*Met*. 13.826). No less amusing than his flowers of speech is Polyphemus's vanity, which becomes more and more conspicuous as his song continues. It is already noticeable near the beginning, where among his praises of Galatea he limits one epithet, *riguo formosior horto*, by the condition *si non fugias* (*Met*. 13.798: "Lovelier than a well-watered garden, if you do not run away"), as if her beauty were dependent on her favorable

---

[52] Homer's contribution to *Met*. 13.827–830 is discussed above. Lines 810–820, with their list of fruits, seem to have been influenced by Homer's famous description of the garden of Alcinous, *Od*. 7.112–132 (see Zarnewski 1925, 17); cf. esp. *Met*. 13.811–812 and *Od*. 7.117–118. Vergil's *Eclogues* provide other examples for the same list: cf. *Met*. 13.812 and *Ecl*. 1.80; *Met*. 13.817 and *Ecl*. 2.53; *Met*. 13.819 and *Ecl* 7.53 (see Holland 1884, 262–263). In addition to the examples mentioned in the text, there is another double allusion to Theocritus and Vergil at *Met*. 13.834–837: *inveni geminos, qui tecum ludere possint, / inter se similes, vix ut dignoscere possis, / villosae catulos in summis montibus ursae; / inveni et dixi "dominae servabimus istos,"* "Atop the hills I found twin cubs of a shaggy bear to play with you, so much alike that you could scarcely tell them apart; I found them and said, 'These I will keep for my mistress'"; τράφω δέ τοι ἕνδεκα νεβρώς, / πάσας μαννοφόρως, καὶ σκύμνως τέσσαρας ἄρκτων, "For you I am rearing eleven fawns, all with collars, and four bear cubs" (Theoc. 11.40–41); *praeterea duo nec tuta mihi valle reperti / capreoli, sparsis etiam nunc pellibus albo; / bina die siccant ovis ubera: quos tibi servo*, "Besides, I have found two roebucks in a hazardous valley, their hides still flecked with white. They drain a sheep's udder twice a day. I'm keeping them for you" (*Ecl*. 2.40–42). Since Ovid's tendency throughout the song is to heighten the comic features of Theocritus's version, he naturally expands the example of bear cubs as gifts for a sea-nymph. Though Vergil, adapting Theocritus's fawns as *capreoli*, omits the bear cubs, Ovid also alludes to his adaptation: *dominae servabimus istos* reflects Vergil's *quos tibi servo*. See Washietl 1883, 131–132. It is worth noting that Theocritus's ἄρκτων comes as a surprise at the end of its line, and Ovid has preserved this effect at *Met*. 13.836. In single lines as well as whole episodes, unexpected conclusions are typical of Ovidian style.

[53] Cicero *Mil*. 53, 66.

response to him. As Dörrie observes, this remark is the turning point from praise to blame,[54] and the list of reproaches ends with a petulant outburst:

> at, bene si noris, pigeat fugisse, morasque
> ipsa tuas damnes et me retinere labores!
> (*Met.* 13.808–809)

> Yet, if you had sense, you would regret running away; you would curse your delays and make an effort to keep me.

Polyphemus's vain self-preoccupation reaches its greatest height in the last part of the song (*Met.* 13.840–869), where he commends his own physical attractions to Galatea, arguing that his apparent defects are in fact elements of beauty. He expands upon his pleasing form with characteristic rhetorical amplification, illustrating by analogical arguments that his size, shagginess, and single eye are preeminently beautiful. The most elaborate of these is the defense of shagginess, where he first formally introduces the topic and the false assumption—that shagginess is ugly—commonly attached to it, then marshals his illustrative analogies and resoundingly announces the sensible conclusion:

> nec, mea quod rigidis horrent densissima saetis
> corpora, turpe puta; turpis sine frondibus arbor,
> turpis equus, nisi colla iubae flaventia velent;
> pluma tegit volucres, ovibus sua lana decori est:
> barba viros hirtaeque decent in corpore saetae!
> (*Met.* 13.846–850)

> Do not think it ugly that my body is shaggy, thick with stiff bristles; a tree would be ugly without its leaves, a horse would be ugly if a mane did not cover its tawny neck; feathers cover birds; wool gives sheep their beauty: a beard and shaggy bristles on men's bodies make them beautiful!

These examples well serve Galatea's purposes in recounting the song to Scylla, since Polyphemus's self-preoccupation is yet another among his many odious characteristics. At the same time, Ovid has the second audience in mind: he skillfully takes advantage of his readers' greater distance from the events to invite them more to laugh at Polyphemus than to share in Galatea's disgust and loathing. In developing Polyphemus's vanity, Ovid exploits familiar sources of humor, well known to Roman readers from their own comic tradition. Plautus, for example, typically portrays the *senex amans* as an unsuccessful suitor, whose self-infatuation

---

[54] Dörrie 1969, 87.

prevents any communication with the youthful object of his desires, and prevents as well any awareness of limits to his own attractiveness.[55] Polyphemus's praise of himself is the most purely comic part of the song. Ovid seems to heighten its ostentatious silliness, encouraging the most facile amusement from his readers at just this point, in order to intensify the shock of Polyphemus's sudden violence.

Violence enters first the Cyclops's language, and immediately afterward his behavior. A change of tone begins when he breaks off his elaborate argumentation (*Met.* 13.855). As Dörrie perceptively remarks, "The Cyclops' increasing agitation is audible in that he speaks ever more choppily, in ever shorter sentences."[56] Though he made no mention of Acis before, and showed no sign that he even knew of any rival, impatience now causes a jealous outburst, and he angrily repeats Acis's name:

> atque ego contemptus essem patientior huius,
> si fugeres omnes; sed cur Cyclope repulso
> Acin amas praefersque meis conplexibus Acin?
> (*Met.* 13.859–861)

> I would better be able to put up with your scorn, if you rejected everybody; but why, after repelling the Cyclops, do you love Acis, and prefer Acis to my embraces?

Polyphemus, incapable of comprehending Galatea's preference, betrays in these lines even greater naivete and arrogance than before. Ovid's presentation still invites laughter, but though the Cyclops's overcharged jealousy and sense of injured merit would well suit a character in a comedy, less than comic are the ugly threats that soon follow:

> modo copia detur,
> sentiet esse mihi tanto pro corpore vires!
> viscera viva traham divisaque membra per agros
> perque tuas spargam—sic se tibi misceat!—undas.
> (*Met.* 13.863–866)

> Give me but the chance, and he will perceive that my strength matches so large a body. I shall tear apart his living guts and scatter his severed limbs across the fields and your own waters—let him join with you that way!

Here, near the end of Polyphemus's song, its tone abruptly alters through its concentration on details of grisly violence. Particularly chill-

---

[55] The most elaborately developed example of the *senex amans* is Lysidamus in Plautus's *Casina*. For a summary of seven Plautine *senes amantes*, see Ryder 1984.
[56] Dörrie 1969, 90.

ing is the pun on *misceat* in the mouth of one who is about to become a murderer because of sexual jealousy. Humor adds a macabre element to Polyphemus's words that increases rather than diminishes the new impression of dangerous cruelty in him.

This sudden development is especially surprising, because throughout Polyphemus's song, as we have seen, Ovid has kept up a pattern of allusion to Theocritus 11 and to *Eclogue* 2. In both, the lover's plaint ends with a resolve to give up the object of hopeless desire:

τί τὸν φεύγοντα διώκεις;
εὑρησεῖς Γαλάτειαν ἴσως καὶ καλλίον' ἄλλαν.
(Theoc. 11.75–76)

Why pursue one who flees? You will find another Galatea, maybe even a prettier one.

invenies alium, si te hic fastidit, Alexin.
(*Ecl.* 2.73)

You will find another Alexis if this one despises you.

Theocritus follows Polyphemus's resolve with an explicit statement of his successful consolation by song:

οὕτω τοι Πολύφαμος ἐποίμαινεν τὸν ἔρωτα
μουσίσδων, ῥᾶον δὲ διᾶγ' ἢ εἰ χρυσὸν ἔδωκεν.
(Theoc. 11.80–81)

Thus Polyphemus nursed his love with song, and fared better than if he had given gold.

In the case of Vergil's Corydon, consolation is absent and the resolve to find another more tentative, but there is no suggestion that despair may harden into violence. Ovid's allusions to Theocritus 11 and *Eclogue* 2 are intentionally deceptive. They induce a comfortable impression of prior familiarity with events and characters of Ovid's story and suggest that the patterns of similarity will carry through to the end. As was noted above, Ovid's Cyclops seems most harmless and laughable just before the irruption of violence.

Homer makes a sudden reappearance in Ovid's account when Polyphemus turns from verbal to physical violence. Polyphemus smashes Acis with a huge rock in a passage clearly modeled on the corresponding part of Homer's narrative, where Polyphemus loses patience with Odysseus and attempts to destroy his ship:

ἧκε δ' ἀπορρήξας κορυφὴν ὄρεος μεγάλοιο
(*Od.* 9.481)

He tore off and threw the crest of a large mountain.

insequitur Cyclops partemque e monte revulsam
mittit.
(*Met.* 13.882–883)

The Cyclops pursued; he tore off part of a mountain and threw it.

Once violence has disrupted a humorous context, humor disrupts the newly grim tone. As was noted earlier, Ovid typically combines humor and gruesomeness without lessening the force of either tonal quality. Here Galatea's *nam cuncta videbam*, "For I saw everything" (*Met.* 13.860), interrupts the narrative with a comical reminder that she and Acis have been Polyphemus's unwilling audience (see also *Met.* 13.786–788). In supplying him with an audience, Ovid again expands upon the situation in Theocritus 11. The change is especially funny because much of the pathos in Theocritus's version results from the lack of any indication that Galatea hears the Cyclops's plaint.[57] A few lines later, Galatea, describing the Cyclops's menacing frenzy and bitter threats against herself and Acis, seems to begin a formal simile to emphasize the loudness of his voice: *tantaque vox, quantam*, "As great a voice, as"—only to replace the expected simile with a baldly flat remark, "As great a voice as an angry Cyclops ought to have": *quantam Cyclops iratus habere / debuit, illa fuit* (*Met.* 13.876–877). A highly inappropriate intrusion of irony occurs when Acis, abandoned by Galatea, flees and pathetically calls for help: he receives the epithet *heros* just as he turns in flight:[58] *terga fugae dederat conversa Symaethius heros*, "The hero, son of Symaethus, turned his back and fled" (*Met.* 13.879). By his ironic use of *heros* in the context of Acis's victimization, Ovid empties the word of meaning. The gruesome slaughter immediately follows this example of significantly indecorous wit (*Met.* 13.882–884), and together they create the intensely grisly/comic mixed tone so characteristic of the *Metamorphoses*. There cannot be detachment

---

[57] Philoxenus's dithyramb included both consolation and a message to Galatea: καὶ Φιλόξενος τὸν Κύκλωπα ποιεῖ παραμυθούμενον ἑαυτὸν ἐπὶ τῷ τῆς Γαλατείας ἔρωτι καὶ ἐντελλόμενον τοῖς δελφῖσιν, ὅπως ἀπαγγείλωσιν αὐτῇ ὅτι ταῖς Μούσαις τὸν ἔρωτα ἀκεῖται, "Philoxenus portrays the Cyclops consoling himself for his love of Galatea, and bidding the dolphins report to her that he is healing his love by the Muses" (Schol. Theoc. 11.1, p. 241 Wendel). Theocritus heightens the pathos of his version by denying Polyphemus the satisfaction of any such communication.

[58] Cf. *Met.* 3.198: *fugit Autonoeius heros*, "The hero, son of Autonoe [i.e., Actaeon], fled." "Ovid characteristically uses *heros* in unheroic contexts" (Anderson 1972, on *Met.* 8.324).

in any just appreciation of the horrific, nor, surely, in that of this ambiguous and complex tone.

Some Scandalous Passages

Seneca the Younger, quoted earlier in this chapter, expressed irritation at intrusions of irreverent humor into Ovid's serious, even sublime description of the flood in Book 1. Such intrusions seldom annoy a critic today, as long as their only casualty is epic seriousness; indeed, it has become customary to call them "charming."[59] The same cannot be said, however, when wit disrupts pathetic contexts, as here in the death of Acis. "Was this a Time to be witty, when the poor Wretch was in the Agony of Death?" Dryden's remarks on Narcissus have an echo in modern censure of Ovidian poetic practice. Galinsky, for example, asks "whether a subject such as human death and suffering should not be exempt from the variety of tone which Ovid successfully strives to achieve," though he has already answered his own question a few pages before: "There are certain events in human life ... whose depiction *per se* requires some *gravitas* and which any sensitive human being, let alone a poet, might be expected to treat accordingly."[60] It is perhaps fair enough for a critic to insist upon decorum, even in such rigid terms, and to fault a poet for not respecting it. But it is less than fair to claim that Ovid lacked sufficient "sensitivity" and "humanity" to portray pathetic incidents in an appropriate manner. Such a claim rests on the assumption that Ovid's personal character can be casually divined from the *Metamorphoses*. Still more misleading are two further assumptions, fundamental to this claim: that Ovid did not write decorously because by nature he could not; and that had he possessed a "sensitive" and "humane" nature, he would have done so. It is possible to substitute for these a less depreciatory assumption: that Ovid wanted his readers to have a wrenching experience from his violations of decorum. He wanted the *Metamorphoses* to be disturbing, and regarded the violation of his readers' sensibilities as a valuable experience for them. Indeed, if there is a didactic purpose to the *Metamorphoses*, it is not so much in the inculcation of positive moral values as in the exposure of the audience to revealing—though sometimes unpleasant—experiences. Ovid makes his readers recognize the power of language to control and manipulate their responses, and exposes to them their susceptibility or willingness—or even craving—to be deceived by comforting and pleasant fictions.

[59] See Wilkinson 1955, 163–164, on charm; and Bernbeck 1967, throughout.
[60] Galinsky 1975, 113, 111. Galinsky devotes a chapter to "Ovid's Humanity: Death and Suffering in the *Metamorphoses*" (110–157).

Ovid's critics generally acknowledge "the essential variety of tone" that Wilkinson perceived in the *Metamorphoses*.[61] Yet they seldom appreciate the clear-eyed thoroughness with which Ovid sought to reflect the variety of human experience in an ever-shifting narrative style. Irruptions of violence, no less than wit, form a consistent pattern of narrative disruption; yet writers on Ovid, if ever they mention violence at all, tend to isolate it as an unfortunate anomaly, explicable only as a sop to the vulgar in Ovid's audience. According to Wilkinson, "There would be some at least among his audience whose jaded taste would respond to any novel sensation of gruesomeness he could inflict, like twentieth-century Parisians at the Grand Guignol. How these must have relished the flaying of Marsyas by Apollo!"[62] Galinsky adapts Wilkinson's censure of Roman readers and directs it at Ovid himself, writing of "Ovid's delight in grotesque cruelty," which he calls "a concession to the taste of the Roman public and a concession that does not seem to have been grudgingly granted."[63] It evidently does not occur to these critics that Ovid could have intended his audience to feel something other than "delight" when reading such passages. They seriously underestimate the emotional range of the *Metamorphoses*.

A particularly impressive example of the emotional power and range of Ovid's narrative is the story of Marsyas (*Met.* 6.382–400)—scarcely a story at all, since Ovid entirely omits the usual introduction of characters and setting, instead plunging his readers without warning into an agonizing description of Marsyas, flayed alive:

> clamanti cutis est summos direpta per artus,
> nec quicquam nisi vulnus erat; cruor undique manat
> detectique patent nervi trepidaeque sine ulla
> pelle micant venae; salientia viscera possis
> et perlucentes numerare in pectore fibras.
> (*Met.* 6.387–391)

> As he screamed, the skin was torn from the surface of his limbs; there was nothing but a wound; blood flowed everywhere, and his uncovered sinews lay exposed; his trembling veins throbbed without any skin; you could count his pulsing innards, and the translucent organ-tissue in his chest.

So severely does Ovid truncate this narrative that he even omits the name of Marsyas until the whole account is finished (*Met.* 6.400). Bernbeck has shown that postponement or omission of names is a common styl-

---

[61] Wilkinson 1955, 159.
[62] Ibid., 162.
[63] Galinsky 1975, 138.

istic feature of the *Metamorphoses*;[64] here initial mention of Marsyas's name would have given warning that an account of his death could be on its way, though even so, one would not have cause to anticipate an account as gruesome as this. There is no mention of how Marsyas came to be flayed; in the standard versions, he receives this punishment for hubris and presumption in challenging Apollo to a musical contest.[65] Ovid does not mention Apollo, and deprives the story of its expected moral context. Since Marsyas's story was well known to the Romans, they would have been struck by Ovid's audacious neglect of what traditionally gave the story its meaning and made Marsyas's agony comprehensible. Without such a context, the violence of his fate becomes the more harrowing and repulsive.

In the preceding story, that of the Lycian Farmers' impiety toward Latona (*Met.* 6.313–381), there is certainly no forewarning of Ovid's treatment of Marsyas: they betray their malicious arrogance in no uncertain terms and obviously deserve their fate when, after muddying the waters of a pool so as to prevent the goddess from drinking, Latona angrily consigns them to the pool forever as frogs.[66] The tone of the story is for the most part light and entertaining, especially toward the end, where Ovid indulges his readers in many amusing details of how the malefactors become frogs, as in his famous imitation of their croaking: *quamvis sint sub aqua, sub aqua maledicere temptant*, "Though now under water, under water they try to utter curses" (*Met.* 6.376). This story, far from suggesting what is to come in the account of Marsyas, is likely to lull its audience into a comfortable state of mild amusement.

So here, as in the tales of Daedalus and Polyphemus, one result of Ovid's manipulation of tone is to soften the audience up for a disconcerting jolt. Yet as in the case of Acis's death, the violent description is no sooner under way than another abrupt change succeeds it. Earlier we noted the play on pronouns (*Met.* 6.385), an intrusive witticism, which, though it complicates the texture, provides no indication of future changes. Who could have expected that close upon the hideous details of Marsyas's flaying there would follow a passage of lovely pastoral, as touching and evocative as its author could make it, and a challenge to anything in Vergil's *Eclogues*?

---

[64] Bernbeck 1967, 44–49; on Marsyas, 48 n. 17. In *Fasti* 6, Minerva recounts Marsyas's fate. Though she does not name him, she identifies him as *satyrus* (*F.* 6.703) and provides the full context of his punishment in a simple summary (*F.* 6.697–710), without disproportionate expansion of the flaying.

[65] For the usual versions, see Anderson 1972, 201; Bömer 3:108–109.

[66] On the moral culpability of the Lycian Farmers, see Anderson 1972, 194–201.

> illum ruricolae, silvarum numina, Fauni,
> et satyri fratres et tunc quoque carus Olympus
> et nymphae flerunt, et quisquis montibus illis
> lanigerosque greges armentaque bucera pavit.
> (*Met.* 6.392–395)
>
> The countryfolk wept for him, woodland divinities, fauns, his brother satyrs,
> Olympus, still his beloved, and whoever on those hills grazed woolly flocks
> and horned herds.

The view that these lines represent "a mere literary topos without any emotive value whatsoever"[67] will not convince readers who are more susceptible to pastoral language and more attentively responsive to generic allusion in these lines, which call to mind earlier experiences of pastoral. In subject matter and diction they recall the gathering of Arcadia's inhabitants to lament Gallus in Vergil's Tenth Eclogue (*Ecl.* 10.13–27). The arrangement of words in *ruricolae, silvarum numina, Fauni*, where an apposition separates adjective and noun, is modeled on two examples in Vergil's *Eclogues*: *densas, umbrosa cacumina, fagos*, "Thick beeches, shady treetops" (*Ecl.* 2.3); *veteres, iam fracta cacumina, fagos*, "Old beeches, now shattered treetops" (*Ecl.* 9.9).[68] Ovid could therefore invite his readers to hear in his imitation a specifically Vergilian bucolic resonance. It is perverse to deny emotional power to these lines of pastoral mourning; short as the passage is, its calm sadness ought to be as affecting in its way as the savage violence that precedes it.

In this passage, as in Ovid's imitation of Homeric violence, allusion requires and presupposes the reader's emotional and intellectual engagement. If we reject "detachment" and regard Ovid's narrative as more powerful and disturbing, then there is no need to explain away the impact of its harrowing passages. Galinsky suggests that some of them may be excused as unfortunate imitations of Homeric violence; the rest he can account for only by inventing a cruel and bloodthirsty personal character for Ovid: "Other episodes for which Ovid encountered no similarly established conventions suggest that he reveled in bloodthirsty and repulsive descriptions of human agony simply because he liked cruelty." Affecting measurement of Ovid's story of Philomela and Tereus against the presumed "spiritual dimension" and "inner qualities" of Sophoclean tragedy, Galinsky in fact condemns it for not fitting conventions of tragic decorum that are traditionally abstracted from Aristotle: "The story is

---

[67] Galinsky 1975, 135.

[68] On the development of this type of apposition, see Norden 1976, 116–117, on *Aen.* 6.7; Skutsch 1956; Solodow 1986; Bömer on *Met.* 6.131. Comparable examples in less notably bucolic contexts are *Met.* 3.420, 4.573, 6.131, 8.372, 9.92, 10.102.

deprived of its tragic spirit, and external aspects predominate. Grotesque actions, hyperbolic gestures, and exaggerated cruelty take the place of the tragic idea, and the reader is treated to a spectacle of gestures rather than moved to pity or fear."[69] It is indeed obvious that Ovid's treatment of death and suffering does not conform to conventional tragic standards. Such criticism does not admit any other proper standards, and so Ovid is doomed to failure. Yet Ovid often seems to have designed his imitation of violent actions to aim at an effect nearly the opposite of Aristotelian tragedy. Aristotle, discussing tragic imitation, writes that painful sights become pleasing in the representation, ἃ γὰρ λυπηρῶς ὁρῶμεν, τούτων τὰς εἰκόνας τὰς μάλιστα ἠκριβωμένας χαίρομεν θεωροῦντες, "for we take pleasure in looking upon likenesses, when they are represented with special accuracy, of things which themselves we look upon with pain" (*Poet.* 1448b10–11). Ovid's violent descriptions, typically deprived of comforting and comprehensible circumstances, become more painful to read the more detailed and specific they are. There is no reason to assume that merely because Ovidian violence is not tragic it consequently lacks "true pathos"[70] and has no real power to move its audience.

Detachment, which is scarcely possible as a response to Ovidian violence, no more convincingly describes the effects of Ovidian wit. As we have seen, Ovid is certainly willing to introduce wit into serious, especially pathetic contexts, and so to disrupt his reader's experience of them. The success of such disruption depends on the reader's engagement with the serious context. Surprise contributes much to Ovidian wit, as when a narrative voice suddenly intrudes with an unexpected comment on the action. Deucalion and Pyrrha, for example, are solemnly discussing the oracle that they have received, and wondering whether to rely on Deucalion's surmise that by the bones of their great parent are to be understood the stones of the earth—*sed quid temptare nocebit?* "What harm will it do to try?" (*Met.* 1.397). This blunt narrative intrusion puts an abrupt halt to all efforts to understand the divine command and calls attention to the practical ease with which Deucalion and Pyrrha can try out their interpretation.[71] And so they throw rocks over their shoulders and almost inadvertently ensure the survival of the human race. Ovid's wit in this example will gain impact on its audience relative to the degree of engagement that the dignified epic context has first achieved. And indeed, Ovid has gone to extra effort in this passage to recall Homeric narrative style, as when he uses nearly the same words to represent Themis's command

---

[69] Galinsky 1975, 129, 132.
[70] Ibid., 123.
[71] Von Albrecht (*WdF* 92, 423) attributes a "genuinely Roman" pragmatism to *sed quid temptare nocebit?* In that case, the thought stands out still more strikingly from its context.

and the performance of it by Deucalion and Pyrrha: *discedite templo / et velate caput cinctasque resolvite vestes*, "Leave the temple, veil your heads and loosen your girt robes" (*Met.* 1.381–382); *discedunt: velantque caput tunicasque recingunt*, "They leave the temple, veil their heads and ungird their tunics" (*Met.* 1.398).[72]

No less vulnerable to intrusive wit are those passages where Ovid makes his most direct appeals to the reader's emotions, in violent and pathetic descriptions. We considered earlier the transformative character of Marsyas's grisly witticism, *quid me mihi detrahis?* "Why do you tear me from myself?" (*Met.* 6.385). If we regard it now for its effect on its context, horror is if anything intensified by wit, and disruption does not invite withdrawal from emotional involvement in the story. Certainly it does not cause the repulsive description of Marsyas's flaying to lose any of its power.

No passage in the *Metamorphoses* provides convincing support for the notion that Ovid expected or wanted emotional disengagement from his readers, not even those passages where he treats a traditionally pathetic subject without the appeal to pathos that such a subject customarily received. Anderson describes Ovid's plague of Aegina (*Met.* 7.523–613) as "a melodramatic episode which is spectacularly amusing and exercises no hold on the audience's emotions."[73] It warrants this description if one expects the audience's emotions to be like those Lucretius intended to evoke by heightening the pathetic features in his adaptation of Thucydides' plague (Lucr. 6.1138–1286), or those Vergil appealed to in contributing a further increase of pathos to adaptation of the subject (*G.* 3.478–566). Ovid, who in his version forestalls the development of pathos wherever it threatens to occur, does not thereby "disengage" the reader and remove all emotional content. Ovid supplies emotional content of a very different nature; his introduction of audacious wit makes his plague an alarming—even hair-raising—as well as amusing experience. Wit makes in this passage yet another assault on the reader's sensibilities, not so much because the subject matter itself demands more decorous treatment as because a complex of allusions keeps the famous plague descriptions of Ovid's predecessors always before the reader's mind, recalling familiar emotions associated with them and thereby heightening the scandalous lack of decorum in Ovid's version. One can easily imagine that readers of Ovid's time were as eager as those of today for sentimental indulgence in familiar emotional thrills, and one can ad-

---

[72] So H-E, on *Met.* 1.398–399.

[73] Anderson 1972, 299 on *Met.* 7.523; cf. Galinsky 1975, 121, on the plague of Aegina: "Ovid is not interested in the subject because he does not want to deal with anything more profound than the externals of the situation."

mire his plague of Aegina for its mockery of this tendency in his own audience.

Whether one admires it or not, calm detachment is unlikely to be one's reaction. Even those modern critics who decry the absence of standard pathos and profundity usually betray petulant irritation at their text and its author, an encouraging sign that they read the *Metamorphoses* with real engagement of the passions. One may wonder whether they can entirely succeed at distancing themselves from Ovid's narrative, or must become vulnerable to its power at last. In any event, Roman readers clearly were affected by Ovid's work, and some of them recorded the strong vexation that it aroused in them.[74] A famous story in the elder Seneca's *Controversiae* (2.2.12) even portrays a confrontation between audience and author: some of Ovid's friends asked him to remove from his works three lines that they objected to; he in turn asked permission to select three that they would not be allowed to touch. They privately wrote down the lines they wanted removed, and he wrote down those he wanted kept safe; the two lists turned out to contain the same lines. Seneca's text preserves two of them, both examples of verbal wit from Ovid's elegiac poetry: *Ars amatoria* 2.24 (a description of the minotaur), *semibovemque virum semivirumque bovem*, "A man half-bull and a bull half-man"; and *Amores* 2.11.10, *et gelidum Borean egelidumque Notum*, "The icy north wind and un-icy south wind." No doubt Ovid chose as his favorite lines those that he reckoned would most appall his audience, and his friends proved him right. For Seneca, the moral of the story is clear: *ex quo adparet summi ingenii viro non iudicium defuisse ad compescendam licentiam carminum suorum sed animum*, "From this it is evident that this highly talented man lacked not the judgment to restrain the excessive freedom of his verse, but rather the intention to do so." The story also suggests that Ovid exploited his insight into his readers' sense of decorum deliberately to thwart its gratification. Surely Ovid would have been pleased to think that after two millennia, a work of his could still amuse readers, arouse their sympathy, and fill them with admiration for its technical virtuosity, its insight into human character, the breadth of experience that it reflects, and much else besides; yet could he have known that after so long his work could still *irritate* its readers, he would probably have felt that his artistic effort could achieve no greater success.

---

[74] Both Seneca the Elder and Seneca the Younger have been quoted above; see also Quint. 10.1.98.

Chapter 3

DISRUPTIVE TRADITIONS

Indecorous Possibilities: Callimachus's Hymn to Artemis and Ovidian Style

In their instability and changeableness, both transgressive witticism and disruptive narrative contribute to make the reader's experience thematic. Ovid's perspectives on the nature of things, characterized by transformation and flux, have a correspondence in the character of his style, which offers multiple and overlapping embodiments of these perspectives. Wit, as we have seen, enacts transformation, and narrative discontinuity renders flux strikingly perceptible. Our discussion of this process has always emphasized allusion, for Ovid never fails to invite his predecessors to participate in his own achievements, engaging to that end his readers' memory and their imaginative reflection upon it. I now ask my readers to take a backward glance at some of Ovid's predecessors and to regard illustrative examples of their narrative patterns. My purpose in considering his predecessors is to show not so much their influence as his exploitation of them. This discussion does not primarily trace stylistic features historically, documenting them as a sort of artistic legacy, though it shares many concerns with literary-historical treatments and has benefited from a number of them.[1] In speaking of Ovid's exploitation of predecessors, I refer not only to his success at making full use of the stylistic resources and techniques bequeathed to him. I extend this notion to address also Ovid's use of his readers' memory of their texts as a constitutive element of his own creative undertaking.[2]

Though the term "allusion" is usually used in discussion of specific expressions and collocations of words that link a later to an earlier work in the reader's awareness, more general stylistic features are at least as likely to establish such a link. Ovid's narrative style itself alludes to earlier unstable, mercurial narrative styles, especially those, I maintain, of Callimachus and Roman elegiac poets. These he adapts to his own thematic purposes, which to some extent he shares with them. The aetiological

---

[1] Of special value for Callimachus and Latin poetry, and Ovid specifically, are Wilkinson 1956; Wimmel 1960; Clausen 1964; Miller 1982.

[2] See Greene 1982, 1: "Once we have noted a so-called model or source, we are only beginning to understand the model as a constitutive element of the literary structure, an element whose dynamic presence has yet to be accounted for."

preoccupations of these writers intersect with Ovid's, and I shall touch upon Ovidian aetiology in the next section. My present concern is to illustrate his refashioning of their narrative patterns to accommodate his characteristic perspectives on transformation and flux. Ovid gives new thematic relevance to the narrative modes of his predecessors, making them part of his own. Through stylistic allusion, through calling our attention to his predecessors' works, Ovid enlists our aid in subsuming them into the *Metamorphoses*, incorporating our recollection of them into our experience of Ovid's work.

Just as the stylistic connections between Ovid, Callimachus, and the elegists are many and various, so, too, are the critical approaches that they can sustain. My own diverges from those most firmly established and widely prevalent, but, I trust, may complement them. Programmatic interpretations of Latin poetry have flourished since Wimmel (1960) and Clausen (1964) emphasized Callimachus's importance in terms of a set of aesthetic attitudes derived from the prologue to the *Aetia* and a few other passages. Brevity, refinement of form, avoidance of epic subjects and epic pomposity, conspicuous and exotic learning—such are the earmarks of Callimachean influence on Latin poetry, observed mainly in the writers of elegy and short epic: "Cinna, Calvus, Catullus, Gallus, Virgil, Propertius—their imaginations were captivated by Callimachus," writes Clausen (including Vergil for the *Eclogues*).[3] Wimmel, focusing on the explicit rejection of epic subjects, also discusses Horace and Ovid's *Amores* in terms of the prologue to the *Aetia*. More recently, the *Metamorphoses* has provided a rich field for programmatic interpretation: Knox (1986), tracing "literary affiliations," represents the Ovid of the *Metamorphoses* as the "Roman Callimachus."[4] Hinds's in-depth reflections on the significance of generic reference include the *Fasti* as well.[5]

Ovid's self-conscious allusion to the craft of writing and its traditions is less my concern than the metaphorical potential of his style, which, viewed rhetorically, creates meanings in its effects on an audience. In his predecessors, as in Ovid, I examine narrative indirection, structural surprise, wit, functional indecorum, and the lostness of the reader. A connection between Callimachus and Ovid in these terms has sometimes been suggested or adumbrated. Wilkinson notes that the "variety of mood" in the *Metamorphoses* "is thoroughly Alexandrian, and particularly

[3] Clausen 1964, 181.
[4] Knox 1986, 10.
[5] See Hinds 1987. On the richly productive tensions between the formal generic associations of the *Fasti* and Ovid's transgressive practice, see Hinds 1992. In the recent work of Keith (1992) and Myers (1994a, 1994b), programmatic concerns are central.

DISRUPTIVE TRADITIONS 133

characteristic of the versatile and mischievous genius of Kallimachos."[6] He mentions as an example of this "variety of mood" Callimachus's third hymn, the Hymn to Artemis, an astonishing work, both amusing and disconcerting, which combines the more severe features of traditional hymns with comic narrative of the divinity's exploits in childhood. That Ovid appreciated the Hymn to Artemis is clear in three conspicuous allusions to it in the *Metamorphoses*.[7] A closer look will suggest what Ovid admired and found useful in its narrative technique, and how our recollection of it may enrich our reading of the *Metamorphoses*.[8]

Callimachus begins in a most traditional fashion, asserting that Artemis is the subject of his hymn; the assertion is interrupted at once by a parenthesis:

Ἄρτεμιν (οὐ γὰρ ἐλαφρὸν ἀειδόντεσσι λαθέσθαι)
ὑμνέομεν.
(H. 3.1–2)

Artemis (for it is not a light thing for singers to neglect her) we shall sing.

The Greek reader will recognize this type of parenthesis as a regular feature of epic style, though not to be expected in the first line of a work;

---

[6] Wilkinson 1956, 237; cf. also 235: "However various the sources of the myths recounted in the *Metamorphoses*, both in organization and spirit, the work as a whole owes most to one man, Kallimachos." See also Wilkinson 1955, 154.

[7] The first and best known of these (H. 3.6ff. and Met. 1.485–487) is discussed below. H. 3.52–53 and Met. 13.851–852 link two portrayals of harmless Cyclopes through a descriptive detail of their single eye. The third allusion, largely unknown, occurs in Met. 10 in the tale of young Cyparissus, whose grief for a stag leads to his own transformation into the cypress. In the opening description of the stag, Ovid alludes to Callimachus's description of the deer that become the prize of Artemis's first hunt. Ovid renders Callimachus's half-line by one of his own: κεράων δ' ἀπελάμπετο χρυσός (H. 3.102); *cornua fulgebant auro*, "The horns shone with gold" (Met. 10.112). This allusion escapes modern commentaries on Ovid and Callimachus; but see Ernesti's edition of Callimachus (1761, 1:112). That it is a specific allusion is assured by the combination of close verbal parallel with appropriate correspondence of context, since both occur in descriptions of deer.

[8] Of great value for the Hymn to Artemis are Wilamowitz 1924; Herter 1929; Bornmann 1968; Haslam 1993; and Bing and Uhrmeister 1994. Haslam's discussion is especially relevant here: in a close reading sensitive to "the constant necessity of making cognitive realignments" (113), he notes, among other features of the narrative texture, "aesthetic fragmentation" (112), paradox and surprise (113), seeming disintegration of structure (114), and "subterfuge" (116). In emphasizing abrupt transition, narrative indirection, and the like, I offer no contradiction to claims for the artistic unity of the hymn, such as that mounted by Bing and Uhrmeister. They take a long view of the hymn as a conceptual totality; my own focus is different, on close observation of the narrative texture as immediately experienced.

the Roman reader will recall that parentheses of this type have established themselves in Latin epic, commonly introduced by *neque enim*:[9]

> Aeneas (neque enim membris dat cura quietem)
> ipse sedens clavumque regit velisque ministrat.
> (*Aen.* 10.217–218)

> Aeneas (for anxiety gave his limbs no rest) himself sat to guide the rudder
> and attend to the sails.

In addition to epic associations, the parenthesis may provide an impression that Artemis is about to be honored as a formidable, even fierce, divinity, jealous of the respect due her; and indeed, the Greeks often so regarded her. If so, the impression is soon dispelled: we next learn of Artemis that "her concern is the bow and the hunting of rabbits"!

> τῇ τόξα λαγωβολίαι τε μέλονται
> καὶ χορὸς ἀμφιλαφὴς καὶ ἐν οὔρεσιν ἑψιάασθαι.
> (*H.* 3.2–3)

> The bow and rabbit hunts are her concern, the wide-spreading dance, and
> playing on the mountains.

Mention of rabbit-hunting introduces a note of comic inappropriateness worthy of Ovid, and reveals that in the dignified, old-fashioned opening of the hymn Callimachus meant deliberately to set his reader up for a surprise. Callimachus shares with Ovid the distinction of having been attacked in antiquity for lack of decorum: Hyginus reports a criticism of this passage: *Callimachum quoque accusari quod, cum Dianae scriberet laudes, eam leporum sanguine gaudere et eos venari dixisset*, "Callimachus also is accused because, when writing the praises of Diana, he said that she rejoices in the blood of rabbits, and hunts them" (*Poet. Astr.* 2.33).[10] The comically intrusive introduction of Artemis λαγωβόλος can be appreciated without specific recollection of the passage in the Homeric Hymn to Aphrodite to which Callimachus's lines principally allude, but the reader who does recall it will observe another aspect to the bold indecorousness of Callimachus's treatment:

---

[9] Two examples (among many) are *Il.* 2.484–487 and Ovid's epic-style imitation of the passage in *Met.* 15.622–625. Other examples in the *Aeneid* are 1.198, 1.643, 2.376, 6.368, 7.195, 7.581, 9.704, 11.684. Von Albrecht (1964, 170–178) discusses the epic associations of this type of parenthesis. It occurs also in elegy (Prop. 4.4.89).

[10] Cf. also the comment of August Meineke in his edition of the Hymns and Epigrams (Berlin, 1861, 156), cited in Herter 1929, 59 n. 32: *parum decore poeta in ipso limine Dianam lepores venari dicit, quorum loco quis non alias feras commemorari expectet*? "Without propriety, the poet at the very threshold says that Diana hunts rabbits. Who would not expect other beasts to be mentioned instead of them?"

DISRUPTIVE TRADITIONS 135

καὶ γὰρ τῇ ἅδε τόξα καὶ οὔρεσι θῆρας ἐναίρειν,
φόρμιγγές τε χοροί τε διαπρύσιοί τ' ὀλολυγαὶ
ἄλσεά τε σκιόεντα δικαίων τε πτόλις ἀνδρῶν.
(*Hymn. Hom.* 5.18–20)

Her delight is the bow, killing wild beasts on the mountains, lyres, dances, piercing shouts, shadowy groves, and a city of just men.

Callimachus takes over the bow and the dances, but "killing wild beasts on the mountains," οὔρεσι θῆρας ἐναίρειν, has given place to "having fun on the mountains," ἐν οὔρεσιν ἐψιάασθαι.[11] In the next two lines it becomes clear that Callimachus means to portray Artemis as a little girl, adapting to his purposes a tradition indeed ancient, but uncommon: one work is known to us, an Aeolic poem evidently by Alcaeus or Sappho, which represents Artemis, probably as a child, adopting perpetual virginity with the approval of Zeus.[12] Not enough remains of this poem to establish its tone, but Callimachus's audience would also know such portrayals of child-divinity as the Homeric Hymn to Hermes, whose largely comic tone the Greeks thought entirely appropriate to hymnal celebration. Also in the background is one of the two Homeric Hymns to Artemis (*Hymn. Hom.* 27); in Callimachus's second line, λαγωβολίαι may call to mind the epithet ἐλαφηβόλος in the second line of that hymn:

Ἄρτεμιν ἀείδω χρυσηλάκατον κελαδεινὴν
παρθένον αἰδοίην ἐλαφηβόλον ἰοχέαιραν.
(*Hymn. Hom.* 27.1–2)

I sing Artemis of the golden spindle, the raiser of shouts, the maiden, the august, the hunter of deer, the shooter of arrows.

Herter perceptively remarks on the connection between the two words: "There is no doubt at all that Callimachus pursues his particular intention in the degradation of ἐλαφηβόλος to λαγωβόλος; he wants to surprise his reader, and whoever had expected from him a hymn in the old style sees himself thoroughly deceived."[13]

Thus even in the first few lines of Callimachus's hymn we can observe a tendency to disappoint expectations aroused by the generic associations of his own text and to disrupt the tone that it had established. In this connection it is interesting that von Albrecht, in his detailed study of parenthesis in the *Metamorphoses*, compares the parenthesis in the first line of the Hymn to Artemis to the "epic" parenthesis in the prooemium

---

[11] The author of *Hymn. Hom.* 5 adapted his expression from *Il.* 21.485: κατ' οὔρεα θῆρας ἐνάρειν.
[12] See Lobel and Page 1952; text also in *Poetarum Lesbiorum fragmenta* 304.
[13] Herter 1929, 59.

to the *Metamorphoses*:[14] *di, coeptis—nam vos mutastis et illa—/ adspirate meis*, "Gods, inspire my undertakings (for you are the ones who changed them)" (*Met*. 1.2–3). If, as von Albrecht has elsewhere maintained, the generic references in Ovid's prooemium are to epic,[15] then Ovid and Callimachus are undertaking a similar stylistic deception of their audience; for Ovid's reader, however impressed by the epic pretensions of the prooemium, will soon find that the *Metamorphoses* is anything but a traditional epic. From the prooemium we can conclude not, as von Albrecht asserts, that "Ovid's intention was without doubt to write an epic,"[16] but only that Ovid may have wanted his readers initially to mistake the *Metamorphoses* for an epic.

Two other features of the lines quoted above from the Homeric Hymn to Aphrodite may affect one's reading of Callimachus's hymn. First, "a city of just men" (δικαίων πτόλις ἀνδρῶν) appears with emphasis at the end of the list of what pleases Artemis—the more noticeably so, because concern for human justice is very seldom attributed to her.[17] Callimachus, about to work up a comic scene between little Artemis and her father, naturally enough leaves out such a concern at this point, but the *doctus lector* may recall its omission here when it suddenly appears, much later, at a most unlikely point: Artemis, having recently acquired her new little bow, tries it out, shooting twice at trees, then at a wild beast; for a fourth try she shoots "a city of unjust men" (εἰς ἀδίκων ἔβαλες πόλιν: *H*. 3.122).

The second feature is the context of the passage in the Hymn to Aphrodite: near the beginning, after a celebration of Aphrodite's power over divinities, human beings, birds, and animals, the poet makes three exceptions—the virgin goddesses Athena, Artemis, and Hestia, "whose hearts Aphrodite cannot win over or deceive" (*Hymn. Hom.* 5.7). In this context the passage occurs. Callimachus picks up its theme of virginity and turns it to comic effect: put into the mouth of a child, who is sitting on her father's knee, a request for perpetual virginity jars with its context:

πατρὸς ἐφεζομένη γονάτεσσι
παῖς ἔτι κουρίζουσα τάδε προσέειπε γονῆα·
"δός μοι παρθενίην αἰώνιον, ἄππα, φυλάσσειν,
καὶ πολυωνυμίην, ἵνα μή μοι Φοῖβος ἐρίζῃ".
(*H*. 3.4–7)

---

[14] von Albrecht 1964, 174. Anderson (1993, 109) now accepts *illa* for *illas* in the manuscripts at *Met*. 1.2, following Kenney (1976) and Kovacs (1988); Tarrant (1982, 350–351) identifies *illa* as a medieval variant.

[15] Von Albrecht 1961; see also Kenney 1976; Feeney 1991, 189–190.

[16] Von Albrecht 1961, 277.

[17] See Bornmann 1968, 60–61, on *H*. 3.122–135.

Sitting on her father's knees, still a child, she addressed her father as follows: "Give me the protection of perpetual virginity, Dad, and many epithets, lest Phoebus rival me."

Callimachus represents Artemis as having acquired her traditional attributes by requesting them one after another in a garrulous and impatient manner characteristic of children. He heightens both characterization and humor by supplying appropriately childish motivations to Artemis's requests: at her age she may have no need for her standard epithet πολυώνυμος, but because of sibling rivalry she certainly wants it: ἵνα μή μοι Φοῖβος ἐρίζῃ. Callimachus audaciously adapts elements of hymnal and epic style to serve new and unexpected purposes. Artemis's insistent repetition of the word δός, for example (6, 8, 13, 18), is stylistically appropriate to a prayer and, as Herter observes, "no less characteristic of childish shamelessness and loquacity."[18] Here Callimachus exploits a traditional genre and its appropriate style, adding comic features that, though not unprecedented in the genre, are certainly unusual in the portrayal of Artemis, and jar with what an audience would commonly expect.

Ovid, no doubt impressed by Callimachus's style of wit, so congenial to his own, alludes to the conversation between Artemis and Father Zeus when Daphne, confronted by her father Peneus's demands for a son-in-law and grandchildren, shrewdly cites Callimachus's hymn against him:

> inque patris blandis haerens cervice lacertis
> "da mihi perpetua, genitor carissime," dixit
> "virginitate frui! dedit hoc pater ante Dianae."
> ille quidem obsequitur.
> (*Met.* 1.485–488)

Clinging to her father's neck with coaxing arms, she said, "Give me the enjoyment of perpetual virginity, dearest father! Diana's father gave her this before." He complied.

As usual, Ovid takes advantage of various features of his original to broaden this passage's humor and intensify its irony. Ovid gives little Artemis's words to "the already nubile Daphne," as Doblhofer remarks,[19] and in her mouth they have a new motivation: struck by Cupid's leaden arrow (*Met.* 1.471–472), she seeks to avoid love and seizes upon Artemis as a rhetorical exemplum. Establishing a parallel between herself and Artemis, she invites Peneus (a river-god and hence only a minor divinity) to imagine himself in the role of Zeus. This subtle flattery does the trick. Yet the actual dissimilarity of Artemis and Daphne soon be-

---
[18] Herter 1929, 64.
[19] Doblhofer 1960, 81.

comes clear enough, as Daphne's newly achieved *virginitas perpetua* does her little good. She immediately becomes the object of Apollo's overheated desires and is saved from rape only by timely metamorphosis into the laurel.

However much Ovid may have learned from Callimachean wit, it is in the creation of unpredictable—sometimes even baffling—narrative movement that Callimachus offered his most important suggestions to Ovid as an author of mythological poetry. The structural scheme of the hymn is superficially simple and clear for its first 109 lines, as Artemis goes about acquiring the objects of her requests—she collects her allotment of Oceanids and nymphs (*H*. 3.40–45), visits the Cyclopes to have them make her little weapons (46–86), then visits Pan in Arcadia to acquire hunting dogs (87–109)—but it is only superficially simple and clear: in fact, the narrative becomes increasingly skewed as it progresses, calculated to lead its audience in unforeseen directions. Artemis had told her father that the Cyclopes would make her a bow and arrows:

ἐμοὶ Κύκλωπες ὀϊστούς
αὐτίκα τεχνήσονται, ἐμοὶ δ' εὐκαμπὲς ἄεμμα.
(*H*. 3.9–10)

At once the Cyclopes shall craft me arrows and a well-bent bow.

So Callimachus could do nothing more straightforward than have her presently arrive at their forge:

αὖθι δὲ Κύκλωπας μετεκίαθε· τοὺς μὲν ἔτετμε
νήσῳ ἐνὶ Λιπάρῃ (Λιπάρη νέον, ἀλλὰ τότ' ἔσκεν
οὔνομά οἱ Μελιγουνίς) ἐπ' ἄκμοσιν Ἡφαίστοιο
ἑσταότας περὶ μύδρον· ἐπείγετο γὰρ μέγα ἔργον·
ἱππείην τετύκοντο Ποσειδάωνι ποτίστρην.
(*H*. 3.46–50)

Straightway she visited the Cyclopes. She found them on the island of Lipara (lately so called; then its name was Meligounis) at Hephaestus's anvils, standing around a mass of metal. They were hastening a great work; they were making a horse-trough for Poseidon.

Yet despite the simplicity and directness of this description, Callimachus is only apparently getting down to business: actually, as Bornmann remarks, "This scene speaks about everything except the making of the arms."[20] Callimachus puts off any mention of the purpose of Artemis's visit by a series of digressions: on the little nymphs' fearful reaction to these perfectly harmless giants (51–63); on the reasons for such fear—

[20] Bornmann 1968, xxix.

divine mothers habitually use the names of Cyclopes to frighten disobedient children (64–71); on an earlier exploit of Artemis, at age three, when she, seated on the Cyclops Brontes' lap, tore out some of his chest hair (72–79). Finally, when the reader may well have lost sight of that purpose altogether, he abruptly dispatches the making of the weapons and the arming of Artemis in less than one line: ἔννεπες· οἱ δ' ἐτέλεσσαν· ἄφαρ δ' ὡπλίσσαο, δαῖμον, "You spoke; they performed the task; at once you were armed, goddess" (*H.* 3.86).

The deliberate distortion of this narrative, though striking enough in itself, becomes even more so by contrast to the Homeric ὁπλοποιΐα (*Il.* 18.369–617), to which the whole scene generally alludes. Homer's much longer narrative preserves the usual Homeric decorum of scale; that is, the most significant events in the narrative receive the longest and most detailed description: Thetis's arrival at Hephaestus's house and formal reception there (369–427); her request for the arms, expanded because of its importance to include an account of Achilles' life and present predicament (428–461); Hephaestus's assent and prompt commencement of work (462–477). Though these sections may be elaborated with explanatory digressions—such as Hephaestus's account of past help from Thetis, which inclines him now to favor her (394–409)—the narrative usually progresses in a linear fashion, and digressions do not compromise the clarity of its progress. Readers need never wonder where Homer is leading them. A very long description of Achilles' shield (478–617) can be inserted without danger of confusion because of its firmly established context.

Callimachus's narrative, by contrast, only begins as if it aimed at Homeric clarity in the lines quoted above. Allusions to Homer's ὁπλοποιΐα emphasize the parallel, such as τοὺς μέν ἔτετμε (*H.* 3.46: Artemis comes upon the Cyclopes), an imitation-with-variation of Homer's τὸν δ' εὗρε (*Il.* 18.372: Thetis comes upon Hephaestus). Thetis finds Hephaestus making robotic (αὐτόματοι) tripods, a marvel to look upon (*Il.* 18.372–377). The "great work" that Artemis finds the Cyclopes working on turns out to be nothing more than a water-trough for Poseidon's horses (*H.* 3.49–50). The prose word ποτίστρη, jarring with its epic adjective ἱππείη,[21] falls at the end of its line as a humorous anticlimax. From this point it is clear that Callimachus's uses of the Homeric ὁπλοποιΐα will include comic adaptation.

By digressively expanding what one would expect to be the beginning of the episode and by reducing the rest of it to barest summary, Callimachus produces a severely unbalanced narrative, one calculated to surprise a reader accustomed in general to Homeric decorum of scale and

---

[21] See ibid., 29, on *H.* 3.50.

familiar in particular with Homer's ὁπλοποιΐα. Similar narrative distortions are common in the *Metamorphoses*, as we have already seen: in the story of Daedalus and Icarus, Ovid deliberately wrecks the elaborately foreshadowed climax, baldly summarizing the tale's conclusion; in that of Marsyas, he omits the beginning of the tale entirely, plunging his readers at once into the violent conclusion. Though virtually any portion of a narrative may be foreshortened, the climax—or what Ovid prepares one to expect will be the climax—is most often so treated. Such narrative distortions, however frequent in the *Metamorphoses*, never lack power to surprise.

One further example will suffice for the present to illustrate Ovid's practice, the encounter of Jason and the fire-breathing bulls (*Met.* 7.100–119), a very free adaptation and condensation of Apollonius's account in the third book of the *Argonautica*. The passage begins in formal epic style with a description of dawn, assembly of the people, and enthronement of King Aeetes (*Met.* 7.100–103). Ovid then describes the bulls with great flamboyance and at some length (*Met.* 7.104–114), including a formal simile. In this description, "static and so menacing," in Kenney's words,[22] Ovid builds tension and suspense toward the coming clash. Jason steps forward—*illis Aesone natus / obvius it*, "The son of Aeson advances to meet them" (*Met.* 7.110–111). The bulls turn toward him: *vertere truces venientis ad ora / terribiles vultus*, "The savage beasts turned their terrible visages toward his face as he advanced" (*Met.* 7.111–112). As the fearful impact approaches, intensified by delay, we suddenly find Jason's "audacious hand" merely stroking the bulls' dewlaps—so bland an activity has replaced the climactic encounter:

> deriguere metu Minyae; subit ille nec illos
> sensit anhelantes (tantum medicamina possunt)
> pendulaque audaci mulcet palearia dextra
> suppositosque iugo pondus grave cogit aratri
> ducere et insuetum ferro proscindere campum.
> (*Met.* 7.115–119)

The Minyae stiffened with fear; Jason advanced and did not feel them panting—such power the potions had—stroked their hanging dewlaps with his bold hand, and yoking them, made them draw the plough's heavy weight and cut the unaccustomed field with the steel ploughshare.

In these lines of rapid summary, all narrative momentum vanishes, as does any chance of heroic behavior on Jason's part. Stylistic anticlimax thus serves to underline Ovid's less-than-heroic portrayal of a traditional

---

[22] Kenney 1973, 137; see also Anderson 1972, 256, on Ovid's "slyly irreverent" treatment of the story.

hero (a characteristic feature of the *Metamorphoses*) in contrast to his source: for if Apollonius's Jason nowhere else behaves in a traditionally heroic fashion, at least in this scene of Book 3 his valor can bear examination by Homeric standards. He must endure the bulls' fierce attack, holding his shield against them, then wrestle them to the ground (*Argonautica* 3.1296–1299, 1306–1313). As if to correct Apollonius, Ovid eliminates Jason's one moment of heroic excellence.[23]

Returning to the Hymn to Artemis, we can observe that the next episode, wherein Artemis visits Pan in Arcadia to acquire hunting dogs and performs her first feat of hunting (*H*. 3.87–109), contains two surprising and unforeseeable developments. The acquisition of dogs is itself unsurprising, since Artemis had indicated in her conversation with Zeus that she needed attendants to take care of her dogs (17). But here, after eight lines give much precise information on the various dogs that Pan provides (90–97), and after we are specifically told that the dogs were following Artemis when she came upon the herd of deer that were to be her first prize (98), it turns out that she did not bother to use them! "To his astonishment," writes Bornmann, "the reader comes to know that the four deer for the chariot were captured without dogs"[24] (νόσφι κυνοδρομίης: *H*. 3.106). The other unexpected development is the very fact that Callimachus represents Artemis performing such a wondrous exploit as the capture of these huge deer, bigger than bulls (102). It was of course traditional to celebrate the amazing achievements of a divinity or hero in childhood, such as we observe in the Homeric Hymn to Hermes (in which baby Hermes invents the lyre and steals Apollo's cattle) or Pindar's First Nemean 35–72 (in which baby Herakles strangles the snakes sent by Hera to destroy him). But those works display from the start a child ready and able to achieve prodigies in the adult world of gods and heroes, whereas in Callimachus's hymn, by contrast, that world has been domesticated and humanized, accommodated, as it were, to fit Artemis. As a result, it comes as a jolt to find Artemis suddenly accomplishing the feats of a traditional child-divinity. As Herter remarks, "Certainly, if Artemis were a goddess of the old stamp, we would credulously accept all wonders from her without further ado; but she was up to now portrayed almost entirely as a human child, from whom we could not expect godly deeds.... When she suddenly appears with really divine capabilities, it is an ἀπροσδόκητον, with which the poet wishes utterly to surprise his listener."[25]

---

[23] See Kenney 1973, 137: "Jason, as Ovid tells the story, is not called upon (or possibly lacks the wit?) even to simulate anxiety or effort."

[24] Bornmann 1968, xxx.

[25] Herter 1929, 87, 89.

Now that Artemis has strangely assumed the role of powerful goddess, and the hymn's subject matter has passed beyond its former narrative boundaries into unknown regions, Callimachus boldly tricks his audience into supposing that the hymn is coming to an end. He adopts a formula of conclusion familiar in the Homeric Hymns—a personal prayer requesting favor and protection for his friends, himself, and his song, followed by a list of agreeable subjects for future hymns to the same divinity (136–141).[26] Instead of concluding, however (the hymn is only a little more than half over), Callimachus manages a transition "in a surprising way," as Wilamowitz observes,[27] to a new narrative section on Artemis's entry into Olympus (142–169). The transition is almost Ovidian in the unpredictability of its goal and the tenuousness of its connective link. While listing Artemis's dogs and bow as subjects presumably for some later song, he mentions the chariot by which she is conveyed to Olympus:

ἐν δὲ κύνες καὶ τόξα καὶ ἄντυγες, αἵ τε σε ῥεῖα
θηητὴν φορέουσιν ὅτ' ἐς Διὸς οἶκον ἐλαύνεις.
(H. 3.140–141)

In that song shall be your dogs, bow, and chariot, which easily carries you, a wondrous sight, whenever you drive to Zeus's house.

Mention of this journey is enough to set off an extended description of Artemis's reception at Olympus, and the hymn takes another unexpected turn. "He who had believed," writes Herter, "that with the conclusion-formula of the old poets Callimachus also wished to end his hymn, sees himself once again deceived."[28]

"Without a connection there follows a section which is calculated to put the reader nearly at an utter loss"—so writes Wilamowitz of the section (H. 3.170–182) that follows Artemis's arrival among the other divinities.[29] Now Callimachus's exploitation of narrative surprise reaches still further extremes. The section begins most traditionally; its subject matter appears to be Artemis as leader of the dance: ἡνίκα δ' αἱ νύμφαι σε χορῷ ἔνι κυκλώσονται, "at the time when the nymphs will encircle you in the dance" (H. 3.170). This opening recalls the Homeric Hymn to Artemis (Hymn. Hom. 27), which contains a simple narrative of the goddess returning from the hunt to lead the Muses and Graces in choral dances. After so beginning his sentence, Callimachus keeps his readers wondering through five lines what the main clause will be, as he lists possible locations for the dance—a traditional feature, but exploited for a

---

[26] For parallels in the Homeric Hymns, see Bornmann 1968, 68, on H. 3.137–141.
[27] Wilamowitz 1924, 2:56.
[28] Herter 1929, 99–100.
[29] Wilamowitz 1924, 2:57.

new purpose: he uses the list to delay, and thereby heighten the effect of, a surprising development. The main clause turns out not to continue the expected narration about Artemis:

μὴ νειὸν τημοῦτος ἐμαὶ βόες εἵνεκα μισθοῦ
τετράγυον τέμνοιεν ὑπ' ἀλλοτρίῳ ἀροτῆρι.
(H. 3.175–176)

> At that time let my oxen not plough a four-acre field for hire under someone else's ploughman.

One may assume for the moment a pious reason for this abrupt request, since interruption of work during Artemis's dances can be thought of as in her honor. The actual explanation comes from a completely different sphere of human activity, commercial investment! The poet's oxen would return lame and sprung-necked from extra hours of work (177–180); the days are longer then, he explains, because the sun stops to watch Artemis's dances (180–182). This burlesque explanation of the prayer in terms of prudential concerns about the renting of livestock causes the serious pretensions of this passage to collapse.[30] Again Callimachus has derived humor from his adopted genre by introducing a strikingly inappropriate feature into it.

These examples are enough to suggest how the Hymn to Artemis offered Ovid narrative characteristics to develop and adapt. In the rest of the hymn there is little narrative (another unforeseeable change); instead, Callimachus shifts to a kind of catalogue-poetry familiar from Homer and the Homeric Hymns, but full of surprises that link this section stylistically with the preceding narrative sections.[31] For our purposes, let it suffice to note that at the end, Callimachus chooses to illustrate the terrible vengeance of Artemis against those who offend her (251–258). Because this is a side of Artemis that the poet has earlier kept in the background, one can observe that the hymn's conclusion makes an extreme contrast to the engaging scenes from childhood that opened it.

Elegiac Contributions: Propertius's Tarpeia and Ovid's Scylla

Propertius's narrative elegies offer Ovid a parallel opportunity for allusive exploitation, for the Roman elegist endows his narratives with formal imbalance and distortion no less striking and memorable than what we

---

[30] See Bornmann 1968, 83, on *H*. 3.175–182; and especially Bing 1984. Herter (1929, 104) concludes of this passage, "That is an entirely unexpected way to perform the task of portraying Artemis as leader of the dance."

[31] "He ostensibly puts questions to the goddess: which city, which mountain, is your favorite.... In reality, he puts them to the listeners, who may guess and then be astonished, when they get an answer that no one hit upon" (Wilamowitz 1924, 2:58).

observed in Callimachus. In maintaining that narrative patterns are part of the allusive power of Ovid's text, I examine connections between elegy and the *Metamorphoses* beyond those usually observed. The work of writers, such as H. Tränkle, who trace elegiac elements in the *Metamorphoses* suggests that amatory themes, treated with stylistic refinement and psychological insight, are Ovid's most important debt to his elegiac predecessors.[32] My discussion will show, drawing upon Propertius's elegy on Tarpeia (4.4) and Ovid's use of it for the story of Scylla in Book 8, that Ovid drew upon Propertius for many of the same narrative features that he alludes to in Callimachus. Ovid did not simply use Tarpeia as a source for his Scylla.[33] His allusions to Propertius's elegy establish many connections in the reader's mind, among them the ethical theme of self-deception, which we earlier touched on with Byblis. Most notably for my purposes, the narrative indirection of Scylla's tale is itself allusive, recalling the dizzying and unstable narrative patterns of Propertius's elegy, and integrating our recollection of that experience with our reading of Ovid's tale.

The elegy recounts the legend of Tarpeia, a Vestal Virgin who, during the siege of the Capitoline hill by the Sabine king Titus Tatius, fell in love with the enemy commander and betrayed the citadel to him expecting to become his consort as a reward; he had her killed instead, and her name became associated with the hill (*mons Tarpeius*). The most conspicuous narrative feature of this elegy is the concentration of all action in its plot to a few lines: except for a brief passage in which Tarpeia, going to fetch water, catches sight of Tatius on the plain and falls in love (15–23), the principal events of the story happen very quickly in eleven lines near the end (81–91). Most of the poem is taken up with scene description and background information, often formally introduced—*lucus erat*, "There was a grove" (3); *urbi festus erat*, "The city was having a festival" (73)—and with Tarpeia's long speech (31–66), which occupies over a third of the poem. Propertius accentuates the resulting imbalance of narrative elements by reducing the climax of the story to extremely condensed summary, with frequent use of asyndeton and ellipsis:

> hoc Tarpeia suum tempus rata convenit hostem:
> pacta ligat, pactis ipsa futura comes.
> (Prop. 4.4.81–82)

> Judging that this was her time, Tarpeia met the enemy. She made her bargain, according to which she herself would be his companion.

---

[32] See Tränkle 1963. The comparisons between elegy and the *Metamorphoses* made by Knox (1986, esp. 9–26 and 48–64) also include similarities in diction and meter.

[33] For sources and parallels, see Hollis 1970, 34–35; Forbes Irving 1990, 226–228.

Even within the eleven lines that resolve the plot, Propertius has plenty of space for setting scenes, since he so abbreviates the actions that occur within them:

> mons erat ascensu dubius festoque remissus:
> nec mora, vocalis occupat ense canis.
> (Prop. 4.4.83–84)

> The hill was difficult of ascent, and unguarded because of the festival. Without delay he killed the loud watchdogs with his sword.

He even includes a digression, recording the amusing fact that Jupiter decided to stay awake that night in order to see his vengeance upon Tarpeia carried out (85–86). Her actual betrayal of the citadel, though announced at the beginning as a principal subject of the poem—*fabor et antiqui limina capta Iovi*, "And I shall tell of the captured threshold of ancient Jupiter" (2)—receives but one line of concise summary; the plot moves swiftly on to her demand for the reward:

> prodiderat portaeque fidem patriamque iacentem,
> nubendique petit, quem velit, ipsa diem.
> (Prop. 4.4.87–88)

> She had betrayed the security of the gate and her country, now defeated; and she asked the date of marriage that she chose herself.

However familiar the basic story may have been to Propertius's audience, his quick-shifting and elliptical narrative style allows him to introduce Tarpeia's death as an abrupt surprise, immediately after Tatius has misleadingly agreed to comply with their pact:

> at Tatius (neque enim sceleri dedit hostis honorem)
> "nube" ait "et regni scande cubile mei!"
> dixit, et ingestis comitum super obruit armis.
> (Prop. 4.4.89–91)

> But Tatius (for not even the enemy honored the crime) said, "Yes, marry, and mount my kingdom's bed!" He spoke, and crushed her beneath his comrades' piled weapons.

Both Propertius's narrative technique in this poem and his aetiological theme offer notable parallels to those of Callimachus. Distortion of scale, abrupt transition, ellipsis, cultivation of surprise—these features, as we have seen, are prominent in his style. We also observe in the elegy on Tarpeia a narrative irony already noted in Callimachus and Ovid, deliberate deception of the audience. At the beginning of the poem Propertius explicitly announces its subject matter:

> Tarpeium nemus et Tarpeiae turpe sepulchrum
> fabor et antiqui limina capta Iovis.
> (Prop. 4.4.1–2)
>
> I shall tell of the Tarpeian grove, Tarpeia's foul sepulcher, and the captured threshold of ancient Jupiter.

Of these three topics, only the last, Tatius's capture of the Capitoline, does Propertius actually discuss, and then only briefly, by the indirect means described above. A grove, introduced in the third line, receives some descriptive details (3–6) and seems to pick up the first topic, but whether this is the grove to be named after Tarpeia remains unexplained. As for "Tarpeia's foul sepulcher," it is never mentioned again. Only by hindsight may one infer a connection between these announced topics and the subsequent narrative—Propertius's audience may well have known of Tarpeia's tomb, and possibly also of her grove, though we have no other references to the latter.[34] In any case, the misleading introduction of *nemus* and *sepulchrum*, an especially audacious example of narrative red-herring, is consistent with the highly elliptical style of the work throughout.

Just so in 4.9, an aetiological elegy on the founding of the Ara Maxima, Propertius initially tricks his audience into supposing that the work concerns the familiar legend of Hercules' encounter with the cattle-stealing monster, Cacus. Propertius formally introduces both characters—*Amphitryoniades*, "Amphitryon's son" (1); *incola Cacus erat*, "Inhabiting the place was Cacus" (9)—and carefully sets the scene by identifying the time (1–4) and place (5–6) of this exciting adventure. Then suddenly the story vanishes in summary (11–16), and this elegy turns out to con-

---

[34] According to Varro and Plutarch, the Capitoline was called *Tarpeius* because Tarpeia was buried there: *hic mons dictus a virgine Vestali Tarpeia quae ibi ab Sabinis necata armis et sepulta*, "This hill received its name from the Vestal virgin Tarpeia, who was killed there by the Sabines' arms, and buried" (*Lingua Latina* 5.41); τῆς μέντοι Ταρπηίας ἐκεῖ ταφείσης ὁ λόφος ὠνομάζετο Ταρπήιος, "Yet the hill was called *Tarpeius* because Tarpeia was buried there" (*Romulus* 18.1). Hence Propertius's readers, aware of this tradition, could infer a connection between *Tarpeiae sepulchrum* (1) and line 93, *a duce Tarpeia mons est cognomen adeptus*, "From Tarpeia, the guide, the hill acquired its name." It is a mistake to assume, as does W. A. Camps (1965, 87), that because Tarpeia's tomb had been removed by Tarquinius Priscus (as Plutarch goes on to report), it could not be the subject of an aetiological work. Callimachus's *Aetia* contains accounts of the origin of rituals and practices that had been long abolished (see Diegesis 3.10–11 on frr. 91–92 Pf., *Melicertes*; Diegesis 4.12–14 on frr. 98–99 Pf., *Euthymus*), and indeed, his *Sepulchrum Simonidis* (fr. 64 Pf.) represents Simonides' shade speaking of the demolition of his tomb. Camps's strained translation of *sepulchrum* as "death," like his acceptance of Kraffert's *scelus* for *nemus*, is unnecessary if we acknowledge that Propertius aims to mislead his audience in announcing Tarpeia's grove and tomb as topics of the poem.

cern another, lesser-known exploit of Hercules, which took place after his encounter with Cacus. Hercules asks for water at the shrine of the Bona Dea; the priestess refuses him, because the shrine is forbidden to men; he breaks down its doors and satisfies his thirst, then declares that the altar that he just established shall always be forbidden to women. The deceptive opening of this work, its disproportionately brief narration of events (as when Hercules assaults the shrine, 61–62), its aetiological subject matter (particularly its account of the origin of a ritual feature that still persists), its half-serious, half-jocular tone—all recall Callimachus.[35]

Propertius's elegy on Tarpeia anticipates the style of the *Metamorphoses* in another important respect. In adopting Callimachus's narrative condensation, ellipsis, cultivation of surprise, and so on, Propertius gave these features the stamp of his own genius; his expansion of the heroine's speech to become the dominant element of the story is a refinement of Callimachean narrative patterns. Ovid's story of Scylla in Book 8, as has long been known, is partly modeled on Propertius 4.4.[36] That Propertius's Tarpeia occurred to Ovid in this context is no surprise, since Propertius probably drew on the legend of Scylla, or other heroines like her, to form his version of Tarpeia.[37] In Livy's account, which evidently represents the earlier version of the legend, Tarpeia betrays the citadel because of her desire for the gold bracelets worn by the Sabines (Livy 1.11.6); in Propertius's account, as in the legend of Scylla, the motive is love for the enemy commander. Ovid's source for the story of Scylla is unknown, but he probably derived from it little more than the incidents of the plot. To organize his narrative, he took over the basic structure of Propertius's elegy on Tarpeia, adapting it to a larger scale. Ovid begins with much background information, including a formal description of place (*Met.* 8.14: *regia turris erat*, "There was a royal tower"), similar to the briefer opening of Propertius's elegy.[38] Next, as in Propertius, the heroine falls in love, sighting the enemy commander at a distance as she looks out from

---

[35] Specific allusion to Callimachus is also a feature of Propertius 4.9: *magno Tiresias aspexit Pallada vates*, "At great cost did the prophet Tiresias look upon Pallas" (57), alludes to the principal subject of Hymn 5; the author's appeal to Sancus for blessing upon his book (72) recalls the similar appeal to the Graces in *Aetia* 1 (fr. 7.13–14 Pf.), a passage imitated also by Ovid (*Fasti* 5.377–378), similarly at the end of a story. On the complexities of tone in Prop. 4.9, see Anderson 1964; Pillinger 1969, 182–189.

[36] See Zingerle 1869–1871, 1:124; H-E on *Met.* 8.1–151, 14ff., 44.

[37] For the other parallels, see Bömer 4:12–14; Hollis 1970, 34–35. Propertius's account of Tarpeia is probably largely his own innovation. Love is the motive also in Simylus (Plut. *Romulus* 17.6), but this version must have been rather different, since Tarpeia betrays Rome to the Gauls, not the Sabines. See Butler and Barber 1933, 343–344; Ogilvie 1970, 74–75.

[38] See H-E on *Met.* 8.14ff.

the walls of the city. Here Ovid expands upon the situation, briefly sketched in Propertius:

> vidit harenosis Tatium proludere campis
>   pictaque per flavas arma levare iubas:
> obstipuit regis facie et regalibus armis,
>   interque oblitas excidit urna manus.
>   (Prop. 4.4.19–22)

She saw Tatius training on the sandy plain, lifting his colorful weapons among the tawny manes. She was astonished at the king's face and royal weapons, and the urn slipped between her forgetful hands.

Ovid adds many details (*Met.* 8.23–37); he represents Scylla admiring Minos in various gear, now throwing his javelin, now shooting his bow; but for the climax of this description, Ovid chooses to expand upon exactly what Propertius identified as the important visual stimuli to desperate passion, *facies et regalia arma*:

> cum vero faciem dempto nudaverat aere
> purpureusque albi stratis insignia pictis
> terga premebat equi spumantiaque ora regebat,
> vix sua, vix sanae virgo Niseia compos
> mentis erat.
>   (*Met.* 8.32–36)

But when, removing his helmet, he bared his face, and all in purple pressed the back of his white horse, conspicuous in its embroidered trappings—then Nisus's daughter was scarcely in control of herself, scarcely in her right mind.

Each heroine now sits down, gazing out at the tents of the enemy camp (*praetoria*, Prop. 4.4.31; *tentoria*, *Met.* 8.43), to deliver her soliloquy. Ovid derives much from the form and content of Tarpeia's speech in Propertius. The speeches are similarly introduced (Prop. 4.4.29–30; *Met.* 8.42–43). Tarpeia's wish to sit as a captive at Tatius's hearth suggested to Ovid the more extreme impulses of Scylla's fantasy:

> o utinam ad vestros sedeam captiva Penatis,
>   dum captiva mei conspicer ora Tati!
>   (Prop. 4.4.33–34)

Would that I could sit a captive at your hearth, so long as I could, as a captive, gaze at Tatius's face!

> o ego ter felix, si pennis lapsa per auras
> Gnosiaci possem castris insistere regis
> fassaque me flammasque meas.
> (*Met.* 8.51–53)

Three times happy would I be, if, gliding on wings through the air, I could stand in the camp of the Cretan king, and confess myself and my flame.

Each heroine addresses much of her speech to her imagined lover, as if he were present to hear and—by a further extension of the fantasy—to approve of her words. This formal feature of the speeches contributes to the exposition of character, since both Propertius and Ovid portray their heroines as wholly self-preoccupied and blind to the realities of their situation, exploiting the power of language for self-deception. Each justifies betrayal of her country on the grounds that it will end the war (Prop. 4.4.59–62; *Met.* 8.56–63, 68); each describes her country as the dowry she brings to her husband (Prop. 4.4.56; *Met.* 8.68). That Ovid establishes these parallels is especially apt, since Tarpeia actually mentions Scylla as a precedent for herself (following a version of the legend in which this Scylla is combined with the sea monster of the same name):

> quid mirum in patrios Scyllam saevisse capillos,
> candidaque in saevos inguina versa canis?
> (Prop. 4.4.39–40)

Is it surprising that Scylla committed outrage against her father's lock, and her white loins were turned to savage dogs?

It is an ingenious irony—and an acute insight into human character—that Propertius has Tarpeia mention Scylla's punishment for her crime without the slightest recognition that she also might come to a bad end. To Tarpeia's mind, the parallel shows only the power of love to alter one's ordinary loyalties and make any sacrifice acceptable, while to Propertius's audience, it can offer a foreshadowing of Tarpeia's own ruin.

The character of the two speeches differs in an important respect. In Propertius's elegy, Tarpeia's resolve to betray the Roman citadel is evidently fixed when she begins her soliloquy; Ovid represents Scylla arriving at the decision to betray Megara during the course of hers. Consistent with his purpose, Ovid gives Scylla a more highly rhetorical style: hers is at first a deliberative speech expressed in formal alternatives:

> "laeter" ait "doleamne geri lacrimabile bellum
> in dubio est: doleo, quod Minos hostis amanti est;
> sed nisi bella forent, numquam mihi cognitus esset."
> (*Met.* 8.44–46)

> It is in doubt whether I should rejoice or grieve that tearful war is being waged. I grieve, because Minos is an enemy to his lover; but unless war had arisen, he would never have been known to me.

For a time she is willing to accede to any demand Minos might make of her except betrayal of the citadel, and thus incidentally reveals that her thought is already turning in that direction. She no sooner states this resolve than she offers an objection:

> nam pereant potius sperata cubilia, quam sim
> proditione potens! quamvis saepe utile vinci
> victoris placidi fecit clementia multis.
> *(Met.* 8.55–57)

> Let the marriage I hope for perish, rather than that I attain my goal by betrayal!—although the clemency of a mild victor has often made defeat advantageous to many.

Feeble as this objection may be, Scylla props it with another, then another, and so on, until from the sheer number of weak but unresisted arguments she comes to a resolution: *coepta placent, et stat sententia tradere mecum / dotalem patriam,* "I like what I have begun, and my resolve stands firm to hand over my country, as a dowry, along with myself" (*Met.* 8.67–68). In the rest of the speech she steels herself for action by various self-gratifying justifications, no longer questioning whether she ought to pursue her desire. As is usual with Ovid, it is when his text is the most elaborately rhetorical and "artificial" that it is the most powerfully convincing as a reflection of human character and experience.

Scylla's two long soliloquies (*Met.* 8.44–80, 108–142) dominate the story as Tarpeia's soliloquy does in Propertius. The principal actions, squeezed in between speeches, occur at breathtaking speed in a condensed style reminiscent of Propertius's elegy and Callimachean narrative:

> thalamos taciturna paternos
> intrat et (heu facinus!) fatali nata parentem
> crine suum spoliat praedaque potita nefanda
> fert secum spolium sceleris progressaque porta
> per medios hostes (meriti fiducia tanta est)
> pervenit ad regem; quem sic adfata paventem est.
> *(Met.* 8.84–89)

> Silently she enters her father's bedchamber and (what a crime!) the daughter robs her father of the fatal lock; now in control of the unspeakable prize, she carries the spoil of crime with her; and passing beyond the gate through the middle of the enemy (so great is her trust in her merit) she reaches the king. He is struck with dread as she addresses him thus.

These lines, packed full of events as they are, abound in small variations of expression and are enriched with descriptive adjectives and parenthetical interruptions. Ovid takes pains to make them neither bare nor overly regular; at the same time he moves the story along as quickly as possible, keeping the clauses extremely short and allowing no pauses to relieve the breathless reader, until suddenly all action freezes again in another speech. He maintains the same style to narrate Scylla's presentation of the lock and Minos's horrified reaction (*Met.* 8.94–96). Minos vanishes from the scene in lines that do not even mention the fall of Megara (*Met.* 8.101–103). Likewise omitted is any reference to Nisus's fate, though one may well have expected some mention of it at this point. Instead Ovid remains true to his indirect and elliptical narrative principles: near the end of the story, just before Scylla's transformation into a sea bird (Ciris), he suddenly interjects, as if by afterthought, a parenthetical reference to Nisus, now transformed into a sea eagle:

> quam [i.e., Scyllam] pater ut vidit (nam iam pendebat in aura
> et modo factus erat fulvis haliaeetus alis),
> ibat, ut haerentem rostro laceraret adunco.
>   (*Met.* 8.145–147)

> When her father saw her (for he already hung in the air, and had lately been
> made a sea eagle with tawny wings), he went to tear her with his hooked
>   beak, as she clung there.

The suddenness of Nisus's appearance as an active participant in the story is appropriate to the introduction of violence—only contemplated in this case, not performed, since Scylla's timely metamorphosis presumably enables her to flee.

Because the narrative style of this story is so strongly reminiscent of Propertius's elegy on Tarpeia, it is important to emphasize how completely Ovid has absorbed the influence of his predecessors into the general stylistic patterns of the *Metamorphoses*. Scylla's story shares elements with others in the work, such as that of Byblis in Book 9, which seem influenced by elegy; so Tränkle characterizes the story of Byblis, mentioning the elliptical nature of its narrative and its concentration on the heroine's passionate soliloquies.[39] Yet such disproportionate development of narrative elements, and consequent distortion of scale, occur everywhere in the *Metamorphoses*, whether or not there is any direct allusion to elegy or reflection of elegiac topics and conventions. Indeed, it is a mistake often made to identify one section of the *Metamorphoses* as "elegiac," another as "epic," another as "comic," another as "tragic," as if Ovid put

---

[39] Tränkle 1963, 460–465.

together a pastiche of genres.[40] Actually, elements of all these genres, and others as well, are as likely as not to appear together in any given story. Ovid's portrayal of Scylla is parallel to that of Byblis, but it is also parallel to that of other heroines in crisis, such as Medea in Book 7 and Althaea later in Book 8. They similarly have critical decisions to make and deliver long speeches at the moment of crisis; but they have no immediate association with the elegiac tradition, and Ovid invites the reader primarily to recall epic and tragic antecedents to their stories. Indeed, in this story Ovid gives Scylla a second soliloquy, after she has stolen the lock, betrayed her city, and met with Minos's rejection (*Met.* 8.108–142). This soliloquy, as subtle and brilliant as the first, is enriched no longer with the parallel to Tarpeia, but with conspicuous allusion to Vergil's Dido, Catullus's Ariadne, and Euripides' Medea.[41]

The parallel to Byblis especially invites us to reflect on the close connections between narrative structure and the significant features of the stylistic surface that we earlier discussed in Byblis's story. Scylla's is another story of self-deception that issues in metamorphosis. In her story as in Byblis's, self-deception is related to metamorphosis in that language—specifically argumentative language addressed to the self—becomes more compelling and more real than the actual circumstances faced by the heroine. There is a link between language and desire in Ovidian narrative structures just as there is in witticism, whose potential for semantic slippage facilitates the generation of fantasy. The intersection of genres in

---

[40] For example, Otis (1970) classifies the early stories of the work as a "divine comedy," and Segal (1978) praises the story of Cephalus and Procris as "tragic."

[41] *Met.* 8.113–116 is a close adaptation of Eur. *Medea* 502–503. Ovid characteristically combines allusion to Catullus and Vergil, as when Scylla thus reproaches the absent Minos: *non genetrix Europa tibi est, sed inhospita Syrtis, / Armeniae tigres austroque agitata Charybdis,* "Europa is not your mother, but the inhospitable Syrtes, Armenian tigers, and Charybdis stirred up by the south wind" (*Met.* 8.120–121). Here Ovid alludes primarily to Catullus's Ariadne, who reproaches the absent Theseus, referring to both the Syrtis and Charybdis (this passage also, like Tarpeia's speech, contains a reference to the other Scylla): *quaenam te genuit sola sub rupe leaena, / quod mare conceptum spumantibus exspuit undis, / quae Syrtis, quae Scylla rapax, quae vasta Charybdis?* "What lioness bore you beneath a solitary cliff, what sea conceived and spit you from its foaming waters, what Syrtis, what grasping Scylla, what vast Charybdis?" (Cat. 64.154–156). Ovid derives the explicit denial of parentage (120) and the tigers as well from Dido's reproach to Aeneas: *nec tibi diva parens generis nec Dardanus auctor, / perfide, sed duris genuit te cautibus horrens / Caucasus Hyrcanaeque admorunt ubera tigres,* "A goddess was not your parent, nor Dardanus your founder, deceitful wretch, but the bristling Caucasus bore you among its hard rocks, and Hyrcanian tigers suckled you" (*Aen.* 4.365–367). It is amusing to note Ovid's subtly ironic use of the Vergilian tigers: Scylla can take the Syrtis and Charybdis in order from Catullus, but it would be injudicious for her mention *Scylla rapax,* even if she could insist on the distinction, so often blurred, between the two Scyllas. Dido's tigers, drawn from the secondary allusion, conveniently fill the gap left by removal of *Scylla rapax.*

Scylla's story, and the multiplication of allusive parallels within it, also contribute to the stylistic embodiment of transformation. Ovid gathers a vast number of mythological tales—and quite a few tales of Roman history—along with the numerous genres in which these tales were known, and makes all these tales and genres tell his story, subsuming them into his own account of transformation and flux. So also, in the cases of Callimachus and Propertius at least, he took over their styles—whose fluid indirection already made them well suited to the representation of flux—and made them transformative.

Epic Distortions: The *Hecale* in the *Metamorphoses*

Propertius, after identifying himself as *Callimachus Romanus* in the introductory poem to Book 4, adapts Callimachus's aetiological mode to his own purposes in the five elegies on Roman subjects (4.2, 4, 6, 9, 10). He seems specifically to have modeled his work on the third and fourth books of the *Aetia*, which comprise separate stories unlinked by the dialogue frame of the first two books.[42] As we have seen, Ovid takes the opportunity to allude to narrative modes of this type in the *Metamorphoses* and to adapt their characteristic distortions of narrative, interweaving allusion to other works and genres as well. Even more than the *Aetia*, the *Hecale* has a stylistic affinity with the *Metamorphoses*. In it Callimachus's innovations in narrative form are at their most extreme, and the field for these innovations, as so often for Ovid's, is the epic genre. For the *Aetia* Callimachus created an essentially new genre (which Ovid found adaptable for his *Fasti*); but for the *Hecale* he wrenched an old one, producing a remarkably extreme distortion of Homeric narrative and pointing the way for Ovid's exploitation of the Latin epic tradition.[43]

Since so much of the work is lost, many details of its narrative development remain unclear. But we can be sure enough of the general progression of events to observe that Callimachus developed and expanded the oddest and most unexpected features of a manifestly traditional heroic story. Theseus, conceived along the lines of Herakles as a destroyer of monsters, tames the bull of Marathon and returns in triumph. This noble exploit provides the outline of the story, which is clearly set out in the extant prose summary:

> Theseus, after escaping Medea's plot, was kept under close watch by his father Aegeus, since the lad had been suddenly restored from Troezen to his father, who had not expected him. Theseus wished to go out against the bull

---

[42] See Pfeiffer 2:xxxv: "In general, Ovid in the *Fasti* appears to have followed the example of *Aetia* 1 and 2, Propertius in the fourth book of elegies the example of books 3 and 4."

[43] On Ovid's use of the *Hecale* in general, see Hollis 1990, 33–34.

that was devastating the area around Marathon, in order to subdue it; prevented from doing so, he left the house secretly, departing at evening. When a rainstorm unexpectedly broke out, he spied on the outskirts the little house of an old woman, Hecale, and there he was received as a guest. Toward dawn he arose, set out for the place, subdued the bull, and returned to Hecale. He unexpectedly found her dead, and groaning that he had been deceived of his expectation, fulfilled what he had promised to do for her after her death as repayment for her hospitality, establishing a deme which he named after her, and setting up a sanctuary of Zeus Hecaleius.[44] (*Diegesis* 10.20–11.7)

Even this brief summary shows an emphasis on unexpected developments in the narrative: the word αἰφνίδιον, "unexpectedly," occurs three times, and there is specific mention of Theseus's arrival as contrary to Aegeus's expectation, and Hecale's death as contrary to Theseus's.[45]

The extant fragments show the author confronting his readers with more surprising twists and turns than even the characters of the plot must handle. He places a dramatic recognition scene at the *beginning* of the story, such as would normally occur near the end of a Euripidean plot. Callimachus may indeed have drawn on Euripides' *Aegeus* for this scene,[46] and in any case it would remind Callimachus's audience of the narrowly averted disasters familiar in Euripides' plays. The events are probably to be reconstructed thus: Theseus is about to drink the poisoned cup provided by Medea, when his father, suddenly recognizing him by birth tokens (a sword and a pair of sandals, fr. 235 Pf., 9 Hollis), strikes the cup from Theseus's lips with the words ἴσχε τέκος, μὴ πίθι, "Stop, my child, do not drink" (fr. 233 Pf., 7 Hollis).

Once the story of Theseus and the bull of Marathon actually begins, the hero's exploit is delayed by the description of his visit to Hecale's hut and his hospitable reception there, which Callimachus evidently expanded to considerable length. It included a *cena rustica*, a "rustic dinner," which became a famous and frequently imitated part of the work, and much conversation between Theseus and Hecale. Theseus, explaining to Hecale the reason for his expedition, evidently questions her about herself and her family (*SH* 285, fr. 40–42 Hollis); she responds with an account of her misfortunes and the death of her near relations. The fragments suggest that one or more of her sons died at the hands of the

---

[44] Pfeiffer 1:227.

[45] See fr. 234 Pf., 8 Hollis: παρὲκ νόον εἰλήλουθας, "You have come contrary to expectation," referred to Aegeus, addressing Theseus in the recognition scene.

[46] See Pfeiffer 1:227: "Most scholars have conjectured that this form of the story goes back to Euripides' *Aegeus*, perhaps rightly; in any event, the tragic poet should have put off the recognition until the end of the play." See also Hollis 1990, 139–140.

bandit Cercyon; Theseus then informs her that he himself earlier killed Cercyon, and other bandits and monsters as well, en route from Troezen to Athens (*SH* 287, fr. 48–49 Hollis). Thus one may be able to perceive a thematic link between this inset narrative and Theseus's upcoming exploit. Yet there can be little doubt that Callimachus placed the greatest emphasis upon the *cena* and Hecale's woeful experiences, reducing the heroic story almost to a framing device or link between episodes.

A comparable distortion of narrative emphasis occurs after Theseus subdues the bull. He returns dragging it along, while the populace rejoices; but the text that describes this event soon becomes a lengthy discourse by a crow to another bird on the afflictions meted out to the bearers of bad news (*SH* 288, 289; fr. 69–74 Hollis).[47] The transition between Theseus's triumph and the crow's oration is unfortunately lost; the interlocutor may be Athena's owl or a younger and less experienced crow; the speaker may be warning her interlocutor against bringing news to Theseus of Hecale's death.[48] Whatever may have linked the crow's discourse to Theseus's triumph, it is clear that the discourse itself dominates this part of the work, pushing Theseus into the background. The discursive crow preoccupies the attention of Callimachus's audience, as well as that of her own interlocutor, with narrative exempla. One of these, the last to be told, concerns events that have yet to occur: the raven, now white, will be turned to black for reporting to Apollo the infidelity of his mistress, Coronis (*SH* 288 [fr. 260 Pf.] 55–61; fr. 74.14–20 Hollis). The longest exemplum is on a subject obviously close to the speaker's heart: crows are denied access to the Athenian acropolis because a crow reported to Athena that the daughters of Cecrops had— contrary to Athena's express command—looked into the box entrusted to them; it contained the baby Erichthonius. During this account, the crow pursues all the ins and outs of her story, including the irregular birth of Erichthonius and the punishment of one of the daughters, Pandrosus, by petrification.

A work so full of indirection and surprise, its narrative progress and tone constantly shifting as tale succeeds tale in unpredictable complexity, its high epic style often strangely at odds with homely subjects and the discourse of garrulous fowl, could not fail to appeal to Ovid. Callimachus's treatment of Theseus and his exploit indeed suggests Ovid's parallel but more extreme treatment of the same hero: Ovid dispatches Theseus to the Calydonian boar hunt (*Met.* 8.303), but principally employs him to link a series of tales only tangentially associated with him (*Met.* 8.547–9.97). Returning from Calydon to Athens, Theseus must

---

[47] See Keith 1992, 9–17.
[48] See Hollis 1990, 224–225 and references; Keith 1992, 16.

halt at the Achelous in flood; accepting the river-god's hospitality, he and his companions recline at the table; their table talk gives rise to the stories of the Echinades, Baucis and Philemon, Proteus, Erysichthon, and Achelous and Hercules. After that, Theseus quickly vanishes from the *Metamorphoses* (*Met.* 9.93–97). Ovid develops Callimachean narrative technique in this sequence of tales by reducing the hero's importance still further than did Callimachus, so that Ovid's reader is likely to lose track of Theseus altogether while enmeshed in the various stories. Appropriate to his reduced role in the narrative is the diminution of his heroism. Callimachus probably granted Theseus a scene of effective valor in his encounter with the bull (frr. 258, 259, 260.1–15 Pf.; frr. 67, 68, 69.1–15 Hollis), just as Apollonius grants one such scene to Jason; but Ovid's Theseus is wholly ineffectual as a warrior, cast in the role of fretful lover even in the midst of the fight: "The great Theseus," writes Anderson, "makes a passionate speech against *virtus*—it is dangerous!—to his beloved Pirithous (405–407), then throws his spear impressively, only to watch it futilely hit a branch (408–10)."[49]

Ovid invites his reader to recall Callimachus's Theseus in the context of his own portrayal, since at the hero's first introduction in Book 7, Ovid summarizes the recognition scene that occurs near the beginning of the *Hecale*. Medea contrives to have Aegeus unwittingly hand his own son a poisoned cup:

> sumpserat ignara Theseus data pocula dextra,
> cum pater in capulo gladii cognovit eburno
> signa sui generis facinusque excussit ab ore.
> (*Met.* 7.421–423)

> Theseus had taken the proffered cup in his unknowing hand, when his father recognized, on the sword's ivory hilt, the tokens of his own family, and dashed the cup of crime from his mouth.

Just afterward, at Aegeus's celebration for the recovery of his son, the populace sings in praise of Theseus (*Met.* 7.433–450), listing bandits and monstrous evildoers killed by the young hero. Here also Ovid adapts the *Hecale*, taking the examples from what was probably Theseus's speech to Hecale in response to her account of Cercyon and the death of her sons.[50] For good measure, Ovid adds the bull of Marathon to the beginning of the list:

---

[49] Anderson 1972, 357–358.

[50] For the relation of the Hecale to *Met.* 7.433–450, see Bömer 3:301, with bibliography.

> te, maxime Theseu,
> mirata est Marathon Cretaei sanguine tauri.
> (*Met.* 7.433–434)

Marathon marveled at you, great Theseus, for the blood of the Cretan bull.

This conspicuous reference to the subject matter of the *Hecale*, together with the preceding recognition scene, establishes the shadowy and intermittent presence of Theseus in the *Metamorphoses*, a purposeful extenuation of his role in Callimachus's little epic.[51]

Ovid's most important and interesting use of the *Hecale* occurs in the last half of Book 2, the tale of the crow and the following sequence, a crucial point in Ovid's manipulation of the audience (*Met.* 2.531–875).[52] He has made the narrative progress of his first book relatively easy to follow: the creation and the four ages occur chronologically; the last age gives rise to the council of gods and the flood that directly results from their consideration of human behavior; the story of Deucalion is naturally part of the flood. Of course, this part of the work is not devoid of surprises:[53] the story of Lycaon, for example, seems on the verge of being told at *Met.* 1.163–167, when we learn that Jupiter is angered by Lycaon's "foul dinner-party":

> facto nondum vulgata recenti
> foeda Lycaoniae referens convivia mensae
> ingentes animo et dignas Iove concipit iras.
> (*Met.* 1.164–166)

Recalling the foul dinner-party at Lycaon's table, which was not yet widely known because the deed was recent, he conceived great anger, worthy of Jupiter, in his heart.

But straightaway Ovid proceeds to the council of gods, delaying for many lines the story of Lycaon (who, as it turns out, served human flesh to his divine guest) until after Jupiter's reaction has been told (*Met.* 1.211–239). Such inversion shows the sequential clarity of Book 1 to be

---

[51] We do not know the context in the Hecale of fr. 298 Pf., which Ovid adapts, just after the song in praise of Theseus, as part of a transition to the stories of Minos and Cephalus: ἐπεὶ θεὸς οὐδέ γελάσσαι / ἀκλαυτὶ μερόπεσσιν διζυοῖσιν ἔδωκεν, "Since the gods did not give laughter to wretched mortals without tears" (fr. 298 Pf., 115 Hollis); *nec tamen (usque adeo nulla est sincera voluptas, / sollicitumque aliquid laetis intervenit) Aegeus / gaudia percepit nato secura recepto: / bella parat Minos*, "And yet (for no pleasure at all is unmixed, but some trouble comes between happy events) Aegeus took carefree joy in the recovery of his son: Minos was preparing war" (*Met.* 7.453–456).

[52] This sequence is now the subject of a full-scale study by Keith (1992).

[53] Anderson (1989) treats its representation of divine justice as a "deceptive paradigm."

less than complete; yet Ovid maintains a predominately linear narrative through the first book and into the second: the very long tale of Phaethon (*Met.* 1.748–2.328) may well convince a reader that the *Metamorphoses* will turn out to be a transparently organized composition after all. If so, the tales of the raven and crow, and all that enters the narrative with them, must correct any such impression. This sequence, which begins as a free reworking and expansion of the crow's discourse in the *Hecale*, seems designed to establish uncertainty and flux as dominant in the reader's experience of this work.

The link between this sequence and the preceding story of Callisto is (as so often) tenuous: Juno, enraged that her husband's mistress has become a permanent fixture in the heavens as a constellation, the Septemtriones, demands of Tethys and Oceanus that they prevent it (or rather her) from ever touching the sea (*Met.* 2.530: *ne puro tingatur in aequore paelex*, "Lest a mistress be dipped in the unsullied sea"). Gaining this satisfaction, Juno rides off in her chariot, drawn by peacocks. Now we learn that peacocks only recently received their colors at the death of Argus, whose hundred eyes now adorn their tails (*Met.* 1.722–723). Just as recently the raven was changed from white to black, and so, as a result of temporal coincidence, we find that the raven is now the subject of the story:

> nam fuit haec quondam niveis argentea pennis
> ales ut aequaret totas sine labe columbas
> nec servaturis vigili Capitolia voce
> cederet anseribus nec amanti flumina cygno.
> (*Met.* 2.536–539)

> This bird was at one time silver-white with snowy wings, so it could equal doves, all spotless, and fell nothing short of geese, who were to save the Capitol with their vigilant cry, nor of swans that love the streams.

In these lines Ovid adapts the exemplum with which Callimachus's crow concludes her speech (*SH* 288 [fr. 260. Pf.] 55–61; fr. 74.14–20 Hollis), and moves a prophecy of future events into the past. Evidently the *Hecale* contained no more than these lines about Apollo's affair with Coronis, her infidelity, and his revenge. Ovid's account is scarcely much longer, but by transposing it, along with the lines on the raven's metamorphosis, to a position near the beginning of the sequence, he gives the impression that a new story is beginning with Coronis, one that promises much longer and more elaborate development than it actually provides. In a standard fashion, the tale opens with a statement of the woman's beauty and identification of the lover who will figure in the events:

> pulchrior in tota quam Larissaea Coronis
> non fuit Haemonia: placuit tibi, Delphice, certe
> dum vel casta fuit vel inobservata.
> (*Met.* 2.542–544)

There was no one more beautiful in all Thessaly than Coronis of Larissa; at least she pleased you, Apollo, as long as she was chaste, or at any rate unobserved.

For all the promise in these lines of a racy and entertaining story, it soon becomes clear that Coronis has been introduced only to be dropped as soon as the raven has subject matter for his tale-bearing. Ovid cuts the tale so short that he omits any mention of Coronis's lover, Ischys (whom Callimachus manages to include), replacing him with summary *adulterium*:

> sed ales
> sensit adulterium Phoebeius, utque latentem
> detegeret culpam, non exorabilis index
> ad dominum tendebat iter.
> (*Met.* 2.544–547)

But Phoebus's bird perceived the adultery, and this inexorable informer hastened to his master to disclose the secret misdeed.

It now appears that the raven will report his news and receive his anticipated punishment in short order. But just as this tale seems about to vanish in summary, it is interrupted by the arrival of the crow:

> quem garrula motis
> consequitur pennis, scitetur ut omnia, cornix.
> (*Met.* 2.547–548)

Whom the chattering crow, with flapping wings, pursued in order to spy out all.

Now another character has taken center stage; the crow begins a speech of advice to the raven, attempting to dissuade him from his plan. Her own punishment for tale-bearing will provide a handy exemplum, and before we know it the crow has introduced, as background to her own experience, yet another story, that of the daughters of Cecrops.

Callimachus's account of Cecrops's daughters, treated at some length in the crow's speech, serves to direct attention away from Theseus and his valorous exploit only for a time. Ovid's account, while preserving the cautionary theme that it had in the *Hecale*, is only one of the many tales that displace each other, and do so in such rapid succession that they seem deliberately designed to leave the reader lost amid ever-disintegrating narrative contexts. No reader, passing through this dizzying series of transitions, which lead only to other transitions, is likely to retain for long a sense of how he or she arrived at any intermediate stage, much less to divine with any accuracy the future progress of the narrative. As if to give his reader less opportunity to regain a sense of narrative bearings, Ovid considerably shortens the story of Cecrops's daughters, summarizing Callimachus's account and omitting many details, such as the origin of Mount Lycabettus (*SH* 289, fr. 261 Pf., 71 Hollis). He concentrates all guilt for the offense in Aglauros, intending, as will later become evident, to tell a further story about her. At this point, however, the crow seems about to recount, or at least to mention, Aglauros's punishment at the hands of Athena:

> abdita fronde levi densa speculabar ab ulmo,
> quid facerent: commissa duae sine fraude tuentur,
> Pandrosus atque Herse; timidas vocat una sorores
> Aglauros nodosque manu diducit, et intus
> infantemque vident adporrectumque draconem.
> (*Met.* 2.557–561)

Hidden in light foliage, from a leafy elm I spied out what they would do. Two kept their trust without deception, Pandrosus and Herse; Aglauros alone, calling her sisters timid, untied the knot; and within they see a baby and a snake outstretched.

Instead, the story of Cecrops's daughters is left strangely unfinished. The crow briefly explains that she reported the events to Minerva; for her pains she lost the goddess's protection and special favor, yielding her position to the owl. The moral she draws from this experience seems to mark the conclusion of her discourse to the raven:

> mea poena volucres
> admonuisse potest, ne voce pericula quaerant.
> (*Met.* 2.564–565)

My punishment can warn birds not to pursue their own danger by talking.

Indeed, her discourse has no legitimate reason for continuing, regarded from the standpoint of its potential interest to the raven, but that fact does not prevent the crow from introducing yet another story. Anticipating an objection that the goddess had not willingly preferred her in the first place, she explains how she came to be *comes Minervae*, "Minerva's companion" (*Met.* 2.588). She was once a beautiful princess, sought by wealthy suitors—this type of formal opening, already familiar here in the second book,[54] becomes grotesquely comic in the mouth of a crow:

---

[54] See *Met.* 2.542–544 just before, and *Met.* 1.478.

DISRUPTIVE TRADITIONS 161

> nam me Phocaica clarus tellure Coroneus
> (nota loquor) genuit fueramque ego regia virgo
> divitibusque procis (ne me contemne!) petebar;
> forma mihi nocuit.
> *(Met.* 2.569–572)

> Coroneus, famous in the Phocian territory, was my father (as is well known); I was a royal maiden and sought by wealthy suitors (do not scorn me). My beauty was my undoing.

When Neptune attempted to rape her, Minerva intervened for the sake of her maidenhood and changed her into the crow; she effected her escape and became Minerva's companion (*Met.* 2.572–588). With this account finished, she proceeds still further to the scandalous tale of her successor in Minerva's favor, Nyctimene, who is now an owl. With bitter malice, the crow pretends to ask the raven whether he knows the details of this story, while in fact supplying them herself:

> an quae per totam res est notissima Lesbon,
> non audita tibi est, patrium temerasse cubile
> Nyctimenen?
> *(Met.* 2.591–593)

> Or have you not heard what is well known throughout all Lesbos, that Nyctimene violated her father's bed?

Now the raven finally responds with a curse upon the crow and rejection of her advice; continuing his flight, he betrays Coronis's infidelity to Apollo (*Met.* 2.569–599). At this point we have every reason to expect the raven's metamorphosis from white to black, especially since it received so much emphasis at the beginning of the sequence. Instead, leaving the raven behind, Ovid proceeds to the love-stricken Apollo and his reaction to the news:

> laurea delapsa est audito crimine amantis,
> et pariter vultusque deo plectrumque colorque
> excidit.
> *(Met.* 2.600–602)

> When he heard this charge against his lover, the laurel slipped from his hair; at the same time the god's expression, plectrum, and color fell.

Apollo abruptly kills Coronis, and Ovid typically complicates the introduction of violence by contributing an element of transformative wit: the syllepsis, *plectrumque colorque / excidit*, is his addition. Now Apollo manages to tear their child "from the flames of the pyre and from its parent's womb" (*Met.* 2.629–630) and entrusts it to Chiron for upbringing; only then do we hear, as if by afterthought, of the raven's punishment. A new story is already under way when his fate receives scant notice:

> sperantemque sibi non falsae praemia linguae
> inter aves albas vetuit consistere corvum.
> (*Met.* 2.631–632)

> Though the raven hoped his true report would get him a reward, Apollo denied him a place among the white birds.

Ovid's sequence of tales, beginning at the introduction of the raven, is now far from over. The discussion above has taken us through only its opening gambit, which Ovid dispatches in scarcely more than a hundred lines. Even so, it is enough to show that the narrative complexities of this sequence, while taking rise from those of the *Hecale*, have proliferated far beyond anything imaginable in that work.

As Ovid proceeds to tell of Ocyroe (Chiron's daughter), her prophecies concerning Aesculapius (the child of Apollo and Coronis), and her transformation into a horse (*Met.* 2.633–675), we seem to have left Callimachus's *Hecale* far behind. The next story offers no reason to doubt this impression. It concerns Mercury's transformation of Battus into a rock (*Met.* 2.676–707), and though Battus's offense is to betray information—he had promised Mercury not to tell where Apollo's stolen cattle lay hidden, then told Mercury himself in disguise—there is little in his story to recall the fate of crow or raven. Yet as Mercury, after inflicting this capriciously severe punishment, flies off to Athens, Ovid suddenly resumes his pattern of allusion to the *Hecale*. For Mercury's arrival, Ovid adapts lines in whose original context the crow described her meeting with Athena:

> Munychiosque volans agros gratamque Minervae
> despectabat [i.e., Mercurius] humum cultique arbusta Lycei.
> (*Met.* 2.709–710)

> As he flew, he looked down on the Munychian fields, the land beloved of Minerva, and the orchards of the cultivated Lyceum.

> ἄστυρον εἰσανέβαινεν [*i. e.*, Athena], ἐγὼ δ' ἤντησα Λυκείου
> καλὸν ἀεὶ λιπόωντα κατὰ δρόμον Ἀπόλλωνος.[55]
> (Fr. 261 Pf. [71 Hollis] 2–3)

> She was arriving at the town, and I met her at the fair and ever-shining race course of Lycaean Apollo.

These lines introduce a surprising return to the daughters of Cecrops, now remote from their original context in the crow's discourse. For Mer-

---

[55] Ovid strikingly preserves Callimachus's anachronistic representation of the Lyceum as already existing in mythical times (see H-E on *Met.* 2.710).

cury aloft espies Herse (named at *Met.* 2.724) as soon as she returns in the Panathenaic procession from the acropolis. He soon conceives a predatory lust for her, and so we come to the story of his attempt to gain access to Herse's chamber, Aglauros's refusal to admit him, and the subsequent petrification of Aglauros (*Met.* 2.730–832).[56]

How Callimachus developed this tale is unknown; but Ovid's innovations in the plot certainly include interrupting the progress of events to occupy our attention with Athena's sudden re-entry into the story, and with the disproportionately long description of Invidia (*Met.* 2.760–811). These developments serve to provide a wholly unexpected conclusion to the crow's tale of Aglauros. The story of Mercury and Herse is well under way: Mercury visits the house of the three sisters; confronted by Aglauros, he asks her to facilitate his access to Herse; Aglauros refuses unless she receives a bribe. Structurally, the plot is now complete on its own terms but for Mercury's removal of Aglauros as an obstacle (whether by payment or force) and his union with Herse; its conclusion requires no reference to other events. Yet the lines that describe Aglauros's reaction to Mercury suddenly bring the earlier tale to notice again:

> adspicit hunc oculis isdem, quibus abdita nuper
> viderat Aglauros flavae secreta Minervae.
> (*Met.* 2.748–749)

> Aglauros looked at him with the same eyes with which she had lately seen the secrets of golden-haired Minerva.

When Aglauros demands the bribe, Minerva—however remote her own interests may be from Mercury's love affairs—enters the story:

---

[56] It appears likely, if one accepts A. Henrichs's re-edition (1983) of a fragment of Philodemus's *De pietate*, that Callimachus wrote of Pandrosus turned to stone. As restored, the text may be translated thus: "Callimachus ... Pandrosus also a stone, because she did not surrender her sister Herse to him." Philodemus's context is an Epicurean attack on poetical conceptions of divinity; in this passage he lists sordid love affairs that the poets attribute to the gods, contrary to the Epicurean view. Philodemus may well have drawn upon the *Hecale* for this story, and it probably occurred in the crow's discourse on the daughters of Cecrops. Ovid's plot corresponds in its barest outline to Philodemus's summary of Callimachus, except that Aglauros, whom Ovid earlier made solely responsible for disobedience to Athena, replaces her sister Pandrosus. This change allows Ovid to take a double advantage of his audience's expectations: he first leaves the story of Aglauros incomplete in the crow's narrative; then, long after there is any likelihood that we will hear of her again, he returns to Aglauros and makes her fate the subject of another story. Ovid associates both stories in his readers' minds with the *Hecale*, sometimes drawing upon it as a plot source, sometimes alluding to specific passages; yet no reader, however familiar with the *Hecale*, could gain from prior knowledge an accurate sense of how Ovid's narrative sequence will develop. Indeed, the more detailed one's recollection of Callimachus, the more false clues and mistaken impressions will complicate the experience of reading Ovid's sequence.

> vertit ad hanc torvi dea bellica luminis orbem
> et tanto penitus traxit suspiria motu,
> ut pariter pectus positamque in pectore forti
> aegida concuteret. subit, hanc arcana profana
> detexisse manu tum, cum sine matre creatam
> Lemnicolae stirpem contra data foedera vidit,
> et gratamque deo fore iam gratamque sorori
> et ditem sumpto, quod avara poposcerat, auro.
> (*Met.* 2.752–759)

The warrior-goddess turned her grim sight toward Aglauros, and sighed deeply, with such agitation that she shook both her mighty breast and the aegis placed upon it. She remembered that Aglauros it was who had disclosed her secrets with an impious hand, when, contrary to the stipulated agreement, she had looked upon Hephaestus's offspring, born without a mother; now Aglauros would please Mercury and her sister, and become rich, receiving the gold which in her greed she had demanded.

Minerva, not Mercury, proceeds to visit Invidia. The passage that follows, with its unforgettable *phantasia* of Invidia crouched over half-eaten snakes and its engrossingly detailed representation of her physical nature, causes its own context, the tale of Mercury and Herse, almost to fade from view.[57] Mercury's love for Herse, the original subject of the story, received much emphasis at the beginning, especially in the simile of the sling and the comical elaboration of Mercury's self-adornment for his tryst (*Met.* 2.726–736). This topic now completely vanishes; we hear nothing about the consummation of the affair, and Mercury re-enters the

---

[57] Though the personification of Invidia probably had no parallel in the *Hecale*, even in this passage Ovid introduces tantalizing allusions to it. When Athena departs, having ordered that Aglauros be infected with envy, Invidia feels pain at the goddess's approaching success, which she herself must cause: *illa deam obliquo fugientem lumine cernens / murmura parva dedit successurumque Minervae / indoluit baculumque capit, quod spinea totum / vincula cingebant*, "As the goddess fled, Envy looked at her with eyes aslant, made small muttering sounds, felt pain at Minerva's success, and took her staff, girded with bands of thorn" (*Met.* 2.787–790). The first of these lines is a close imitation of fr. 374 Pf., 72 Hollis: ἡ δὲ πελιδνωθεῖσα καὶ ὄμμασι λοξὸν ὑποδράξ / ὀσσομένη, "And she, turning pale, glaring with eyes aslant." *Illa* corresponds to ἡ δὲ, *obliquo lumine* to ὄμμασι λοξὸν ὑποδράξ, and *cernens* to ὀσσομένη; Ovid omits only πελιδνωθεῖσα, perhaps because he had just identified pallor as a permanent characteristic of Invidia (*Met.* 2.775: *pallor in ore sedet*). Callimachus's lines may possibly refer to Athena; in any case, Ovid adapts to an abstraction what originally described a person or divinity. Hence the allusion has a transformative function in the reader's apprehension of it: to recognize the allusion is to participate in reification of the abstraction. Likewise, when Invidia takes a staff, Ovid achieves psychological symbolism in its *spinea vincula*; and he also adapts to an abstraction what had a personal reference of some kind in the *Hecale*: γέντο δ' ἐρείκης / σκηπάνιον, "She took a staff of heath" (fr. 355 Pf., 66 Hollis).

story only to turn Aglauros into stone (*Met.* 2.814–818). Herse, moreover, whose youthful beauty received so much notice at the beginning (*Met.* 2.722–725), then disappears from Ovid's account altogether except as a tormenting vision of happiness set by Invidia before Aglauros's eyes (*Met.* 2.803–807). Such a role for Herse is hardly what Ovid induced his readers to expect by the amatory topoi with which he initially regaled them! The story turns out to concern Invidia and its terrible consequences for Aglauros, described in terms of poison and psychological torture; it ends with a description of her petrification (*Met.* 2.820–832).

Three times before this, our consideration of Ovid's style has brought us to this point in Aglauros's story. A sylleptic pun initiates her petrification, as Mercury, with his aggressively literal-minded joke, misinterprets and realizes Aglauros's words:

> "desine!" dixit,
> "hinc ego me non sum nisi te motura repulso."
> "stemus" ait "pacto" velox Cyllenius "isto!"
> (*Met.* 2.816–818)

> "Stop!" she said, "I will not leave this place until you have been driven away." "Let us agree upon these terms," replied swift Mercury.

In the personification of Invidia, Ovid transfers conceptual abstractions into the physical sphere through the power of *phantasia*, as he does also with the *imago* of Herse's happiness. Now narrative distortion, achieved by unexpected amplification and ellipsis of events, renders our progress through the tale thematically changeable, an image of flux. The conclusion of Aglauros's tale well exemplifies the convergence and interconnectedness of all elements of Ovid's transformative style. This sequence of tales has been taken to show the "unsatisfactory" results of Ovid's focus on metamorphosis: "It is evident once more that Ovid had to utilize metamorphosis in other ways if he wanted to achieve a more satisfying narration and a more adequate appearance of unity."[58] One may rather suggest that the sequence can prove satisfactory, indeed richly rewarding, to readers who come to it with different expectations. The notions of "unity" here applied may be better left in store for other works by other authors. Whatever relevance or value one may find in them, I wish to emphasize that Ovid does not "utilize" metamorphosis as an externally introduced device to unify disparate tales, whose subject matter may be various and not necessarily related to it. Rather, he reveals its presence in every feature of every tale. To Ovid's genius, no subject is intractable. In

---

[58] Galinsky 1975, 95–96. Keith (1992, 2–7) ably addresses this criticism, insisting on the interest and importance of embedded narratives in the sequence.

this sequence Ovid has brought to bear all the resources of his art, including wordplay, personification, and as intricate and convoluted a narrative style as had ever been achieved, for purposes often comic, but never trivial: he aims in this sequence to impress upon his readers, through their own experience, a more powerful and compelling image of change.

Chapter 4

DEEPER CAUSES: AETIOLOGY AND STYLE

> His word is more than the miraculous harp.
> —*The Tempest* 2.1.83

Aetiological Wordplay

In calling to our minds the stylistic character of his predecessors' works, Ovid associates his tales with their aetiological preoccupations. At the end of the *Hecale*, Theseus establishes an annual banquet in Hecale's honor and a precinct of Zeus Hecaleius, also naming a deme after her.[1] These are instituted to persist into later times, and so for Callimachus's readers—whatever their awareness of Attic institutions—the narrative offers an explanation of them through an account of their farthest origins. In the story of Tarpeia, Propertius offers a way of understanding the origin of her grove and tomb, and how her name came to be associated with the *mons Tarpeius*. Ovid has other aetiological claims to make, and his re-imaginings of these works engage their contribution to his efforts. Though the *Metamorphoses* includes the origins of quite a few religious, cultural, and historical phenomena, Ovid's is principally an account of cosmological origins, explaining natural phenomena through metamorphosis: "Ovid always maintains among his primary purposes a concern with how things came to be the way they are and how we are to understand the world that has been given us. The *Metamorphoses* is a grandly cosmological work that attempts to bridge all the orders of creation by understanding heaven and earth, animate and inanimate beings, physical laws, and human emotions through a series of parallel explanations."[2]

Ovid's aetiological concerns, pervasive in the *Metamorphoses* and *Fasti*, and extensive in his other works, have an immeasurably complex relationship with aetiological traditions of the literary and cultural context: his concerns both arise from these traditions and decisively reshape them. The vastness of the topic precludes anything but a selective treatment here. In this chapter I pursue some thematic reflections relevant to other

---

[1] On these institutions, see Hollis 1990, 268–269 on fr. 83 (264 Pf.); 356 on the aetiological conclusion of the *Hecale*.
[2] Barkan 1986, 27.

topics already discussed, which I re-address with a shift in the angle of vision. Fortunately, the recent work of K. S. Myers goes far to map out the aetiological background of the *Metamorphoses*, and to define the place of Ovid's work in aetiological traditions, both Hellenistic and Roman.[3] As always, Ovid ranges over a domain larger than our view of it. I choose a few corners to explore, and describe some exemplary cases, especially those in which the stylistic surface embraces even matters of such cosmic import.

Regarding the stylistic embodiment of aetiological themes, we can observe that although Ovid's work resembles that of the authors whose narrative styles he exploited, such as Callimachus and Propertius, in having aetiological goals, his goals are largely different; and those who did compile tales of transformation, such as Nicander and Boios, did not do so in a style that much resembles Ovid's. As is often pointed out, their works are in every sense catalogue-poetry.[4] Ovid may have exploited Nicander's *Heteroiumena* for more than details of plot, and the two books of Boios's *Ornithogonia* provided "fairly slight stories," as Forbes Irving remarks, "crammed with *aitia* for different sorts of birds."[5] Yet only in the abstract do these suggest a parallel to Ovid's achievement, as when Athenaeus characterizes the aetiological scope of Boios's work: καθόλου δὲ ὁ ποιήσας ταῦτα τὰ ἔπη πάντα τὰ ὄρνεα ἀνθρώπους ἱστορεῖ πρότερον γεγονέναι, "The author of this epic work explains that all birds without exception were once human beings" (Ath. 9.393F).

However learned, allusive, and refined aetiological poetry may be, it is by definition not a self-enclosed artistic artifact, not art for art's sake. For it insists on a direct connection with the reader's extraliterary experience, claiming to offer an explanation of causes for phenomena already familiar or potentially so, known or at least knowable outside the text. Offering a radical challenge to any separation between "poetry of experience" and "artistic poetry," much less an antinomy between them,[6] aetiological poetry invites us to extend its vision, its perspective on artistic subjects, to the world outside.

The Romans' awareness of the *mons Tarpeius* in their ordinary visits to the Capitoline may be changed by their reading of Propertius, their experience of their city influenced by his artistic meanings. Ovid offers a parallel to his own readers in those characters within the work who, observing a bird or other creature of the natural world, learn that it was once a human being with a story. The story follows, and unexpectedly deepens

---

[3] Myers 1994b, a comprehensive discussion of aetiology in the *Metamorphoses*, with rich bibliographical resources.
[4] E.g., Galinsky 1975, 150; Hollis 1970, xxii–xxiii.
[5] Forbes Irving 1990, 19.
[6] Galinsky 1975, 151.

the observer's perspective on nature, suffusing it with a complex of human meanings that were formerly opaque to the observer's gaze. So Ceyx, calling Peleus's attention to the hawk's savage behavior, explains that it was once his brother. Nature may appear simply natural, but in fact, Ovid tells us, it is largely human in origin, and aetiological narrative reveals how it has absorbed human qualities. Because of the *animi constantia* that characterizes Ovidian metamorphosis, these qualities remain expressed in their natural form:

> forsitan hanc volucrem, rapto quae vivit et omnes
> terret aves, semper pennas habuisse putetis:
> vir fuit et (tanta est animi constantia) iam tum
> acer erat.
> (*Met.* 11.291–294)

> Perhaps you may suppose that this bird, which lives on prey and terrifies all birds, always had feathers: it was a man, and (so great is continuity of mind) even then was fierce.

Illustrating the direct transfer of qualities from human to natural, Ceyx goes on to describe his brother Daedalion's warlike character in this way:

> illius virtus reges gentesque subegit,
> quae nunc Thisbaeas agitat mutata columbas.
> (*Met.* 11.299–300)

> Its valor then subdued kings and peoples, which now, transformed, harasses the doves of Thisbe.

At the end of the tale, when Daedalion attempts to kill himself out of grief at his daughter's death, Apollo changes him into the hawk. He passes into nature, like so many others, at his most intense level of emotional distress; and this distress remains fixed forever in an unresolved state:

> oraque adunca dedit, curvos dedit unguibus hamos,
> et nunc accipiter, nullis satis aequus in omnes
> saevit aves aliisque dolens fit causa dolendi.
> (*Met.* 11.342–345)

> He gave him a hooked beak and curved hooks to his nails; and now a hawk, friendly to none, he treats all birds with savagery; in pain himself, he becomes a cause of pain to others.

A parallel case, where we, along with an internal audience, learn of causal origins, occurs shortly thereafter. One old man points out to another a sea bird, remarks that it has a royal ancestry, and details its family stemma. The bird is in fact Priam's son and Hector's brother:

> frater fuit Hectoris iste:
> qui nisi sensisset prima nova fata iuventa,
> forsitan inferius non Hectore nomen haberet.
> (*Met.* 11.758–760)
>
> He was Hector's brother, and had he not experienced a strange fate in early youth, perhaps he would have a name not less than Hector's.

There follows the tale of Aesacus, whose amorous pursuit of Hesperie leads to her death, whereupon, overcome by remorse, Aesacus attempts to kill himself. As in the equally grim conclusion of Daedalion's story, transformation thwarts suicide: *et optatae non est data copia mortis*, "And he had no opportunity for the death he wished" (*Met.* 11.786). Aesacus becomes the *mergus*, "diver," a bird who repeatedly plunges into the sea out of suicidal guilt: *letique viam sine fine retemptat*, "And without end he tries again to take the path of death" (*Met.* 11.792).[7]

In revealing, as causes for the phenomena of the *mundus*, a vast number of human stories—usually stories of misfortune—Ovid offers a vision of the nature of things. As an interpretive view of the cosmos, one may imagine the *Metamorphoses* as a challenge to other views—that of Lucretius's *De rerum natura*, for example; but the *Aeneid* comes most often to mind. The *Aeneid* also presents itself as "poetry of explanations," accounting for city and empire by tracing their origins in a narrative of the distant past.[8] Vergil has a considerable stake in the aetiological traditions exemplified in the smaller-scaled works of Callimachus and Propertius, to which he brings a larger national and cosmic perspective. "Vergil's interest in cosmological origins can here be seen to link up with the Alexandrian taste for aetiological poetry; the *Aeneid* is indeed a poem of foundation, a *ktisis*."[9]

There is any number of ways in which one could summarize the differences between Ovid's and Vergil's aetiological preoccupations. Vergil wrote an account of Roman origins that embraced cosmic perspectives, Ovid an account of cosmic origins that embraced perspectives on Rome. The Trojan royal family is of interest to Vergil because it provides through Aeneas a path to the first beginnings of the Roman people among the gods (through Venus) and in Italy, the home of Dardanus. Ovid found the Trojan royal line of interest because, among other things, it provided the *mergus* to the host of shore birds, through which one can trace the presence of human anguish deep within nature's realm.

---

[7] For background on Daedalion and Aesacus, see Forbes Irving 1990, 241–242, 223–224.

[8] Horsfall (1991) associates the *Aeneid* with "the poetry of explanations."

[9] Hardie 1986, 68. Hardie (380) briefly represents the *Metamorphoses* as Ovid's "imitation, with variation, of Virgil's conception of a universal epic."

Such summaries and exemplifications do not put an end to the matter, but only begin to describe the character of aetiological concerns in both the *Aeneid* and the *Metamorphoses*; for these concerns are deeply interfused in elements of style. Some features of Vergilian style Ovid could almost directly adapt to non-Vergilian purposes, and this process of adaptation enriches the reading of Ovid's text with a wealth of Vergilian reminiscences. Our understanding of these is poorly served by metaphors of "indebtedness" or "borrowing," since they actively contribute to oppose Ovid's thematic aims and vision to our recollection of Vergil's.[10] One of these features is etymological wordplay, the allusion, explicit or implicit, to a word's derivation. Etymological wordplay abounds in Vergil's works, and Vergilian examples illustrate how the derivation of a word or name may be significantly appropriate, "because it corresponds to some essential feature of the thing named, or gives the true explanation (*etymos logos*) of the thing."[11] In suggesting a radical connection between word and thing, etymological wordplay becomes an intimate expression of Vergil's aetiological preoccupations.[12]

That Latium takes its name from *latere*, because Saturn hid there in exile (*Aen.* 8.322–323), is only one example of one type of wordplay; but it is enough to show how a connection between words can be a figure for thematic historical claims. The effort to understand this instance of wordplay requires Vergil's readers to recognize at once a semantic link between two words and a further conceptual link between a region familiar from their own experience and the narrative of Saturn's exile. They participate in granting Latium as they know it a meaningful connection to the remote past. Wordplay also makes the name Latium thematically resonant in another sense, associating the place with exile as a theme both of the immediate context—for Evander is speaking of his own exile, with Saturn as a parallel—and of the larger work, filled as it is with tales of displaced persons, immigrants, and exiled wanderers.

---

[10] See Kenney 1973, 118, on the pervasive presence of Vergilian reminiscences in Ovid's work: "Closer analysis . . . shows that this is not a matter of straightforward borrowing and adaptation, but rather that what might be called a consistent and calculated process of denaturing has been at work."

[11] O'Hara 1996a, 3. O'Hara impressively documents etymological wordplay throughout Vergil's works. In a subsequent discussion of Ovid, O'Hara finds "many overlaps between Vergilian and Ovidian wordplay," concluding that "many Ovidian passages allude to and interact with instances of etymological wordplay in Vergil, in ways that are meant to be recognized, and that should be a part of our understanding of each poet's goals and methods" (O'Hara 1996b, 255).

[12] As O'Hara (1996a, 109) remarks, "There is a significant overlap of the *Aeneid*'s general concern with the origins of the Roman people and its frequent concern for the origins of words or names, for in its interest in aetiology the *Aeneid* is simultaneously most Roman and most Alexandrian."

In parallel fashion, Ovid through etymological wordplay engages his readers in an active appreciation of transformation and flux, inviting them to participate in his vision of natural and cosmic origins. This is not the place to attempt a survey of all of his modes of etymological wordplay, yet a few examples may begin to suggest the richness of this feature of the stylistic surface.[13] We learn the origin of dew when, at the death of Memnon on the plains of Troy, his mother Aurora mourns for him; thereafter, her tears mark her daily passing as the dew, a natural expression and eternal reminder of her grief. The formulaic *nunc quoque,* "even now," reflects a recurring appeal to us to recognize metamorphosis as a cause for elements of our present-day surroundings, as Ovid's aetiological narrative claims once again to expound meanings inherent in a familiar phenomenon:

> luctibus est Aurora suis intenta piasque
> nunc quoque dat lacrimas et toto rorat in orbe.
> (*Met.* 13.621–622)

> Aurora, intent on her own grief, even now sheds maternal tears, causing dew over the whole world.

As a stylistic embodiment of the *aition, rorat* offers an etymology of Aurora's name.[14] The name of Aurora is shown to have had its origin in her grief, just as the dew began and continues as a reminder of that grief. In recognizing that her name derives from this event, we can see the name as a phenomenon parallel to the dew itself; for both names and things bear the memory of their origins. All names and things, we may be tempted to conclude, are potentially interpretable in terms of their causes, if only the aetiological poet will tell their stories.

As we saw earlier, Ovid makes puns transformative, and the language of puns offers him a variety of transformative opportunities. The etymological connection between *ros* and *Aurora* remains within the Latin language, as do some parallel examples;[15] but bilingual puns, that bridge the Greek and Latin languages, are more common in the *Metamorphoses.* Their conspicuous presence is fitting, for they are another trope of metamorphosis.[16] One could also call them metaphrastic puns, puns of transla-

---

[13] On etymological wordplay in the *Metamorphoses,* see Rosati 1983, 161–166; many examples in Ahl 1985; Hinds 1987; Weber 1990; Keith 1992; Myers 1992 and 1994a; O'Hara 1996b; and Wheeler 1997; for the *Amores,* McKeown 1987, 32–37, 45–62; for the *Fasti,* Porte 1985, 197–264.

[14] Kenney 1986, 451. As H-E suggest on *Met.* 13.621, the *aition* is probably original with Ovid; so may be the etymological wordplay.

[15] E.g., the origin of bats, *vespertiliones*: *tenent a vespere nomen,* "They have their name from the evening" (*Met.* 4.415).

[16] For the term "bilingual pun," see Kenney 1986, 417, on *Met.* 7.418–419; McCartney 1919, 354. Myers 1994b, 37–39, 47 (Tages), provides a valuable collection of examples.

DEEPER CAUSES 173

tion, because they cross over the gap between languages. Once again Ovid engages the reader's mind to participate in transformative acts: the mental process of translation is an experiential symbol of the metamorphosis that is occurring in each case. Such a shift occurs, for example, at the birth of Ocyroe ("swift-flowing"), later to become the horse:[17]

> fluminis in rapidi ripis enixa vocavit
> Ocyroen.
> (*Met.* 2.637–638)

Giving birth on the banks of a swift stream, she named her Ocyroe.

Before transformation, Battus is true to his name in Greek, "the chatterer," by informing on Mercury to the god himself in disguise; after transformation, he is true to his Latin name *index*, "the informer," a name that his petrified form still retains:[18] *qui nunc quoque dicitur index*, "Which even now is called the informer" (*Met.* 2.706).

Sometimes Ovid alludes to the etymology of a Greek name without explicitly mentioning it, thereby requiring a still more productive cooperation on the reader's part. To adopt Servius's critical vocabulary, Ovid "suppresses" the name.[19] So Venus uses the Latin language with great authority to provide the etymology of her Greek name (Aphrodite from ἀφρός), linking it to an account of her own origin:

> in medio quondam concreta profundo
> spuma fui Graiumque manet mihi nomen ab illa.
> (*Met.* 4.537–538)

I was foam, congealed long ago in the midst of the sea, and my Greek name remains derived from foam.

In a similar case of suppression, Medea aloft espies the house of Eumelus, *lugentis in aere natum*, "Grieving for his airborne son" (*Met.* 7.390), who had been transformed into a bird. The son's name receives no mention, but as Kenney remarks, "There is a bi-lingual wordplay in the Latin: *in aere natum* alludes to the name of the bird (*aeropus*) into which Apollo in pity changed the boy."[20] Another bilingual pun occurs shortly thereafter, when Medea prepares the cup for young Theseus that has been poisoned with aconite. Ovid renders this Euripidean and Callimachean story transformative by tracing the aconite to froth cast from

---

[17] See H-E on *Met.* 2.633: "Ovid himself at line 637 gives the etymology of her name."
[18] H-E on *Met.* 2.707 note that the wordplay is Ovid's invention.
[19] Servius on *Georgics* 2.126: *supprimens nomen* (see O'Hara 1996a, 81 and n. 336). "Suppression" is an important category in O'Hara's account of Vergilian wordplay; see 79–82.
[20] Kenney 1986, 417, on *Met.* 7.390. For sources and background, see Forbes Irving 1990, 226, on Botres, the boy's original name.

Cerberus's jaws, and by tracing the word *aconitum* to ἀκόνη, "whetstone," glossed by *cautes*, "rock":[21]

> rabida qui concitus ira
> inplevit pariter ternis latratibus auras
> et sparsit virides spumis albentibus agros;
> has concresse putant nactasque alimenta feracis
> fecundique soli vires cepisse nocendi,
> quae quia nascuntur dura vivacia caute,
> agrestes aconita vocant.
> (*Met.* 7.413–419)

Roused to savage anger, he filled the air with three simultaneous barks, and spattered the green fields with white foam; they suppose that this congealed and, gaining nourishment from the fertile and productive soil, took on the power to harm. Because it grows and flourishes on hard rock, the countrymen call it aconite.

Two more examples of aetiological wordplay will suffice to illustrate its intimate connection to transformation. In both, Ovid suppresses a Greek name to be supplied from the reader's memory. He links Hecuba's canine transformation to the local *aition* of Cynossema, the "dog's tomb," a headland on the Thracian coast, known to geographical writers as Hecuba's tomb:[22]

> locus exstat et ex re
> nomen habet, veterumque diu memor illa malorum
> tum quoque Sithonios ululavit maesta per agros.
> (*Met.* 13.569–571)

The place is conspicuous, and has its name from the event; and long mindful of her old injuries, even then she howled in sadness through the Thracian fields.

Scholars of myth debate about the appropriateness of the dog as the animal into which Hecuba is changed,[23] but for Ovid the case is clear. What was a metaphor in *Iliad* 24.212–213, where Hecuba desires, animal-like, to devour Achilles, becomes physically realized in Ovidian metamorphosis.[24] Once again, the figurative becomes literal in a parallel

---

[21] Kenney 1986, 417, on *Met.* 7.418–419, offers further etymological suggestion in *a-conitum*, "dustless, soilless."

[22] Strabo 13.1.28; Diodorus Siculus 13.40; see Forbes Irving 1990, 207.

[23] See Forbes Irving 1990, 208: "The transformation is a particularly mysterious one, and there is no obvious simple explanation for it."

[24] Euripides (*Hecuba* 1263–1273) had preceded Ovid in describing Hecuba's transformation, and Ovid alludes frequently to this play in the preceding narrative (H-E on *Met.* 13.399–575).

process of change. Hecuba passes from human to nonhuman as her words turn to barks: *rictuque in verba parato / latravit conata loqui*, "As her open mouth shaped itself for words, trying to speak, she barked" (*Met.* 13.568–569).

When, at the end of Book 10, Adonis's blood, spilled on the ground, rises from it as a flower, the anemone, many thematic and stylistic elements of the *Metamorphoses* converge in a few richly evocative lines. Pointing out that Persephone was permitted to change a nymph into the mint plant, Venus claims the same privilege for herself, now that her lover Adonis has died.[25] She adds some nectar to his blood:

> nec plena longior hora
> facta mora est, cum flos de sanguine concolor ortus,
> qualem, quae lento celant sub cortice granum,
> punica ferre solent, brevis est tamen usus in illo;
> namque male haerentem et nimia levitate caducum
> excutiunt idem, qui praestant nomina, venti.
> (*Met.* 10.734–739)

There was a delay not longer than a full hour, when a blood-red flower arose from his blood, the color pomegranates have, which hide their seeds beneath a pliant rind. Yet the enjoyment of it is brief: its petals cling but poorly, falling off in their light fragility; the same winds shake them off that give the flower its name.

Following Ovid's pattern of suppression in etymological wordplay, Orpheus, whose narrative song is now ending, omits the name anemone, but alludes to it metaphrastically in *venti*, ἄνεμοι.[26] There is a symbolic link, as Anderson observes, between Adonis and the anemone established by the brief time in which each is allowed to flourish.[27] Yet the terms of the passage pass beyond symbolism to the stylistic enactment of metamorphosis. For the origin of the anemone occurs at the same moment that the winds perform at once a physical and a conceptual action: they shake the anemone's petals from it while providing it with its name.

---

[25] The tale is doubly aetiological, for the origin of the anemone follows the cult-*aition* of the Adonia (*Met.* 10.724–727). For background on the story, see Forbes Irving 1990, 279–280.

[26] In similar fashion, Ovid ends Book 11 by providing the etymology of the *mergus*, "diver," into which Aesacus was transformed, without mentioning the word itself: *aequora amat, nomenque manet, quia mergitur, illo*, "He haunts the sea's surface, and has his lasting name because he dives into it" (*Met.* 11.795). Ovid suppresses *mergus* here in conscious and deliberate recognition of this mode of etymological wordplay: he is perfectly willing to use the word in other contexts, e.g., *Met.* 8.625. See Varro *Ling.* 5.78: *mergus quod mergendo in aquam captat escam*, "The diver, because it gets its food by diving into the water." Myers (1994b, 37) notes the parallel etymology of κολυμβίς from κολυμβάω, "to plunge headlong."

[27] Anderson 1972, 535, on *Met.* 10.738–739.

Ovid's sylleptic habit of mind once again renders his stylistic expression transformative, achieving here a juncture of aetiological metamorphosis, sylleptic expression, and bilingual wordplay.

When Ovid describes the winds as granting a name to the flower, we may notice that he has omitted human participation in the naming of things. This is by no means always the case: aconite, for example was originally so named by the local countrymen (*Met.* 7.419: *agrestes*). One could easily imagine a human observer naming the anemone after witnessing the loss of its petals to the winds. That this is not the case carries a symbolic suggestion: that the natural world already may possess its own meanings, and can be read like an author's text; that the aetiological poet functions like a commentator, identifying sources and providing background information to the reader. Venus refers to the festival that shall always celebrate her Adonis as *luctus monimenta*, "A memorial of my grief" (*Met.* 10.725). As a ritual re-enactment, the *monimenta* must be interpreted in terms of the causes behind its original institution, if it is to be properly understood by its participants and observers. It demands such interpretation. The same is true of a *monumentum* of stone, bearing an inscription that summons the passerby to read,[28] or other physical reminders. Servius provides us with an etymology for the word: *monumenta autem a mentis admonitione sunt dicta*, "Monuments were named from their admonition of the mind" (Servius ad *Aen.* 3.486). He refers to Vergil's application of the word to the fine garments and other gifts exchanged at leave-taking, which recall persons long departed to the observer's recollection.[29] Nature in the *Metamorphoses* functions as a *luctus monumentum* in this sense, a reminder of the grief that gave rise to so many of its features. These can even bear a written inscription to admonish the reader's mind, as when the blood of Hyacinthus, accidentally killed by Apollo, gives rise to the hyacinth.[30] The flower bears the letters AI AI, "Alas," a natural imitation in Greek of Apollo's grief. Normally we would need to divine this expression metaphrastically from the Latin that Ovid (through Orpheus the narrator) supplies him: *flosque novus scripto gemitus imitabere nostros*, "And as a new flower you will imitate my

---

[28] Varro (*Ling.* 6.49) mentions sepulchral inscriptions in deriving *monumentum* from *memoria*.

[29] In this context, Andromache's gifts to Aeneas will remind him of her, just as Ascanius in person reminds her of Astyanax. In a more violent context, Pallas's sword-belt functions as *saevi monimenta doloris*, "a reminder of cruel pain," for Aeneas at *Aen.* 12.945; see Servius, ad loc., for a similar derivation. For derivations from both *memoria* and *monere*, see Maltby 1991, s.v. *monumentum*.

[30] As with Adonis, a festival, the Hyacinthia, memorializes Hyachinthus in Sparta: *honorque / durat in hoc aevi*, "The rite honoring him remains to the present age" (*Met.* 10.217–218).

groans in written form" (*Met.* 10.206). But in this case Nature and Ovid offer us identical texts:[31]

> non satis hoc Phoebo est (is enim fuit auctor honoris):
> ipse suos gemitus foliis inscribit et AI AI
> flos habet inscriptum funestaque littera ducta est.
> (*Met.* 10.214–216)

That was not enough for Phoebus (for he originated the honor): he wrote his own groans on the leaves, and the flower still has "Alas!" inscribed on it; a letter of mourning was fashioned there.

Ovid's Little *Aeneid*

> ταράσσει τοὺς ἀνθρώπους οὐ τὰ πράγματα, ἀλλὰ
> τὰ περὶ τῶν πραγμάτων δόγματα.
>
> Things do not give people trouble, but ideas about things.
> —Epictetus *Enchiridion* 5

Etymological wordplay is but one feature of Vergilian style that Ovid transforms for his own ends, one thematically significant mode of recalling the *Aeneid* to his readers' minds. The points of comparison between the *Aeneid* and *Metamorphoses* are innumerable, and each reader at each successive reading can expect to discover new ones. Because indecorous wit and the narrative indirection of the *Metamorphoses* have engaged our attention, let us now maintain this focus as we consider, in stylistic and narrative terms, how the *Metamorphoses* is a reaction to the aetiological thrust of the *Aeneid*. Ovid himself provokes us to consider the two works together: he even includes a remarkably distorted version of Vergil's plot in Books 13–14, reducing most of it to summary as a frame for largely

---

[31] For a valuable discussion of this natural text, sensitive to its memorializing function, see Janan 1988, 122: "Further, the flower-text Apollo creates functions because of the basic paradox that informs written language. The flower-text is an absent-presence: it affirms that Hyacinthus is *not* there (thus not a threat to Apollo's control) at the same time that it denies this fact (thus assuaging Apollo's guilt). The flower-text reflects what it memorializes—the absent-presence of the beloved, a loss and an absence represented to the lover so keenly and constantly as to become a 'presence' (*semper eris mecum*). Accordingly, the ultimate monument to Hyacinthus—ultimate because more permanent and widely publishable—is a material Absent-Presence: a text, composed of present material representatives (written signifiers) of absences (signifieds). Apollo creates this by inscribing the words for his mourning cries on the hyacinth."

unrelated tales. Thus he invites comparison more explicitly than do any of the later writers of Latin epic, who all wrote for audiences steeped in the *Aeneid*; for none of these others undertook to rework its specific subject matter. By an odd paradox, most critics of the *Metamorphoses* feel called upon to compare it to the *Aeneid*, attributing significance of some sort to the comparison, yet find little of interest in Ovid's refabricated *Aeneid*. Fränkel goes so far as to suggest that Ovid should have quit after Book 11; for him, the later books of the *Metamorphoses* show Ovid striving unsuccessfully to achieve epic sublimity along the lines of Homer and Vergil.[32] Galinsky, in the most extreme interpretation of these books, takes the opposite view of Ovid's purposes. On the subject of Aeneas, Galinsky remarks, "Ovid simply tells this story, as he tells all others, in other ways than did some of his predecessors."[33] According to this view, Ovid aimed—here as elsewhere—at nothing more than superficial innovation. This simple achievement, not surprisingly, appears much diminished in comparison to the works of Ovid's epic predecessors, which by contrast possess meaningful content. In Vergil, for example, "It is the meaning of events that matters, not the events themselves"; the "events themselves" are, according to Galinsky, all we get in Ovid, whose choice of metamorphosis as a theme "intrinsically leads to a neglect of moral and metaphysical questions."[34]

It is worth emphasizing that Ovid does empty the story of Aeneas of its Vergilian themes, but only to replace them with others. Ovid chooses to rework the subject matter primarily of Books 3 and 6, the prophetic books, in which the *Aeneid* becomes most explicitly a providential history. In Ovid's version, the hand of providence is conspicuously lacking, as is any connection between plot and cosmic order, such as one comes

---

[32] Fränkel 1945, 101: "When he had composed eleven books, he seems to have realized that his themes had grown stale. At that juncture, he might gracefully have brought his biggest and greatest work to a swift conclusion, but once more he was unable to part with what he had under his hands." Fränkel goes on to assert that "with the Twelfth Book the epic changes its character.... Enchanting caprice gives way to an ambition for grandeur." Ovid now tries his hand "at the truly heroic manner of epic."

[33] Galinsky 1975, 219.

[34] Ibid., 238, 239. Galinsky claims not to evaluate the *Metamorphoses* harshly: "Myth can survive by being told vividly and palpably and without the Vergilian sense of mystery and metaphysics. The narrative emphasis on myth takes its place next to the speculative one and both exist in their own right, though separately" (242). Nevertheless, the reader who accepts Galinsky's mode of comparison is likely to conclude that the *Metamorphoses* is trivial— inferior *because* it lacks "mystery and metaphysics," not to mention "profundity," "meaning," and other features attributed by Galinsky to the *Aeneid*. See also Solodow (1988), who includes a section entitled "Narrative Without Morality," in which he claims that Ovid's "stories, singly and collectively, lack meaning" (157). What Galinsky and Solodow miss in Ovid's Little *Aeneid* is *Vergilian* meanings, which they assume to be the only genuine article.

to expect from Vergil. In its place Ovid offers an answer to the *Aeneid*, subsuming its plot and characters to illustrate the universal prevalence of flux.

It may at first seem strange that out of all the events in the *Aeneid*, Ovid should select the wanderings of Aeneas to retell, and make more use of Vergil's Book 3 than any other book, especially as it lacks the dramatic and emotional thrills of Books 2 and 4, the fall of Troy and the love story. Yet Book 3 has much of a more abstractly thematic character to contribute, for Vergil, while enumerating the many places visited by Aeneas's fleet, devotes much space to prophecies received along the way. These prophecies reinforce a complex of themes of great importance in the *Aeneid*, for they invite associations in the reader's mind between the events of Vergil's story and the schemes of fate reflected in Rome's later history. In other words, prophecy is the one feature of the *Aeneid* that most explicitly invites allegorical interpretation. Though it may be wrong to exaggerate allegorical elements in the *Aeneid*, it is certainly easy to do so: Romans comfortable with the Augustan settlement must have found it convenient to see in the *Aeneid* a presentation of Rome's remote past as a prophecy of its present national greatness. On this view, Aeneas's mission becomes a divinely ratified pattern applicable to the understanding of contemporary political events and to the comprehension of the future as well.[35] Thus the *Aeneid* can offer its readers a providential interpretation of their national existence.

So extreme an allegorical reading, of course, ignores much of what Vergil wrote and deflects attention from his persistent emphasis on the blood and suffering that were the cost of Rome's founding.[36] Yet political allegory can easily be abstracted as *the* meaning of the *Aeneid*, excluding all else that may qualify or contradict it. Sophisticated readers may observe that political allegorization of the *Aeneid* is intellectually complacent and false to the experience of reading; it reduces the work to conceptual simplicity and endows it with a dishonest invitation to emotional comfort. Yet there are aspects of the work that give rise to this interpretation: it is more exaggeration than mistake. As we shall see, Ovid concentrates our attention on the "prophetic" aspects of the *Aeneid*, thereby making important thematic reflections upon it, and upon its reception among his contemporaries in a peaceful and complacent time. If, on the one hand, audiences could receive the *Aeneid* in a simplified and reduced providential interpretation, Ovid could seize upon simplification and reduction as rhetorical techniques, to offer those same audiences a

---

[35] Hardie (1986) discusses Vergil's use of analogies between cosmological order and political order; see also Quint 1993.

[36] On this theme, see O'Hara 1990.

parodic version, eliminating some prophetic elements of Aeneas's story and reducing others to burlesque. Thus one reductive reading generates its opposite as a mirror image.

On the level of narrative style, the symmetry and linear progress of the *Aeneid* most strongly invite providential interpretation. As Servius notes, the work falls into two halves, six of its books modeled on the *Odyssey* and six on the *Iliad* (Servius ad *Aen.* 7.1). One does not need the charts and tables superimposed on the work by some critics to perceive that Vergil employs symmetry and parallelism as structural principles.[37] The analogy between order in the nature of things and order in artistic representation can be traced as far back as Aristotle, who, assailing the metaphysical systems of others, remarks that "from the observable facts it appears that nature is not a series of episodes, like a bad tragedy" (*Metaph.* 14.1090b20). Aristotle's statement reflects an idea of decorum, and decorum on a similarly cosmic scale contributes much to the stylistic and thematic character of the *Aeneid*. The narrative style of the work is appropriate to Vergil's goal of setting Aeneas's journeys and battles in the context of the Fates' design, a design always comprehensible to the reader, if not always to characters in the story.

Before turning to the specifics of Ovid's Little *Aeneid*, let us examine a prominent prophecy of *Aeneid* 3, both as an illustration of narrative style and as a specific subtext to Ovid's version. When Aeneas puts in at Buthrotum and visits Helenus, priest and king, he receives a prophecy whose great length endows it with special importance and emphatic impact (*Aen.* 3.374–462). Like other prophetic speakers in the *Aeneid*, Helenus has plenty to say about the unfolding of fate, and so informs Aeneas from the start:

> nam te maioribus ire per altum
> auspiciis manifesta fides; sic fata deum rex
> sortitur voluitque vices, is vertitur ordo.
> (*Aen.* 3.374–376)

> For it is clearly a trustworthy conclusion that you are crossing the sea under higher auspices. So the king of the gods casts the lots of fate and disposes events; so turns the order of things.

But the content of Helenus's prophecy is less cosmic and more practically useful than any Aeneas has yet heard, since it supplies him with much specific information about his itinerary from western Greece around Sicily to Cumae. This new feature contributes significantly to narrative style as a reflection of theme, for once Helenus's prophecy is over, it immediately begins to be fulfilled. We learn along with Aeneas that the

---

[37] Schematic charts are prominent in Otis, both on Vergil (1964) and on Ovid (1970).

prophet's information can be trusted. What he tells Aeneas about Scylla and Charybdis, for example, enables the Trojans to avoid these monsters without trouble about 120 lines later (*Aen.* 3.420–432, 554–569). Helenus also foretells an important event to be narrated later in the story, Aeneas's visit to the Sibyl (Book 6), and he includes some entirely accurate information about the content of her prophecies, which will take up, conveniently enough, where he left off (*Aen.* 6.441–460). Thus, in fulfilling prophecy, events of the plot enable us to witness those events as the working out of orderly pattern.

Abstract habits of mind are a favorite target of Ovid's ridicule; against them his debunking manner is the perfect weapon. By reworking *Aeneid* 3 and 6 in his own narrative style, Ovid renders their events incapable of sustaining the providential interpretations familiar to readers of Vergil. He does so partly by reducing those events to severely summarized form. A typical example occurs near the beginning of Ovid's Little *Aeneid*, where four-and-a-half lines of Ovid cover seventy-nine lines of Vergil at dizzying speed (*Aen.* 3.1–79). The comical effect will remind modern theatergoers of Tom Stoppard's *Fifteen-Minute Hamlet* and other parodic abbreviations of Shakespearean tragedy, where the humor is created by reductive editing. Vergil's gradually unfolding narrative patterns give way to precipitate forward movement:

> profugaque per aequora classe
> fertur ab Antandro sceletaque limina Thracum
> et Polydoreo manantem sanguine terram
> linquit et utilibus ventis aestuque secundo
> intrat Apollineam sociis comitantibus urbem.
> (*Met.* 13.627–631)

And with his exiled fleet he is carried from Antandros and leaves behind the crime-stained thresholds of the Thracians and the land that flowed with Polydorus's blood and with serviceable winds and favoring tides enters Apollo's city with his shipmates accompanying him.

Moreover, such summary references to *Aeneid* 3 are scattered over a vast space of 473 lines (*Met.* 13.623–14.77), forming a frame for much material—such as the long account of Polyphemus, Acis, and Galatea—that has noticeably little to do with the *Aeneid*. Ovid's narrative principles do not change in these later books; in fact, he uses the wanderings of Aeneas much as he used Theseus's journeys in Books 8–9, and the Muses' discourse to Minerva in Book 5. Fränkel's notion, that Ovid's use of earlier epic was meant to raise the tone of the later books, is implausible, both because we are allowed to forget about Aeneas for hundreds of lines at a stretch and because here, as elsewhere, Ovid treats Vergilian subjects

182   CHAPTER 4

with irreverent humor, calling attention to the absence of Vergilian themes. The Little *Aeneid* begins thus:

> non tamen eversam Troiae cum moenibus esse
> spem quoque fata sinunt; sacra et, sacra altera, patrem
> fert umeris, venerabile onus, Cythereius heros.
> de tantis opibus praedam pius eligit illam
> Ascaniumque suum.
> (*Met.* 13.623–627)

Yet nonetheless the fates did not permit Troy's hope to be overthrown along with her walls. The hero, son of Venus, carries on his shoulders the sacred objects and that other sacred object, his father, a venerable load. Out of such vast treasures the dutiful man chooses this piece of booty, and his Ascanius too!

Fata ostentatiously announces a connection with thematic content of the *Aeneid*, but the following lines fail to maintain it. Instead, we witness a familiar Ovidian reaction to abstract and grandiose interpretive possibilities: literalizing humor. Associating Anchises first with *sacra*, then with *onus*, then most audaciously with *praeda*, Ovid invites rather disrespectful attention to matters not emphasized by Vergil. Vergil's image of Aeneas carrying his father, along with the *penates*, from the ruins of Troy invites us to consider parallels with other father-son pairs in the work, and to recognize symbolic resonances: in various senses, the image symbolizes Rome's mission, as well as *pietas*. Thus Vergil tends to guide our view away from the physical realities of the situation. But in Ovid's version, Anchises stubbornly remains a heavy, if valuable, object.[38] "Out of such vast treasures the dutiful man chooses this piece of booty"—and we are invited to think of Aeneas, as he makes his hasty exit, passing over so many cauldrons and tripods in favor of this "venerable load," his father. After all, one can only carry so much. Satirists commonly concentrate on the physical in order to call attention to the highly selective views of reality upon which "higher truths" are frequently propped. So does Ovid here.

Coincident with satirical debunking in this passage is play on the conceptual and physical, which, as we have so often seen, suffuses the whole work and reaches to the very core of Ovidian metamorphosis. In the first

---

[38] Although Vergil's Aeneas twice refers to Anchises as his *onus*, "burden," when narrating in detail the circumstances of his departure from Troy (*Aen.* 2.723, 729), Vergil's terms do not exploit the contrast of physical and conceptual in which Ovid delights. On the contrary, Anchises' weight serves as an image and exemplum of the labors imposed on Aeneas, thereby subordinating our apprehension of Anchises' physicality to its higher significances.

line of the Little *Aeneid*, syllegtic wordplay reveals that Vergil's tale has now become radically transformative: Troy's *hopes* will not be overturned along with her *walls*; *eversam* must serve both conception and object. Comparable in its thematic impact, we may recall, is a classic case of Ovidian syllepsis in Book 14, where Ovid reduces *Aeneid* 4 to four lines of summary: *excipit Aenean illic animoque domoque*, "There Dido received Aeneas into her heart and house" (*Met.* 14.78). That story, too, has been comically subsumed into the *Metamorphoses*.

Since some have denied that Ovid's Little *Aeneid* is at all parodic,[39] we may usefully measure this passage against Linda Hutcheon's definition in *A Theory of Parody*, a valuable clarification of critical terms that are often vague and muddled in application. "Parody," according to Hutcheon, "is related to burlesque, travesty, pastiche, plagiarism, quotation, and allusion, but distinct from them." The distinctive feature is *repetition* of another text, "repetition that includes difference" and "a critical ironic distance" from the text parodied. Since Ovid repeats Vergil's plot, in an exploded version, taking over characters and even thematic value-terms like *fata* and *pietas*, his Little *Aeneid* well fits the description of a parodic text: "A formal synthesis, an incorporation of a backgrounded text into itself," in which the textual doubling "functions to mark difference."[40] Though, according to Hutcheon, "there is nothing in *parodia* that necessitates the inclusion of a concept of ridicule," ridicule often is the function of parody's ironic distance: "Satire frequently uses parodic art forms for either expository or aggressive purposes."[41]

Ovid's exploitation of reductive wit has a powerful aggressive force, yet there is more than simple debunking in his treatment, for he is building the *Metamorphoses* out of the resulting ruins. The ironic distance between his version and Vergil's provides him with an opportunity to reinforce the thematic foundations of his own work, reusing the dismantled *Aeneid* as raw material. Thematic preoccupations of the *Metamorphoses* confront the reader in this Little *Aeneid*, jarring with the Vergilian associations of their context. Ovid now introduces a story told by Anius, familiar in *Aeneid* 3 as king of Delos and an old guest-friend of Anchises. Anchises questions Anius about his son and two daughters (who are not mentioned in the *Aeneid*), and Anius begins to tell what happened to them with a significant interpretive comment: *tanta homines rerum inconstantia versat*, "Human beings are subject to so great inconstancy in their

---

[39] In Ovid's adaptation of Vergilian episodes, "The result is not parody," according to Galinsky (1975, 247). Remarkably, Galinsky admits parody of Vergil in other parts of the *Metamorphoses*, but not in the Little *Aeneid* of Books 13–14 (250).

[40] Hutcheon 1985, 43, 37, 53.

[41] Ibid., 32, 43. Hutcheon illustrates parody without ridicule mainly in twentieth-century examples, which are her principal focus.

affairs" (*Met.* 13.646). This *inconstantia*, as the events will show, reflects Ovid's great theme of universal flux, here set in contrast to Vergilian providence. Apollo gave prophetic powers to Anius's son, and to his daughters Bacchus gave the ability to turn anything to grain, wine, and olive oil. Agamemnon, finding out about the daughters' gifts, seizes them and commands them to feed his army; they escape to the island of Andros, ruled by their brother. Agamemnon's forces arrive, threatening war. Betrayed by their brother and about to be put into chains, they appeal to Bacchus for help and are turned into doves (*Met.* 13.640–674). At the point where Anius's son hands the daughters over to Agamemnon, Ovid introduces that familiar Vergilian theme, *pietas*, to show its utter defeat in this context. He explicitly contrasts the son with Aeneas:

> victa metu pietas: consortia corpora poenae
> dedidit, et timido possis ignoscere fratri:
> non hic Aeneas, non, qui defenderet Andron,
> Hector erat, per quem decimum durastis in annum.
> (*Met.* 13.663–666)

> Duty was conquered by fear. He handed over his sisters' bodies to their punishment. You could forgive the timid brother: there was no Aeneas here; to defend Andros there was no Hector, who enabled you to endure into the tenth year.

The arbitrary exercise of brute force by Agamemnon, the weak timidity of the son, the helplessness of the daughters—such aspects of human character and experience Ovid presents in a deliberately inappropriate context, one that we have been accustomed to associate with virtuous heroism operating within the Fates' beneficent scheme. The reader is now left to ponder which version of the Trojans' visit to Delos may have the greater ring of truth.

By eliminating prophecy from his version of *Aeneid* 3, Ovid eliminates the most obvious manifestations of divine purpose and the corresponding structural comprehensibility of events granted by Vergil to his reader. *Aeneid* 6 offers Ovid an opportunity to achieve a similar result, since Vergil in that book again occupies much of our attention with prophetic exposition. The account of future history given to Aeneas by Anchises in the underworld (*Aen.* 6.756–886) completely vanishes in Ovid's version. Ovid does, however, include a new look at the Cumaean Sibyl. To the familiar picture of Aeneas and the Sibyl in the underworld, Ovid adds some irreverently physical complications, which Vergil, in preserving the serious tone appropriate to his purposes, could not afford to mention. Foot travel in Hades is tiring, especially on the upward path. Ovid denies his hero any quick exit through the ivory gate (*Aen.* 6.893–899); instead, Aeneas must trudge along, beguiling the time in conversation with his tour guide. *Evadere ad auras* turns out here to be truly *labor*: *inde ferens lassos adverso tramite passus / cum duce Cumaea mollit sermone laborem*, "As he dragged his weary steps away from there on the upward path, he softened the effort by conversation with his Cumaean guide" (*Met.* 14.120–121).[42] In Vergil, Aeneas promises the Sibyl a temple, in which the Sibylline books will one day be kept; she then delivers an accurate, if temporarily ambiguous, prophecy of the coming war in Latium. In Ovid's version, the Sibyl flatly rejects any association of herself with a divine nature:

> respicit hunc vates et suspiratibus haustis
> "nec dea sum," dixit, "nec sacri turis honore
> humanum dignare caput."
> (*Met.* 14.129–131)

The prophetess looked back at him, and, sighing deeply, said, "I'm no goddess! Do not consider a human being worthy of sacred incense."

Instead of proceeding to prophesy, Ovid's Sibyl tells how she, though only human, came by her extreme longevity. Apollo attempted to bribe her to endure his love; she asked for and got a life span to equal in number of years the grains of sand in a handful, but could not keep Apollo off except by rejecting his offer of eternal youth. She now has lived seven generations and must endure another 300 years of old age. The story ends with rueful reflections on the consuming power of time:

> tempus erit, cum de tanto me corpore parvam
> longa dies faciet, consumptaque membra senecta
> ad minimum redigentur onus, nec amata videbor
> nec placuisse deo; Phoebus quoque forsitan ipse
> vel non cognoscet vel dilexisse negabit:
> usque adeo mutata ferar nullique videnda,
> voce tamen noscar, vocem mihi fata relinquent.
> (*Met.* 14.147–153)

There will be a day, when from so large a body the length of time will make me small. My limbs, consumed by old age, will be reduced to the smallest weight. No one will think it likely that I was loved and pleased a god. Maybe even Phoebus himself will not recognize me or will deny that he

---

[42] Galinsky (1975, 226–227), pursuing his thesis that Ovid's only goal is *referre idem aliter*, ignores the humorous and parodic aspects of Ovid's treatment. Galinsky does, however, recognize the pathos in the Sibyl's personal narrative (228–229). Lines 104–115 of this story receive detailed discussion in Bömer 1959, 278–286 (= *WdF* 92, 187–199).

loved me. To such great changes shall I pass. Though visible to no one, I will be recognized by my voice: the fates will leave me a voice.

Instead of the Vergilian Sibyl's frenzied outbursts, Ovid's Sibyl, in straightforward, measured utterance, produces a grimly matter-of-fact account of her victimization—victimization so thoroughgoing that though she rejected Apollo's love, she now cannot describe her loss of beauty except in terms of his reaction. Apollo enters the story not as the god of prophecy, but as another example of casually destructive power, creating disastrous consequences for a human being. Consistent with the aetiological preoccupations of the *Metamorphoses*, Ovid pursues his subject farther back into the past than did Vergil, revealing deeper causes behind familiar phenomena (in this case, phenomena familiar in all legendary and historical accounts of the Sibyl and her prophecies, including the *Aeneid*). Temporal priority of events increases the impact of Ovid's thematic suggestions: that Vergil's story is not the whole story, that arbitrary power and unintelligible suffering are more deeply embedded in the nature of things than are providential order and the working out of beneficent fate.

Ovid does include some prophecies near the end of his work, at a point where they—unlike Vergil's prophecies, which occur mostly in the first six books—can offer no structural signposts to the reader, nor any interpretive guidance of the sort familiar in Vergilian prophecy. A prophecy of Helenus suddenly occurs, where one would least expect it, in the discourse of Pythagoras. Pythagoras provides an entertainingly, often comically, exhaustive list of examples to prove that his (and Ovid's) great theme, *omnia mutantur*, "All things change" (*Met.* 15.165), possesses universal inclusiveness. Having mentioned such cases as the lynxes of India, whose urine turns into gemstones, and coral, which also hardens at the touch of air (*Met.* 15.414–417), Pythagoras moves on to human nations, some of which are always gaining, some losing, strength. This consideration introduces a list of cities, once great, that have now fallen, and one that is now rising, Rome:

> clara fuit Sparte, magnae viguere Mycenae,
> nec non et Cecropis, nec non Amphionis arces:
> vile solum Sparte est, altae cecidere Mycenae;
> Oedipodioniae quid sunt, nisi nomina, Thebae?
> quid Pandioniae restant, nisi nomen, Athenae?
> nunc quoque Dardaniam fama est consurgere Romam,
> Appenninigenae quae proxima Thybridis undis
> mole sub ingenti rerum fundamina ponit.
> haec igitur formam crescendo mutat et olim
> inmensi caput orbis erit.
> (*Met.* 15.426–435)

Sparta was famous, and great Mycenae powerful; so was the citadel of Cecrops, Athens, and that of Amphion, Thebes. Sparta is now cheap land; lofty Mycenae has collapsed. What is Oedipus's Thebes, except a name? What remnant is there now of Pandion's Athens, except a name? Now there is also a report that Dardanian Rome is rising, which with huge effort sets its foundations by the waters of the Tiber that flows from the Apennines. This city, therefore, is changing its shape by its increase, and someday will be the head of the vast world.

The rhetorical structure of this passage requires that Pythagoras prophesy the decline of Rome, in order to complete the parallel now established between Rome and the other cities.[43] But remembering a prophecy once given to Aeneas by Helenus, he abruptly inserts that instead. Combining legendary and historical topics, Helenus predicts Aeneas's survival, then Rome's greatness, and ends with Augustus's career:

> hanc [i.e., urbem Romam] alii proceres per saecula longa potentem
> sed dominam rerum de sanguine natus Iuli
> efficiet; quo cum tellus erit usa, fruentur
> aetheriae sedes, caelumque erit exitus illi.
> (*Met.* 15.446–449)

Over the long ages, other chieftains will make Rome powerful, but one born from Iulus's blood will make her mistress of the world. When earth has derived its benefit from him, the heavenly seats shall do so, and heaven shall be his end.

The content of Helenus's prophecy resembles Jupiter's to Venus at *Aeneid* 1.257–296, and Aeneas is represented, as so often in the *Aeneid*, in tears and afflicted with doubt:

> quantumque recordor,
> dixerat Aeneae, cum res Troiana labaret,
> Priamides Helenos flenti dubioque salutis.
> (*Met.* 15.436–438)

This much I recall: when Troy was tottering, Priam's son Helenus spoke to Aeneas, who was weeping and uncertain of his safety.

Ovid even imitates Vergil in briefly granting the reader a larger perspective on events than Aeneas: but in doing so he turns Vergilian style against itself, for the thematic context—that cities, once risen, inevitably

---

[43] Anderson (1963, 27) notes that "his juxtaposition of rising Rome to the fallen cities of the past, nothing but names (15.429ff.), indicates clearly what he foresaw for his city." To be sure, Ovid's authorship of lines 426–430 has often been questioned; see references in Bömer 7:366–368 on *Met.* 15.426–430. For instructive parallels and a discussion of Pythagoras as narrator, see Barchiesi 1989, 86–90.

fall—qualifies rather than reinforces the prophetic message. Our greater awareness does not expand the application of prophecy (as it does in the *Aeneid*), but limits it. Ovid can count on our recognizing—after fourteen-and-a-half books of continuous metamorphosis, as well as after the immediately preceding lines—that even Rome's destiny must yield to change. The Romans possessed historical awareness well beyond earlier builders of empire and could easily imagine their city in decline and collapse. They were not conceptually bound to identify their national destiny with the ultimate goal of teleological patterns in the cosmos, and could read in Polybius's *Histories* how Scipio, whose defeat of the Carthaginians left Rome unrivaled in the western Mediterranean, wept bitterly as Carthage was consumed by flames. When Polybius asked him why he was thus moved, he said, "Because I am reflecting on the changeableness incident to fortune: perhaps some day a time will come when a similar experience will befall Rome."[44]

Ovid's Vergilian language and allusive associations in the prophecy of Helenus acquire a greatly ironic resonance in context: the passage shows how Ovid's narrative style and thematic aims necessarily obstruct providential interpretation of legend and history. The same fact is also manifest in Jupiter's prophecy to Venus near the end of the *Metamorphoses* (*Met*. 15.807–842). Ovid's version of the exchange between these two divinities must again call to mind Vergil's well-known prophecy of Jupiter to Venus in *Aeneid* 1. Though Ovid's scene is full of Vergilian reminiscences, its position near the close of the work (as we saw also in the Ovidian prophecy of Helenus) renders it incapable of contributing to our overall interpretation in Vergil's manner. Instead, the interpretive weight of nearly fifteen books will affect our understanding of the prophecy. Its immediate context exhibits narrative indirection typical of the *Metamorphoses*: once Aesculapius has arrived in Rome as a snake, the subject changes to the apotheosis of Julius Caesar by a very tenuous connection: *hic tamen accessit delubris advena nostris: / Caesar in urbe sua deus est*, "Yet he was added as a newcomer to our temples, while Caesar is a divinity in his own city" (*Met*. 15.745–746). Yet no sooner has the divine Julius been established as subject than Ovid deflects our attention to Augustus, attributing Julius's deification less to his own achievements than to the fact that his offspring was Augustus: *neque enim de Caesaris actis / ullum maius opus, quam quod pater exstitit huius*, "For of Caesar's acts there was no greater accomplishment than this, that he became the father of this man" (*Met*. 15.750–751). This notion, while it ostensibly may be praise of the *princeps*, may also call attention to the fact that Julius was not really Augustus's *pater* at all (later he is more accurately referred to in the

---

[44] Diodorus Siculus 32.24, based on Polybius 38.21: see Walbank 1979, 722–725.

phrase *nominis heres* (*Met.* 15.819). More importantly, Ovid pursues his explanation for Julius's apotheosis with that ostentatiously naive literal-mindedness typical of humor in the *Metamorphoses* and familiar from countless earlier examples. Augustus, in order to be divine himself, had to acquire a divine father: *ne foret hic igitur mortali semine cretus / ille deus faciendus erat*, "The former had to become a god in order that the latter not be born from mortal seed" (*Met.* 15.760–761). We are already well acquainted with apotheosis as an occasion for Ovidian humor, and may recall how in Book 14 Venus had won deification for her son Aeneas: apart from an appeal to Jupiter's grandfatherly pride (*Met.* 14.588–589), her argument consists of nothing more than the observation that one visit to hell is enough: *satis est inamabile regnum / adspexisse semel, Stygios semel isse per amnes*, "It's enough to have viewed that unlovable realm once, and once to have crossed the Stygian river" (*Met.* 14.590–591). Venus entirely carries the day with this reasoning; even Juno has to agree (*Met.* 14.592–593).

Once narrative indirection, accompanied by tonal instability, has provided a thoroughly un-Vergilian context for Jupiter's prophecy, this indirection carries over into the prophecy itself and jars with all Vergilian associations. Jupiter, in answering Venus's appeal for Julius's life, soon changes the subject to Augustus as well, and spends much of the speech summarizing Augustus's military and political career (*Met.* 15.822–839). He returns to Julius only at the end, "as if by an afterthought," as Otis rightly remarks,[45] by which time one may well have forgotten that the much-neglected Julius is the ostensible subject of the narrative: *hanc animam interea caeso de corpore raptam / fac iubar*, "Meanwhile, make this soul, snatched from its murdered body, into a constellation" (*Met.* 15.840–841).

The fact that this scene has obvious associations with the *Aeneid* allows Ovid to exploit Vergilian themes for comical exaggeration, just as we would expect from the rest of the *Metamorphoses*. Vergil's Jupiter, for example, is resigned to the higher demands of fate: he touchingly explains to Hercules that he could not even save his son Sarpedon's life when the Fates required it (*Aen.* 10.467–472), and refuses to intervene in the Latin war with the remark *fata viam invenient* (*Aen.* 10.113). Ovid outdoes Vergil at his own game by supplying the Fates with a regular archive-house, a *tabularium*—reminiscent of the huge structure familiar to the Romans in their own forum—which Jupiter visits to consult the archival records:

> sola insuperabile fatum,
> nata, movere paras? intres licet ipsa sororum
> tecta trium: cernes illic molimine vasto

---

[45] Otis 1970, 304.

> ex aere et solido rerum tabularia ferro,
> quae neque concussum caeli neque fulminis iram
> nec metuunt ullas tuta atque aeterna ruinas:
> invenies illic incisa adamante perenni
> fata tui generis. legi ipse animoque notavi
> et referam, ne sis etiamnum ignara futuri.
> (*Met.* 15.807–815)

> Do you intend all alone, my daughter, to move invincible fate? You are permitted to enter the three sisters' dwelling yourself: you will there perceive the archive-house of events—a vast pile, made of bronze and solid steel, which fears neither heaven's crash nor the lightning's anger: safe and eternal, it fears no kind of collapse. There you will find, engraved in eternal adamant, the fate of your family. I've read it myself and made some mental notes. I'll recount it, lest you be any longer ignorant of the future.

This invitation to regard Jupiter's dealings with the *veteres sorores* as a bureaucratic and institutional procedure adds just that note of grotesque absurdity needed to bring the tone of Jupiter's prophecy within the stylistic traditions of the *Metamorphoses*.[46] Ovid does not aim, as Fränkel and Otis maintain, "to give dignity and solemnity"[47] to his conclusion by turning the *Metamorphoses* into serious Vergilian epic at the last minute. Such a goal would be impossible to achieve at this stage: the sudden introduction of fate, prophecy, the future, and Augustan propaganda cannot cancel out fifteen books of metamorphosis, though Bömer, in the most recent volume of his commentary, again defends the notion that Ovid includes Julius's apotheosis and the passages on Augustus "in all seriousness."[48] Bömer provides a list of critical works that question the sincerity or success of Augustan elements in Book 15 and dismisses them all with the remark, "Here the observation is worth making, with a view to the modern problem of 'non-Augustanism,' that Ovid employs the official terminology in an entirely loyal fashion."[49] Though many of these works could fairly be accused of conceptual crudity,[50] Bömer's answer is more misleading: he treats the Augustan passages as if they were isolated

---

[46] "Jupiter you see is only Library-Keeper, or *Custos Rotulorum* to the Fates," says Dryden, quoting Ovid's lines in his note on *Aen.* 10.622; see Frost 1987, 6:831.

[47] Otis 1970, 281.

[48] Bömer 7:453–454, on *Met.* 15.745ff.

[49] Ibid., 250, on *Met.* 15.1.

[50] Many "anti-Augustan" discussions of the *Metamorphoses* are scornful of Ovid's achievement, for example, Little 1972. Little resorts to biographical fantasy to explain the thematic emptiness he sees in the *Metamorphoses*: "The spoilt favorite of a sophisticated and idle coterie whose business in life was pleasure, he can be excused for thinking that life was a game" (401).

fragments, without a context to affect interpretation of their "official terminology."

In fact, Ovid's aim is to subsume even contemporary features of poetical and political discourse in general and universal flux. Now that change has been established as the only constant, Ovid can bring ideas traditionally bound to eternal fixity—*ferrea decreta sororum* (*Met.* 15.781); *incisa adamante perenni / fata* (*Met.* 15.813–814)—within the scope of his theme. Depriving them of their attachment to coherent contextual support, Ovid sets them loose to toss and swirl in the vortex of universal change. Whereas Vergil subordinates all to fate, from Jupiter down, reflecting cosmic order in the hierarchical patterning of his narrative, Ovid throws fate onto the heap along with everything else, reflecting the ubiquity of change in what we may call a cumulative narrative, to which, conceivably, any example—from the urine of lynxes to the destiny of Rome—could be added.

Aetiology and the Nature of Flux

Now that we have considered Ovidian flux and change in opposition to providential interpretations of the *Aeneid*, the cosmological ambitions of the *Metamorphoses* deserve further description and emphasis, for they in particular ought to be recognized as offering a thematically and conceptually rich alternative to the worldviews of Vergil and other epic writers. The *Metamorphoses* is a creation story from beginning to end: the creation of the cosmos does not occupy only a few lines at the beginning of Book 1, but continues throughout this vast collection of aetiological stories.[51] These stories, culled from every quarter, with a wide array of subject matter, tone, and scale, purport to explain how various natural phenomena came to be so, and at the same time interpret these phenomena in symbolically significant terms. The ancients could, of course, explain the nature of things in ways that left mythology far behind, even approaching what moderns would consider scientific explanation. But mythological aetiology could still provide a significant image of the cosmos, a natural context for human life that itself reflects human meanings. Ovid creates such a conceptual framework, and within it aims at great variety in its subjects and treatments, augmenting that variety by the sheer num-

---

[51] On the aetiological ambitions of the *Metamorphoses*, see Schmidt 1991, 70–78; and Myers 1994b, 27: "The cosmogonic themes with which Ovid's epic begins and ends are not abandoned in the central portions of the poem. Throughout the *Metamorphoses* many of Ovid's marvelous metamorphic tales account for and explain the origins of various existing natural and geographical phenomena and thus, like Pythagoras in Book 15 who teaches *rerum causas* (*Met.* 15.68), they continue in a manner the natural-philosophical themes that introduce the poem."

ber of tales, in order to produce a cumulatively compelling impression that his subject is nothing less than the origin of the natural world.

The story of Cyparissus, which just precedes that of Hyacinthus and is parallel to it, begins and ends with emphasis on its aetiological theme, that is, on the connection between the story and present aspects of experience available to Ovid's reader. Cypresses came to exist as a result of this incident:

> nunc arbor, puer ante deo dilectus ab illo,
> qui citharam nervis et nervis temperat arcum.
> (*Met.* 10.107–108)

> Now a tree, then a boy loved by the god who strings both lyre and bow with sinews.

What is now *cupressus*, a common natural feature, was once Cyparissus, a particular human being. In Apollo's remark at the end of the story we learn that Apollo's grief over the death of Cyparissus is the origin of the cypress's present-day association with mourning:

> "lugebere nobis
> lugebis alios aderisque dolentibus" inquit.
> (*Met.* 10.141–142)

> "I will grieve for you, and you for others; and you will attend them in their grief," he said.

Ovid's Roman readers could daily observe cypresses planted around tombs, just as we can today.

Similarly, an emphatic statement of aetiological theme begins and ends the story of Daedalus and Perdix, discussed above. When the partridge makes its shocking appearance at the funeral of Icarus, Ovid briefly delays his explanatory narrative with a remark that at that time there was only one partridge, since its transformation had but recently occurred:

> unica tunc volucris nec visa prioribus annis,
> factaque nuper avis, longum tibi, Daedale, crimen.
> (*Met.* 8.239–240)

> At that time it was the only such bird, unseen in earlier years, and but lately made a bird—a charge of long standing against you, Daedalus.

At the end of the story it becomes clear, as usual in Ovidian metamorphosis, that this new creature is the ancestor of the species now familiar. The behavior of partridges eternally expresses the trauma suffered by the original human Perdix, and their name also memorializes his suffering:

> nomen, quod et ante, remansit.
> non tamen haec alte volucris sua corpora tollit,
> nec facit in ramis altoque cacumine nidos;
> propter humum volitat ponitque in saepibus ova
> antiquique memor metuit sublimia casus.
> (*Met.* 8.255–259)

> The name that it had before remains. Yet this bird does not lift its body aloft. It does not make its nest in the branches and high treetops; it flies along the ground and sets its eggs in hedges, and mindful of its ancient fall, it fears the heights.

In this appeal to the extraliterary experience of the reader, Ovid not only establishes a connection between our awareness of partridges (whatever that may amount to) and the story of their origin, but also colors that awareness with the grim and troubling character of his narrative. That is, Ovid's uniquely disruptive narrative style, by which he initially offers a sentimental and appealing portrayal of Daedalus, then reveals Daedalus's horrible crime and its embodiment in nature, makes a powerful interpretive comment on the natural context of human life. As we read the *Metamorphoses*, Ovid invites us to regard everyday phenomena symbolically in the light of the work's aetiological preoccupations, and see behind the outward face of nature an origin in human suffering and passion.

Since Ovid's stories suggest that events in the remote past endow features of present reality with lasting significance, one may think of aetiological passages in the *Aeneid* as in a sense parallel. Yet their thematic character is wholly different. When Vergil represents Aeneas establishing ancient precedent for the Actian games, for example (*Aen.* 3.274–280), the narrative serves to ratify and legitimate a contemporary institution, suggesting that the Fates' beneficent design, explicit in the *Aeneid*, may implicitly embrace contemporary institutional and political realities as well. By contrast, Ovid's account of Cyparissus invites us to interpret a common natural and—in its use around tombs—cultural feature as signifying continuity of unresolved grief. The apparent permanence of the cypress and of its association with mourning does not make it any less rooted in accident and inexplicable disaster, which in so many Ovidian tales seem to characterize human experience. In the case of Perdix, *antiqui memor casus*, "mindful of his ancient fall," it is his emotional state at the moment of disaster—desperate fear—that defines the permanent behavior of partridges.

Aetiological metamorphosis typically causes some human passion or state of suffering to become suddenly a part of the nature of things, and often, as we noted in Daedalion's case, does so when a character's emotions have reached their highest conceivable pitch. In Philomela, raped and mutilated by Tereus, and her sister Procne, Ovid portrays extremes of cruel treatment that engender an all-consuming passion for revenge, a passion that transcends all other aspects of their characters. They become birds just as that passion achieves its terrible goal: serving up Tereus's and Procne's son to him in a grisly meal, they triumph in their revenge (*Met.* 6.653, 659–660). E. M. Waith notes that "when Tereus discovers what vengeance has been taken on him, he too is transported by overmastering emotions. At this moment of crisis the feelings of the three characters are alike in intensity, though as different as exultant vengeance mixed with fear is from grief mixed with rage. In each case the emotion is unbearable; the character is literally beside himself. And this is the moment in which all three are metamorphosed."[52] Metamorphosis takes place with characteristic suddenness and, considering the length of the story—more than 250 lines—makes a hasty conclusion in eight lines:

> corpora Cecropidum pennis pendere putares:
> pendebant pennis. quarum petit altera silvas,
> altera tecta subit; neque adhuc de pectore caedis
> excessere notae, signataque sanguine pluma est.
> ille dolore suo poenaeque cupidine velox
> vertitur in volucrem, cui stant in vertice cristae,
> prominet inmodicum pro longa cuspide rostrum:
> nomen epops volucri, facies armata videtur.
> (*Met.* 6.667–674)

> You would think the bodies of Cecrops's daughters were held aloft on wings: they *were* held aloft on wings. One of them sought the woods, the other the rooftops. Not yet have the spots of gore vanished from their breasts, and their plumage is still marked with blood. He, made swift by his pain and desire to punish, turns into a bird whose head bears a crest; an enormous bill projects and serves him as a sword. The bird's name is the hoopoe, and its face appears armed.

We have often noted that Ovid abruptly abandons a narrative, taking the reader by surprise; now we can further observe that his manner of stopping a tale with an inconclusive conclusion perfectly complements the aetiological theme, and vice versa. By bringing violent emotion in human characters to a peak, and then transferring them instantly into nature, with the emotional crisis unresolved, Ovid reflects chaotic violence on all fronts simultaneously: in the disintegration of character and humanity portrayed in the story, in the truncated events of its plot, and in the symbolic potential of nature, whose phenomena now offer grim signs by

[52] Waith 1957, 41; on the role of passion in transformations, see also Anderson 1963.

which to understand their meaning—the birds' plumage is still marked with blood. Thus, in Ovidian metamorphosis, the world is being continually created through change; yet at the same time, flux is frighteningly perceptible just below the structures of creation. By a strange paradox, chaos still prevails in the forms of nature, and its violence seems to become more deeply embedded in the cosmos with each new change.[53]

It is fair to speak of the "permanent" and "lasting" character of transformed phenomena, for Ovid uses *manere* ("to remain"), *durare* ("to endure"), and the like in describing the aetiological consequences of metamorphosis. Yet these terms lack the absoluteness that other authors may claim for them in other works; for Ovid's *Metamorphoses* is the epic of change, and his own use of stock aetiological language affects its meaning. Its terms become less terminal, giving way at the edges to the fluidity of their context. Expressions such as *nunc quoque* ("now also") and *etiam nunc* ("even now") are indeed formulas, but one should not imagine that therefore they could readily be tranferred from one work to another and still mean the same thing. When Ovid appeals to us to connect our experience of a natural phenomenon with his explanatory narrative, he invites us to recognize that the lasting effects of metamorphosis are signs of flux. Permanence is illusory if thought to be absolute; what appears permanent is a reminder of change. Just as Ovid subordinates Fate to flux in his revision of Jupiter's speech to Venus, so also he subordinates the traditional claims of permanence attached to aetiological arguments. He does so by taking advantage of a two-way rhetorical force that they had always possessed. If one views such arguments from past to present, the past event defines features that persist; the author reveals causes, granting the audience a clear understanding of what had been obscure. If one views the same arguments from present to past, the narrative, composed long after the fact, defines the past event in terms of the author's vision; having reshaped and redefined the past, the author offers his vision to the audience as an interpretive guide.

It would be a mistake to suppose that readers of aetiological narrative are naively aware only of the first and not of the second perspective. Most readers of the *Aeneid*, for example, know that it is the author's imaginative power that grants him authority to construct an interpretively charged account of the remote past. Ovid's paradoxical mode, subsuming permanence to change, calls somewhat more attention to the process, lest anyone suppose that words like *manere* and *durare* refer to something outside the realm of change. In the *Metamorphoses*, trans-

---

[53] As Myers (1994b, 158) remarks, "In the end, the cosmos, like Pythagoras' speech, is shown not to be rational, but rather a chaos, and thus both philosophic and poetic narrative are stripped of the power adequately to explain the world in all its arbitrariness."

formed phenomena are like the seashells that, as Pythagoras evocatively reminds us, one can observe lying far from the sea, or like an anchor found high in the mountains:

> vidi ego, quod fuerat quondam solidissima tellus,
> esse fretum, vidi factas ex aequore terras,
> et procul a pelago conchae iacuere marinae,
> et vetus inventa est in montibus ancora summis.
> (*Met.* 15.262–265)

> I myself have seen what was once very solid ground become sea; I have seen land made from sea. Seashells lay far from the sea, and an ancient anchor has been found on the mountaintops.

To an observer, these may appear tranquil sights, apparently unchanging; but the effort to comprehend the presence of these objects in their incongruous settings requires one to recognize the presence of change behind phenomena, and to acknowledge its dominion. What appears stable and distinct, as the mountains and sea are distinct, was not always so, and will not always be so.

It would be easy to measure Ovid's tales against the more balanced and closed structures employed by others, and to decry the absence of more positive and comforting meanings appropriate to such structures;[54] but, to return to Tereus, Procne, and Philomela, it would be more fruitful to regard Ovid's adaptation of this tragic story as parallel to his adaptations of Vergilian narrative, and (like them) wholly successful. Just as Ovid replaces providential history in his version of the *Aeneid* with a more disquieting vision, so here he eliminates the potentially more comforting consequences of Sophoclean heroic characterization. To what extent Ovid used Sophocles as a source is unknown, but relatively unimportant: what matters more is the fact that Sophocles' version was the preeminent one and therefore most likely to be lodged in the reader's memory. Enough of the *Tereus* remains to show that it had plenty of violence and cruelty, but these features were probably qualified and transcended by a defiant heroism, such as we meet often in Sophocles' main characters.[55] Indeed, Procne appears to have resembled Antigone in her fierce integ-

---

[54] Galinsky 1975, 132: "Sophocles wrote a *Tereus* and we can be sure that, in accordance with the nature of Greek tragedy and Sophoclean tragedy in particular, inner qualities took precedence over external events or manners. Ovid's version is another example of untragic presentation of tragic material. . . . Grotesque actions, hyperbolic gestures, and exaggerated cruelty take the place of the tragic idea, and the reader is treated to a spectacle of gestures rather than moved to pity and fear." These remarks are ostensibly unevaluative, but in such terms Ovid's is a much diminished achievement.

[55] On Ovid's sources, see Otis 1970, 406–410; on the reconstruction of the *Tereus*, Pearson 1917, 2:221–226.

rity. A section of a speech, probably Procne's speech in this play, survives, in which she describes the miserable lot of women (fr. 583); and her helplessness, along with the injuries done her by her husband Tereus, evidently provided a starting point for an almost miraculously powerful defiance such as we observe also in Antigone. Since her revenge on Tereus takes the form of killing their child, she resembles Medea as well. Procne's heroic integrity would have offered a suggestion of human possibilities above the horrors of the plot, and would have tended to palliate (as heroic interpretations of human behavior usually do) the monstrous cruelty of her actions. Furthermore, tragedy's formal regularity would have provided the heroic theme with aesthetic corroboration. Neither Sophocles' theme nor his style was acceptable in the *Metamorphoses*: for Ovid, heroism of any kind is the least convincing of human pretensions, and readers willing to face Ovid's ultimately bleaker view of human existence will recognize the thematic appropriateness of his open-ended and unpredictable narrative movement, so unlike that of Sophoclean tragedy.

Whereas the formal perfection of Sophocles' tragedies contributes to the powerful impact of his themes upon an audience, Ovid overwhelms his audience with accumulated examples: the story of Tereus, Procne, and Philomela, no longer a clearly delimited aesthetic whole, becomes part of a seamless continuum of change.[56] For all their variety, most of Ovid's transformations prove to be aetiological in the end. The principal exception is shape-shifting by divinities, such as Jupiter in his many disguises, and Proteus (*Met.* 8.730–737): gods exercise some control over metamorphosis and can return to their original or favorite forms; but human beings cannot, and usually remain part of the natural scene. As we noted before, Ovid emphasizes the fact by recurring expressions like *nunc quoque* and *etiam nunc*, which signal the aetiological nature of a transformation by asserting that its consequences can be verified by present observation. The first occurrence of *nunc quoque* in the *Metamorphoses* helps to characterize Lycaon in his new form; its context, wherein Lycaon's ethical and emotional character becomes permanently recognizable in wolves, is the first of a vast number of similar transformations:[57]

> in villos abeunt vestes, in crura lacerti:
> fit lupus et veteris servat vestigia formae:

---

[56] Sophocles' *Tereus* included a report of the metamorphosis of its main characters (fr. 581).

[57] *Nunc quoque* occurs in a specifically aetiological sense in the following instances in the *Metamorphoses*: 1.235, 1.706, 4.561, 4.602, 4.750, 4.802, 5.328, 5.677, 7.467, 7.656, 9.226, 9.664, 10.160, 11.144, 13.622, 14.73. A comparable expression, εἰσέτι καὶ νῦν, occurs at Callimachus *H.* 3.77; for similar expressions see Apollonius Rhodius 2.717, and in prose Herodotus 7.178. 2. See Myers 1994b, 63–67, "Aetiological Phraseology in the *Metamorphoses*."

> canities eadem est, eadem violentia vultus,
> idem oculi lucent; eadem feritatis imago est.
> (*Met.* 1.236–239)

His clothes pass into fur, his arms into forelegs; he becomes a wolf, and preserves traces of his old shape: he has the same gray hair, the same violent expression, and the same gleaming eyes; he bears the same image of wildness.

In addition to regular formulas like *nunc quoque,* there are almost innumerable forms of expression by which Ovid contrasts someone's human past with his or her natural present, as in the case of Caeneus, who, changed from a woman into a man, becomes a bird at last: *maxime vir quondam, sed avis nunc unice, Caeneu!* "Caeneus, once an excellent man, now a unique bird!" (*Met.* 12.531).

In order to get a clear sense of Ovid's thematic originality and to emphasize how consistent are the results of his investigation into natural causes, it will be worthwhile to note a few examples of significantly developed aetiological ideas in two of his predecessors, Homer and Callimachus. Already in Homer, aetiological metamorphosis has a sophisticated thematic function.[58] The story of Niobe in the *Iliad* ends with an explanation that she, though turned to stone, still broods over the ills she suffered from the gods; moreover, for the benefit of the audience, Homer carefully provides a report of her location on Mount Sipylus, a place well known:

> νῦν δέ που ἐν πέτρῃσιν, ἐν οὔρεσιν οἰοπόλοισιν,
> ἐν Σιπύλῳ, ὅθι φασὶ θεάων ἔμμεναι εὐνὰς
> νυμφάων, αἵ τ' ἀμφ' Ἀχελώϊον ἐρρώσαντο,
> ἔνθα λίθος περ ἐοῦσα θεῶν ἐκ κήδεα πέσσει.
> (*Il.* 24.614–617)

Now, among the rocks, among the solitary mountains, in Sipylus, where they say are the sleeping-places of the nymphs, who dance along the Achelous, there turned to stone, she nurses her woes.

Ovid can easily adapt this specificity of place, with its appeal to the reader's recognition (*Met.* 6.149: *Sipylum colebat,* "Sipylus was her home"). But Homer's attendant details—the sleeping-places of the nymphs, who dance by the streams of Achelous—too much suggest stability and peace in the divine and natural order, and seem to comprehend Niobe's grief in a consolatory context. Such an impression reinforces the themes at issue in Homer's context: Achilles tells the story of Niobe in order to convince Priam to eat, as Niobe did, and break the hold of

---

[58] On Homeric metamorphosis, see Fauth 1975; on Niobe, see Kakridis 1930.

mourning upon him. Ovid's aim in his version of this same metamorphosis is the opposite of consolation: to disturb his readers by heightening the intensity of Niobe's suffering at great length, until at its highest pitch her powers of speech, once so luxuriantly employed (*Met.* 6.170–202), fail in a choking paralysis attributable at once to grief on the emotional level, and to petrification on the physical:

> ipsa quoque interius cum duro lingua palato
> congelat, et venae desistunt posse moveri.
> (*Met.* 6.306–307)

> Even her tongue within her grows stiff, along with her hard palate; her veins stop being able to move.

Meanwhile, the mystery of transformation is stylistically registered. We have observed the anadiplosis and division of Niobe's name earlier (*Met.* 6.273); here, the semantic range of *venae* expands to embrace both veins of the human body and those of rock.

G. S. Kirk writes, "Not many Greek myths were explicitly aetiological, at least before the Hellenistic poets and mythographers decided to remedy the defect." Kirk uses "defect" with some sarcasm, since, as he later remarks, "complex and elaborate myths, . . . especially if they are strongly imaginative and fantastic, rarely have as their purpose just the provision of a concrete and specific aetiology."[59] Of course, Hellenistic versions of myths also do not have only this purpose, and they are often as "imaginative and fantastic" in their way as the more remotely ancient versions that interest Kirk and other students of myth. Yet it is true that among Hellenistic writers, interest greatly increased in aetiological myths of a "concrete and specific" character, which explain "the names, origins and functions, of plants, animals, men, cults, rituals, customs, institutions, cliffs, caves, mountains, rivers." We can understand some of this interest in the function assigned by Kirk to aetiological myths in general: they are "part of the process of binding the volatile present to the traditionally and divinely sanctioned regularity of the past."[60] So formulated, this value for aetiological myths can apply to those of all peoples. But the distinctive craving for such myths among the Greeks after Alexander's time must result at least partly from the displacement of culture that occurred in the period, when the Greek homeland lost economic and cultural importance, as well as population, to Alexandria and other centers of Hellenistic civilization overseas. An interest in origins—particularly those of rituals and customs—flourished as a prop to cultural identity.[61]

---

[59] Kirk 1970, 227–228, 258.
[60] Ibid., 257, 258.
[61] P. Bing (1988, 74) traces the allusiveness of the Alexandrian poets to "an obsessive

One section of Callimachus's *Aetia* dramatizes with special force his own urgent preoccupation, and that of his contemporaries, with the origins of custom and ritual. Fr. 178 Pf. (Icus), as we know from its own details and from Athenaeus 11.477C, was introduced by an account of an Athenian named Pollis, now residing in Egypt, who even there celebrates the festivals of his native Athens at their proper times. Difficult as it must have been to observe rites that were bound by their very nature to locale and the participation of the community, Pollis allows none of them to escape his notice, as we are told at the beginning of the fragment. On this occasion, he has invited Callimachus to a feast, the Aiora, in honor of Erigone, at which it is customary for Athenians to host their friends. This culturally defensive context, where a member of an ancient community tries to maintain its religious traditions in a new and foreign place, provides the perfect symbolic as well as literal setting for an aetiological story. Callimachus gets to know a fellow guest on the same dining-couch—a merchant from the island of Icus, whose abhorrence of heavy drinking shows him to be a sympathetic man of culture—and asks why the inhabitants of Icus revere Peleus, and what connection there is between Icus and Thessaly, Peleus's homeland. The explanation seems to be just beginning as our fragment breaks off.[62]

Callimachus's aetiological narrative may well have appealed to an emotional craving in his audience not unlike that which prompted Pollis's diligence. As a native of Cyrene, Callimachus frequently reminds his countrymen of the antiquity of their city, Greek from a time long before Alexander. In the Hymn to Apollo, he employs well-known cultic associations of Apollo—with Delos and the famous altar of horns—to introduce the foundation of Cyrene by Battus, guided by Apollo (*H.* 2.60–68); and among Apollo's various epithets he selects the one, Carneius, that connects the god with Cyrene and its colonization from Thera (*H.* 2.69–79).[63] Callimachus provides cultural reassurance to his countrymen, and to other inhabitants of Ptolemaic Egypt, calling attention to connections in myth between the new and the old homeland. In the Hymn to Delos, Leto, after looking for a place to give birth to her divine offspring, finally is granted one by Delos and sits down by the stream of Inopus on that island. There Callimachus gains an opportunity to remind

---

sense of rift," and further remarks (75), "The allusiveness of these poets was, I submit, not merely fashionable erudition. Rather it reflects the profound desire to compensate for a perceived epigonality and artistic disjunction. Social and geographical isolation in Alexandria could only have intensified this desire, for the burden of asserting one's cultural identity in such an old and alien civilization would have been especially onerous."

[62] See fr. 43.12–17 Pf., and Pfeiffer on 16: Callimachus may in this fragment also be describing a *convivium*, where he heard what he now reports on the cities of Sicily (*Aet.* 2).

[63] On Thera and Cyrene, see also fr. 716 Pf.

his readers of subterranean channels that supposedly link the Nile to Delos's little river; so that notions, however extravagant, about a natural phenomenon can reflect a significant religious connection:

ἡ δ' ἀρητὸν ἅλης ἀπεπαύσατο λυγρῆς,
ἕζετο δ' Ἰνωποῖο παρὰ ῥόον, ὅντε βάθιστον
γαῖα τότ' ἐξανίησιν, ὅτε πλήθοντι ῥεέθρῳ
Νεῖλος ἀπὸ κρημνοῖο κατέρχεται Αἰθιοπῆος.
(*H.* 4.205–208)

Gladly she left off her mournful wandering, and sat by the stream of Inopus, which the earth issues forth at its deepest when the Nile in full flow descends from the cliffs of Ethiopia.

So important an event as Athena's birth from the head of Zeus occurred by the lake (or river) Tritonis in Cyrenaic territory (fr. 37 Pf.); and a marsh is called Pallantias because the nymphs of Libya there washed the newly born goddess (see Pfeiffer on fr. 584). In Cyrene is a hill of the Muses (fr. 673 Pf.), and further examples could be cited to attest Callimachus's aim to endow local places and peoples with familiar associations in myth and story.[64]

From early times, the Romans found themselves in a position of having to reconcile divergent sources of cultural identity, traced on the one hand to local traditions, and on the other to the Greeks; consequently, aetiological myth and speculation flourished among them. Cato's immensely influential *Origines* provided the history of Rome up to recent times with an aetiological background, drawing heavily on Hellenistic foundation-legends as well as local sources. Cato includes Aeneas in his first book, and devotes two of his seven books to accounts of the foundation of various Italian cities.[65] The attempt to trace the origin of Rome and other settlements in Italy to ancient civilizations, which were already well endowed with a mythical past, parallels the Alexandrians' attempts; it does so not merely because Hellenistic models lay to hand, but because it served a similar need among Roman audiences. The Romans' aetiological preoccupations helped to control a deep uneasiness about their relation to older civilizations and to gratify an at times almost obsessive desire to establish cultural legitimacy for their traditions and institutions. Cicero gives powerful expression to a sense of cultural lostness in a pas-

---

[64] Callimachus several times mentions Cyrene, the eponymous nymph of his city; see *H.* 2.94–95; *H.* 3.206; and Bornmann 1968, ad loc. At fr. 1.22 Pf., Apollo may be called *Lycius* because of his connection with this nymph: *transfiguratus in lupum cum Cyrene concubuit*, "Transformed into a wolf, he lay with Cyrene" (Servius ad *Aen.* 4.177). Other fragments relating to the city and region of Cyrene include frr. 484, 706, 795, 810 Pf.

[65] On Cato's *Origines*, see R. Helm in *RE* s.v. Porcius 22.1.156–162.

sage of his *Academia posteriora*. He represents himself addressing M. Terentius Varro, whose *Antiquitates* comprised probably the vastest and most ambitious investigation of Rome's cultural origins ever undertaken: "When we were roaming and wandering like strangers in our own city, your books brought us home, so to speak, so that at last we were able to recognize who and where we were." After this compelling image of the cultural need that gives impulse to a passion for aetiology, Cicero goes on to list the various aspects of Roman life whose origins Varro has revealed in the *Antiquitates*, then significantly remarks on the light thereby brought to Roman poets and literature (only philosophy, Cicero's present subject, has Varro slighted):

> nam nos in nostra urbe peregrinantis errantisque tamquam hospites tui libri quasi domum reduxerunt, ut possemus aliquando, qui et ubi essemus, agnoscere. tu aetatem patriae, tu discriptiones temporum, tu sacrorum iura, tu sacerdotum, tu domesticam, tu bellicam disciplinam, tu sedem regionum, locorum, tu omnium divinarum humanarumque rerum nomina, genera, officia, causas aperuisti plurimumque idem poetis nostris omninoque Latinis et litteris luminis et verbis attulisti atque ipse varium et elegans omni fere numero poema fecisti philosophiamque multis locis inchoasti, ad impellendum satis, ad edocendum parum. (*Acad. post.* 1.3)
>
> You have revealed the life of our country, its chronology, the laws of its rituals, priestly institutions, institutions at home and in war, the site of its regions and districts, the terms, classifications, duties, and causes of divine and human institutions; you have brought much light to our poets, to Latin literature and language generally; you yourself have written varied and refined poetry in nearly every meter; you have touched upon philosophy in many passages—enough to encourage the student, but not to give complete instruction.

None of the poets was to make more thoroughgoing and elaborate use of Varro's subjects and themes than Ovid, who in the *Fasti*, following the earlier efforts, on a small scale, of Propertius in his fourth book, draws heavily on the *Antiquitates*.[66] Ovid's *Fasti* is also, with its many formal adaptations of Callimachus's *Aetia*, an ambitious attempt on his part to adapt Callimachus's aetiological mode; yet one may well doubt that it reinforces in readers' cultural awareness a reassuring sense of permanence. C. Newlands contrasts Ovid's narrator with that of Callimachus: "The Ovidian narrator seems to lack the scholarly authority of his influential predecessor."[67] This gap in authority is of great consequence for

---

[66] For sources of the *Fasti*, see Bömer's commentary (1957–1958, 1:22–32); on Callimachus and the *Fasti*, see Miller 1982; on its aetiological character, Porte 1985.

[67] Newlands 1992, 37; on Ovid and Callimachus, see ibid., 41–42.

the narrator's function: Ovid's narrator is tentative and sometimes at a loss, confessing to indecision in the presence of multiple explanations. Newlands argues that Ovid in the *Fasti* abandons claims to narrative authority, and thereby in effect destabilizes traditional views of the Roman past.[68] Ovid takes over Callimachean forms of argument that were designed to trace causes and uncover origins, and that were well suited to reveal some sense of permanence in human affairs, manifest in the temporal continuity of custom and rite. But he turns these forms from their traditional function: by denying his own narrative authority, he denies the cultural stability and permanence to which his arguments could lead. Stability and permanence are as much illusions here as in the *Metamorphoses*.

Ovid can follow Callimachus along a great many of his aetiological paths, but does not follow them to their conclusion. One can attribute to Ovid a failure to complete the journey, or, as I would prefer, a refusal to continue it. His beginnings often suggest a Callimachean end, an attempt to do for the Romans what Callimachus had done for his countrymen: to help validate the cultural identity of the audience by tracing its customs and traditions to the remote past, and often legitimizing them by association with venerable foreign places:

> dicite, Pierides, sacrorum quae sit origo,
> attigerit Latias unde petita domos.
> (F. 2.269–270)

> Tell, Muses, what is the origin of the rites; from what place were they acquired, and came to Latin homes.

This appeal begins Ovid's derivation of the Lupercalia from Arcadia. Like Callimachus, Ovid will often describe not only the myth associated with a rite, but also the details of the rite itself, as if knowledge of them had been lost, or was in danger of becoming so. A typical example is his account of rituals connected with the Lemuria, or Ghost Festival of May, a month "which even now retains part of its ancient custom," *qui partem prisci nunc quoque moris habet* (F. 5.428). The customs themselves occupy nearly half of Ovid's account (F. 5.419–444); for the rest he summons Mercury to explain the origin of the Lemuria and its name (F. 5.445–484). Like Callimachus at Pollis's banquet, Ovid often describes himself actively searching out information: on one journey he witnesses a procession to the grove of the mildew-goddess, Robigo, and turns aside to

---

[68] See ibid., 47: "The narrator's heavy reliance on variant explanations and stories and his frequent refusal to choose among them calls attention to the multiplicity and ambiguity of tradition and challenges the authoritarian view of Rome's history and its heroes promulgated by current Augustan propaganda."

investigate—*protinus accessi, ritus ne nescius essem*, "I approached nearer, so as not to be ignorant of the rite" (*F.* 4.909)—and on another learns an aetiological tale from his host along the way:

> hac ego Paelignos, natalia rura, petebam,
>   parva, sed adsiduis uvida semper aquis.
> hospitis antiqui solitas intravimus aedes:
>   dempserat emeritis iam iuga Phoebus equis.
> is mihi multa quidem, sed et haec narrare solebat,
>   unde meum praesens instrueretur opus.
>   (*F.* 4.685–690)

> By this way I was heading for the Paeligni, my native countryside, a small place but moist with unfailing streams. I entered the usual lodging of my old host; Phoebus had already taken the yokes from his resting horses. The host always told me many stories, among them the following, with which to build my present work.

The information, from which a sense of the past may be thus fashioned, not only is fugitive and difficult of access, but also tends to produce multiple *causae* for the same phenomenon. Among the various ways of understanding these multiple explanations, one is that by them Ovid means to qualify his aetiological impulse to explain with a sense of the uncertainty of human cause-finding. C. Martin emphasizes "the often arbitrary, obscure conceptualizations by which man orders his existence," to which he contrasts "the eternal fixity of the stars."[69] Whether one agrees that Ovid's treatment of astronomical subjects in the *Fasti* really endows it with so encouraging a thematic character ("a modest celebration of the heavenly perfection standing above all mortal formulation"), Martin well brings out the tentative nature of its aetiological explanations.[70] W. R. Johnson sees no such assertion of eternal fixity and order in it. The concluding pages of his discussion describe Ovid "pleading for the dead and dying pieties" of traditional Roman religion; the poet's task is ultimately hopeless, because "the humble, authentic pieties of the past" have long since become irrecoverable. Johnson closely connects this idea both with the work's incompleteness and with his evaluation of it as Ovid's "only failure."[71] For Johnson, the futility of Ovid's aetiological

---

[69] Martin 1985, 262; on the multiplicity of *causae*, see 264–267. Miller (1992, 27) accounts for variant aetiologies in terms of etiquette in addressing divinities; by offering, for example, four different explanations for Minerva's epithet of *capta*, "captured" (*F.* 3.835–848), Ovid "gives responsibility for deciding among them (and any others not mentioned) to Minerva herself."

[70] Martin 1985, 270.

[71] Johnson 1978, 17, 16, 8. Returning to the *Fasti*, Johnson (1992) characterizes its author as a "satirist" (174) and contrasts his multivalent language in this work with Au-

quest left the *Fasti* without a thematic center and, when Ovid recognized the fact, caused him to abandon the task half-finished. With a different emphasis, D. C. Feeney also proposes that Ovid altered his purposes for the *Fasti* during its composition. Because Ovid continued to work on the *Fasti* after his exile, Feeney sees changes in the work in response to the author's fate. Ovid had misjudged the shifts in Augustus's tolerance of free speech, so in exile he rewrote parts of it: "What I do want to suggest is that important sections of the poem were re-written from exile so as to make the *Fasti* read like a poem whose *licentia* had been suppressed, which has not been allowed to keep speaking, which has become *nefas*." Thus the *Fasti* becomes "a mute reproach to the constraints set upon the poet's speech."[72]

Whether or not one agrees that *licentia* has the prominence that Feeney assigns it, he rightly calls attention to change in the potential significance of works for their author. Ovid's revision of the *Fasti* in exile gives it to some extent a new identity. Now transformed into a poem of exile, the *Fasti* becomes more radically and more significantly incomplete. Its incompleteness now possesses a symbolic parallel to the author's broken state. The life of an exile is denied wholeness; and fittingly, his work can embody its author's lack, until such time as he shall be recalled. It still serves this function.

A number of tales occur in both the *Fasti* and the *Metamorphoses*, and Ovid probably worked on both aetiological productions in the same period.[73] It is instructive to observe that a story will appear in the *Fasti* as a link between the Roman past and the prestigious mythical traditions of Greece, whereas in the *Metamorphoses* the same story is subsumed into a vaster, more cosmic scheme. Most readers would now acknowledge, against Heinze's view, that the narrative style of the tale of Proserpina in the *Metamorphoses* exhibits as much discontinuity, indirectness, and tonal complexity as Ovid's other version of the same story in the *Fasti*, or perhaps even more.[74] But the aetiological character of these stylistically similar narratives is very different. In the *Fasti*, the origins explained are those

---

gustan "imperial jargon" (179): "To this unitary, centripetal and artificial system of codes, here in its religious dialect, Ovid opposes his own idiom of centrifugal and polyphonic coruscations" (178). That the *Fasti* is a multivalent work, offering multiple voices and multiple interpretive options, is a theme of Barchiesi 1994.

[72] Feeney 1992, 15, 19.

[73] Syme (1978, 21) claims priority for the *Fasti* over the *Metamorphoses*, "putting the six extant books between the years 1 and 4." See also Fränkel 1945, 142–143.

[74] Heinze 1919, 1–10; see also the revision and refinement of Heinze's generic criticism in Hinds 1987, 99–114. Since the stories of Cyane (*Met.* 5.425–437) and Arethusa (*Met.* 5.577–641) interrupt the account in the *Metamorphoses*, one could argue that the version in the *Fasti* is the more linear and straightforward, marking a less radical departure from epic narrative—a conclusion the opposite of Heinze's.

of rites and customs associated with Ceres' worship. When her wanderings in search of her daughter bring her to Aetna, she procures fire from the mountain to continue the search by night. Hence torches are still employed in her rites:

> illic accendit geminas pro lampade pinus:
> hinc Cereris sacris nunc quoque taeda datur.
> (F. 4.493–494)

> There she lit two pine trees as a lamp: hence even now at Ceres' rites a torch is handed out.

An aetiological interest in the Eleusinian mysteries has influenced the focus of the plot, most of which concerns Ceres' reception by the rustic Celeus and her consecration of his son Triptolemus to be the inventor of agriculture (F. 4.502–560). Here we learn the origin of the *saxum triste* "stone of sorrow" (504), still to be seen at Eleusis, and the reason why the initiates break their fast at nightfall (535–536). Ovid includes a reflection, typical of the *Fasti*, on the ancient and primitive character of a place so famous and greatly changed:[75]

> fors sua cuique loco est: quod nunc Cerealis Eleusin
> dicitur, hoc Celei rura fuere senis.
> (F. 4.507–508)

> Each place has its own fate: what now is called Ceres' Eleusis then was the farmland of old Cereus.

Ovid connects the story of Ceres and Eleusis with Rome by flamboyantly far-fetched geographical means reminiscent of Callimachus's undersea Inopus: as Ceres leaves Eleusis to pursue the search in her dragon-borne chariot, she eventually visits even the western rivers, and finally the Tiber:

> nunc adit Hesperios Rhenum Rhodanumque Padumque
> teque, future parens, Thybri, potentis aquae.
> (F. 4.571–572)

> Now she approaches the western rivers, the Rhine, the Rhone, the Po, and you, Tiber, some day to be the parent of mighty waters.

Like Callimachus, Ovid in the *Fasti* improves every opportunity to link the most diverse mythical locales to his own city.

None of these details occurs in Proserpina's tale in the *Metamorphoses*,

---

[75] Ovid repeatedly emphasizes Rome's rural past: *F.* 1.243–244, 1.502, 2.280, 3.71–72, 5.93–94. In these expressions he recalls Tibullus 2.5.25–26 and the *locus classicus*, Propertius 4.1.1ff.

where the aetiologies are, as we would expect, of natural phenomena: the first salamander and owl occupy prominent sections of the story, as do the Sirens, who, if they are not exactly natural, but semi-divine creatures, nevertheless have a familiar and permanent place along the seacoasts of legendary settings. As usual in the *Metamorphoses*, those mythological beings who are traditionally the most sinister and destructive turn out originally to have had humanly understandable and often praiseworthy motives. The Sirens were Proserpina's companions, and Ovid explicitly raises doubts about whether they deserved to be turned into monsters. Remarking on the comparative justice of Ascalaphus's transformation into the owl—the consequence of tale-bearing—he brings in the Sirens as a contrast:

> hic tamen indicio poenam linguaque videri
> commeruisse potest: vobis, Acheloides, unde
> pluma pedesque avium, cum virginis ora geratis?
> an quia, cum legeret vernos Proserpina flores,
> in comitum numero, doctae Sirenes, eratis?
> (*Met.* 5.551–555)

He can appear to have deserved punishment for his tale-bearing tongue, but as for you, daughters of Achelous, from what cause are your feathers and birds'-feet, while you still have the faces of maidens? Is it because, learned Sirens, you were among Proserpina's companions, when she gathered spring flowers?

Their only crime was to be present at her ravishment and wish for wings to extend the search for her by sea. Hence they received wings and the feet of birds, retaining the human faces and lovely voices they originally possessed. The well-known destructive consequences of this metamorphosis do not enter the picture:

> quam postquam toto frustra quaesistis in orbe,
> protinus, ut vestram sentirent aequora curam,
> posse super fluctus alarum insistere remis
> optastis facilesque deos habuistis et artus
> vidistis vestros subitis flavescere pennis;
> ne tamen ille canor mulcendas natus ad aures
> tantaque dos oris linguae deperderet usum,
> virginei vultus et vox humana remansit.
> (*Met.* 5.556–563)

After you sought her in vain over the whole world, straightaway you prayed to be able to go on wings over the waters, so that the sea could also feel your concern. The gods complied, and you saw your limbs turn yellow with

> sudden feathers; yet lest your song, born to soothe the ear, so great a gift of mouth and tongue, lose its function, your maiden faces and human voice remained.

The unexpected sympathy that Ovid evokes in his readers for the Sirens may call to mind the earlier experiences of Medusa—likewise terrible and destructive in a familiar story, but once beautiful and sought after by many suitors (*Met.* 4.793–803). Neptune rapes her in the temple of Minerva, and though Medusa is clearly not to blame, Minerva's punishment for the crime takes the form of changing Medusa's hair, once her special glory, to snakes.

We may contrast unexpected nobility of character in the Sirens with Ceres' surprising cruelty and indulgence in spite—not traditional features of the story, but prominent here, and reminiscent of many other examples in the *Metamorphoses*. After a sympathetic description of Ceres, anxious and unresting, wandering the world in search of her daughter, Ovid brings her to a humble cottage; there an old woman serves her a sweet posset containing polenta. When the woman's irritating little boy, *duri puer oris et audax*, "A hard-faced and bold youngster" (*Met.* 5.451), laughs at her for drinking so greedily, she throws the drink over him, shrinking him into a salamander; the grains of polenta become his spots (*Met.* 5.446–461). As often in Ovidian tales of divine vengeance, the disparity between trivial crime and severe punishment is shocking; so here is the lack of fellow-feeling, which one might expect Ceres, having lost her own child, to extend to the old woman. As if to make the story even more harshly unpleasant, Ovid adds a pathetic description of the old woman's reaction to her boy's transformation:

> mirantem flentemque et tangere monstra parantem
> fugit anum latebramque petit.
> (*Met.* 5.459–460)

> As she marveled, wept, and prepared to touch the prodigy, he fled from the old woman and sought hiding.

In the case of the Sirens and of Medusa, Ovid searches back beyond the best-known conceptions of these figures to a more remote and ancient event, a terrible transformation that left some aspect of the mythical or natural world changed. This constant pursuit of deeper causes deserves emphasis because it defines the aetiological conception behind Ovid's reworkings of his major epic predecessors—reworkings that so occupy our attention in the later books of the *Metamorphoses*. Viewing these books superficially, one could maintain that Ovid simply ransacked the *Iliad*, *Odyssey*, and *Aeneid*—and legends connected to their plots—for metamorphoses, adding also much extraneous material of an un-epic nature. But the aetiological character of these metamorphoses, whether epic in origin or not, shows a consistent purpose in the selection: to replace whatever was their original thematic character with the inevitably grimmer and more disquieting perspectives of the *Metamorphoses*.

Scylla in the *Odyssey* destroys some of Odysseus's men (*Od.* 12.245–259). To ask why would presumably be irrelevant, and no explanation is given: Homer's audience was evidently satisfied to regard it as the nature of such monsters to be destructive. In the *Metamorphoses*, amorous causes are revealed: we learn of events farther back in time than those of the *Odyssey*, events simultaneously comical and sinister: how Glaucus was in love with Scylla, and, when he naively tried to get Circe's help in his suit, only succeeded in inadvertently arousing her passion for him; how Circe in jealous cruelty changed Scylla into a monster, only to be rejected by Glaucus anyway (*Met.* 13.898–14.69). At this point, the subject matter of the *Odyssey* suddenly enters the story, and Scylla's behavior in that work now becomes explicable in terms of an elaborate context: she, powerless against a goddess, could at least vent her bitter resentment on the goddess's lover, Ulysses:

> Scylla loco mansit, cumque est data copia primum
> in Circes odium sociis spoliavit Ulixen.
> (*Met.* 14.70–71)

> Scylla remained in that place, and, as soon as she had the chance, in her hatred for Circe she robbed Ulysses of his companions.

Scylla's motives become at this point strangely understandable, and with understanding evocative, perhaps, of sympathy in the reader—who again, though with no less astonishment, is constrained to recognize an unaccustomed familiarity of mind and a glimmer of fellow-feeling with another of the worst monsters of traditional mythology.

Of all the characters in the *Odyssey*, Circe has the most to contribute to the Ovidian picture. She and her dangerous temptations have a well-defined part to play in the events of the Homeric plot; then she disappears, abandoned by Odysseus in pursuit of the greater good, and by the reader in pursuit of the happier ending. In the *Metamorphoses* she assumes a more sinister narrative presence. She dominates large sections of Book 14, pervasively and—from the perspective of one reading—with uncertain limits; she sometimes seems to vanish, and sometimes reappears, in a manner consistent with the work's narrative unpredictability. In Book 14, Ovid brings his subjects closer and closer to home, as more Roman tales become interwoven with the Greek. As we experience this shift, it is interesting to observe the great play Ovid gives to Circe's malignant power. Her preeminence suggests that in the Ovidian conception of Rome's origins, her influence goes back farthest, and it the most pervasive.[76]

When at the beginning of Book 14 Glaucus leaves Aetna and proceeds north along the west coast of Italy (*Met.* 14.1–10), his journey is strangely reminiscent of Aeneas's in the *Aeneid*. Should the reader not notice this fact, Ovid's narrative soon explicitly returns to Aeneas, long abandoned at Zancle (*Met.* 13.728): immediately after Scylla's metamorphosis, we read of Aeneas heading north on a parallel voyage (*Met.* 14.75–90). Aeneas's story, of course, takes him past Circe, on to Cumae and Latium—and in the *Aeneid* Vergil vividly and quickly portrays her land of dangerous enchantments, and the Trojan fleet coasting safely by (*Aen.* 7.10–24). But Ovid's readers may only suppose, once the sordid transformation of Scylla has ended, that they will now leave Circe behind. Aeneas's reappearance, laden with recollections of Vergilian providential history, soon gives way, first to Achaemenides and his grisly account of the Cyclops (both will recall *Aeneid* 3), and then, unexpectedly, to Circe's triumphant return (*Met.* 14.241ff.). At this point, not only do we learn all about the encounter of Ulysses' men with Circe, their transformation into beasts and back again (*Met.* 14.241–307), but we also hear the tales, developed at length, of Picus and Canens, both of whose lives were ruined by Circe.

Picus and Canens are especially notable, as Fränkel briefly remarks, since with them Ovid begins the shift to Roman subjects.[77] These stories are thematically interesting in that they show the cosmological emphasis of the *Metamorphoses* in general becoming subtly combined with local aetiologies reminiscent of the *Fasti*. Ovid subsumes the origins of Rome into those of the cosmos, in both cases locating their most ancient sources in the power of Chaos and Old Night.

In the story of Picus (*Met.* 14.320–415), Circe falls desperately in love with another young man, just as she did with Glaucus shortly before. When he rejects her advances, she turns him into a woodpecker. The tale is narrated by Macareus, a former crewman of Ulysses', to whom, in Ovid's simultaneous re-casting of events in *Aeneid* 3 and the *Odyssey*, Achaemenides has told his adventures. Macareus then responds with an account of his own experiences: while Ulysses and his crew linger in Circe's domain, one of her maids answers Macareus's aetiological questions about the statue of a young man with a woodpecker on his head; the statue has its own shrine and plenty of votive garlands (*Met.* 14.312–

---

[76] Otis (1970, 288) briefly but perceptively remarks of Circe, "Her baneful magic now dominates the second half of the Aeneas section."

[77] Fränkel 1945, 104. On the tale of Picus and Canens, see Myers 1994b, 104–113.

319). "The reader infers," observes Fränkel, "that Circe kept worshiping like a god the Picus that was, even after she had savagely robbed him of his human shape and beauty."[78] Since the Romans revered Picus as a native divinity, they, as readers of this tale, may well have been troubled to observe an unwholesome origin for their worship in the means Circe chose to indulge her thwarted passion. Once this aetiological introduction has established a connection between the tale and religious traditions familiar to the Roman audience, we learn the maid's purpose in telling it—to show Circe's power:

> "accipe" ait, "Macareu, dominae potentia quae sit
> hinc quoque disce meae; tu dictis adice mentem!"
> (*Met.* 14.318–319)

> "Pay attention, Macareus," she said, "and learn also from this how great is
> my mistress's power; and ponder my words."

Through his narrator, Ovid makes much of the story's setting in the fields and woods of Latium. Its opening line begins to localize the story:

> Picus in Ausoniis, proles Saturnia, terris
> rex fuit.
> (*Met.* 14.320–321)

> Picus, the offspring of Saturn, was king in the Ausonian territory.

Ovid includes his standard introduction to a love story, but with the genders reversed: many sought Picus's hand; one, in this case Canens, will be significant in the plot—she is to become his bride. Ovid lists dryads, "born on the Latian hills," fountain nymphs, and naiads, expanding the last category into a catalogue, and dwelling on the names of streams and lakes in the vicinity of Rome. The catalogue serves not only to emphasize Picus's desirability, but also to bring home to the audience the fact that this story concerns events to be associated, for all their antiquity, with familiar ground, events that occurred, so to speak, just beyond the garden gate or the edge of the road:

> ille suos dryadas Latiis in montibus ortas
> verterat in vultus, illum fontana petebant
> numina, naiades, quas Albula quasque Numici,
> quas Anienis aquae cursuque brevissimus Almo
> Narve tulit praeceps et opacae Farfarus undae,
> quaeque colunt Scythicae stagnum nemorale Dianae
> finitimosque lacus; spretis tamen omnibus unam

---

[78] Fränkel 1945, 105.

ille colit nymphen, quam quondam in colle Palati
dicitur Ionio peperisse Venilia Iano.
(*Met.* 14.326–334)

His face attracted the notice of dryads born on the Latin hills; divinities of springs sought him, as did the naiads that the Albula bore, and the waters of the Numicius and the Anio, the Almo, shortest of streams, the rushing Nar, Farfarus with its dark waters, and those that inhabit the woodland pool of Scythian Diana and the neighboring lakes; yet scorning them all, he cherished that nymph alone, whom Venilia, they say, once bore to Ionian Janus on the Palatine hill.

The local emphasis is reminiscent, of course, of the *Fasti*, as is the fancied etymological connection of Janus, in the last line quoted, with Ionia.[79] But any positive and celebratory ideas connected with Rome's place and past, such as Ovid may have set out in the *Fasti*, here lose force in the direction the story next takes. When Picus goes out boar-hunting "into the Laurentian fields" (*Met.* 14.342), Circe catches sight of him and is instantly consumed with desire:

obstipuit: cecidere manu, quas legerat, herbae,
flammaque per totas visa est errare medullas.
(*Met.* 14.350–351)[80]

She was astonished: the herbs, which she had gathered, fell from her hand,
and a flame seemed to spread through all her marrow.

Just before these lines, Ovid further develops the thematic potential of local reference by representing Circe leaving the *Circaea arva* and advancing into Latium to cull herbs for her enchantments:[81]

venerat in silvas et filia Solis easdem,
utque novas legeret fecundis collibus herbas,
nomine dicta suo Circaea reliquerat arva.
(*Met.* 14.346–348)

The daughter of the sun had come into those same woods, and, in order to gather fresh herbs on those fertile hills, had left the Circaean fields, so called from her own name.

---

[79] On *Ianus Ionius*, see Bömer 7:117–118, on *Met.* 14.344.
[80] The situation and language recall Propertius's elegy on Tarpeia, Prop. 4.4.21–22.
[81] Circe is linked with Tusculum, the *Circaea moenia* (*Met.* 14.253; cf. Hor. *Epod.* 1.30), which was founded by Telegonus, her son with Ulysses; see Ogilvie 1970, 199, on Livy 1.49.9. Circe has an etymological connection with Circei (Monte Circello); Cicero *De natura deorum* 3.48: *Circen quoque coloni nostri Cercienses religiose colunt*, "Our farmers of Cercei scrupulously worship Circe"; see Pease 1955–1958, 2:1077–1079. Henry (1873–1889, 3:467) quotes the early nineteenth-century traveler Bonstetten that in his time no inhabitants of Monte Circello would enter the grotto of "la maga Circe."

In this place the story takes its course: Circe sends a false boar to draw Picus deep into the woods, then confronts him with her love; he rejects her, loyal to Canens; and again, as in her action against Scylla, Circe uses metamorphosis as a weapon of jealous anger. Picus becomes the first woodpecker, and like so many other examples in this work, he expresses as a bird his lasting resentment and frustration at the cruel change, piercing the wood of trees and giving wounds to their branches. The difference is only that here the process takes place in *silvae Latiae*, "The woods of Latium," providing a reminder, in connection with the general aetiological themes, that not only distant places, but even the neighboring woods resound with the evidence of such cruelty:

> seque novam subito Latiis accedere silvis
> indignatus avem duro fera robora rostro
> figit et iratus longis dat vulnera ramis.
> (*Met.* 14.390–392)

And enraged that he was suddenly being added, a new bird, to the woods of Latium, he pierced the wild trunks with his sharp beak, and in his anger gave wounds to the long branches.

Once Circe has turned Picus's companions into various animals (*Met.* 14.397–415), her banefulness claims another victim in Canens, whose distress over Picus's disappearance drives her to madness:

> nec satis est nymphae flere et lacerare capillos
> et dare plangorem (facit et tamen omnia) seque
> proripit ac Latios errat vesana per agros.
> (*Met.* 14.420–422)

It was not enough for the nymph to weep, tear her hair, to wail (though she did all those things); she also rushed off, wandering distracted through the fields of Latium.

Exhausted with grief and wandering, she comes to the banks of the Tiber and dissolves into nothingness in a manner familiar from other stories (that of Echo, for example, in *Met.* 3.393–401), but here perhaps sadder:

> luctibus extremis tenues liquefacta medullas
> tabuit inque leves paulatim evanuit auras.
> fama tamen signata loco est, quem rite Canentem
> nomine de nymphae veteres dixere Camenae.
> (*Met.* 14.431–434)

At the end of her struggle she dissolved, her light marrow wasting away, and she gradually vanished into thin air. Yet her story left its mark on the place, which the nymphs, the ancient Muses, duly called Canens after her own name.

This incident becomes the more significant in that metamorphosis overtakes Canens in the vicinity of Rome—perhaps, if *Camenae* is a correct reading,[82] before the very gates of the city. For Ovid's association of the Camenae with a place, otherwise unknown, called Canens suggests that it is to be located near the grove dedicated to these native muses just outside the Porta Capena. If so, this story completes the advance of Circe's malignant power: she not only occupies the hills and field of Latium, but extends her influence to the site of Rome. A coincidence might occur to some of Ovid's readers, that the might of Carthage also came this far: for Livy reports that Hannibal, with only two companions, "rode right up to the Porta Capena, in order to scout out the site of the city" (*Hannibal . . . cum duobus milibus equitum usque ad ipsam Capenam portam, ut situm urbis exploraret, obequitavit*: *Per.* 26).

The tales of Circe, Glaucus, Picus, and Canens take place before Aeneas's arrival in Latium. They are in the *Metamorphoses* the larger and more deeply significant events between which his brief journey forms a tenuous link.[83] Romulus, too, plays a little part in Ovid's account of Roman origins (*Met.* 14.799–828); but the poisonous malignancy of Circe tends to engulf all else. The role Ovid writes for her is consistent with his cosmological ambitions in this work: Circe enables Roman legend and history to be accommodated to the account of natural causes through metamorphosis, all brought about by the arbitrary exercise of divine power. Also as a result of this thematic principle, events of the *Odyssey* appear without its theme of ultimate homecomings, events of the *Aeneid* without its providential pattern; even incidents of Ovid's own *Fasti* appear, but without the provisional satisfactions to be gained from pondering the greatness and antiquity of one's city. As he appealed to his readers' recollection of his own and his predecessors' works, Ovid aimed to transform familiar notions and familiar experiences, suffusing them with a more pervasive wit and deeper sadness.

---

[82] Anderson reads *coloni* for *Camenae*; see H-E on *Met.* 14.434 for the etymological and topographical associations of Canens; on the Camenae, see Rodríguez Almeida in Steinby 1993, 216.

[83] The journey of Macareus is parallel to the journeys of Glaucus, Aeneas, Circe, and Canens in its movement toward Rome. Macareus retells events of the *Odyssey*. But while Odysseus made an outward journey, from the point of view of Homer's audience, into unknown and remote places, Macareus's retelling moves the setting inward, from the perspective of Ovid's audience, ever closer to Rome. Macareus places events and people of the *Odyssey* in firmly localized Italian settings, familiar to Ovid's audience: the city of the Laestygones (*Met.* 14.233–234), for example, is Formiae in Latium; see H-E on *Met.* 14.10 and 14.233.

CONCLUSION

F. KERMODE, in *The Sense of an Ending*, discusses ways in which fictional creations organize the materials of existence. Near the beginning, Kermode remarks that his topic "is infallibly interesting, and especially at a moment in history when it may be harder than ever to accept the precedents of sense-making—to believe that any earlier way of satisfying one's need to know the shape of life in relation to the perspectives of time will suffice."[1] The works Kermode discusses are mostly twentieth-century fiction. Yet Ovid, looking back on the fictional structures prevalent in his own day, and their corresponding perspectives on reality, might have been struck by the same thought, especially when he regarded the extraordinary appeal and pervasive influence of the *Aeneid*. In some ways, the *Metamorphoses* resembles the modern works that Kermode characterizes, for Ovid's reaction to the dominant narrative structures available to him and his audience has many modern parallels: he keeps traditional structures and their ordered perspectives always before his readers' minds, while embodying them in disturbingly fragmentary structures of his own creation. He deliberately disrupts the experience of reading by bringing to mind structurally consolatory perspectives, only to thwart their development and the familiar gratifications associated with them. At the same time, witticisms and wordplay have a parallel function on the narrative surface. After the sense of a word or phrase seems stable and complete, Ovidian wit introduces unexpected semantic perspectives, demanding a re-understanding of the expression, a new mental grasp on a text that demands interpretation, yet always suggests that our interpretations will never be stable or complete—a perfect figure of eternal change.

To make comparisons between ancient and modern narratives requires a great deal of abstraction. So many of their obvious differences must be overlooked that comparison can only be partial and provisional; yet when Kermode describes Robert Musil's *The Man Without Qualities* as "multidimensional, fragmentary, without the possibility of narrative end,"[2] Ovid's modern reader may be impressed by the fact that this description could apply to the *Metamorphoses* as well. So many elements of its style encourage an expectation of conventional resolution and conven-

---

[1] Kermode 1967, 3.

[2] Ibid., 127. Kermode goes on to remark that Musil "was prepared to spend most of his life struggling with the problems created by the divergence of comfortable story and the non-narrative contingencies of modern reality" (127–128).

tional understanding, only to defeat any such expectation. There is an astringent quality in the reading of such works that some may mistake for detachment, forgetting, in the case of the *Metamorphoses* at least, that the work has always engrossed its readers.

Ovid's lack of sentimentality, and his ability to engage his readers' emotions without inviting complacency and intellectual slumber, make his work particularly precious and remarkable. It is tempting to suppose that he wrote for a time not unlike our own: aesthetically awash in sentimentality and nostalgia, with audiences unwilling or unable to bear the taste of even a little artistic accommodation to contemporary realities; with artists, for their part, frequently at fault for brutalizing their audiences, rubbing their faces in unmediated horrors—just as Ovid is sometimes accused of doing in his depictions of violence. Ovid most likely did not wish to affect his audiences that way, but he did wish to astonish them and fill them with wonder. And this goal, so often represented as a reaction within the work to its events—commonly by such expressions as *obstipuit*, or *obstipuere omnes*, "He or she was astonished"; "They were astonished"[3]—is connected to the work's representational purposes. When Ovid impresses an image of the nature of things upon his readers, their wonder is both means and end, since it both engages them in the narrative and permits their experience to escape reduction to familiar patterns and stale habits of emotional indulgence. His readers can wonder at the beauty, violence, and all else besides that is set before them in so vast a work, and yet be unseduced by comparatively paltry interpretive frameworks. Reading the *Metamorphoses* is analogous to what our experience of the natural world might be if it were possible to free it from the weight of romantic interpretation, which still constrains people to deliver themselves of banal profundities and suffer secondhand spiritual yearnings, whenever they enter the fields and woods. Yet how can one's mind not assign reductive meanings to every aspect of experience, and instead arrive at a more receptive sense of wonder? It would take a powerful narrative to do that.

[3] *Obstipescere* in the perfect tense occurs thirteen times in the *Metamorphoses*; twelve of these occur at the beginning of a line.

Appendix A

G. J. VOSSIUS ON *SYLLEPSIS ORATORIA*

THE *Commentarii rhetorici* of G. J. Vossius (1577–1649) established *syllepsis oratoria* as a trope. Because of its unrecognized influence on syllepsis as now commonly used, I quote the opening of Vossius's discussion (Vossius 1695–1701, 3:196–197, with his marginal notes in brackets):

> Est autem rhetoribus σύλληψις, cum vox anceps usurpatur communiter; sive, cum verbo ambiguo res unâ plures significantur. Quod inprimis in comparativis fieri solet. Ut in illo Homeri de ira [*Il.* σ], ac alibi [*Il.* α] de Nestoris oratione, γλυκίων μέλιτος [Melle dulcior]. Nec non hoc Maronis Ecl. VII.
>
> > *Nerine Galatea, thymo mihi dulcior Hyblae.*
>
> Nam γλυκίων, et *dulcior*, de melle proprie; de ira, & oratione, & Galatea, improprie sumuntur. Sic eâdem eclogâ:
>
> > *Imo ego Sardois videar tibi amarior herbis.*
>
> Ac mox:
>
> > *——Et somno mollior herba.*
>
> Simile etiam est illud Plauti Epidico [Act. 3 sc. 2]: *versutiores, quam rota figularis*. Ubi *versutus* tum proprie de rota, tum metaphorice de Epidico servo accipitur. Quamquam vix puto *versutus* de rota dici posse. Interim negari nequit, proprie rotam *verti*: a vertendo autem *versutus*. Atque hoc suffecit Comico, ut voce eâ luderet.

The rhetoricians, moreover, have *syllepsis*, when a word of various meanings is used without discriminating between them, or, when several things are signified at the same time by an ambiguous word. It occurs with special frequency in comparatives, as in the passage of Homer on anger [*Il.* 18.109], and elsewhere [*Il.* 1.249] on Nestor's speech, "sweeter than honey." There is also this example in Vergil's *Ecl.* 7.37: "Nereus's daughter Galatea, sweeter to me than thyme of Hybla." For "sweeter" is taken properly of honey; improperly of anger, speech, and Galatea. So in the same eclogue [*Ecl.* 7.41]: "I will seem to you more bitter than Sardinian herbs." And a little later [*Ecl.* 7.45], "Grass softer than sleep." Similar also is the expression of Plautus in the *Epidicus* (371): "Craftier/more swiftly turning than a potter's wheel," where *versutus* is first taken properly of the wheel, then metaphorically of the slave Epidicus; though I scarcely think that *versutus* can be said of a wheel. Still, one must admit that a wheel properly turns [*verti*]: and *versutus* is from turning [*vertendo*]. That sufficed for the comic poet to play on the word.

Vossius's *metaphorice* shows that he recognizes the metaphorical nature of this trope, though he does not, as Dumarsais was later to do, class it as a kind of metaphor (Vossius classes it under *Ironia*). Douay-Soublin, on Dumarsais ([1730] 1988, 278), is mistaken in regarding his "syllepse oratoire" as a new trope with an original label.

Appendix B

SYLLEPSIS AND ZEUGMA

ANCIENT GRAMMARIANS define syllepsis and zeugma variously (see Lausberg 1990, §701–708; Frécaut 1969, 30 n. 2). They typically apply zeugma to a single verb with multiple objects, for each of which it is understood in a different sense; cf. Charisius (Keil 1:280–281), Diomedes (Keil 1:444), Donatus (Keil 4:397), Pompeius (Keil 5:300–301), and Sacerdos (Keil 6:456), all of whom cite the same example: *Troiugena, interpres divum, qui numina Phoebi, / qui tripodas, Clarii laurus, qui sidera sentis / et volucrum linguas et praepetis omina pennae*, "Trojan-born, interpreter of the gods, you who perceive the divine will of Phoebus, his tripods, the laurel of the Clarian god, the constellations, the tongues of birds, and omens of swift bird-flight" (*Aen.* 3.359–361). Some modern authorities accept, with variation, ancient definitions of zeugma, e.g., Smyth (1956, §3048): "A form of brachylogy by which two connected substantives are used jointly with the same verb (or adjective) though this is strictly appropriate to only one of them." This definition of zeugma is well exemplified by Vergil (*G.* 1.92–93): *ne tenues pluviae rapidive potentia solis / acrior aut Boreae penetrabile frigus adurat*, "Lest thin rains or the keener force of the harsh sun or the penetrating cold of the north scorch the soil." Ancient grammarians typically apply syllepsis to *ad sensum* construction of singular subjects with plural verbs, and plural subjects with singular verbs; cf. Charisius (Keil 1:281), Diomedes (Keil 1:444–445), Donatus (Keil 4:397), Pompeius (Keil 5:301–302), and Sacerdos (Keil 6:457).

Zeugma and syllepsis, as defined by ancient grammarians, are of value chiefly for conciseness of expression. The grammarians discuss literal and figurative uses of words under metaphor (e.g., Quintilian 8.6.5–6), which they class separately from other tropes. It remained for Dumarsais to make rhetorical syllepsis "a kind of metaphor." So redefined, the trope continues to achieve conciseness, but is much bolder in its joining of literal and figurative senses, and corresponds more precisely to Ovid's usage than do the ancient definitions. Conciseness is characteristic of Ovid's style in general (see Kenney 1973, 132), but he makes this trope accomplish much more than conciseness.

According to Kenney (1972, 40), "There is a useful distinction between syllepsis, which is extremely common in Ovid, and zeugma, which I doubt if he ever affects. If the first is to be called by the name of the second, we are left without a term for (e.g.) Virg. *G.* i.92–3, *A.* ii.780, v.340–1." While I accept this functional distinction, it is worth emphasizing that the use of either syllepsis or zeugma to describe usage like Ovid's is a modern convention. Dumarsais's definition was widely disseminated in handbooks and dictionaries, and remains so today (e.g., Littré 1961, 7:647, s.v. *syllepse*).

Though the value of the modern distinction between syllepsis and zeugma may be admitted, the use of ancient terms with modern refinements is bound to produce some absurdity and confusion. Pseudo-Rufinianus, for example, gives syllepsis a definition very similar to that assigned by Smyth to zeugma! σύλληψις *est, cum duabus diversisque sententiis et rebus unum datur verbum minime utrisque conveniens*: "Syllepsis is when two different clauses and things are given one verb, which is not appropriate to both of them," but to only one of them (Ps.-Iulius Rufinianus *lex.* 2 [p. 48 Halm]).

On syllepsis in Ovid, see Fränkel 1945, 197 n. 10; H-E on *Met.* 9.135; Frécaut 1969; Bömer vol. 1 on *Met.* 1.750; Kenney 1973, 149 n. 76; Galinsky 1975, 143, 156 (n. 37), 248; Mack 1980, 105–106; Rosati 1983, 154–155. Of the types of syllepsis classified by Lausberg (1990, §701–708), those most relevant to Ovidian usage are §707.1, Außermenschliches/Menschliches, and §707.4, Konkretum/Abstractum. Of prose examples, the most dazzling is in Tacitus: *Germania . . . a Sarmatis Dacisque mutuo metu aut montibus separatur*, "Germany is separated from the Sarmatians and Dacians by mutual fear or else by mountains" (*Germania* 1).

Appendix C

FURTHER EXAMPLES OF SYLLEPSIS IN OVID

SYLLEPSIS is pervasive in Ovid's writings. A complete list of examples is not possible, for additions could always be made to it. The following are some illustrative examples to supplement those already quoted: 1.526 (*cumque ipso verba inperfecta reliquit*, "She left him and left his words unfinished"); 2.470 (*quo simul obvertit saevam cum lumine mentem*, "To whom she directed her savage mind along with her gaze"); 2.601–602 (*plectrumque colorque / excidit*, "His plectrum and color fell"); 4.469 (*causas odiique viaeque*, "The causes of her hatred and her journey"); 4.569 (*malis annisque graves*, "Weighed down by injuries and by years"); 6.2 (*carminaque Aonidum iustamque probaverat iram*, "She approved of the Muses' songs and of their just anger"); 7.133 (*demisere metu vultumque animumque Pelasgi*, "The Greeks' faces and spirits sank with fear"); 7.347 (*cecidere illis animique manusque*, "Their spirits and hands fell"); 7.493 (*Cephalum patriaeque mandata ferebat*, "The ship carried Cephalus and his country's instructions"); 8.134–135 (*an inania venti / verba ferunt idemque tuas, ingrate, carinas?* "Or do the same winds carry away your empty words and your ships, ungrateful wretch?"); 8.177 (*amplexus et opem Liber tulit*, "Bacchus brought embraces and assistance"); 8.388–389 (*addunt / cum clamore animos*, "They raised the level of courage and of noise"); 8.584 (*pariterque animis immanis et undis*, "Equally huge in my anger and my waters"); 9.279 (*thalamoque animoque receperat Hyllus*, "Hyllus received her into his bedchamber and heart"); 9.633 (*patriam fugit ille nefasque*, "He fled country and crime"); 10.50 (*hanc simul et legem Rhodopeïus accipit heros*, "Orpheus received her and also the stipulation"); 10.414 (*tremulasque manus annisque metuque*, "Her hands trembling from years and fear"); 10.473–474 (*inlato lumine vidit / et scelus et natam*, "Bringing in a light, he saw both the crime and his daughter"); 11.674 (*lacrimas movet atque lacertos*, "She set her tears and arms in motion"); 14.78 (*excipit Aenean illic animoque domoque*, "There she received Aeneas in heart and home"); 14.377 (*ille ferox ipsamque precesque relinquit*, "Fiercely he abandoned her and her entreaties"); 14.417–418 (*et frustra coniunx oculis animoque Canentis / expectatus erat*, "In vain had Canens watched for/expected him with eyes and mind"). In the *Fasti*: F. 3.545–546 (*arserat Aeneae Dido miserabilis igne, / arserat exstructis in sua fata rogis*, "Wretched Dido had burned with a fire [of love] for Aeneas and had burned on a pyre constructed for her fate"); *F.* 3.549 (*praebuit*

Aeneas et causam mortis et ensem, "Aeneas provided the cause of her death and also the sword"). For further examples in other works of Ovid, see Frécaut 1969.

There are also less striking expressions that play on the physical and conceptual: 1.142 (*bellum, quod pugnat utroque*, "War that fights with both iron and gold"); 2.146 (*consiliis, non curribus utere nostris*, "Use my advice, not my chariot"); 8.210 (*inter opus monitusque*, "Amid the work and instruction"); 8.560–561 (*"utar" que "Acheloe, domoque / consilioque tuo" respondit, et usus utroque est*, "He answered, 'I'll use both your house and advice, Achelous,' and he used both." Many mildly sylleptic expressions also occur, some with only a slight suggestion of the metaphorical, some with only a slight suggestion of the literal.

Comparable to syllepsis are cases of wordplay like that at 1.750 (*animis aequalis et annis*, "Equal in high spirits and in years"). Here two different spheres of reference are joined, but not the literal and figurative or the physical and conceptual. The effect of such expressions is analogous to that of syllepsis, for they result not merely in brevity of expression, but in semantic stretching as well—here of *aequalis*, which is perfectly appropriate to both *animis* and *annis*, but would normally serve two separate conceptions. Comparable cases are 3.658 (*nec enim praesentior illo / est deus*, "No god is more serviceable than he"), where Ovid plays on two senses of *praesens*, "present" and "helpful" (see Rosati 1983, 105); and 3.645 (*meque ministerio scelerisque artisque removi*, "I removed myself from the furthering of their crime/the performance of my skill").

REFERENCES

Ahl, F. 1985. *Metaformations: Soundplay and Wordplay in Ovid and Other Classical Poets*. Ithaca, N.Y.
———. 1988. "Ars est Caelare Artem (Art in Puns and Anagrams Engraved)." In Culler 1988, 17–43.
von Albrecht, M. 1961. "Zu Ovids Metamorphosenproem." *RhM* 104:269–278.
———. 1963. "Ovids Humor und die Einheit der Metamorphosen." *AU* 6, 2:47–72. (Reprinted in *WdF* 92, 405–437.)
———. 1964. *Die Parenthese in Ovids Metamorphosen und ihre dichterische Function*. Spudasmata 7. Hildesheim.
von Albrecht, M., and E. Zinn, eds. 1982. *Ovid*. Wege der Forschung 92. 2d ed. Darmstadt.
Anderson, W. S. 1963. "Multiple Change in the *Metamorphoses*." *TAPhA* 94:1–27.
———. 1964. "Hercules Exclusus: Propertius IV, 9." *AJPh* 85:1–12.
———, ed. 1972. *Ovid's* Metamorphoses: *Books 6–10*. Norman, Okla.
———. 1989. "Lycaon: Ovid's Deceptive Paradigm in Metamorphoses 1." *ICS* 14:91–101.
———. 1993. "Form Changed: Ovid's *Metamorphoses*." In A. J. Boyle, *Roman Epic*, 108–124. London and New York.
Arnaldi, F. 1958. "La 'retorica' nella poesia di Ovidio." In Herescu 1958, 23–31.
Barchiesi, A. 1989. "Voci e instanze narrative nelle *Metamorfosi* di Ovidio." *MD* 23:55–97.
———. 1994. *Il poeta e il principe: Ovidio e il discorso augusteo*. Rome and Bari.
Barkan, L. 1986. *The Gods Made Flesh: Metamorphosis and the Pursuit of Paganism*. New Haven, Conn.
Barthes, R. 1977a. *Image-Music-Text*. Trans. S. Heath. New York.
———. 1977b. *Roland Barthes by Roland Barthes*. Trans. R. Howard. New York.
Bernbeck, E. J. 1967. *Beobachtungen zur Darstellungsart in Ovids Metamorphosen*. Zetemata 43. Munich.
Bing, P. 1984. "Callimachus' Cows: A Riddling Recusatio." *ZPE* 54:1–8.
———. 1988. *The Well-Read Muse: Present and Past in Callimachus and the Hellenistic Poets*. Hypomnemata 90. Göttingen.
Bing, P., and V. Uhrmeister. 1994. "The Unity of Callimachus' Hymn to Artemis." *JHS* 114:19–34.
Binns, J. W., ed. 1973. *Ovid*. London and Boston.
Bömer, F. 1957–1958. *P. Ovidius Naso, Die Fasten*. 2 vols. Heidelberg.
———. 1959. "Ovid und die Sprache Vergils." *Gymnasium* 66:268–288. (= *WdF* 92, 173–202.)
Bömer, F., ed. 1969–1986. *P. Ovidius Naso: Metamorphosen*. 6 vols. Heidelberg.
Bornmann, F., ed. 1968. *Callimachus, Hymnus in Dianam*. Florence.
Boyle, A. J., ed. 1988. *The Imperial Muse*. Ramus Essays on Roman Literature of the Empire, vol. 1. Berwick, Victoria. (= *Ramus* 16 [1987].)

Brenkman, J. 1976. "Narcissus in the Text." *Georgia Review* 30:293–327.
Butler, H. E., and E. A. Barber, eds. 1933. *The Elegies of Propertius.* Oxford.
Cameron, H. D. 1970. "The Power of Words in the *Seven Against Thebes.*" *TAPhA* 101:95–118.
Camps, W. A. 1965. *Propertius, Elegies Book IV.* Cambridge.
Clausen, W. V. 1964. "Callimachus and Roman Poetry." *GRBS* 5:181–196.
Conte, G. B. 1986. *The Rhetoric of Imitation.* Ithaca, N.Y.
Culler, J. 1981. *The Pursuit of Signs: Semiotics, Literature, Deconstruction.* Ithaca, N.Y.
———, ed. 1988. *On Puns: The Foundation of Letters.* Oxford.
Davis, G. 1983. *The Death of Procris: "Amor" and the Hunt in Ovid's* Metamorphoses. *Instrumentum Litterarum* 2. Rome.
Dickie, M. W. 1975. "Ovid, *Metamorphoses* 2.760–64." *AJPh* 96:378–390.
Doblhofer, E. 1960. "Ovidius Urbanus: Eine Studie zum Humor in Ovids Metamorphosen." *Philologus* 104:63–91, 223–235.
Dörrie, H. 1969. "Der verliebte Kyklop." *AU* 12, 3:75–100.
Due, O. S. 1974. *Changing Forms: Studies in the* Metamorphoses *of Ovid. Classica et Medievalia, Dissertationes* 10. Copenhagen.
Dumarsais. [1730] 1988. *Des tropes, ou des différents sens.* Ed. F. Douay-Soublin. Paris.
DuRocher, R. J. 1985. *Milton and Ovid.* Ithaca, N.Y.
Erasmus, Desiderius. 1969–a. *Opera omnia.* Amsterdam.
———. 1969–b. *Collected Works of Erasmus.* Toronto.
Ernesti, J. A., ed. 1761. *Callimachi Hymni, Epigrammata et Fragmenta, quibus accedunt Ezechielis Spanhemii commentarii, et notae nunc primum editae Tiberii Hemsterhusii et Davidis Ruhnkenii.* 2 vols. Leiden.
Fantham, E. 1979. "Ovid's Ceyx and Alcyone." *Phoenix* 33:330–345.
Fauth, W. 1975. "Zur Typologie Mythischen Metamorphosen in der Homerischen Dichtung." *Poetica* 7:235–268.
Feeney, D. C. 1991. *The Gods in Epic: Poets and Critics of the Classical Tradition.* Oxford.
———. 1992. "*Si licet et fas est*: Ovid's *Fasti* and the Problem of Free Speech Under the Principate." In Powell 1992, 1–25.
Ferrari, G.R.F. 1987. *Listening to the Cicadas: A Study of Plato's* Phaedrus. Cambridge.
Fish, S. 1980. *Is There a Text in This Class? The Authority of Interpretive Communities.* Cambridge, Mass.
Forbes Irving, P.M.C. 1990. *Metamorphosis in Greek Myths.* Oxford.
Fränkel, H. 1945. *Ovid: A Poet Between Two Worlds.* Berkeley and Los Angeles.
Frécaut, J.-M. 1969. "Une Figure de style chère à Ovide: Le Zeugma ou attelage." *Latomus* 28:28–41.
———. 1972. *L'Ésprit et l'humour chez Ovid.* Grenoble.
Frost, W., ed. 1987. *The Works of Virgil in English.* Dryden's *Works,* vols. 5–6. Berkeley and Los Angeles.
Galinsky, G. K. 1975. *Ovid's* Metamorphoses: *An Introduction to the Basic Aspects.* Berkeley and Los Angeles.
Ghisalberti, F. 1933. "L'Ovidius Moralizatus di Pierre Bersuire." *Studij Romanzi* 23:5–136.

Glare, P.G.W., ed. 1968–1982. *Oxford Latin Dictionary*. Oxford.
Gow, A.S.F. 1952. *Theocritus*. 2 vols. Rev. ed. Cambridge.
Grafton, A. 1991. *Defenders of the Text: The Traditions of Scholarship in an Age of Science, 1450–1800*. Cambridge, Mass.
Greene, T. M. 1982. *The Light in Troy: Imitation and Discovery in Renaissance Poetry*. New Haven, Conn.
Haedicke, W. 1969. "Die Nicht-Metamorphose." *AU* 12, 3:73–74.
Hardie, P. 1986. *Virgil's Aeneid: Cosmos and Imperium*. Oxford.
———. 1992. "Augustan Poets and the Mutability of Rome." In Powell 1992, 59–82.
Hartman, J. J. 1920. "Ad Ovidii Met. XIII, 133." *Mnemosyne* 48:433.
Haslam, M. W. 1993. "Callimachus' Hymns." In M. A. Harder, R. F. Regtuit, and G. C. Wakker, eds., *Callimachus*, Hellenistica Groningana 1, 111–125. Groningen.
Haupt, M., O. Korn, H. J. Müller, R. Ehwald. 1966. *P. Ovidius Naso, Metamorphosen*. 2 vols. Rev. M. von Albrecht. Dublin and Zurich.
Heinze, R. 1919. *Ovids elegische Erzählung*. Berichte über die Verhandlungen der Sächsischen Akademie der Wissenschaften zu Leipzig, Philologisch-historische Klasse 71.7. Leipzig. (= *Vom Geist des Römertums*, 3d ed., ed. E. Burck [Stuttgart, 1960], 308–403.)
Henderson, J. 1988. "Lucan / The Word at War." In Boyle 1988, 122–164.
Henrichs, A. 1983. "Die Kekropidensage im PHerc. 243: von Kallimachos zu Ovid." *CronErc* 13:33–43.
Henry, J. 1873–1889. *Aeneidea, or Critical, Exegetical, and Aesthetical Remarks on the* Aeneis. 4 vols. London, Edinburgh, Dublin.
Herescu, N. I., ed. 1958. *Ovidiana*. Paris.
Herter, H. 1929. "Kallimachos und Homer: Ein Beitrag zur Interpretation des Hymnos auf Artemis." In *Xenia Bonnensia: Festschrift zum 75 jährigen Bestehen des Philologischen Vereins und Bonner Kreises*, 50–105. Bonn. (= *Kleine Schriften*, ed. E. Vogt [Munich, 1975], 371–416.)
———. 1980. "Verwandlung und Persönlichkeit in Ovids *Metamorphosen*." In *Kulturwissenschaften: Festgabe für Wilhelm Perpeet zum 65. Geburtstag*. Bonn.
Higham, T. F. 1958. "Ovid and Rhetoric." In Herescu 1958, 32–48.
Hinds, S. 1987. *The Metamorphosis of Persephone: Ovid and the Self-Conscious Muse*. Cambridge.
———. 1988. "Generalizing About Ovid." In Boyle 1988, 4–31.
———. 1992. "Arma in Ovid's *Fasti*: Part 1 (Genre and Mannerism); Part 2 (Genre, Romulean Rome and Augustan Ideology)." *Arethusa* 25:81–153.
Holland, G. R. 1884. *De Polyphemo et Galatea*. Leipziger Studien zur klassischen Philologie 7:139–312.
Holland, R. 1902. *Die Sage von Daidalos und Ikaros*. Leipzig.
Hollis, A. S. 1970. *Ovid*, Metamorphoses, *Book VIII*. Oxford.
———, ed. 1990. *Callimachus, Hecale*. Oxford.
Holtsmark, E. B. 1966. "Poetry as Self-Enlightenment." *TAPhA* 97:253–259.
Hopkins, D. 1988. "Dryden and Ovid's 'Wit Out of Season.'" In Martindale 1988, 167–190, 276–279.
Horsfall, N. 1991. "Virgil and the Poetry of Explanations." *G & R* 38:203–211.

Hutcheon, L. 1985. *A Theory of Parody: The Teachings of Twentieth-Century Art Forms*. New York and London.
Iser, W. 1978. *The Act of Reading: A Theory of Aesthetic Response*. Eng. trans. Baltimore. (Originally published Munich, 1976.)
Janan, M. 1988. "The Book of Good Love? Design and Desire in *Metamorphoses* 10." *Ramus* 17:110–137.
Jauss, H. R. 1982. *Aesthetic Experience and Literary Hermeneutics*. Trans. M. Shaw. Minneapolis. (Originally published Munich, 1977.)
Johnson, W. R. 1978. "The Desolation of the *Fasti*." *CJ* 74:7–18.
———. 1992. "The Return of Tutunus." *Arethusa* 25:173–180.
Kakridis, J. Th. 1930. "Die Niobesage bei Homer." *RhM* 79:113–122.
Keil, H. 1857. *Grammatici Latini*. 8 vols. Leipzig.
Keith, A. 1992. *The Play of Fictions: Studies in Ovid's* Metamorphoses *Book 2*. Ann Arbor.
Kennedy, D. F. 1993. *The Arts of Love: Five Studies in the Discourse of Roman Love Elegy*. Cambridge.
Kenney, E. J. 1964. Review of von Albrecht 1964. *Gnomon* 36:374–377.
———. 1972. "*Materie superatur opus*." Review of Bömer 1969–1986, vol. 1. *CR* 22:38–42.
———. 1973. "The Style of the *Metamorphoses*." In Binns 1973, 116–153.
———. 1976. "Ovidius Prooemians." *PCPhS* 22:46–53.
———. 1986. Introduction, Historical Sketch, and Explanatory Notes. In A. D. Melville, trans., *Ovid: Metamorphoses*. Oxford.
Kermode, F. 1967. *The Sense of an Ending: Studies in the Theory of Fiction*. Oxford.
Kinsley, J., ed. 1962. *The Poems and Fables of John Dryden*. Oxford.
Kirk, G. S. 1970. *Myth: Its Meaning and Functions in Ancient and Other Cultures*. Berkeley and Los Angeles.
———. 1990. *The Iliad: A Commentary*. Vol. 2. Cambridge.
Knox, P. E. 1986. *Ovid's* Metamorphoses *and the Traditions of Augustan Poetry*. Cambridge.
Konstan, D. 1991. "The Death of Argus, or What Stories Do: Audience Response in Ancient Fiction and Theory." *Helios* 18:15–30.
Kovacs, D. 1988. "Ovid *Metamorphoses* 1.2." *CQ*, n.s. 37:458–465.
Lafaye, G., ed. and trans. 1928–1930. Ovide, *Les Métamorphoses*. 3 vols. Paris.
Lanham, R. A. 1976. *The Motives of Eloquence: Literary Rhetoric in the Renaissance*. New Haven, Conn., and London.
Lateiner, D. 1990. "Mimetic Syntax: Metaphor from Word Order, Especially in Ovid." *AJPh* 111:204–237.
Lausberg, H. 1990. *Handbuch der literarischen Rhetorik: eine Grundlegung der Literaturwissenschaft*. 3d ed. Munich.
Leach, E. W. 1988. *The Rhetoric of Space: Literary and Artistic Representations of Landscape in Republican and Augustan Rome*. Princeton.
Lee, A. G., ed. 1953. *Ovid, Metamorphoses I*. Cambridge.
Leutsch, E., and F. G. Schneidewin. 1839–1851. *Paroemiographi Graeci*. 2 vols. Göttingen.
Little, D. 1972. "The Non-Augustanism of Ovid's *Metamorphoses*." *Mnemosyne* 25:389–401.

Littré, E. 1961. *Dictionnaire de la langue française*. 7 vols. Reprint. Paris.
Lloyd-Jones, H., and P. Parsons. 1983. *Supplementum Hellenisticum*. Texte und Kommentare 11. Berlin and New York.
Lobel, E., and D. L. Page. 1952. "A New Fragment of Aeolic Verse." *CQ* 46 (= n.s. 2):1–3.
McCartney, E. 1919. "Puns and Plays on Proper Names." *CJ* 14:343–358.
Mack, S. 1980. "'The Single Supplie': Some Observations on Zeugma with Particular Reference to Vergil." *Ramus* 9:101–111.
———. 1988. *Ovid*. New Haven, Conn., and London.
McKeown, J. C. 1987. *Ovid, Amores*. Vol. 1, *Text and Prolegomena*. Liverpool.
Magnus, H., ed. 1914. *P. Ovidi Nasonis Metamorphoseon Libri XV*. Berlin.
Maltby, R. 1991. *A Lexicon of Ancient Latin Etymologies*. ARCA Classical and Medieval Texts, Papers, and Monographs 25. Leeds.
Martin, C. 1985. "A Reconsideration of Ovid's *Fasti*." *ICS* 10:261–274.
Martindale, C., ed. 1988. *Ovid Renewed: Ovidian Influences on Literature and Art from the Middle Ages to the Twentieth Century*. Cambridge.
Mewalt, J. 1946. "Antike Polyphemgedichte." *AAWW* 83:269–286.
Miller, J. F. 1982. "Callimachus and the Augustan Aetiological Elegy." *ANRW* 2.30, 1:371–417.
———. 1992. "The *Fasti* and Hellenistic Didactic: Ovid's Variant Aetiologies." *Arethusa* 25:11–31.
Mondi, R. 1983. "The Homeric Cyclopes." *TAPhA* 113:17–38.
Montaigne, Michel de. [1595] 1993. *Michel de Montaigne, The Complete Essays*. Trans. M. A. Screech. London.
Moss, A. 1982. *Ovid in Renaissance France: A Survey of the Latin Editions of Ovid and Commentaries Printed in France Before 1600*. Warburg Institute Surveys 8 London.
Murray, W. M., and P. M. Petsas. 1989. *Octavian's Campsite Memorial for the Actian War*. Transactions of the American Philosophical Society 79, pt. 4. Philadelphia.
Myers, K. S. 1992. "The Lizard and the Owl: An Etymological Pair in Ovid, *Metamorphoses* Book 5." *AJPh* 113:63–68.
———. 1994a. "*Ultimus Ardor*: Pomona and Vertumnus in Ovid's *Met*. 14. 623–771." *CJ* 89:225–250.
———. 1994b. *Ovid's Causes: Cosmogony and Aetiology in the* Metamorphoses. Ann Arbor.
Nagle, B. R. 1983. "Byblis and Myrrha: Two Incest Narratives in the *Metamorphoses*." *CJ* 78:301–315.
Newlands, C. 1992. "Ovid's Narrator in the *Fasti*." *Arethusa* 25:33–54.
Norden, E. 1976. *P. Vergilius Maro* Aeneis Buch VI. 6th ed. Stuttgart.
Ogilvie, R. M. 1970. *A Commentary on Livy, Books 1–5*. Oxford.
O'Hara, J. J. 1990. *Death and the Optimistic Prophecy in Vergil's* Aeneid. Princeton.
———. 1996a. *True Names: Vergil and the Alexandrian Tradition of Etymological Wordplay*. Ann Arbor.
———. 1996b. "Vergil's Best Reader? Ovidian Commentary on Vergilian Etymological Wordplay." *CJ* 91:255–276.

Otis, B. 1964. *Virgil, A Study in Civilized Poetry*. Oxford.
———. 1970. *Ovid As an Epic Poet*. 2d ed. Cambridge.
Owen, S. G., ed. 1924. *P. Ovidi Nasonis Tristium Liber Secundus*. Oxford.
Pauly, A., G. Wissowa, et al. 1893–1978. *Real-Encyclopädie der classischen Altertumswissenschaft*. Stuttgart.
Pearson, A. C. 1917. *The Fragments of Sophocles*. Cambridge.
Pease, A. S. 1955–1958. *M. Tulli Ciceronis De natura deorum*. 2 vols. Cambridge, Mass.
———. 1963. *M. Tulli Ciceronis De divinatione libri duo*. Reprint. Darmstadt.
Peradotto, J. J. 1969. "Cledonomancy in the *Oresteia*." *AJPh* 90:1–21.
Petrone, G. 1988. "*Nomen/omen*: poetica e funzione dei nomi Plauto, Seneca, Petronio." *MD* 20/21:33–70.
Pfeiffer, R. 1949–1953. *Callimachus*. 2 vols. Cambridge.
Pianezzola, E. 1979. "La metamorfosi ovidiana come metafora narrativa." In D. Goldin, ed., *Retorica e poetica*, Quaderni del circolo filologico linguistico padovano 10, 77–91. Padua.
Pillinger, H. E. 1969. "Some Callimachean Influences on Propertius." *HSCP* 73:171–199.
Porte, D. 1985. *L'Étiologie religeuse dans les* Fastes *d'Ovide*. Paris.
Pöschl, V. 1959. "Kephalos und Prokris in Ovids *Metamorphosen*." *Hermes* 87:238–243.
Powell, A., ed. 1992. *Roman Poetry and Propaganda in the Age of Augustus*. London.
Quilligan, M. 1979. *The Language of Allegory: Defining the Genre*. Ithaca, N.Y.
Quint, D. 1993. *Epic and Empire: Politics and Generic Form from Virgil to Milton*. Princeton.
Redfern, W. 1984. *Puns*. Oxford.
Regio, R., ed. 1493. *P. Ovidii Metamorphosis cum integris ac emendatissimis Raphaelis Regii enarrationibus et repraehensione illarum ineptiarum quibus ultimus Quaternio primae editionis fuit inquinatus*. Venice.
Riffaterre, M. 1980. "Syllepsis." *Critical Inquiry* 6:625–638.
Rosati, G. 1983. *Narciso e Pigmalione: Illusione e spettacolo nelle Metamorfosi di Ovidio*. Florence.
Roscher, W. H. 1884–1937. *Ausführliches Lexikon der griechischen und römischen Mythologie*. 7 vols. Leipzig.
Rudd, N. 1988. "Daedalus and Icarus (i): From Rome to the End of the Middle Ages; (ii): From the Renaissance to the Present Day." In Martindale 1988, 21–53.
Russell, D. A. 1964. *"Longinus": On the Sublime*. Oxford.
Ryder, K. C. 1984. "The *Senex Amator* in Plautus." *G & R* 31:181–189.
Schawaller, D. 1987. "Semantische Wortspiele in Ovids *Metamorphosen* und *Heroides*." *GB* 14:199–214.
Schmidt, E. A. 1991. *Ovids poetische Menschenwelt: die Metamorphosen als Metapher und Symphonie*. Sitzungsberichte der Heidelberger Akademie der Wissenschaften, Philosophisch-historische Klasse 2. Heidelberg.
Segal, C. P. 1978. "Ovid's Cephalus and Procris: Myth and Tragedy." *GB* 7:175–205.

———. 1985. "Ovid: Metamorphosis, Hero, Poet." *Helios* 12:49–63.
Skutsch, O. 1956. "Zu Vergils Eklogen." *RhM* 99:198–199.
Smyth, H. W. 1956. *Greek Grammar*. Rev. ed. Cambridge, Mass.
Snyder, J. M. 1980. *Puns and Poetry in Lucretius'* De rerum natura. Amsterdam.
Solodow, J. B. 1986. "*Raucae, tua cura, palumbes*: Study of a Poetic Word Order." *HSCP* 90:129–153.
———. 1988. *The World of Ovid's* Metamorphoses. Chapel Hill, N.C.
Steinby, E. M. 1993. *Lexicon Topographicum Urbis Romae*. Vol. 1. Rome.
Syme, R. 1978. *History in Ovid*. Oxford.
Tarrant, R. J. 1982. "Editing Ovid's *Metamorphoses*: Problems and Possibilities." *CP* 77:342–360.
Tillyard, E.M.W. 1951. *Studies in Milton*. New York.
Tissol, G. 1992. "An Allusion to Callimachus' *Aetia* 3 in Vergil's *Aeneid* 11." *HSCP* 94:263–268.
Tompkins, J. P. 1980. "The Reader in History." In J. P. Tompkins, ed., *Reader-Response Criticism*, 201–232. Baltimore.
Tosi, R. 1991. *Dizionario delle sentenze latine e grece*. Milan.
Tränkle, H. 1963. "Elegisches in Ovids Metamorphosen." *Hermes* 91:459–476.
Verducci, F. 1985. *Ovid's Toyshop of the Heart*: Epistulae Heroidum. Princeton.
Vossius, G. J. 1695–1701. *Opera*. 6 vols. Amsterdam.
Waith, E. M. 1957. "The Metamorphosis of Violence in *Titus Andronicus*." *Shakespeare Survey* 10:39–49.
Walbank, F. W. 1979. *A Historical Commentary on Polybius*. Vol. 3. Oxford.
Walde, A., and J. B. Hofmann. 1938–1956. *Lateinisches Etymologisches Wörterbuch*. 3 vols. Heidelberg.
Walter, H. 1963–1986. *Lateinische Sprichwörter und Sentenzen des Mittelalters in Alphabetischer Anordnung*. 8 vols. Göttingen.
Washietl, J. A. 1883. *De similitudinibus imaginibusque Ovidianis*. Vienna.
Weber, C. 1990. "Some Double Entendres in Ovid and Vergil." *CP* 85:209–214.
Wheeler, S. M. 1997. "Changing Names: The Miracle of Iphis in Ovid, *Metamorphoses* 9." *Phoenix* 51.
Wilamowitz-Moellendorf, U. von. 1924. *Hellenistische Dichtung in der Zeit des Kallimachos*. 2 vols. Berlin.
Wilkinson, L. P. 1955. *Ovid Recalled*. Cambridge.
———. 1956. "Greek Influence on the Poetry of Ovid." In *L'Influence grecque sur la poésie latine*, Entretiens Fondation Hardt 2, 223–243. Geneva.
Williams, G. 1978. *Change and Decline: Roman Literature in the Early Empire*. Berkeley and Los Angeles.
Wimmel, W. 1960. *Kallimachos in Rom: die Nachfolge seines apologetischen Dichtens in der Augusteerzeit*. Hermes Einzelschriften 16. Wiesbaden.
Winkler, J. J. 1985. *Auctor and Actor: A Narratological Reading of Apuleius's* The Golden Ass. Berkeley and Los Angeles.
Zarnewski, K. 1925. "Die Szenerieschilderungen in Ovids Metamorphosen." Diss., Breslau.

Zeitlin, F. I. 1982. *Under the Sign of the Shield: Semiotics and Aeschylus' Seven Against Thebes*. Rome.

Zingerle, A. [1869–1871] 1967. *Ovidius und sein Verhältnis zu den Vorgängern und gleichzeitigen römischen Dichtern*. 3 vols. Reprint. Hildesheim.

Zumwalt, N. 1977. "*Fama subversa*: Theme and Structure in Ovid *Metamorphoses* 12." *CSCA* 10:209–222.

INDEX LOCORUM

Antoninus Liberalis, 34.4: 42
Apollonius Rhodius, 3.636: 45
Apuleius, *Metamorphoses* 11: 106–107
Aristarchus, *Schol. Graec.* 2.111 Erbse: 72n.114
Aristotle
  Metaph. 14.1090b20: 180
  Poet. 1448b10–11: 128
  Sophistici Elenchi 177a20, 177b20: 55–56n.82
Athenaeus, 9.393F: 168; 11.477C: 200

Boios, *Ornithogonia*: 103n.26, 168

Callimachus
  Aetia frr. 64, 91–92, 98–99Pf.: 146n.34; fr. 178Pf.: 200
  Hecale fr. 233Pf., 7 Hollis: 154; fr. 234Pf., 8 Hollis: 154n.45; fr. 261Pf., 71 Hollis, 2–3: 162; fr. 298Pf., 115 Hollis: 157n.51; fr. 355Pf., 66 Hollis: 164n.57; fr. 374Pf., 72 Hollis: 164n.57; *Diegesis* 10.20–11.7: 153–154
  Hymn, 3.1–2: 133; 3.2–3: 134; 3.4–7: 136–137; 3.9–10: 138; 3.46–50: 138; 3.46: 139; 3.86: 139; 3.102: 133n.7; 3.106: 141; 3.122: 136; 3.140–141: 142; 3.170: 142; 3.175–176: 143; 4.205–208: 201
Cassiodorus, *Expositio in psalmum* 87, 10: 13
Catullus, 64.154–156: 152n.41
Charisius, Keil 1:280–281: 219
Cicero
  Acad. post. 1.3: 202
  De divinatione 1.103: 31n.46; 2.84: 32
  De finibus 2.8.24: 21n.25
  De natura deorum 2.138: 70n.112; 3.48: 212n.81
  Mil. 53, 66: 119n.53

Diodorus Siculus, 32.24: 188
Diomedes
  Keil 1:301: 57n.87
  Keil 1:444–445: 219

Donatus, Aelius
  Keil 4:377: 57n.87
  Keil 4:397: 219

Epictetus, *Enchiridion* 5: 177
Euripides
  Aegeus: 154
  Hippolytus 309ff.: 40n.62

Herodotus, 1.30.4: 38n.58
Homer
  Il. 1.249: 217; 18.109: 217; 21.485: 135n.11; 24.614–617: 198
  Od. 6.107: 72n.115; 9.246–249: 118n.50; 9.275: 115; 9.481: 123; 9.509: 116
Horace
  C. 1.3.34: 101
  Ep. 1.18.71: 44
  Ars P. 29–30: 95–96; 139: 96n.10
Hyginus, *Poet. Astr.* 2.33: 134
Hymni Homerici, 4. 145–147: 35; 5.7: 136; 5.18–20: 135; 27.1–2: 135

Livy, 5.32.6: 33n.48; 5.55.1–2: 30–32; *Per.* 26: 214
Longinus. *See* Ps.-Longinus
Lucan, 6.257: 31n.46; 7.721–722: 32n.46
Lucretius, 6.1138: 69; 6.1142: 70n.111

New Testament
  Matt. 11.5: 56
  Hebr. 11.5: 24n.33

Ovid
  Am. 2.11.10: 130; 2.13.15–16: 73n.119; 2.19.19: 20; 3.11.48: 20n.24
  Ars Am. 1.615–616: 22n.27; 2.24: 130
  Her. 18(19).149–150: 73–74n.119
  Met. 1.1–2: 136; 1.142: 222; 1.164–166: 157; 1.236–239: 197–198; 1.292: 95; 1.302: 96; 1.304: 95; 1.305–306: 96; 1.381–382: 129; 1.397: 128; 1.398: 129; 1.485–488:

Ovid, *Met.* (*cont.*)
137; 1.526: 221; 1.584: 63; 1.641: 61n.93; 1.750: 222; 2.25: 85; 2.146: 222; 2.283: 62; 2.302–303: 62; 2.312–313: 19; 2.383: 61n.93; 2.470: 221; 2.505–506: 19; 2.530: 158; 2.536–539: 158; 2.542–548: 159; 2.557–561: 160; 2.564–565: 160; 2.569–572: 161; 2.588: 160; 2.591–593: 161; 2.600–602: 161; 2.601–602: 221; 2.609: 73n.119; 2.629–630: 161; 2.631–632: 162; 2.637–638: 173; 2.649–654: 57; 2.695–697: 35–36; 2.704: 61; 2.706: 35–36, 173; 2.709–710: 162; 2.748–749: 163; 2.752–759: 164; 2.775: 164n.57; 2.775–777: 66; 2.778–782: 65–66; 2.787–790: 164n.57; 2.800–801: 70; 2.803–806: 66–67; 2.815–819: 34–35; 2.816–818: 165; 2.817: 17–18, 65; 3.5: 15; 3.99–100: 19; 3.181–182: 72n.115; 3.198: 123n.58; 3.202–203: 60; 3.378: 17; 3.385–392: 15–16; 3.417: 83; 3.466: 11, 13, 69, 94; 3.473: 74; 3.645: 222; 3.658: 222; 4.175–176: 19; 4.415: 172n.15; 4.461: 61n.93; 4.469: 221; 4.496–498: 71; 4.537–538: 173; 4.569: 221; 5.451: 208; 5.459–460: 208; 5.546: 60; 5.551–555: 207; 5.556–563: 207–208; 6.2: 221; 6.149: 198; 6.273: 57–58; 6.306–307: 199; 6.376: 126; 6.385: 15, 59, 129; 6.387–391: 125–126; 6.392–395: 127; 6.635: 15, 39; 6.667–674: 194; 7.110–112: 140; 7.115–119: 140; 7.133: 221; 7.340: 15; 7.347: 221; 7.390: 173; 7.413–419: 174; 7.419: 176; 7.421–423: 156; 7.433–434: 157; 7.453–456: 157n.51; 7.493: 221; 7.687–688: 28; 7.688–689: 28nn.42, 44; 7.814–815: 27n.38; 7.821: 27n.38; 7.821–824: 26; 7.830: 27; 7.835–836: 29; 7.837: 26; 7.856–858: 29; 7.863: 28; 8.14: 147; 8.32–36: 148; 8.44–46: 149–150; 8.51–53: 149; 8.55–57: 150; 8.67–68: 150; 8.84–89: 150–151; 8.120–121: 152n.41; 8.134–135: 221; 8.145–147: 151; 8.155–156: 97; 8.177: 221; 8.183–185: 97–98; 8.191–192: 98; 8.195–200: 99; 8.199–200: 98; 8.210: 222; 8.210–216: 99–100; 8.213–214: 103; 8.223–225: 100–101; 8.225–231: 101; 8.231–232: 55, 58; 8.233–240: 102–103; 8.239–240: 192; 8.254–255: 20; 8.255–259: 193; 8.256–259: 103; 8.359: 96n.10; 8.388–389: 221; 8.458–459: 53–54; 8.463–464: 53, 57, 58; 8.476–477: 14, 52; 8.506–508: 53; 8.507: 67; 8.513–517: 54; 8.518: 52n.78; 8.522–525: 54–55; 8.529–530: 58–59; 8.560–561: 222; 8.573: 63n.98; 8.584: 221; 8.585: 58; 8.785–786: 68; 8.791–792: 69; 8.799–808: 68–69; 8.814–815: 68; 8.818–820: 70; 8.831–832: 69; 8.838–842: 69; 8.862–863: 61; 9.126: 26n.36; 9.134–135: 19; 9.279: 221; 9.408: 15; 9.409: 19; 9.454: 52n.77; 9.461: 45; 9.466–467: 45; 9.470: 45; 9.474: 45; 9.477–478: 43; 9.487: 45; 9.493–494: 43; 9.514–516: 43–44; 9.515–516: 47; 9.522–524: 44; 9.528: 44; 9.530–534: 44–45; 9.564–566: 46; 9.575: 48; 9.597: 46; 9.601–609: 46–47; 9.630: 43; 9.633: 49, 221; 9.659–664: 50; 9.664–665: 49–50; 10.50: 221; 10.107–108: 192; 10.112: 133n.7; 10.141–142: 192; 10.152–154: 36; 10.206: 176–177; 10.214–216: 177; 10.217–218: 176n.30; 10.283–284: 80n.127; 10.298–299: 38; 10.315: 38; 10.321–323: 38–39; 10.332–333: 39; 10.337–340: 37–38; 10.346–348: 37; 10.364–367: 39–40; 10.368–369: 41n.64; 10.369: 41; 10.395: 41n.64; 10.401: 40; 10.409–410: 40; 10.414: 41n.64, 221; 10.441: 40; 10.445: 36–37; 10.467–468: 40; 10.473–474: 41, 221; 10.482–487: 41–42; 10.499–500: 41; 10.500: 50; 10.557: 26n.36; 10.564–566: 60; 10.725: 176; 10.734–739: 175; 11.47–48: 63; 11.85–179: 3–4; 11.157–159:

63; 11.291–294: 169; 11.299–300: 169; 11.342–345: 169; 11.386–388: 73; 11.429: 84; 11.544–546: 74; 11.562–567: 75; 11.586–588: 76; 11.588: 78; 11.594–602: 76; 11.608–609: 77; 11.613–615: 78; 11.619–621: 77–78; 11.626: 78; 11.635–641: 78–79; 11.641–645: 79; 11.652–656: 81; 11.654: 78; 11.658–660: 82; 11.666–668: 82; 11.674: 221; 11.674–676: 82–83; 11.684–689: 83; 11.700–701: 83–84; 11.705–707: 84; 11.742: 73; 11.758–760: 170; 11.786: 170; 11.792: 170; 11.795: 175n.26; 12.29–30: 56; 12.32–34: 25; 12.39–42: 86; 12.44–48: 85–86; 12.49–55: 87; 12.56–58: 86; 12.59–60: 85; 12.531: 198; 12.621: 58n.88; 13.133–134: 22–23; 13.284–285: 23; 13.383: 24; 13.388–390: 59; 13.568–569: 175; 13.569–571: 174; 13.621–622: 172; 13.623–627: 182; 13.627–631: 181; 13.632–633: 25–26; 13.646: 183–184; 13.663–666: 184; 13.730–731: 111; 13.733–739: 112; 13.740–745: 113–114; 13.750–752: 114; 13.760–761: 115; 13.763–764: 114; 13.765–769: 115; 13.770–775: 20–21, 116; 13.780: 117; 13.781: 114; 13.789–793: 118; 13.798: 119–120; 13.808–809: 120; 13.824–826: 119; 13.829–830: 117–118n.50; 13.834–837: 119n.52; 13.846–850: 120; 13.859–861: 121; 13.860: 123; 13.863–866: 121; 13.865–866: 24; 13.876–879: 123; 13.882–883: 123; 14.61–65: 60–61; 14.70–71: 209; 14.78: 183, 221; 14.120–121: 185; 14.129–131: 185; 14.147–153: 185–186; 14.253: 212n.81; 14.318–321: 211; 14.326–334: 211–212; 14.346–348: 212; 14.350–351: 212; 14.377: 221; 14.390–392: 213; 14.417–418: 221; 14.420–422: 213; 14.431–434: 213–214; 14.580: 61n.93; 14.590–591: 189; 14.649–650: 25; 14.679–680: 61; 15.68: 191n.51; 15.165: 93, 186; 15.262–265: 196; 15.426–435: 186–187; 15.436–438: 187; 15.446–449: 187; 15.599–600: 61; 15.745–746: 188; 15.750–751: 188; 15.760–761: 189; 15.781: 191; 15.807–815: 189–190; 15.813–814: 191; 15.819: 189; 15.840–841: 189; 15.879: 49

F. 2.269–270: 203; 3.545–546: 221; 3.549: 221–222; 4.493–494: 206; 4.504: 206; 4.507–508: 206; 4.571–572: 206; 4.685–690: 204; 5.428: 203

Tr. 2.296: 34n.49

Philodemus, *De pietate*: 163n.56
Plato
  Cratylus 407E-408A: 35
  Phdr. 275D-E: 47–48; 276A: 47
Plautus, *Epidicus* 371: 217–218
Pliny the Elder, *N. H.* 15.83: 32
Plutarch
  Ant. 65.3: 33n.47
  Camillus 32.2: 32–33
  Romulus 18.1: 146n.34
  Mor. 622C: 110n.43
Polybius, 38.21: 188
Pompeius, Keil 5:300–302: 219
Propertius, 3.10.15: 20; 4.4.1–2: 146; 4.4.2: 145; 4.4.3: 144; 4.4.19–22: 148; 4.4.33–34: 148; 4.4.39–40: 149; 4.4.73: 144; 4.4.81–82: 144; 4.4.83–84: 145; 4.4.87–91: 145; 4.9.1: 146; 4.9.9: 146; 4.9.57: 147n.35
Ps.-Iulius Rufinianus, *lex.* 2 (p. 48 Halm): 220
Ps.-Longinus, 15.1: 64, 67

Quintilian, *Inst.* 6.2.29: 64; 8.6.4: 24n.33; 8.6.10: 9

Sacerdos, Keil 6:456–457: 219
Scriptores Historiae Augustae, 24 (*Tyr. Trig.*), 10.3–7: 31n.46
Seneca the Elder, *Controv.* 2.2.12: 5–6, 130; 9.5.17: 5–6
Seneca the Younger, *QNat.* 3.27.13–14: 95
Servius
  on Vergil, *Georg.* 2.126: 173n.19
  on Vergil, *Aen.* 3.486: 176

INDEX LOCORUM

Servius (cont.)
  on Vergil, *Aen.* 4.177: 201n.64
  on Vergil, *Aen.* 7.1: 180
  on Vergil, *Aen.* 12. 945: 176n.29
Sophocles, *Tereus*: 196–197; fr. 581: 197n.56
Suetonius, *Aug.* 96.2: 33–34

Tacitus, *Germania* 1: 220
Theocritus, 7.152: 110n.40; 11.1–6: 109; 11.12–13: 114; 11.15–16: 110; 11.17–18: 117; 11.19–21: 118; 11.36–37: 117n.50; 11.40–41: 119n.52; 11.75–76: 122; 11.80–81: 122
  Schol. Theoc. 11.1 (p. 241 Wendel): 123n.57
Tragoedia incerta, fr. 35 Ribbeck: 9

Varro, *Ling.* 5.41: 146n.34; 5.78: 175n.26; 6.49: 176n.28

Vergil
  Catal. 5.1: 92n.3
  Ecl. 2.3: 127; 2.22: 117n.50; 2.40–42: 119n.52; 2.73: 122; 7.37: 217; 7.41, 45: 217; 9.9: 127; 10.13–27: 127
  Georg. 1.92–93: 219
  Aen. 1.315: 112; 1.501: 72n.115; 1.684–688: 71–72; 2.772–773: 75n.120; 3.359–361: 219; 3.374–376: 180; 3.390: 96n.10; 3.420–421: 111; 3.426–427: 111–112; 4.9: 45n.68; 4.365–367: 152n.41; 5.508: 19; 6.30–33: 100, 104n.30; 7.341: 70; 7.351: 70; 8.43: 96n.10; 8.322–323: 171; 10.113: 189; 10.180–181: 58; 10.217–218: 134; 12.945: 176n.29

Zenobius, 6.28: 89–90
Zonaras, 10.30: 33n.47

INDEX

Achelous, 58, 63n.98, 156
Acis, 21, 24, 114, 122–124
aconite, 173–174, 176
Actaeon, 60
Adonis, 175–176
Aegeus and Medea, 153–154, 156
Aeneas, 75n.120, 180–187, 201
Aesacus, 169–170, 175n.26
aetiology, 10, 103; and cultural identity, 199–206; in the *Fasti*, 202–206; and flux, 191–214; and wordplay, 167–177. *See also* aition
Agamemnon, 56
Aglauros, 17–18, 34–35, 40, 65–67, 160, 163–166. *See also* Cecrops, daughters of
aition, 101, 102, 172, 174. *See also* aetiology
Aius Locutius, 33n.48
Ajax, 59
Alcmaeon, 6, 19
Allecto, 70–71
allegory: aesthetic, 3–4; artistic, 49, 80; moralizing, 8; and personification, 64–65
allusion, generic, 131–166; and instability of tone, 109; as trope, 108. *See also* elegy; epic; tragedy
Althea, 14–15, 17, 22, 52–55, 57–58
Amata, 70
anadiplosis, 58–59
Anchises, 182
Anius, 25, 183–184
Apollo and the Sibyl, 186
Apollonius Rhodius, 140–141
Apuleius, 106–107
Ardea, 61n.93
Ariadne, 97
Aristotle, 55–56, 127–128, 180
Artemis. *See* Diana
Ascalaphus, 60, 207
Atalanta, 60
Athena. *See* Minerva
Atlas, 63
audience: deception of, 104–105, 142, 145–147, 157–166; engagement of, 12, 27–28, 89–97, 105–106, 127; and multiple readings, 106–108; multiplicity of, 7–8; and written language, 47–48. *See also* narrative, disruption of
Augustus (Octavian), 187–190; and divinatory wordplay, 33–34
Aurora, 29, 172

Battus, 35–36, 61, 162, 173
Bersuire, P., 8
Boios, 168
Byblis, 6, 36, 42–52, 84, 151–152

Caeneus, 198
Caesar, C. Julius, 32n.46, 188–189
Callimachus: and aetiological perspectives, 167–168, 198–203; and indecorum, 131–135; and Ovidian narrative, 131–166; and Propertius's narrative style, 146n.34, 147
Camenae, 214
Camillus, 30–33
Canens, 210–214
Cato the Elder, 201
Catullus, 152
Caunus, 42–49
Cecrops, daughters of, 17–18, 155, 159–160, 162–166. *See also* Aglauros
Cephalus and Procris, 26–30, 55, 73, 98
Cercyon, 155–156
Ceres, 67–69, 206–208
Ceyx: and Alcyone, 72–84; and Peleus, 73, 169
Chaucer, G., 11, 52n.77
Cicero, 201–202
Cinyras, 38–41
Cipus, 61
Circe, 209–214
cleavage of identity, 56–62
"comic relief," 11–12, 18, 21
conduplicatio, 58–59
cornix. *See* crow
Coronis, 155, 158–162
corvus (raven), 158–162

Crassus, M., 32
Cratinus, 110
Creusa, 75n.120
crow (*cornix*), discourse of: in Callimachus's *Hecale*, 155; in Ovid's *Metamorphoses*, 157–163
Cyparissus, 192–193

Daedalion, 169–170, 193
Daedalus: and Icarus, 55, 58, 98–105; and Perdix, 97–105, 192–193
Daphne, 137–138
decorum. *See* indecorum, stylistic
Demosthenes, 89–92
Deucalion and Pyrrha, 128–129
Diana (Artemis), 72n.115; in Callimachus's Hymn to Artemis, 131–143
Dido, 11, 13, 45n.68, 71
divided sense of terms, 55–57
Dryden, J., 6n.5, 11, 13, 23, 58–59, 78–79, 84, 94–95, 124, 190n.46
Dumarsais (César Chesneau, Sieur du Marsais), 18, 55–56, 218–220

Echo. *See* Narcissus
elegy, generic allusion to, 143–153
engagement. *See* audience: engagement of
Ennius, Q., 96n.10
epic, generic allusion to, 15, 135–136, 208–209; in Callimachus and Ovid, 153–166; and divine representation, 34; and Homeric style, 128–129; and personification, 63–64, 70–72, 85–88; and Vergilian style, 25–26, 178, 181–182, 190. *See also* Apollonius Rhodius; Homer; Vergil
Epicharmus, 110
Erasmus, D., 38n.58, 89–90
Erysichthon, 67–70
etymology. *See* wordplay and puns: etymological
Eumelus, 173
Euripides, 40n.62, 110, 152, 154
Eutychus and Nicon, 33–34
Evander, 171

Fama, 63, 85–88
Fames, 63, 64n.101, 67–71
flux, thematic and stylistic: and aetiology, 191–214; and instability of tone, 101; and metamorphosis, 4, 10, 88; and narrative texture, 153, 158, 165, 179; and permanence, 195–196; and Vergilian providential history, 184; and wordplay, 172

Galatea. *See* Polyphemus
Glaucus, 209–210

Hecale, 154–156, 167
Hecuba, 174–175
Helenus, 111, 180–181, 186–188
Hercules, 19; and Cacus, 146–147
Hermes. *See* Mercury
Herse. *See* Cecrops, daughters of
Historia Augusta, 31n.46
Homer: and aetiological perspectives, 198–199; allusion to, 108–111, 115–124, 139–140, 209; and divine representation, 72
Hyacinthus, 176–177

imago, 16, 45, 53, 66–67, 75, 78, 81–82, 165
Inachus, 63
indecorum, stylistic, 3, 5–6, 11–13, 15, 22–26, 62, 91–97, 124, 131–135
Invidia, 63, 65–68, 70, 164–165
Io, 61n.93
Iphigenia, 25, 56
Iris, 75, 77–78
Ixion, 61n.93

Janus, 212
Jason, 140–141
Juno, 62, 75, 78
Jupiter and Venus, 187–191, 195

kledonomancy. *See* wordplay and puns: divinatory

Lavinius, P., 8
Lemuria, 203
Livy, 30–33
Lucan, 31–32n.46
Lucretius, 170
Lupercalia, 203
Lycaon, 157
Lycian Farmers, 126

Macareus, 210, 214n.83
Mars Ultor, 34n.49

Marsyas, 15, 59–60, 125–127, 129
Medea: and Aegeus, 153–154, 156; and Theseus, 173–174
Medusa, 208
Meleager, 52–55, 58
Memnon, 172
Mercury (Hermes), 17–18, 34–36, 162–166
metamorphosis: and figurative language, 9, 50, 53–55, 57n.86; and metaphor, 174; and narrative texture, 4, 194–197; and paradox, 41–42, 52–61; and personification, 61–88; and unresolved distress, 169–170, 193–199; and wordplay, 21–22, 24, 27, 37, 172–177; and written language, 43–50
metaphor, 9, 18, 54, 219; and wordplay, 24; and metamorphosis, 174
Midas, 3–4
Milton, J., 21n.25
mimetic syntax, 57
Minerva (Athena), 72, 160, 162–163
Minos, Pasiphae, and the minotaur, 97–98, 100
Mnestra (daughter of Erysichthon), 61
Montaigne, Michel de, 80n.127
Morpheus, 78–82
Myrrha, 36–44, 48, 50–51

Narcissus, 11, 13–17, 67, 69, 74, 83, 94, 124; and Echo, 6, 15–18, 40
narrative, disruption of, 89–130; and allusion, 108–123, 131–166; and "detachment," 92–94, 111, 127, 130; and engagement, 105, 108; and instability of tone, 97–105, 124–130; and metamorphosis, 194–197; and multiple readings, 106–108; and parody of Vergil, 187–191; and surprise, 4, 9–10, 94, 101–102, 105–107, 134, 141; and violence, 121–124
Nicander, 28n.43, 42, 168
Niobe, 57–58, 198–199
Nisus, 151
Nyctimene, 161

Octavian. See Augustus
Ocyroe, 173; and Chiron, 57
Oeneus, 58–59
Olenos and Lethaea, 6

omen. See wordplay and puns: divinatory
Orpheus, 51, 63, 175
Ovide moralisé, 8

Pandrosus. See Cecrops, daughters of
paradox, 9, 13–15, 22n.27, 37–38, 40, 49, 62, 73–75, 83, 101; and metamorphosis, 41–42, 52–61; and personification, 67–69
parody, 15, 180–183
paronomasia, 23n.31, 24–25, 58
Perdix, 19–20, 97–105, 192–193
personification, 29n.48, 61–88; and allegory, 64–65
Phaedra, 40n.62
Phaethon, 19
phantasia, 61–88, 164–165
Phantasos, 79
Philomela. See Tereus, Procne, and Philomela
Philoxenus, 110, 123n.57
Picus, 210–214
plague of Aegina, 129–130
Plato, 35, 46–48; and Ovid, 51–52
Plautus, 120–121
Plutarch, 32–33
Pollis, 200
Polyphemus, 20–22, 108–124; and Galatea, 24, 113–124
Pomona. See Vertumnus and Pomona
Procne. See Tereus, Procne, and Philomela
pronouns, play on, 59–62, 77–78, 84
Propertius: and aetiological perspectives, 167–168; and Ovidian narrative, 143–153
prophecy in narrative, interpretive consequences of, 179–191
Proserpina, 205–207
prosopopoeia, 64
proverb, 47–49, 89–90
pun. See wordplay and puns
Pygmalion, 3–4, 80
Pythagoras, 186–187, 191n.51, 195n.53, 196

Quintilian, 8–9

raven (*corvus*), 158–162
Regalianus (Regilianus), 31n.46
Regio, R., 8, 55n.81, 64–65, 77, 85
Robigo, 203–204

Saturn, 171
Scipio (P. Cornelius Scipio Aemilianus), 188
Scylla (daughter of Nisus), 51, 143–144, 147–153
Scylla (nymph/monster), 60–61, 111–114, 209–210
Seneca the Elder, 5–6, 92, 130
Seneca the Younger, 95, 124
Sibyl, 181, 184–186
Sirens, 207–208
Socrates, 35, 47
Sol, 61n.93
Somnus, 63, 72–80
Stoppard, Tom, 181
surprise. *See* narrative, disruption of
syllepsis, 3, 9, 18–26, 41, 46, 60, 116, 161, 176, 183, 217–222; and wordplay, 22–26; and zeugma, 18, 219–220

Tarpeia, 143–153, 167
Tatius, Titus, 144–147
Telemus, 20–21
Tellus, 61–62
Tereus, Procne, and Philomela, 6, 40n.62, 127–128, 194–197
Theocritus, allusion to, 108–111, 113–124
Theseus, 153–157, 167, 173–174
Tisiphone, 71
Tmolus, 63
tone, instability of, 4, 96–105, 112, 123–130, 133, 189
tragedy, generic allusion to, 25–26, 28, 39–40, 98n.17, 127–128, 196–197
transformation. *See* metamorphosis

Ulysses, 20–21, 22–24

Varro, M. Terentius, 202
Venus, 173; and Adonis, 175–176; and Amor, 71–72; and Jupiter, 187–191, 195
Vergil: and aetiological perspectives, 170–171; allusion to, 10, 25, 63, 100, 117–119, 127, 152n.41; and anadiplosis, 58; parody of, 111, 177–191; and personification, 70–72; and providential history, 170, 178–181, 186, 188–191, 193; and stylistic decorum, 11, 13, 94; and syllepsis, 19
Vertumnus and Pomona, 24–25, 61
Vossius, G. J., 18, 217–218
Vulcan, 19, 34n.49

wit. *See* audience: deception of; cleavage of identity; divided sense of terms; indecorum, stylistic; narrative, disruption of; paradox; parody; pronouns, play on; syllepsis; tone, instability of; word order, symbolic; wordplay and puns; written language: and metamorphosis
word order, symbolic, 52, 57–58, 68, 71, 74, 84
wordplay and puns, 6, 9, 12–13, 16, 60, 92; aetiological, 167–177; bilingual, 172–176; divinatory, 30–36; etymological, 171–177; and irony, 36–42; and metaphor, 24; and misunderstood speech, 26–30; and personification, 61–88; and syllepsis, 20–26, 116, 122; "tasteless," 62; and written language, 42–52
written language: and metamorphosis, 43–50; and wordplay, 42–52

zeugma, 18, 219–220

About the Author

Garth Tissol is Associate Professor of Classics at Emory University.